Law Office Management
for Paralegals

◆ ◆ ◆

ASPEN PUBLISHERS

Law Office Management for Paralegals

◆ ◆ ◆

Laurel A. Vietzen

Elgin Community College

Wolters Kluwer
Law & Business

AUSTIN   BOSTON   CHICAGO   NEW YORK   THE NETHERLANDS

Aspen Publishers
Attn: Permissions Department
76 Ninth Avenue, 7th Floor
New York, NY 10011-5201

To contact Customer Care, e-mail customer.care@aspenpublishers.com,
call 1-800-234-1660, fax 1-800-901-9075, or mail correspondence to:

Aspen Publishers
Attn: Order Department
PO Box 990
Frederick, MD 21705

Printed in the United States of America.

1 2 3 4 5 6 7 8 9 0

ISBN 978-0-7355-8507-2

Library of Congress Cataloging-in-Publication Data

Vietzen, Laurel A.
    Law office management for paralegals / Laurel A. Vietzen.
        p. cm.
    Includes index.
    ISBN 978-0-7355-8507-2
    1. Law offices — United States. 2. Legal assistants — United States — Handbooks, manuals, etc. I. Title.
    KF318.V54 2009
    340.068 — dc22

                                                                2009021353

About Wolters Kluwer Law & Business

Wolters Kluwer Law & Business is a leading provider of research information and workflow solutions in key specialty areas. The strengths of the individual brands of Aspen Publishers, CCH, Kluwer Law International and Loislaw are aligned within Wolters Kluwer Law & Business to provide comprehensive, in-depth solutions and expert-authored content for the legal, professional and education markets.

CCH was founded in 1913 and has served more than four generations of business professionals and their clients. The CCH products in the Wolters Kluwer Law & Business group are highly regarded electronic and print resources for legal, securities, antitrust and trade regulation, government contracting, banking, pension, payroll, employment and labor, and healthcare reimbursement and compliance professionals.

Aspen Publishers is a leading information provider for attorneys, business professionals and law students. Written by preeminent authorities, Aspen products offer analytical and practical information in a range of specialty practice areas from securities law and intellectual property to mergers and acquisitions and pension/benefits. Aspen's trusted legal education resources provide professors and students with high-quality, up-to-date and effective resources for successful instruction and study in all areas of the law.

Kluwer Law International supplies the global business community with comprehensive English-language international legal information. Legal practitioners, corporate counsel and business executives around the world rely on the Kluwer Law International journals, loose-leafs, books and electronic products for authoritative information in many areas of international legal practice.

Loislaw is a premier provider of digitized legal content to small law firm practitioners of various specializations. Loislaw provides attorneys with the ability to quickly and efficiently find the necessary legal information they need, when and where they need it, by facilitating access to primary law as well as state-specific law, records, forms and treatises.

Wolters Kluwer Law & Business, a unit of Wolters Kluwer, is headquartered in New York and Riverwoods, Illinois. Wolters Kluwer is a leading multinational publisher and information services company.

Summary of Contents

Contents

1
◆ ◆ ◆

Law Firm Structure and Regulation in the Legal Profession

2

◆ ◆ ◆

About Technology

3

◆ ◆ ◆

Law Office Communications: The Medium

4

◆ ◆ ◆

Law Office Communications: The Message

5

◆ ◆ ◆

Law Office Systems: Conflicts and Calendars

6

◆ ◆ ◆

Law Office Accounting

7
◆ ◆ ◆

Office and Equipment

8

◆ ◆ ◆

Records Management

9

◆ ◆ ◆

Employees

10

◆ ◆ ◆

Personal and Professional Development

11

◆ ◆ ◆

Attracting and Retaining Clients

Foreword

In preparing to write this book, I experienced quite a bit of anxiety about what should be included. Law Office Management for Paralegals — as a lawyer since 1981 I know quite a bit about law offices; as a professor in the business division of a community college since 1989, I know a fair amount about management; as the coordinator of an ABA-approved paralegal program for 20 years, I know quite a bit about paralegals. But what is the essential combination of this knowledge and experience that should be taught in a law office management course? I started at the website of the American Association for Paralegal Education and found that the organization categorizes core paralegal competencies into nine classifications: Critical Thinking Skills; Organizational Skills; General Communications Skills; Legal Research Skills; Legal Writing Skills; Computer Skills, Interviewing and Investigation Skills; Knowledge of the Paralegal Profession and Ethical Obligations; and Law Office Management Skills. The description of Law Office Management Skills reads as follows:

> Basic knowledge of the fundamentals of law office management and organization is essential to the entry-level paralegal. This knowledge can be presented through a stand-alone course or as part of the general program curriculum. Paralegal education programs should be able to demonstrate that their graduates can:
>
> 1. Identify and explain basic principles of management;
> 2. Explain issues relating to employment and promotion of paralegals;
> 3. Identify and describe the different types of law offices including organization, management and personnel structure;
> 4. Identify and explain the different management, administrative and support roles performed by lawyers and non-lawyers in the law office;
> 5. Describe law office billing practices, accounting systems and methods used for determining cost of legal services;
> 6. Understand administrative systems used in law practice, including client relation systems, conflict management, personnel, docket/calendaring systems, billing systems and risk management systems; and
> 7. Explain the role of technology in the management and administration of the law office.

http://www.aafpe.org/p_about/core_comp.pdf

I knew that my book could easily cover those essential seven competencies, but I thought it could do much more. I have studied paralegal program curriculum for years, in connection with developing the program I direct and in connection with visiting other programs seeking ABA approval or re-approval. I know that most paralegal programs have separate Legal Research and Legal Writing classes but many do not have separate classes in Critical Thinking, Organization, General Communication, Management Concepts, Computers and Technology, or Ethics. These skills are so important that they should be incorporated into every class and students should be able to identify and quantify what they are learning, not only to build their confidence, but to enable them to describe what distinguishes them from persons with no formal education in the field. I have, therefore, included assignments related to these competencies throughout the book. The assignments are crucial because they enable students and teachers alike to assess the students' learning.

Laurel A. Vietzen

June 2009

Acknowledgements

I would like to thank:

J.R. Phelps of the Florida Bar Association
Tabs3 technical support

1

Law Firm Structure and Regulation in the Legal Profession

As a Manager

You will be responsible for ensuring that the chain of command within your firm is effective, efficient, and fair; that employees understand and respect that structure; and that employees know the legal and ethical limitations on what they do.

Objectives

After completing this chapter, you will be able to

- Identify the body that regulates the legal profession in your state.
- Find ethical rules enforced by that regulatory body.
- Describe the types and structures of law offices.
- Describe the roles of lawyers and non-lawyers in a firm.
- Describe the importance of an organizational chart in defining those roles and create an organizational chart.
- Describe the importance of an office procedures manual.
- Create a page for procedures manual concerning the functions of a notary public.
- Describe the impact of outsourcing in the legal field.

A. Law Office . . . Management?
B. Front Office/Back Office
C. Regulation of the Practice of Law
D. Non-lawyers and Regulation

A.   Law Office . . . Management?

The position of law office manager is not the same in every law office. The United States Bureau of Labor Statistics does not have a separate classification for law office managers. Without a defined set of competencies, how do people know when they are ready to become law office managers, and how do they get those positions?

The most common scenario is for a law office manager to rise from some other position in a law firm, learning on the job.[1] Success is a delicate balance between knowledge of business and knowledge of the practice of law. In one article detailing the rise of the legal management specialty, Cheryl Leone, a longtime law office manager who now runs a management contracting business, explains during her interview:

> "[M]anagers must have some business education or background, like bookkeeping and projections. . . . They must also know and understand the law behind their jobs. For example, they must be familiar with employment regulations." And while business training is extremely helpful, some legal background may be a job-saver. "We've placed a gentleman with great business experience but no understanding of law firms," Ms. Leone recounted. "He didn't think running a firm would be different from running any other business — and he only lasted a few months." Knowing how law firms work and understanding the legal environment is essential for would-be business managers. Ursula Furi-Perry, Holding the Firm Together: Business Managers on the Rise, http://www.lawcrossing.com/article/index.php?id=543 (last visited Feb. 9, 2009).

You may come to this course with some of the necessary skills. You may be familiar with legal terminology and ethics because you have taken paralegal classes or worked in a law office. You may have business skills, such as bookkeeping and record management, from work experience or education. If some of the material is a review for you, try to look at it from a different perspective. Remember: many definitions of "management" refer to accomplishing goals by supervising and leading other people. As a law office manager, you will likely have to explain business practices and law office functions to other employees. When you come to material that seems to be a review or "common sense" to you, consider how you would explain it to the new receptionist or the temporary worker hired for a major project.

---

[1]JOHN P. WEIL & COMPANY — Law Practice Management Consultants http://weilandco.com/new/article8.html

All of them have to bring people—each of them possessing a different knowledge—together for joint performance.

—Peter Drucker, the "guru" of modern management, discussing why all organizations have managers and what all managers have in common, in *Managing in a Time of Great Change* (1995)

You may have already started to assemble a portfolio of your school work for your future job search; if you have not done so, start with this course (and with Exhibit 1-1). Nothing is better than a well-organized portfolio of work to show a potential employer what you can do. Your portfolio can be a binder with tabs to organize written work, a CD with files containing your work, or a website to which you upload your work. Resources to help you assemble a portfolio can be found at http://jobsearch.about.com/cs/resumes/a/portfolio.htm.

The contents of your portfolio will differ, depending on the type of job you are applying for. For example, a portfolio for a litigation support position might contain your resume, a sample of an objective memo you wrote after conducting legal research, and samples of pleadings, notices, deposition summaries, and other litigation-related documents you drafted. If you are applying for a law office management position, the employer would likely be more interested in seeing samples of pages from an office procedures manual you have compiled, a memo assessing options for a technology purchase, and a memo describing a new office policy.

Exhibit 1-1
Your Portfolio of Management Skills

The Association of Legal Administrators has compiled lists of competencies for legal administrators (http://www.alanet.org/education/knowledgesurvey.aspx). The following topics were based on those lists. Consider organizing your law office management portfolio accordingly. By completing the assignments in this book, you will create an item for each category. (If you wish to focus on assignments that focus on management competencies, look for the heading "Management Portfolio.")

1. Business Planning
2. Records Management
3. Conflict Management
4. Legal Industry Trends
5. Ethics
6. Marketing
7. Electronic Privacy
8. Employee Benefits & Motivation
9. Technology
10. Communications
11. Financial & Accounting
12. Business Systems

B. Front Office/Back Office

front-office
Systems that deal directly with the client (i.e., practice of law)

back office
Systems that do not deal directly with client

Paralegals
Person qualified by education, training, or experience to perform substantive legal work under supervision of an attorney; also called "legal assistant"

The **front-office** functions of law, dealing with clients and actually practicing law, get all the glamour. Television shows and movies depict drama in the courtroom, brilliance during strategizing sessions, and compassion in personal relationships. Those front-office functions cannot occur, however, without a **back office** that is running smoothly to make the practice functional and, in most cases, profitable. **Paralegals** support lawyers in the practice of law, as you will learn in other classes, but they also perform the many back-office functions that are the focus of this book.

The back office bills the clients, balances the books, orders supplies, keeps equipment operating, handles the mail and phone messages, pays the bills, manages employees, keeps the library current, manages files, handles scheduling, and much more. In the smallest firms, a single lawyer may handle both front-office and back-office functions; in most firms, at least one non-lawyer handles most of the back-office functions. Some large firms have people for each function: mailroom people, bookkeepers, a receptionist, secretaries, technology support people, human resource professionals, and others. Regardless of how big each part of this team is, neither can function without the other, and the two must be in balance. Law cannot be practiced without cash flow, but the back-office drive for profit must never take precedence over ethical practice and putting the clients first.

malpractice
Negligence in the performance of professional duties; may be a basis of civil liability

The purpose of this book is to educate the unsung heroes of that balancing act—paralegals—on how to best achieve equilibrium between the two functions and how to comply with the rules of professional responsibility[2] in doing so. Although the structures and operations of law firms vary widely, certain systems and procedures are common to all because those systems and procedures are necessary to avoid violation of the ethical rules, resulting in **malpractice**.

C. Regulation of the Practice of Law

bar associations
Professional organization of lawyers, responsible for regulation in some states

American Bar Association (ABA)
National association of attorneys; has a program for approval of paralegal programs

Model Rules
Ethical rules promulgated by American Bar Association

While the practice of law is generally a business intended to generate a profit, it is unlike most businesses in that lawyers are regulated and subject to ethical rules on a state-by-state basis. Many people believe that **bar associations** regulate lawyers and are responsible for deciding whether a lawyer should be investigated and disciplined, but that is not necessarily true. For example, although the **American Bar Association (ABA)** has a code of professional responsibility, the organization has no regulatory authority over lawyers. Lawyers are not required to belong to the ABA, and many do not. The ABA has established **Model Rules**, which have served as the basis for rules enforced by the states. (To see the ABA Model Rules, visit http://www.abanet.org/cpr/mrpc/model_rules.html.)

The highest court in each state is ultimately responsible for the practice of law in that state. How the court handles that responsibility differs from state to

---

[2]In this book, the terms "ethical rules" and "rules" or "code" of professional responsibility are used interchangeably.

state. Some courts are very active in making rules to regulate the practice of law; others delegate authority to the state legislature. In some states, responsibility is shared: the legislature enacts laws dealing with the practice of law, which are supplemental to the court's regulation. However the rules are made, they are directly applicable to licensed lawyers and, as will be discussed later, indirectly applicable to those employed by lawyers.

How the court implements those rules also depends on the states. In states with **integrated (or unified) bar associations**, membership in the state bar association is mandatory, and the bar association is responsible for investigating lawyers charged with violations of ethical rules and holding hearings. In other states, the courts use governmental administrative agencies to perform those functions. In those states, membership in bar associations is generally voluntary, and the bar associations, while able to police their members, have no way of disciplining non-members. In addition, the lower courts of the state may have authority to discipline lawyers or to punish the unauthorized practice of law.

Discipline imposed on lawyers for failure to comply with ethical rules can include a reprimand, probation, suspension, or disbarment. A **reprimand** may be private, communicated to only the attorney, or may be public. An attorney placed on **probation** or **suspension** may be required to meet specific conditions to be returned to full privileges. Conditions might include supervision, reporting, submitting to audits, participation in a treatment program, or completion of a course or a test. **Disbarment**, the most serious disciplinary measure, terminates the attorney's license to practice law, although it is possible to apply for reinstatement. A lawyer might also be required to make **restitution**.

The definition of the term "practice of law" is subject to ongoing debate (discussed in later sections of this book), but it is easy to identify who is a lawyer and is therefore regulated. The terms "lawyer" and "attorney" are interchangeable. A person who wants to become a lawyer typically earns a (four-year) bachelor's degree, which can be in any field, and then applies to law school[3] to earn a **J.D.**, or juris doctorate degree. Most states require that prospective lawyers take and pass a **bar exam** and undergo a rigorous background check after completing law school. The bar exam generally consists of multistate and state-specific sections and is part essay and part objective test.

Once a lawyer passes the bar exam and background check, he is **licensed** by a particular state. A lawyer licensed in multiple jurisdictions will typically note that licensing on his or her letterhead and cards. Some states offer **reciprocity** for lawyers who have practiced in one state for a specific amount of time, so that they do not have to take another bar exam to practice in a new state. To remain a licensed attorney (avoid being disbarred or suspended), the lawyer must comply with the rules of professional conduct, pay an annual licensing fee, and, in most states, attend **continuing legal education (CLE)**.

Some countries have different types of lawyers, but the United States does not. In the United Kingdom, **barristers** plead in the higher courts and give expert opinions on points of law, while **solicitors** interact with clients and do

---

[3]It may surprise you to learn that some states have alternative ways to qualify for the bar exam. For example, the state of Washington still allows candidates to "read law" while working with licensed attorneys, like Abraham Lincoln did. The American Bar Association has extensive information about becoming a lawyer on its website (http://www.abanet.org).

integrated (or unified) bar associations
Bar association that has regulatory authority over lawyers in the state

reprimand
Censure or rebuke

probation
Discipline under which attorney may practice, with supervision or conditions

suspension
Temporarily removed

Disbarment
Act of being officially removed from practice as an attorney

restitution
Reparations; restoring what was taken

J.D.
Juris Doctor, the degree most commonly earned in law school

bar exam
Test taken after law school, before becoming a licensed attorney

licensed
Having governmental permission to perform certain acts

reciprocity
Recognition of licenses issued by other states

continuing legal education (CLE)
Often required as part of licensing or certification; if mandatory called MCLE

barristers
Lawyer licensed to practice in court (generally in England or Wales)

solicitors
Lawyer authorized to give advice and prepare documents, but not to go to court, in England or Wales

abogado
Spanish for "attorney"

notario
In Spanish-speaking countries, authorized to perform official functions and transactional types of legal practice

notary public
Authorized to witness signatures, verify identity, administer oaths

transactional work. In many Spanish-speaking countries, an **abogado** is a lawyer who can act as an advocate in court, while a **notario** is a public official (not an advocate) authorized to prepare and certify official documents; a notario must be involved in certain property conveyances, marriages, wills, the establishment of limited companies, and the buying and selling of businesses. This sometimes creates confusion for individuals new to this country, who may believe that a **notary public** is qualified to handle legal problems.

With the exception of a special bar exam for those wishing to practice patent law, board certification of lawyers as "specialists" is a relatively new trend. Many states still have no program for designating lawyers as specialists in particular fields. A lawyer may generally advertise availability to practice (or unwillingness to practice) in a particular field, but may not indicate special certification unless state ethical rules permit.

Assignment 1-1
Research Regulation Questions

Starting at the American Bar Association Center for Professional Responsibility website (http://www.abanet.org/cpr/links.html#States), identify the body responsible for regulation of lawyers in your state. Next, find your state's rules for professional conduct. On the same site, you may find a link to ethical opinions for your state. Bookmark or add each of these to your Favorites; you will need them for future assignments. You should also bookmark or add to your Favorites Cornell's American Legal Ethics Library (http://www.law.cornell.edu/ethics), which will help with future assignments.

strict liability
Responsibility without regard to fault

lawyers' assistance program (LAP)
Counseling program for lawyers with substance abuse or other personal problems

1. Find the rule that makes lawyers responsible for the conduct of their employees. Is this a **strict liability** rule? Is the lawyer responsible for employee misconduct regardless of how careful she was in attempting to run an ethical office?
2. Determine whether the body that regulates lawyers in your state requires CLE for lawyers and how lawyers must report their CLE (see http://www.abanet.org/cle/mcleview.html).
3. Determine whether your state has a **lawyers' assistance program (LAP)** (see http://www.abanet.org/legalservices/colap). What is the purpose of a LAP?
4. Is your state a unified bar state? How does your state rank in terms of number of lawyers? Find out at http://www.abanet.org/barserv/stlobar.html and http://www.abanet.org/marketresearch/2007_Natl_Lawyer_FINALonepage.pdf.

D. Non-lawyers and Regulation

A law firm may employ a variety of individuals who are not lawyers but who perform vital functions that require a high level of knowledge and skill. Large firms often employ investigators, law librarians, messengers, docket clerks, accountants, bookkeepers, and even **IT specialists**. Firms that have specialized practices may even hire individuals with special substantive knowledge, such as nurse-legal consultants.

IT specialists
Expert in information technology (IT)

A firm may also employ managers and administrators to perform and oversee the functions described in this book. Does the title "manager" or "administrator" make a difference? Not really; the important thing is to understand the authority that has been given. Is the manager or administrator authorized to make large purchases, to hire and fire employees, and to make significant policy decisions? A large firm might even have several administrators or managers, including a human resources manager, a systems manager, a paralegal manager, and a marketing manager.

Many firms employ highly skilled legal secretaries for their high speed and accuracy in keyboarding and ability to take dictation. Most firms also hire paralegals, also called legal assistants, who are qualified by education, training, or work experience to perform **substantive legal work** that would otherwise be performed by attorneys. Large firms may have several levels or tiers of paralegal employment, ranging from entry-level to senior or manager paralegals.

substantive legal work
Requires knowledge of legal concepts; not clerical work

Example

Is there a difference between a legal secretary and a paralegal? Yes! The duties of people with these titles in a particular law firm sometimes overlap, but courts distinguish between paralegal tasks and secretarial tasks in fee awards (discussed in depth in a later chapter). "The relevant inquiry for requested paralegal fees is 'whether the work was sufficiently complex to justify the efforts of a paralegal, as opposed to an employee at the next rung lower on the payscale ladder.' *People Who Care v. Rockford Bd. of Educ., Sch. Dist. No. 205*, 90 F.3d 1307, 1315 (7th Cir. 1996). Accordingly, the district court should disallow time spent on what are essentially 'clerical' or secretarial tasks. Id. In this case, the tasks for which Spegon's counsel sought an award of paralegal fees included organizing file folders, document preparation, and copying documents. The district court concluded that only one-half hour of the paralegal's time was for 'reasonable and necessary administrative tasks that could not be performed by a secretary.' Spegon offers no evidence to suggest that the court erred in reaching this conclusion. Because we afford great deference to the district court's determination that these sort of tasks do not justify the efforts of a paralegal, we find that the court did not abuse its discretion in reducing the requested number of hours for the paralegal." *Spegon v. Catholic Bishop*, 175 F.3d 544, 553 (7th Cir. 1999).[4]

---

[4]A discussion of paralegal tasks that are appropriate for separate billing is included in the Accounting chapter.

Paralegals are indirectly regulated by the authorities that regulate their employers (lawyers), but are they subject to direct regulation? That depends on the state and on how the terms "paralegal" and "regulation" are defined. In this book, the term "paralegal" is used to describe a person working under the supervision of a licensed attorney; "regulation" is used to refer to standards mandated by governmental authority. The term "certification" is used to refer to a voluntary program for determining compliance with standards. While no state currently requires a license as a prerequisite to doing traditional paralegal work, a few have **registration** or certification for those who call themselves paralegals. (See Exhibit 1-2 for more on how licensure, certification, and registration differ.) To find the status of paralegals in your state, visit the **National Federation of Paralegal Associations (NFPA)** website (http://www.paralegals.org) and search the chart of regulation by state.

registration

Process of collecting names of individuals or firms performing certain tasks

National Federation of Paralegal Associations (NFPA)
Umbrella organization under which many local associations operate

Some people use the term "paralegal" or "independent paralegal" to describe people performing legal work for their own clients, without lawyer supervision. Paralegals working without lawyer supervision are beyond the scope of this book and, in many states, may be in violation of laws prohibiting unauthorized practice of law. (The unauthorized practice of law is discussed further at the end of this chapter.) In a few states, independent paralegals may provide document preparation and other limited services without violating prohibitions on unauthorized practice of law.

Paralegals in states without direct regulation of their job-related conduct are, of course, subject to the criminal laws that govern all of us. In addition, a paralegal could be sued by her employer if the lawyer suffers financial loss in a civil suit as a result of **vicarious liability** for the paralegal's negligent actions or is subject to discipline for an ethical violation by the paralegal. Attorneys remain responsible for legal work delegated to paralegals and must supervise paralegals' work.

vicarious liability
Liability imposed for actions of another

Example

Courts have interpreted the Washington Rules of Professional Conduct regarding confidential information to apply equally to paralegals as to attorneys. "This section [RPC 5.3] charges attorneys with the responsibility of ensuring that non-attorney staff members follow the same ethics rules that apply to attorneys." *Daines v. Alcatel*, 194 F.R.D. 678 (E.D. Wash. 2000). For purposes of disqualification, courts have therefore treated paralegals and other non-attorneys as having the same ethical responsibilities regarding confidential information as attorneys. *Richards v. Jain*, 168 F. Supp. 2d 1195, 1201 (D. Wash. 2001).

Whether traditional paralegals should be regulated and whether paralegals should be allowed to work directly for their own clients are very controversial issues. Regulation of traditional paralegals might not serve any purpose in protecting the public, but it could increase the recognition and utilization of paralegals, which could, in turn, reduce the cost of legal services. Regulation could also make law office management easier by simplifying the hiring process. Most law offices currently look at some mix of factors to hire paralegals: education, experience, certification, and references. On the other hand, regulation might be costly and complicated and might prevent some people from entering the field.

Exhibit 1-2
Defining Terms of Regulation

Even lawyers get confused about what terms such as "certification" and "registration" describe when referring to paralegals. Lawyers may advertise for a **certified** paralegal when they want a paralegal with a certificate in paralegal studies from a reputable school.

Registration is a process by which individuals list their names with a private association or governmental agency. Registration may require that individuals meet certain education, training, or bonding requirements and it often overlaps with certification. At the time of this writing, at least one private association refers to those who meet its certification standards (see below) as "registered" and a few states have programs for registration of paralegals. For example, in Texas, paralegals who wish to be recognized as specialists have the option of registering with the state if they meet stated criteria.

Certification programs are typically voluntary and are usually administered by private organizations, such as the NFPA, the **National Association of Legal Assistants (NALA)**, the **American Alliance of Paralegals (AAPI)**, or the **Association for Legal Professionals (NALS)**. The Ohio State Bar Association has recently implemented a voluntary certification program. Certifications are discussed in the chapter on professionalism. Certification is intended to validate an individual's skills and knowledge by setting standards for education, requiring testing, and, in some cases, requiring continuing education. Certification is typically not required to gain employment in a particular field.

In California it is unlawful to use the title "paralegal" unless the individual meets specified standards. The California system does not amount to licensure, in the opinion of some people, because an individual who does not meet the requirements could perform the same work , as long as he does not use the title "paralegal."

Licensure is the process by which an agency or branch of the government grants permission to persons meeting educational and testing requirements to engage in an occupation. Licensure is a mandatory requirement for employment in the field and is generally enacted by legislation. All states license lawyers, for instance, but none currently license paralegals.

Here are just some of the job titles given to non-lawyers in firms, in addition to "secretary," "paralegal," and "legal assistant." Remember too that some of these have levels (junior, clerk, senior, chief, head).

certified
To have it acknowledged that specific standards have been met

National Association of Legal Assistants (NALA)
Professional association, offers CLA designation

American Alliance of Paralegals (AAPI)
An association of individual paralegals, has a certification program

Association for Legal Professionals (NALS)
Association of individuals in legal service professions

Administrator	Facilities Manager	Marketing
Calendar Clerk	File Clerk	Office Services Manager
Case Clerk	Financial Officer	Operations Officer
Chief Operating Officer	Human Resources Manager	Records Clerk
Conflicts Clerk	Information Systems or Tech	Recruitment Manager
Controller	Librarian	
Docket Clerk	Manager	

The quality and structure of educational programs for paralegals varies widely. Some programs provide a few hours of training, while others require completion of a college degree (two- or four-year); some offer a certificate for completion of paralegal specialty courses and may (or may not) require completion of a college degree before completion of the certificate. Some programs offer college credit; some do not. Some programs are offered as distance education (online, correspondence, teleconferencing), while others are traditional. No wonder employers are confused! Attorneys usually do not have time to research the options, so they often rely on whether the educational program is ABA-approved. A program not approved by the ABA can be of very high quality, but an employer can hire a graduate of an ABA-approved program and know, without checking, that the program meets certain standards.

Despite the general lack of mandatory regulation, paralegals generally want to conform to the aspirations of a true profession. The national paralegal organizations, including NFPA and NALA, have promulgated codes of conduct for their members.

Assignment 1-2

Research Paralegal Issues

1. Using the NFPA website as a starting point (http://www.paralegals.org), write a short explanation of any statutes in your state that concern the work of paralegals. If your state has any type of scheme for registration or regulation, does it include any rules governing conduct?

2. Find the NALA Code of Ethics on that organization's website (http://www.nala.org/code.htm). What is the penalty for violation of the Code? Find the Code definition of "paralegal" and note how Canons 1 and 10 tie into the state ethical rules for lawyers.

Management Portfolio

Exempt employees
Exempt from some wage/hour laws; usually salaried

3. **Exempt employees** are those who are exempt from certain wage and hour laws (e.g., overtime pay). The designation usually applies to administrative, executive, or professional employees who receive an annual salary, in equal payments weekly, biweekly, or at some other specified time interval. You have just been hired by the newly formed partnership of Rodan & Stosh; partner Ed Rodan has a big project coming up and wonders whether he will have to pay his paralegal overtime. Use the Internet to research whether paralegals are generally considered exempt employees. A good starting point would be the NFPA website. Use the Search box. Write a short business memo explaining your findings to Mr. Rodan. (If you are not familiar with the format or style of a business memo, visit http://owl.english.purdue.edu/owl/resource/590/01. The site is an excellent resource that can help you with a variety of writing challenges.)

E. Types of Law Offices

A private law office may consist of a single lawyer (often called a **sole practitioner**) with no support staff or it may consist of hundreds of lawyers, paralegals, and other support staff with several **satellite offices**. As you might imagine, there are hundreds of options in between those two ends of the spectrum. Determining the type of environment in which you will function best and be happy is an important step in achieving success in the field. For example, in a small firm, a paralegal is likely to wear many hats and perform functions ranging from clerical to heavy client contact. In a larger firm, there is likely to be more specialization; while the type and level of the work may be more consistent, some people might find the consistency boring.

Some lawyers are **generalists** who will take almost any kind of case. A **boutique practice** is a firm that specializes in a particular area of law. "**Captive**" firms work only for a particular client or clients. A large full-service firm may have **practice groups** engaged in various specialties. Some lawyers and firms handle both **litigation** and **transactional law**; others handle only one or the other. Within the world of litigation, some firms handle both **civil** and **criminal** cases; others handle one or the other. The types of work the firm handles obviously determines the type of work assigned to paralegals. Consider: do you prefer the excitement of litigation or the orderly routine of transactional law? Do you like to work on a variety of matters or to be an expert in a few fields?

Some private firms refer to themselves as **clinics** and attempt to fill the need for affordable legal services. Other legal service clinics are funded by government, operated as part of a law school, or privately funded as not-for-profit operations. Many lawyers do not work in private law firms but in governmental **administrative agencies** or **in-house** corporate law departments. The "head" attorney in a corporate legal department is called **general counsel**. Corporate legal departments tend to focus on preventative legal work. For litigation and other unusual problems, the corporation will often turn to **outside counsel**. Agencies and corporate law departments also employ paralegals and can provide unique career opportunities. For example, a paralegal can often advance within a corporation without having to earn a law degree. A paralegal in an administrative agency is often given responsibilities that would not be delegated in a law firm, such as participation in adversarial proceedings. Although many law firm paralegals say that they would not give up the relationships they have with clients and the feeling of being an essential part of a team, employment in a law department or agency can also mean fewer "emergencies," more regular hours, and no need to keep track of time so that it can be billed to a client.

The letterhead in Exhibit 1-3 indicates that Med-Law is a **partnership** operating under a **trade name**. Some firms are structured as **business entities**, such as **professional corporations (PC)**, **professional associations**, **limited liability companies (LLC)**, or **limited liability partnerships (LLP)**, depending on what state law allows. Structuring the firm as a corporation or limited liability entity is intended to protect attorneys from vicarious liability for the actions of other lawyers and may have tax consequences.

As a practical matter, the choice of partnership or entity may make little difference in the operation of the firm. Certain lawyers have a financial interest in

sole practitioner
Attorney who does not have partners

satellite offices
Small office apart from the main office

generalists
Practices in various legal specialties

boutique practice
Often a small firm; has a particular focus or area of expertise

"Captive"
Firm that provides services to only one or a select group of clients

practice groups
Structure of law firm in which those working on certain types of legal problems are grouped together

litigation
Lawsuit; practice of law that involves courts

transactional law
Practice of law that does not typically involve going to court

civil
Area of law dealing with private disputes, such as property, contract, and tort matters

criminal
Area of law under which government prosecutes individuals for violation of criminal statutes

clinics
Law office with mission of providing affordable services

administrative agencies
Governmental entity created by statute, responsible for administering a particular law; a state department of children and family services; or a local zoning authority

in-house
Legal department within a larger organization

general counsel
Head attorney in a corporate legal department

outside counsel
Firm to which corporate law department refers work

partnership
Business in which partners share control, profits, and losses

trade name
Name under which business operates; also called an "assumed name"

business entities
Business recognized as having a legal existence separate from its owners

professional corporations (PC)
Entity owned and controlled by professionals (e.g., lawyers) that provides some protection from liability

professional associations
Entity owned and controlled by professionals (e.g., lawyers)

limited liability companies (LLC)
Business entity that provides members with protection from liability

limited liability partnerships (LLP)
Business entity that provides partners with protection from liability

managing partner
Partner responsible for firm operations

pro bono
Work done by a lawyer at a reduced rate or for free, "for the public good"

partners
An owner, shares in profits, losses, control

the business and a corresponding right to make business decisions; others are employees. A firm may have an autocratic style, with one or two decision makers, or a democratic culture in which many have input into decisions.

In large firms, the decision makers often operate through a **managing partner** or by committee. A firm might have a single management committee; separate management committees for internal affairs (hiring, technology) and external affairs (marketing, pro bono work); or several committees, including, for example, a hiring committee, a social committee, a technology committee, a **pro bono** committee, a compensation committee, and more. There is no standard structure. Increasingly, however, law firms are recognizing the value of having trained non-lawyers in administration and management positions. Lawyers typically have not been trained in management and finance and are most profitable to their firms when they are practicing law and billing clients!

F. Classifications of Lawyers Within a Firm

If you have ever examined a letter sent by a large law firm (e.g., Exhibit 1-3), you have probably noticed "the line." Names above the line are generally **partners**, who are the owners and decision makers for the firm. In Exhibit 1-3, note the years following the name of partner Sam Qureshi, indicating that Mr. Qureshi is deceased. The ethical rules of most jurisdictions allow a firm to retain the name of a deceased partner.

Must all of the owners of a firm be licensed lawyers? In most states, the answer is yes, but **multidisciplinary practice** is a hot issue. Ethical rules that prohibit lawyers from sharing fees with non-lawyers make non-lawyer ownership — as characterized by sharing in profits — impossible. These ethical rules are discussed in greater detail in another chapter.

Associates are lawyers who do not share in ownership or control and are generally employees of the partners; they typically hope to "make partner" after working for several years. While some firms still have an **up-or-out** policy for associates, other firms have determined that routinely offering associates partnership is no longer financially practical. It is increasingly common for firms to hire "permanent" associates, sometimes called **staff attorneys**, with the understanding that they will not be eligible for partnership.

Not all partners are equal. Some firms have junior or non-equity partners whose share of ownership and decision-making capacity is less than the full or **equity partners**. Even among the equity partners, some have more influence within the firm, typically because they are top **rainmakers**. People often call these "heavy hitters" or "corner office" partners.

In addition to partners and associates, a firm may employ **independent contractors** who are not actually employees; **law clerks**[5]; and non-lawyers, including paralegals and clerical workers, and individuals from other fields, such as accountants. Under the ethical rules in many states, non-lawyers cannot become

---

[5]Some lawyers use the term "law clerk" very loosely, to describe any non-lawyer employee, but in this book the term refers to law students working part-time in law firms.

owners of the firm, so a lawyer and a non-lawyer may not operate as a partnership by sharing legal fees.

Hiring independent contractor, "contract," or **freelance** lawyers and para-legals can work well for a firm. Sometimes the firm wants to "test drive" a potential new employee before making a commitment; other times the firm does not have a regular workload to justify a permanent hire. In addition, independent contractors are not entitled to any benefits the firm may offer, and must account for and pay their own taxes. Employers must be careful in determining whether a worker is an employee or an independent contractor:

> Employers who misclassify workers as independent contractors can end up with substantial tax bills as well as penalties for failing to pay employment taxes and failing to file required forms information. . . .
>
> Generally, whether a worker is an employee or an independent contractor depends upon how much control you have as a business owner. If you have the right to control or direct not only what is to be done but also how it is to be done then your workers are most likely employees. If you can direct or control only the result of the work done, and not the means and methods of accomplishing the result, then your workers are probably independent contractors.
>
> Three broad characteristics are used by the IRS to determine the relationship between businesses and workers—Behavioral Control, Financial Control, and the Type of Relationship. Behavioral Control covers facts that show whether the business has a right to direct or control how the work is done through instructions, training, or other means. Financial Control covers facts that show whether the business has a right to direct or control the financial and business aspects of the worker's job. The Type of Relationship factor relates to how the workers and the business owner perceive their relationship. U.S. Department of the Treasury, Internal Revenue Service, Independent Contractor vs. Employee, http://www.irs.gov/newsroom/article/0,,id=173423,00.html (last visited Feb. 9, 2009).

Note the designation of Ms. McCulloch on Exhibit 1-3. The term **of counsel** is used in so many different contexts that it has no single meaning. The term might be used to describe a relationship between a law firm and a lawyer who works part-time for the firm and also works at a separate solo law practice, law teaching, or a totally unrelated business.

Issue: A Rose by Any Other Name . . .

Law firms label individuals as partners, associates, independent contractors, and so on, but does that label bind outside parties, such as government agencies? For example, many law firms are "top heavy" according to race and/ or sex. Can a firm avoid liability under laws prohibiting discrimination against employees by calling lawyers partners rather than associates? Not always![6]

The of-counsel attorney might be an employee or might be a self-employed independent contractor in performing work for the firm; the attorney might be compensated on a **space for services** basis rather than with money. The term "of

---

[6]*See Clackamas Gastroenterology Assoc., P.C. v. Wells,* 123 S. Ct. 1673 (2003).

multidisciplinary practice
Joint practice and fee sharing between lawyers and nonlawyers

Associates
Lawyer who does not share in ownership or liability of firm; typically an employee

up-or-out
Policy requiring that an employee who does not achieve promotion leave the firm

staff attorneys
Permanent associate

equity partners
Attorney with ownership interest

rainmakers
Person who generates substantial business for the firm

independent contractors
Provides services but is not an employee

law clerks
Typically a law student

freelance
To work as an independent contractor

of counsel
Attorney's relationship with law firm; can mean many things

space for services
Arrangement under which a lawyer is given office space in return for performing legal services

counsel" can also be used to describe the relationship between a law firm and an expert in an area of law in which the firm does not think of itself as being particularly well qualified. The term can be used to describe retired partners who do not actively practice law on a full- or part-time basis, but occasionally consult with their former firm; probationary partners-to-be; or lawyers who have attained a permanent status within a firm but do not expect to attain full partner status. Might any ethical problems arise from the firm sharing space with someone not a member of the firm? Perhaps. An obvious risk is disclosure of confidential information. The firm must ensure that people not associated with the firm do not have access to client files, mail, messages, faxes, and e-mail, and cannot overhear verbal communications between lawyers and clients. Appropriate steps may include keeping all files in closed or locked files or in lawyers' offices; ensuring that correspondence, fax transmissions, and similar documents are received/ transmitted and handled from a place and in a way that prevents inadvertent disclosure; restricting access to telephones, fax machines, and computers by unauthorized personnel; dividing office space to create privacy; and training personnel. It is especially important that shared staff understand the separate entities and the need for special procedures. Even accidental disclosure of confidential communications between lawyer and client can result in discipline.

Sharing space can also create conflicts of interest. Circumstances may arise when the relationships between the lawyers may prevent them from effectively representing their respective clients or when confidential information is so sensitive that the lawyers sharing space cannot adequately ensure the appropriate degree of protection.

Lawyers sharing space, whether as part of a space-for-services arrangement or just as a matter of convenience and economy, must not mislead the public about the relationship. Careless communication or office setup could make people believe that the lawyers are affiliated when that is not the case. The public may assume that lawyers are part of the same firm unless specific efforts are made to clarify that they are practicing as separate entities. If the relationship between lawyers exists only to share office space, equipment, or other resources, they should not create a single name, such as "Roe & Doe" for signs, cards, or advertising. They must not share the same letterhead. Using disclaimers such as "not a legal partnership" does not necessarily solve the problem.

Example

Sufficient accessibility to confidential information by each lawyer can lead to an actual conflict; however, such permeability between the practices is not assumed. See *In re Sexson*, 613 N.E.2d 841 (Ind. 1993) ("firm" found when even though two lawyers practiced separately, they (1) used common letterhead; (2) shared office space, phone lines, and office personnel; and (3) had apparent access to each other's confidential information). However, when two practitioners present themselves to the public in a way suggesting that they are a firm or associated in the practice of law or otherwise conduct themselves in such a manner, they should be regarded as an association or a firm. *See United States v. Agboola*, 2001 U.S. Dist. LEXIS 25105, 11-12 (D. Minn. Oct. 31, 2001); Model R. Prof'l Conduct 1.10 (2001).

**Exhibit 1-3
Med-Law Letter**

MED-LAW
1056 Spartan Drive
Elgin, IL 00123
Phone: 947-697-0000
Fax: 947-697-0001
Website: www.medlawelgin.com

PARTNERS:

Sam Qureshi 1929-2006   Sheila Abrams
Joseph W. Hallock   Lynn O'Donnell
Andrew L. Sosonowski   Marie Kostelny
Dana Biegel

ASSOCIATES:
Gail Hendry
Pat McNerney   **Of Counsel:**
Robert K. Warski   Sharon McCulloch
Jude Kullenberg

September 24, 2009

Rene Miller
140 S. Wood Dale Rd.
Wood Dale, ND 00191

Dear Ms. Miller:

Welcome aboard! This letter is to confirm that we have hired you as our new paralegal and office manager, pursuant to the terms discussed during your interview last week. We look forward to seeing you at 8:30 a.m. on Monday, October 8. At that time I will introduce you to the staff, show you your office, and acquaint you with our procedures.

Sincerely,

Sheila Abrams
SAA: fat

Paralegals:
Stacy Herrmann   Mike Kalland   Joan Lehmann   Jean Walters

co-counsel
Lawyers working together on a matter

Lawyers who are not in the same firm may, from time to time, work together as **co-counsel** on a matter and share legal fees. Often they send separate bills to avoid the impression that they are in the same law firm, but they may send out a joint bill or a bill from one of the firms with an appropriate explanation. Sharing of fees by lawyers not in the same firm is subject to special ethical rules. Generally, fees must be divided in a way proportional to the services performed by each lawyer, or the lawyers must assume joint responsibility for the matter, and the client must be informed.

Assignment 1-3

Research Ethical Issues

Using the ethical rules for your state (which you bookmarked or added to your Favorites as part of an earlier assignment), do the following:

1. Identify all the sections relating to lawyers' sharing office space.
2. Find the sections relating to law firm names. May a firm continue to use the name of a deceased partner? Suppose that a partner or associate becomes a judge and the firm has lots of preprinted stationary in the supply room that includes the name of that partner or associate. Suppose that the firm also just paid a hefty fee to have the names of all the lawyers painted on the front of its building. Is there a problem with continuing to use that stationary or leaving the painting on the building unchanged?
3. Would a law firm in your state be permitted to use a trade name, such as "DUI Specialists"?
4. What do the rules require if the firm has offices in several states, but some lawyers are not authorized to practice in each state in which the firm's offices are located?
5. Does your state prohibit lawyers from entering into partnership with non-lawyers (multidisciplinary practice)?
6. Exhibit 1-3 includes the names of the firm's paralegals. Would this be lawful in your state? May paralegals be identified on letterhead, the firm's website, and business cards? The issue is not addressed by the rules of professional conduct in every state, so you may need to look at ethical opinions, such as Florida Ethics Opinion 86-4 (1986), http://www.floridabar.org/TFB/TFBETOpin.nsf/0/d3129e3c314163ad85256b2f006cab14?OpenDocument, or Utah Bar Opinion 131 (1993), http://www.utahbar.org/rules_ops_pols/ethics_opinions/op_131.html.

G.   Understanding the Chain of Command

It is very important to know the names and roles of the people within the firm that employs you from your first day on the job. One of the quickest ways to gain a person's attention and respect is to use the person's name. Understanding the status of the various individuals who assign projects can help you understand the firm's priorities and your relationship to your coworkers.

An **organizational chart** is essential to understanding the workings of a large law firm. Such a chart describes the structure of an organization in terms of rank or function. While a small firm may not need a formal chart, it does need to define its "chain of command" and clarify responsibilities. In large firms the chart can be very complicated and is, therefore, sometimes dissected into smaller charts for each individual department or practice area or to accommodate separate offices, known as **satellite offices**. While an organizational chart often includes the names of individuals who fill particular positions, the chart should reflect the functions of the firm and the positions that have responsibility for each function, so that functions don't "fall between the cracks" when people change jobs or are absent from work.

Titles and chain of command are important to more than efficient delegation of work and good working relationships. The ABA Model Rules obligate partners to make reasonable efforts to ensure ethical behavior by those they supervise (Rule 5.1) and obligate all lawyers to make reasonable efforts to ensure ethical behavior by non-lawyers they supervise (5.3). Employers are generally vicariously liable for the job-related negligence of their employees. On the other hand, an employee is not vicariously liable for the actions of another simply because she worked as an employee for the firm.[7]

In addition to understanding the chain of command, employees in a law firm should have clear descriptions of their responsibilities and, when appropriate, instructions on how to perform those responsibilities. A **job description** is valuable for hiring, assessing performance, evaluating compensation, and re-solving disputes among employees. A **procedures manual** describes how specific tasks should be performed, in order to ensure compliance with ethical rules, maintain uniformity, control quality, and allow others to perform an employee's job with minimum disruption.

For example, assume that the receptionist at Med-Law is responsible for greeting clients in person and by phone; taking messages; ensuring that the copier has paper and toner and completing large copy jobs; handling mail, pickups, and deliveries; keeping coffee available; overseeing the fax machine; and "stripping" closed files.[8] Simple enough, right? But now suppose that the re-ceptionist is taken ill and the firm has to bring in a receptionist from a **temporary agency**. Would a temporary employee instinctively know that these are the functions of the job? Would he know how to operate the copier, the phone system, and fax? Does he know how the firm protects the confidentiality of clients in handling phone calls, mail, and faxes? Does he know which delivery service the firm uses? Would he know which papers can be safely removed from a closed file

organizational chart
Describes the structure of an organization in terms of rank or function

satellite offices
Small office apart from the main office

job description
Detailed identification of job responsibilities and qualifications

procedures manual
Detailed descriptions of how to perform tasks in compliance with office policy

temporary agency
Business that provides workers on a temporary basis

---

[7] *Standage v. Jaburg & Wilk, P.C.*, 866 P.2d 889 (Ariz. Ct. App. 1993).
[8] This task is described in Chapter 8 on records management.

and how to dispose of those papers? Does the office manager want to spend the day answering questions about how mail should be distributed and how the coffee maker works?

Assignment 1-4
Organization Chart, Procedures Manual

Management Portfolio

1. Examine the organization chart for Med-Law, shown in Exhibit 1-4, and discuss the following:
   a. Med-Law has decided that it needs only one secretary to support four professionals (lawyers and paralegals) because the lawyers and paralegals are quite good at using technology and do much of their own keyboarding, filing, and similar clerical work. Why do you think the secretaries are listed under the control of the office manager, rather than one per practice group? What kinds of problems might this cause or avoid?
   b. Is there any difference in the structure of the malpractice group as compared to the other two practice groups? If you see a difference, can you explain why it might be done differently?
   c. Do you see any potential problems for the paralegals in the regulatory affairs and real estate groups, based on the chart?
2. What problems are avoided by having distinct practice groups, as opposed to a structure in which all of the paralegals work for all of the lawyers?
3. Job applicants often dread the inevitable "Do you have any questions?" Based on what you have learned about law firm structure and operations so far, formulate three to four questions that would help you determine whether you would like to work for a particular firm.
4. Examine job opportunities within federal agencies. Visit http://www.usajobs.gov and search "paralegal." Next, try to find a similar site that lists jobs in your state agencies.
5. Are you ready for management? Do some online research to determine the characteristics of a good manager. For example, look at Stephen Covey's *Seven Habits of Highly Effective People*. Can the traits be learned, or are they part of a basic personality type?

Management Portfolio

6. Earlier in this chapter, you learned that people from other countries are sometimes confused about the functions of a notary public. To learn more about the issue, visit http://www.nationalnotary.org/news/index.cfm?Text=newsNotary&newsID=152. Using the same website, determine how to become a notary public in your state. Next, find your state's online

information about notaries and write a page for an office procedures manual, describing how a new employee can become a notary, what functions a notary public serves, and what procedures a staff member should follow in notarizing documents while on the job.

Because you will create several such pages for the manual in future assignments, use an easy-to-read format that you can use for all procedures manual pages. An outline format, for instance, could work well (see the example below). To see more examples of formatting, visit the Microsoft Templates site, which includes templates that can be used for many assignments in this book as well as for other situations: http://office. microsoft.com/en-us/templates/FX100595491033.aspx. Enter "office procedures" in the search box. You will find that even a form for substitute teachers could be used to create a contact sheet for a procedures manual.

Exhibit 1-4
Organization Chart

For assistance in preparing a professional-looking chart, see http://office. microsoft.com/en-us/visio/HA011588171033.aspx.

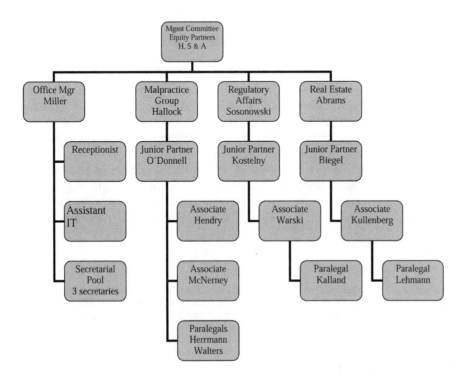

Example

Notary Procedures:

1. **How to become a notary**
   a. **Contact information**
   b. **Qualifications**
2. **Functions of a notary**
3. **Procedures to be followed when you are asked to notarize a document**

H.   Outsourcing

outsourcing
Having work performed by individuals or companies outside the firm

Many law firms, like other businesses, have always outsourced some of their non-substantive functions such as accounting or technology support. Some have also outsourced a portion of their substantive functions to independent contractor lawyers and freelance paralegals (described below). This type of **outsourcing** has not been controversial (unless you lost your job because of it!) because it generally has meant that the firm was able to obtain the use of expertise and equipment that it could not otherwise afford. It often results in savings for clients and in new jobs at other local businesses.

offshoring
Outsourcing to workers outside the United States

Recently, however, substantive legal work is being outsourced to providers outside the United States (**offshoring**). This trend allows law firms and corporate law firms to have entry-level work, normally done by new paralegals and associates, to be done at a much lower cost in countries like India and Australia, where there are many English-speaking people, trained in law, willing to work at a much lower wage doing things like document review, contract review, discovery support, and legal research. Some large firms have established their own overseas offices. Others rely on outsourcing services that establish offices, train and supervise employees, and, of course, work for the firm only when needed. The need to transport huge quantities of often irreplaceable documents prevented offshoring until the mid-1990s; use of electronic documents and instant communication by means of the Internet has made it possible and economical. For many firms, the bottom line is keeping costs down.

In addition to the possible loss of U.S. jobs,[9] offshoring presents other compelling issues. How will new paralegals and associates gain the hands-on experience they need to move into upper-level and supervisory positions? It is not a simple question. In 2008 the ABA gave its approval to the practice of

---

[9]An estimated 12,000 legal jobs moved offshore in 2004 alone. Krysten Crawford, Outsourcing the Lawyers, CNNMoney.com, Oct. 15, 2004, http://money.cnn.com/2004/10/14/news/economy/lawyer_outsourcing/?cnn=yes. The trend is expected to continue. On November 26, 2008, the Wall Street Journal reported that "Forrester Research Inc., Cambridge, Mass., estimates that 35,000 U.S. legal jobs will be moved offshore by 2010 and 79,000 will move by 2015." For more information about the trend, the services available, and costs, see http://www.mindcrest.com/ and http://www.paralegals.org/associations/2270/files/outsourcing.pdf.

offshoring. Those who promote offshoring argue that by making firms more efficient and profitable, they actually create additional jobs in the United States.

Perhaps the most important questions are these: Are offshore employees, who are typically not licensed lawyers in the United States, truly being supervised as needed to avoid **unauthorized practice of law (UPL)**? Does the practice provide less protection for confidential information or even create conflicts of interests in certain situations?

unauthorized practice of law (UPL)
Doing things that only a lawyer should do, while not licensed as a lawyer

Every state has laws regulating the practice of law; UPL refers to performing work in violation of those statutes. As of this writing, every state except Arizona has a UPL statute that makes it illegal for anyone other than a licensed lawyer to practice law. While the definition of "practicing law" is very ambiguous and may vary from location to location, the ambiguity is not usually problematic in the context of the responsibilities of a traditional paralegal, working under supervision of an attorney. A freelance paralegal, working as an independent contractor for attorneys, can still be a traditional paralegal, as long as her customers are lawyers. It is generally agreed that, under supervision of a lawyer, a paralegal can do anything a lawyer can do except

- Establish the attorney-client relationship and set fees;
- Represent a party in an adversarial hearing in a court or other tribunal that does not provide for non-lawyer representation, although a paralegal can assist at trial and, in many jurisdictions, appear in court on non-contested matters;
- Give legal advice, which can be defined as suggesting a course of action or predicting a result based on knowledge of an individual's factual situation and substantive law, although a paralegal can communicate legal advice.

The situation is more troublesome when it involves an individual who is not a traditional paralegal and can range from the former legal secretary who advises her neighbor to lock the no-good husband out of the house, to the real estate agent who advises a seller to sign a contract for deed and not record it, to business operations providing a range of legal services without involvement of an attorney. These services are sometimes called pro bono or document preparation services and may claim to provide only clerical services to parties representing themselves. How states deal with UPL varies widely.

Should lawyers and traditional paralegals be concerned about UPL? Yes: innocent clients could be hurt, the reputation of the legal field could suffer, and law firms might lose business. On a more practical level, the ethics rules in many states hold a lawyer responsible for engaging in UPL by practicing in a state in which she is not licensed and for assisting in UPL by failing to properly supervise paralegals and other non-lawyers. Proper education and supervision of non-lawyer employees is essential to meeting the ethical requirements of the practice of law.

Assignment 1-5
Research Unauthorized Practice

---

1. Learn more about it: The American Bar Association tracks developments on UPL (http://www.abanet.org/rpte/section_info/upl/home.html), and several state bar associations have sections devoted to UPL. NFPA has a position paper on non-lawyer practice (http://www.paralegals.org/associations/2270/files/non_lawyer_practice.pdf). NALA states that "[a] legal assistant/paralegal cannot give legal advice, represent a client in court, set a fee, or accept a case, which functions are generally considered the practice of law. Working under the supervision of an attorney, the legal assistant's work product is merged with and becomes part of the attorney work product. In communications with clients and the public, the legal assistant's non-lawyer status must be clear." NALA, What Is a Paralegal? http://www.nala.org/whatis.htm (last visited Feb. 9, 2009). Using a search engine such as Google, enter the name of your state and "unauthorized practice of law" to find out how the issue has been dealt with in your state.

Management Portfolio

discovery
Exchange of information and evidence before trial

2. Your new firm, Rodan & Stosh, is involved in a huge products liability case. Ed Rodan is considering using a company based in India to handle the thousands of documents that will be sent and received during **discovery**. Leona Stosh is not sure it is a good idea; she has heard the paralegals grumbling that this is why new graduates cannot find entry-level jobs and is afraid that it will be bad for office morale. Use the Internet to research legal outsourcing. The ABA website (http://www.abanet.org) is a particularly good source of information; you should be able to examine a 2008 ethical opinion entitled Lawyer's Obligations When Outsourcing Legal and Nonlegal Support Services (Formal Ethics Op. 08-451 (2008)). First, identify at least two companies that provide legal outsourcing using personnel in India. Next, write a one- to two- page memo addressing alternatives to offshoring this work and how the partners should proceed if they decide to use the company in India.

Out There — Paralegal Profile
The Value of Diverse Experiences

Denise Hawthorne earned a BS degree in anthropology; held jobs in the corporate world, in retail, and in real estate; and was an at-home mother before earning her paralegal certificate from an ABA-approved program. While in school, Denise was awarded a paid internship with the federal Securities and Exchange Commission (SEC).

"Working for the government was exciting and challenging. The positions are salaried so there was no pressure to keep billable hours. I learned a lot about administrative law as well as how to survive in a large and accountable chain of command. I did substantive work for eight attorneys under the direction of one supervising attorney. She coordinated their projects and gave assignments on a weekly basis. Each attorney had a precise way of doing things and could be quite explicit about the expected result. The advantage was the exposure to many different procedures as each attorney represented a different level in the investigative process. The disadvantage was that I worked on one small piece of a job and did not always see how it fit into the whole project. There  was no 'conception to completion' fulfillment in this position. Another challenge was working with the variety of personalities and communication styles. That is where my supervisor would step in to advise and direct. A major emphasis with the internship was the ongoing training I received regarding federal agency regulations. The government paid a generous internship salary and provided a public transportation stipend. The greatest fulfillment for me was working for the 'good guy' so to speak. The agency also had an IT section — I had to call on them regularly! Security was of utmost importance and I was sharply aware of confidentiality and the importance not to comment or say anything about my work. The legal research using Westlaw and EDGAR brought me to greater depths of the law. Almost every attorney not only took the time to explain what they wanted but provided constructive criticism for revisions. I personally grew from the feedback of my supervisor and attorneys. They set aside the time to review and invest in me."

"After the agency experience, I sought a job where I would have more client contact. I found a job with a single attorney. This kind of a job requires wearing many hats! I do my own clerical work—being proficient with computer software is essential. One 'downside' to this type of firm is that the lawyer's style and personality are part of every aspect of the office. I also miss having colleagues with whom to discuss problems and solutions. On the other hand, I have learned to work independently and learned a lot about several new areas of law on my own; handling billing and other financial matters have rounded out my paralegal experience. I thoroughly enjoy meeting with clients and using the time-billing database."

What's next for Denise? She is thinking of trying a corporate law department.

Chapter Review

Discussion Questions

1. What is outsourcing, and what issues does the practice implicate?
2. What are independent contractors? How does use of independent contractors benefit an employer? Might it benefit the worker?
3. How are lawyers regulated in your state?
4. What are the different meanings that might attach to the designation "of counsel"?
5. What is vicarious liability, and why is it a concern to partners? How might concerns about vicarious liability effect lawyers' decisions in delegating high-level work?
6. Describe some of the back-office functions of a medium to large law office.
7. In some firms, new associates are immediately assigned to a practice group; in other firms, they are not. Identify advantages to each system.
8. Would you prefer to work as a paralegal for a government agency, a corporate law department, a sole practitioner, a small firm, or a large firm? Why?
9. Discuss some of the procedures that should be implemented to prevent ethical problems when sharing office space.
10. Why would a paralegal care whether he or she is classified as an exempt or non-exempt employee?
11. Identify three activities in which a paralegal should not engage, even under supervision of an attorney, to avoid the appearance of unauthorized practice of law.

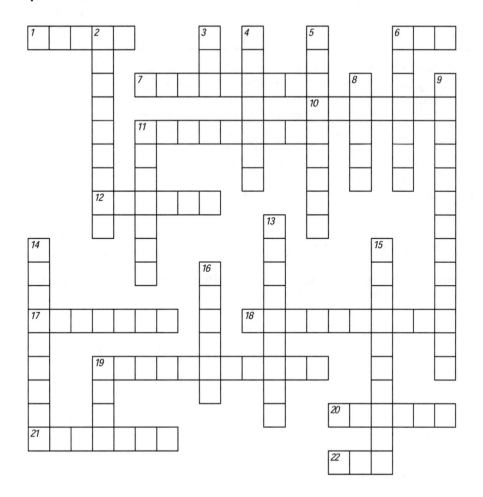

Across

1. typically a law school student
6. initials, most lawyers must attend
7. _____ liability for actions of another
10. an owner of the firm
11. lawyer-employee
12. partner's ownership interest
17. Spanish for "attorney"
18. practice that involves going to court
19. legal work, not clerical
20. _____ public, witnesses signatures under oath
21. obtained by meeting mandatory qualifications to engage in profession
22. _____exam

Down

2. brings in lots of business
3. initials, approves paralegal education programs
4. also called integrated bar association
5. license to practice law has been revoked temporarily
6. of _____, describes relationship of attorney to firm
8. _____ name, also called assumed name
9. a lawyer who prepares contracts, handles real estate matters, writes wills, or does similar type of work
11. analyzes risk using math

Terms and Definitions

American Alliance of Paralegals, Inc. (AAPI): An association of individual paralegals, has a certification program

American Bar Association (ABA): National association of attorneys; has a program for approval of paralegal programs

abogado: Spanish for "attorney"

administrative agency: Governmental entity created by statute, responsible for administering a particular law; a state department of children and family services; or a local zoning authority

associate: Lawyer who does not share in ownership or liability of firm; typically an employee

Association for Legal Professionals (NALS): Association of individuals in legal service professions

back-office: Systems that do not deal directly with client

bar association: Professional organization of lawyers, responsible for regulation in some states

bar exam: Test taken after law school, before becoming a licensed attorney

barrister: Lawyer licensed to practice in court (generally in England or Wales)

boutique practice: Often a small firm; has a particular focus or area of expertise

business entity: Business recognized as having a legal existence separate from its owners

captive: Firm that provides services to only one or a select group of clients

certified: To have it acknowledged that specific standards have been met

continuing legal education (CLE): Often required as part of licensing or certification; if mandatory called MCLE

civil: Area of law dealing with private disputes, such as property, contract, and tort matters

clinic: Law office with mission of providing affordable services

co-counsel: Lawyers working together on a matter

criminal: Area of law under which government prosecutes individuals for violation of criminal statutes

disbarment: Act of being officially removed from practice as an attorney

discovery: Exchange of information and evidence before trial

equity partner: Attorney with ownership interest

exempt employee: Exempt from some wage/hour laws; usually salaried

freelance: To work as an independent contractor

front-office: Systems that deal directly with the client (i.e., practice of law)

general counsel: Head attorney in a corporate legal department

generalist: Practices in various legal specialties
IT specialist: Expert in information technology (IT)
in-house: Legal department within a larger organization
independent contractor: Provides services but is not an employee
integrated (or unified) bar association: Bar association that has regulatory authority over lawyers in the state
J.D.: Juris Doctor, the degree most commonly earned in law school
job description: Detailed identification of job responsibilities and qualifications
lawyers assistance program (LAP): Counseling program for lawyers with substance abuse or other personal problems
law clerk: Typically a law student
licensed: Having governmental permission to perform certain acts
limited liability company (LLC): Business entity that provides members with protection from liability
limited liability partnership (LLP): Business entity that provides partners with protection from liability
litigation: Lawsuit; practice of law that involves courts
malpractice: Negligence in the performance of professional duties; may be a basis of civil liability
managing partner: Partner responsible for firm operations
Model Rules: Ethical rules promulgated by American Bar Association
multidisciplinary practice: Joint practice and fee sharing between lawyers and nonlawyers
National Association of Legal Assistants (NALA): Professional association, offers CLA designation
National Federation of Paralegal Associations (NFPA): Umbrella organization under which many local associations operate
notario: In Spanish-speaking countries, authorized to perform official functions and transactional types of legal practice
notary public: Authorized to witness signatures, verify identity, administer oaths
of counsel: Attorney's relationship with law firm; can mean many things
offshoring: Outsourcing to workers outside the United States
organizational chart: Describes the structure of an organization in terms of rank or function
outside counsel: Firm to which corporate law department refers work
outsourcing: Having work performed by individuals or companies outside the firm
paralegal: Person qualified by education, training, or experience to perform substantive legal work under supervision of an attorney; also called "legal assistant"
partner: An owner, shares in profits, losses, control
partnership: Business in which partners share control, profits, and losses
practice groups: Structure of law firm in which those working on certain types of legal problems are grouped together
pro bono: Work done by a lawyer at a reduced rate or for free, "for the public good"
probation: Discipline under which attorney may practice, with supervision or conditions
procedures manual: Detailed descriptions of how to perform tasks in compliance with office policy
professional association: Entity owned and controlled by professionals (e.g., lawyers)

professional corporation (PC): Entity owned and controlled by professionals (e.g., lawyers) that provides some protection from liability

rainmaker: Person who generates substantial business for the firm

reciprocity: Recognition of licenses issued by other states

registration: Process of collecting names of individuals or firms performing certain tasks

reprimand: Censure or rebuke

restitution: Reparations; restoring what was taken

satellite office: Small office apart from the main office

sole practitioner: Attorney who does not have partners

solicitor: Lawyer authorized to give advice and prepare documents, but not to go to court, in England or Wales

space for services: Arrangement under which a lawyer is given office space in return for performing legal services

staff attorney: Permanent associate

strict liability: Responsibility without regard to fault

substantive legal work: Requires knowledge of legal concepts; not clerical work

suspension: Temporarily removed

temporary agency: Business that provides workers on a temporary basis

trade name: Name under which business operates; also called an "assumed name"

transactional law: Practice of law that does not typically involve going to court

unauthorized practice of law (UPL): Doing things that only a lawyer should do, while not licensed as a lawyer

up-or-out: Policy requiring that an employee who does not achieve promotion leave the firm

vicarious liability: Liability imposed for actions of another

2

About Technology

As a Manager

You will be responsible for ensuring that your firm is using the most effective technology to meet client needs. You will regularly evaluate what technology the firm is using, research and propose purchases, plan for implementation of new technology and systems, arrange for employee training, and, most important, set policies to ensure the security of data.

Objectives

This chapter is intended for students who have not had an "Introduction to Computers" class or who had such a class long ago and have not used computers extensively in their work.

After completing this chapter, you will be able to

- Explain what the terms "operating system" and "applications software" mean.
- Discuss the purposes of computer networks, intranets, and extranets, as well as the problems inherent in those setups.
- Describe how and why backups are done in a law firm.
- Conduct research on the Internet and evaluate the credibility of websites.
- Know which listservs may benefit your career and understand how to manage e-mail.
- Know the functions and capabilities of word processing, spreadsheet, database, and presentation programs and the terminology associated with each.
- Understand the features of printers, fax machines, copiers, scanners, digital cameras, and personal digital assistants and be able to evaluate the features needed for a particular use.
- Manage changes in technology.

"But I'm a language and people person, not a technical person!" Many drawn to legal careers would say this, and it is a good thing. Pepperdine University's Graziadio School of Business and Management reports that the skills needed for success as a twenty-first-century manager include these:

- Communication and interpersonal skills
- An ethical or spiritual orientation
- The ability to manage change
- The ability to motivate
- Analytic and problem-solving skills
- Being a strategic/visionary manager

Mark Mallinger, *Management Skills for the Twenty First Century*, Graziadio Business Report, http://gbr.pepperdine.edu/982/skills.html (last visited Feb. 10, 2009).

But how will you communicate, manage change, motivate, and solve problems? Most likely you will accomplish those things using a computer. As early as 1989, experts recognized that

> [m]anagers plan and coordinate the destinies of their companies through intelligent use of the information that pumps through the organization's arteries. Today managers systematize the gathering and distribution of data and information through computerized networks. Increasingly, with the aid of computer-driven, statistics-oriented decision support systems, managers exert their influence from their own personal work stations. Lester R. Bittel, *The 36-Hour Management Course* (1989).

During the last 15 years of the twentieth century, technology transformed every aspect of the practice of law. Even the relationships of people within firms changed: the traditional legal secretary's skills, such as taking dictation, high-speed typing, and filing, became less important. Different skills became important — the skills described in the Foreword of this book.

Many of the changes have made the practice of law more efficient. On the other hand, acquiring the latest technology is expensive, and learning to use it is time-consuming. Technology has also raised the bar. Courts and clients are less tolerant of mistakes and delays. Legal professionals have access to so much more information — but do they have the time to use it or the ability to organize it?

Some legal professionals were initially frightened by technology and convinced that they could not and did not have to learn to use it. They hoped that their knowledge of substantive law would be enough and that they could avoid the revolution. The time of such thinking has passed. There is no getting around it: entry into the legal profession absolutely requires the ability to use technology.

There are several difficulties with this reality. Which technology? What level of ability? How do established workers trying to enter a new field compete with colleagues who have used computers since early childhood?

Some of you are those people who have used technology since early childhood. Others are people who have learned on the job or taken classes. You likely know far more about technology than the author of this book. You could do all of the assignments in this book without reading this chapter. If you are one of those people — congratulations! Never stop learning! You already know one of the important secrets of dealing with technology:

ONCE YOU HAVE SOME BASIC COMPUTER SKILLS AND KNOW WHAT TECHNOLOGY CAN DO, YOU CAN FIGURE OUT HOW TO DO IT.

This is a very important statement because you don't know which programs will be in use at the firm that hires you. In addition, technology changes every day. You cannot learn all of it. Because of the expense of acquiring licenses, you may not have an opportunity to work with particular software before starting at a firm that uses it.

The goal of later chapters in this book is to teach you what technology is available, what that technology can do, and how to perform the same functions using your basic skills and the tools available to you. The goal of this chapter is to introduce you to (or reacquaint you with) the basic skills. Some assignments in this book are intended to teach or reinforce specific technology skills, but most of the information on technology is intended to teach you the terminology, the available functions, and the particular law office applications. Some of the information in this chapter is repeated in later chapters, as it is relevant to the law office management competency under discussion.

A. Your Computer: The Basics

operating system
Software that allows computer to run applications

The computer you use now and the computer you will use on the job have some things in common. Each has an **operating system** that, among other things,

applications programs
Software designed for a particular task, such as word processing

allows you to run **applications programs**. The most common operating systems currently in use are Microsoft Windows, the Macintosh operating system, Linux, and Solaris. Because Windows is most commonly used in law offices, this book gives examples using the applications found in Microsoft Office, a bundle of applications commonly found on business computers.

For More Information

Because Microsoft is the most commonly used operating system, this book refers to many Microsoft programs and tutorials and gives websites for further information. If you want more information about another type of operating system or its applications, visit one of these websites:

- http://www.apple.com/business/solutions/legal.html. Law office applications for the Mac
- http://www.themaclawyer.com. Blog on using Macs in the practice of law
- http://maclawstudents.com/blog. Mac for law students
- http://lawtech.wordpress.com/2007/07/10/ubuntu-linux-law-office. Blog on using Linux in law offices
- http://www.linux.com/articles/113155. Information about Linux
- http://www.linux.org. More information about Linux/Unix and applications
- http://www.sun.com/software/solaris/index.jsp. Information about Solaris and applications
- http://www.google.com/google-d-s/tour1.html. How to create documents, spreadsheets, and presentations online
- http://www.nytimes.com/2006/06/17/technology/17money.html. How to find free software online
- http://www.nextstudent.com/the-students-blog/archive/2007/07/19/the-mac-software-you-need-to-get-through-college.aspx. Excellent site for and articles on Mac freeware

---

freeware
Software available for free download; also called "open source"

license
Permission to use copyrighted software

The basic functions in the Microsoft Office suite can be found elsewhere, even in **freeware**, so the examples and assignments will have value even if you do not work with Microsoft. Software is protected intellectual property. A **license** is a contract between a software publisher and a user; it grants the user permission to use and/or copy the software so that the use is not an infringement of the publisher's rights under copyright law. Freeware is software that can be used without paying for a license.

This book assumes at least some familiarity with the concept of networked computers, finding information on the Internet, sending and receiving e-mail, word processing, data management using a spreadsheet or database, and presentation software such as PowerPoint. This introduces or reviews those concepts.

network
Group of connected computers and hardware

1.　Networks, Intranets, and Extranets

A computer **network** is simply an interconnected group of computers and other hardware, such as printers, fax machines, and scanners. In a peer-to-peer network, one of the workstation computers acts as **server**, but in a larger network, one or more dedicated servers may be needed to manage communication and/or resources of the network with adequate memory and speed. A server is simply a computer that has been configured to share its resources with or run software for other computers. A large firm might have a single multiprocessing server or different servers for different jobs, which might include an applications server, on which applications are stored and run; a file server, on which files are stored; a mail server for e-mail; a print server that manages the printers; and a database server.

Network connections can be wired or wireless. Networking computers allows users to communicate easily and to share hardware and data. Networked computers can be used to establish an **intranet**, essentially a private version of the Internet under the control of a single administrative entity and generally available to a limited group, such as the employees of the organization.

A law firm's intranet would typically allow individual users to access the firm's forms and documents, calendar, client information, internal directory, and more. An intranet is not necessarily accessible from outside the office by means of the Internet, but such access can be extremely valuable to users who are away from the office. If the firm does provide offsite access, it must be particularly careful about security, as described below.

An **extranet** is a network that has limited connections to the networks of one or more other trusted organizations. Most of you have used an extranet when you have logged onto a site, such as Federal Express, to track the progress or location of a package or logged onto a site to check your bank balance and transfer money. The advantages of an extranet include less use of expensive delivery services, better security than some other means of sharing information, instant access to information (elimination of telephone tag!), and reduced need to print documents.

A law firm extranet can have tremendous value in improving communication with clients, who can use it to check their bills, verify important dates, or examine documents. Similarly, a corporate client may establish an extranet so that its law firm can have access to documents and other information. **Mega-firms**, with offices in many cities or even different countries, often use extranets to connect the various offices. Other uses for an extranet include setting up a common worksite with another firm when working as co-counsel or even setting up a site accessible to opposing counsel for mandatory sharing of information and documents.

As you might imagine, any technology with such potential for improving the practice of law also has the potential for problems. Poor design causes many of the most common minor problems of intranets and extranets, so that the site is not user-friendly or includes graphics that make it slow to open. Some firms overuse their extranets for marketing, which may discourage clients from using the site. Another extranet problem is the "Wizard of Oz" factor—clients "look behind the curtain" and expect to see constant and regular work on their matters. The biggest problem with respect to extranets (and, to some extent, intranets) is security. No intranet or extranet (or even local group of networked computers) should be considered completely impenetrable to outsiders, sometimes called **hackers**, but various tools can be used to make the system very secure. With respect to these outsiders, the law firm's goal is twofold: to keep them out and to

server
A central computer that manages computer network resources; a file server stores files for users; a print server manages printers; a network server manages network traffic

intranet
Private version of Internet within organization

extranet
Private intranet extended to select outsiders

Mega-firms
Extremely large firms

hackers
Computer user who intentionally gains access to confidential information

make the system difficult to enter so that they turn their attention to sites without security. Security tools can be expensive and can make the system slower and more difficult to use, so the firm must carefully evaluate its needs before implementing particular tools.

A firm with only an intranet, without offsite access, is typically concerned only with restricting access to the system, while a firm with an extranet or an intranet with offsite access must also consider how to protect information in transit.

Outside hackers get more attention, but many experts agree that the biggest threat is from insiders. Firms should screen employees before giving them access to the system and monitor use once employees have access. Larger firms often establish an information security office to manage sensitive client documents and implement practices to protect confidentiality. Many firms require employees to sign a policy stating that they understand that there is no expectation to privacy when using any of the employer's computers or related resources.

The most common way of restricting access is by requiring use of passwords. Unfortunately, when employees choose their own passwords, they often pick easy-to-guess words, use the same password for years, and even share their passwords with others. On the other hand, using hard-to-remember computer-generated passwords and requiring frequent password changes can result in employees writing their passwords on sticky notes on their monitors. The firm should have policies that establish how often passwords should be changed and prohibit employees from giving their passwords to others. Firms can also assign different levels of access to supervisors, administrators, trusted users, vulnerable users, and guests, according to the respective needs of those users.

Some firms combine a password selected by the employee along with a "token," an electronic device about the size of a poker chip that has a serial number listed on the back and a display on the front with a six-digit number that changes every 60 seconds. The server, which runs the same number-generating program as the token, recognizes the serial number based on the employee entering the password and determines whether the number entered is correct for the employee at that time before allowing access to the server.

Another approach is **encryption**, or "scrambling" of information on the site by the use of software so that it is not accessible to anyone without a "key." Encryption, discussed in more detail in Chapter 3, is usually thought of as a method to protect information in transit, but it also protects very sensitive information in storage on your intranet. It is also possible to **partition** information so that an intruder hacking into one database does not have access to other sections. **Digital signatures**, which verify the identity of the party seeking access or originating material, also typically involve encryption. The future? Perhaps **biometrics**; users could be identified by fingerprint, eye scan, or some other physical trait.

Other methods of controlling access include **firewalls** and **web configuration**. A firewall is a device or software that inspects network traffic and denies or allows passage based on a set of rules. The rules typically involve assigning "trust levels" to communication sources. Web server configuration is a way of telling a server to allow access only from certain **domain names** or certain IP addresses (the numbers that go along with domain names, like 204.10.154.83).

Finally, there is physical security. Having a server on which important data and work can be saved eliminates the worry that individual computers will crash or be destroyed or stolen, but the server itself must be protected. Servers and storage

encryption
Process of transforming information using an algorithm to make it unreadable to anyone except those possessing a key

partition
To divide into parts

digital signatures
Method of authenticating electronic message using cryptography

biometrics
Science of identification by personal characteristics

firewalls
Security to limit access from outside computer or network

web configuration
Arrangement of components to achieve particular function

domain names
Identifies computers on Internet

devices should be in controlled environments, such as in a locked room. With increased awareness about the need for disaster planning, firms are now aware of the need for regular (for most firms, daily) **backup** of their electronic information.

backup
Copies of data for restoration

2. Backing Up

How a firm backs up its electronic information depends on a number of factors. Some of the variables include the following:

- Configuration of computers can range from individual, non-networked computers in a very small firm, to networked computers in a larger firm, to a server with many **client computers** in large firms.

client computers
Connected to a server in a network

- Even if the firm has a network server, some users may save information locally to their hard drives so that the individual computers have to be backed up as well as the server.
- If the firm has a server, it may have a "mirror drive" or a "virtual drive" that backs up users' work every time they click Save.
- If a firm does not have an **IT** staff or another staff member comfortable with the task, it may have to use the services of a consulting firm.

IT
Information technology

- A firm may choose to do only an incremental backup daily, capturing the new files that have been created, rather than backing up the entire system; the entire system should be backed up at least weekly.
- When backing up older files, a firm should consider whether the files are compatible with new formats and systems. In the event of a disaster, could they be recovered using new equipment and systems? If not, these files should be saved using the new formats.
- A firm can back up files using a physical medium or an online backup service. If a physical medium is used, it must be stored in a secure spot offsite. When it is retired, it must be destroyed or completely erased so that client information cannot be accessed. Physical mediums include the following:
  - Tape has tremendous storage capacity and is generally used for server backup. Magnetic tapes wear out and must be retired periodically.
  - CDs and DVDs are effective to back up an individual computer. Many desktop and notebook computers come with built-in CD burners and DVD burners. Blank reusable discs that can be overwritten are easily purchased almost anywhere.
  - External hard drives, zip drives, and other **USB[1]-enabled** external drives have the capacity to store file and system backups.

USB-enabled
Capable of being connected to computer by universal serial bus, a standardized interface socket

- There are many online backup services competing for law firm business. These services have the advantages of freeing law firm staff from conducting backup and can usually provide whatever level of storage space a firm needs. Online backup is particularly helpful in the event of an area-wide disaster such as Hurricane Katrina. The information is online, so users can get their data anywhere there is an Internet connection. Of course, the firm must determine that the service it uses has adequate security in place to protect its information.

---

[1]USB stands for "universal serial bus."

Internet
Worldwide, publicly accessible series of interconnected computer networks

e-mail
Electronic mail

World Wide Web (WWW)
Sites accessible by Internet containing images, documents, services

hyperlinks
Navigation elements that connect user to another spot in the same document or to another document or website

uniform resource locators (URLs)
Web addresses

3. The Internet

The **Internet** is a worldwide, publicly accessible series of interconnected computer networks, consisting of millions of smaller domestic, academic, business, and government networks. Those smaller networks carry information and services, such as **e-mail** (electronic mail), file transfer, online chat, online gaming, and the interlinked webpages and other resources of the **World Wide Web (WWW)**. People sometimes use the terms interchangeably, but the Internet and the Web are not the same thing. The Web is a service accessible by the Internet; it consists of documents, images, and other resources, connected by **hyperlinks** to **uniform resource locators (URLs)**, or web addresses (see Exhibit 2-1). A **browser**, such as Internet Explorer, Firefox, or Netscape, is used to access the resources of the Web; the browser connects to the Internet by one of several methods, including landline **broadband**, dial-up phone line, satellite, **wi-fi**, and even cell phones.

The Internet and the Web provide law firms with low-cost ways of reaching a large audience of potential clients (online marketing is discussed in Chapter 12) and of communicating with existing clients. They allow legal professionals to work from remote locations and work with people and resources at other locations without travel.

Exhibit 2-1
URLs

URLs are complicated. In the simplest terms, http://www.elgin.edu/library means:

http://	*www.*	*elgin*	*.edu*	*/library*
Indicates that hypertext transfer protocol was used in posting the site.	Indicates that the site is on the World Wide Web (as opposed to, for example, an intranet or extranet).	Domain name.	Suffix or type identifier. A URL ending with a suffix such as .edu, .com., or .gov generally will lead you to a site's **homepage**.	Path, which identifies the directory in which specific pages are stored. Could include additional levels (for example, the name of a particular document). With the exponential growth in the number of websites, expect changes to this system and new suffixes!

homepage
Mainpage of a website

The Web is also an excellent resource for factual and some legal research. Internet research is conducted by using a **search engine**, which may be included with your browser. Other popular search engines are Yahoo!, AltaVista, Excite, and Google (see Exhibit 2-2). There are many specialty search engines, including some for legal information, such as the Internet Legal Research Group (http://www.ilrg.com) and LawCrawler (http://lawcrawler.findlaw.com). A "terms and connectors" search will result in a list of URLs; clicking on the hyperlink takes you to the site.

browser
User interface on computer; allows navigation

broadband
Method of data transmission

wi-fi
Wireless technology used for networking

Exhibit 2-2
Examples of a Search

Suppose your employer asked you to use the Web to research an issue concerning legal malpractice insurance.

Although search engines do not all use the same connectors, they perform similarly. Entering the words *malpractice insurance* will retrieve sites that contain either the word *malpractice* or the word *insurance*, with priority given to sites that include both words, but not necessarily together. Entering the words in quotes — *"malpractice insurance"* — should retrieve only sites that contain that phrase, while entering *malpractice w/5 insurance* will retrieve sites on which the word *malpractice* appears within 5 words of the word *insurance*. You might also consider *malpractice w/5 insurance w/5 attorney OR lawyer* or *malpractice w/5 insurance AND NOT medical*. Consult the Help or Advanced Search feature to learn the functions of connectors. On Google, for example, clicking Advanced Search opens a template so that you can enter your search terms with the connectors you want with no guessing.

Using Google's Advanced Search feature, a search of:

> *attorney OR lawyer AND "malpractice insurance" BUT NOT medical*

brought up the following results in the top five:

LPL - ABA

The committee surveyed insurers that provide legal **malpractice insurance** about the . . . Audio CLE Available-Contract Lawyering Risks: An Ethics, **Lawyer** . . . www.abanet.org/legalservices/lpl/ - 25k - Cached - Similar pages

Consumer's Guide to Legal *Malpractice Insurance*

Problems can still arise, particularly in gaps when a **lawyer** changes insurance . . . for an insurer to offer a disabled or free tail to a disabled **attorney**. . . . www.cobar.org/group/display.cfm?GenID=361 - 30k - Cached - Similar pages

---

EXHIBIT 2-2
(continued)

---

*Lawyer Professional Liability / **Attorney** Malpractice / Legal . . .*

We specialize in California **Lawyer's** Professional Liability Insurance. California attorneys need legal **malpractice insurance**. We will shop your **attorney** . . . www.**lawyer**sprofessionalinsurance.com/ - 21k - <u>Cached</u> - <u>Similar pages</u>

Virginia State Bar - About the Bar - **Lawyer Malpractice Insurance**

About the Bar **Attorney** Records Search. Clients' Protection Fund Conferences CRESPA . . . **Lawyer Malpractice Insurance**. 2007–2008 Committee . . . www.vsb.org/site/about/**lawyer**-malpractice-insurance/ - 18k - <u>Cached</u> - <u>Similar pages</u>

Virginia State Bar - Meetings and Events - VSB **Lawyer Malpractice** . . .

About the Bar **Attorney** Records Search. Clients' Protection Fund Conferences CRESPA . . . VSB **Lawyer Malpractice Insurance** Committee. May 7, 2008 . . . www.vsb.org/site/events/item/vsb-**lawyer**-malpractice-insurance-committee5/ - 12k - <u>Cached</u>–

---

search engine
Used to find information on Internet

Internet service provider (ISP)
A company or organization through which users access the Internet

Anyone can post information on the Web without any check on its accuracy. To ensure that you are finding reliable information, evaluate websites before you use them. Ask the following questions:

- What does the URL tell you?
  - Government sites use the suffix .gov or .mil; educational institutions use .edu; .org generally indicates a not-for-profit organization, but there is no enforcement; .com indicates a commercial site; .net generally indicates an Internet service provider. Some suffixes, such as .uk (United Kingdom), indicate a country, although there is no guaranty of accuracy.
  - Does the domain name indicate that it could be a personal website? For example, use of a personal name or location on an **Internet service provider** (**ISP**) site such as AOL or Geocities often indicates a personal site.
  - Is the site sponsored by a credible institution?
- Is the information dated?
- Is the author identified? Can you verify the credentials of the author, perhaps by an independent search?
- Does the site include links to independent authorities?

For More Information

The Internet Corporation for Assigned Names and Numbers (ICANN) is responsible for creating the suffixes that identify the type of site, registering domain names, and arbitrating disputes concerning domain names. For more information, visit http://www.icann.org.

---

4. E-mail

The Internet allows people to send messages and transfer files by e-mail. To send and receive e-mail, a person must have an e-mail address, provided by an ISP. E-mail addresses consist of a user name, the symbol @, the domain name of the ISP or company, and a suffix (for example, lvietzen@foxvalley.net). While there is no equivalent of a phone book for e-mail addresses, it is often possible to determine a person's e-mail address if you know the URL of the organization for which that person works. For example, the website for the college at which this book's author works is http://www.elgin.edu; all employees are assigned addresses that consist of their first initial, last name @ elgin.edu (for example, lvietzen@elgin.edu). Most companies have similar patterns.

For More Information

Ethics and etiquette for using e-mail are discussed in depth in Chapter 3 and 4. If you do not have basic e-mail skills (sending and receiving messages, attaching a document or picture), there are many sources of information on the Internet. A good starting point is http://www.ctdlc.org/remediation.

Legal professionals often use their e-mail accounts to join **listservs** so that they can receive announcements or participate in discussions relevant to their work. There are many such groups for paralegals.

Managing e-mail can be time-consuming, especially if the user subscribes to listservs. Many firms use **filters** to manage e-mails. Filters typically identify and discard messages that contain sexual language or profanity or that have the characteristics of **spam**. Even if incoming mail has been filtered, the user must decide whether to save or delete messages and which messages should be printed and saved as **hard copy**.

listservs
E-mail mailing list

filters
Security devices that sort e-mail according to rules

spam
Unsolicited, unwanted e-mail

hard copy
Printed document

Assignments 2-1: Internet and Extranets

1. Use the Internet to identify at least two listserv groups for paralegals.
2. Conduct an Internet search to find an article concerning electronic signatures on contracts. Determine whether there is a law governing such

signatures and, if so, where that law can be found. What is meant by the term "certificate authority," and what factors should be considered in choosing a vendor to provide that service? Are there any kinds of documents or agreements that cannot be signed electronically? Can clicking the "I agree" box on a website constitute a signature? Write a one- to two-page paper addressing those questions and how you chose the website that is your source: what was the date, what made you think the source was credible?

3. List the elements you would include on an extranet designed to facilitate work with co-counsel on a medical malpractice case.

B. Applications

1. Word Processing

Word processing — the use of a computer to create, edit, and print documents — is probably the most common law office application of technology. The majority of law offices use Microsoft Word, which is part of Microsoft Office. (For more specific information about Word, including demonstrations and online training, visit http://office.microsoft.com/en-us/word/FX100487981033.aspx.) Regardless of which word processing program you use, make sure you are familiar with the following basic features:

word wrap
Word processing feature in which text automatically advances to next line

- Creating and printing a document. (The text in word processing programs automatically advances to the next line, a feature called **word wrap**. Also, most word processors are WYSIWYG ("what you see is what you get"); the document will appear on the display screen exactly as it will look when printed.)
- Inserting text into or deleting text from what you have already created.
- Selecting text in the document and cutting, moving, copying, inserting, or deleting it.
- Defining page size and margins and readjusting them.
- Searching for a particular word or phrase and, if you want, having the program automatically replace it with another word or phrase. (You will use the Search feature for an assignment later in this chapter relating to conflicts of interest.)

Most word processing programs also have the following more sophisticated features:

fonts
Typeface

clipart
Premade images for insertion into electronic documents

- Formatting — the ability to change **fonts**; make text bold, italicized, or underlined; insert page numbers, headers and footers, footnotes, comments, graphics (including **clipart**), graphs, tables, charts, and photographs; and lay out pages with different margins, indentations, or other design features.
- Utilities — spell-check, thesaurus, dictionary, and word-count capabilities.

- File management — functions that allow you to create, delete, organize, move, and search for files.
- **Macros** — essentially shortcuts; characters or words that represent a series of keystrokes that can represent text or commands.
- Merges — merging text from one file into another is particularly useful for generating many files that have the same format but different data. Generating mailing labels is the classic example of using merges.
- Tables of contents and indexes — by inserting codes into the document, you can automatically create a table of contents and index.

Many law firms supplement their word processing software with **document assembly software**, which can create templates by reviewing existing documents in your word processing program. Users can also create original templates or purchase templates to avoid having to reinvent the wheel anytime a pleading, contract, or trust is needed. Standard phrases and paragraphs can be saved and stored for later use. Examples include HotDocs (http://www.hotdocs.com), Qshift (http://www.evdense.com), and Ghostfill (http://www.ghostfill.com).

Word processing skills are essential to success in school and on the job. If your skills are not adequate, you can improve them by using an online tutorial, such as the one found at http://www.ctdlc.org/remediation/indexWord.html.

Special Concerns — Documents Stored in Electronic Format

Virtually all business documents are now created on a computer, and many are never printed but exist in electronic form only. If your firm handles litigation, you are likely to receive electronically stored information (ESI) from clients, witnesses, and opposing parties. ESI consists of traditional documents, such as briefs and pleadings, as well as e-mail, text messages, websites visited, and much more. ESI also includes **metadata**, which records the history of the information, such as when and on which computer it was created, when and on which computer it was altered, and other properties. Metadata can also be found on cell phones, smart phones, portable computers, and other devices.

The importance of this data-behind-the-data cannot be overemphasized. The Federal Rules of Evidence[2] provide that ESI is subject to discovery (**e-discovery**); that clients must preserve and produce ESI; that lawyers must request, protect, review, and produce ESI; and that courts rectify abusive or obstructive electronic discovery. A party receiving ESI with metadata intact obtains far more than information typically found on the face of conventional documents. The emerging field of **computer forensics** enables experts to find documents and e-mails that have been deleted, to determine who had access to information at specific times, to determine when calls were made to particular numbers, and to establish that information has been subject to tampering. Because of fears of accidental **spoliation** of evidence, many firms now **outsource** their computer forensic needs and even their management of information coming in or being produced (sent) as part of discovery.

Firms may produce information in electronic form during discovery, or, if they produce paper copy, the receiving firm may **scan** documents as they are received and number them as part of the scanning process. Scanning can even create searchable **OCR** images so that documents can be retrieved by looking for certain words.

macros
Character or word that represents a command or a series of keystrokes

document assembly software
Creates templates for legal documents

metadata
Data describing the properties and history of electronic documents

e-discovery
Electronic discovery

computer forensics
Specialized form of e-discovery in which an investigation is carried out on the contents of the hard drive of a specific computer

spoliation
Destruction, alteration, or mutilation of evidence, especially by a party for whom the evidence is damaging

outsource
To send tasks outside the organization for completion

scan
To convert a physical document or image to electronic form, using a scanner

OCR
Optical character recognition, electronic conversion of printed text into editable format

---

[2]*See* Fed. R. Evid. 26, *available at* http://www.uscourts.gov/rules/EDiscovery_w_Notes.pdf.

native format
Format in which document
was originally created

image format
Preserves document as an
"image" that cannot be
edited

Scanning documents into certain formats also allows the originator to "lock" the content so that it cannot be altered. A client may send a document to its law firm in **native format**, such as Microsoft Word or Corel WordPerfect, but the firm may want to save it in an **image format**, such as a PDF or TIFF document, to prevent changes.

2. Data Management

Management of the vast amount of information needed to operate a law firm is generally accomplished by use of computer databases and spreadsheets. A **database** is a structured collection of records or data, stored in a computer system, that relies on software for organization and retrieval. A law firm might use a database to store, organize, and retrieve information about clients to check for conflicts of interest or mail newsletters.

database
Organized collection of data
in electronic format

*For an interesting example of
how a law firm used a
database to help a client
organize information about
its franchise operations, see
http://elmorelaw.com/wp/?
page_id=9.*

A **spreadsheet** is the computer equivalent of a paper worksheet. It displays cells that together make up a grid consisting of rows and columns, each cell containing text, numeric values, or a formula that defines how the contents of that cell will be calculated based on the contents of any other cell (or combination of cells) each time any cell is updated. Spreadsheets are frequently used for financial information because they can recalculate the entire sheet automatically after a change to a single cell.

spreadsheet
Software application that
does mathematical
calculations

cell
Box for holding data or
formula in a spreadsheet

A **cell** is like a box for holding data. A single cell is usually referenced by the intersection of its column and row (A2 is the cell in the sample spreadsheet below containing the number 100). Columns C and D of the sample spreadsheet contain values that were calculated by inserting a formula that makes reference to other cells. For example, the number in cell C2 is the result of the formula[3] =A2+B2 or =sum(A2:B2).[4] The formula is not generally visible in the cell, but appears in the toolbar at the top of the sheet when the cell is "selected." Sophisticated software allows for complicated formulas and even use of conditions (if F2 >100 . . .). Sophisticated users can program the sheet to retrieve data from other sources and even to automatically update that data and recalculate as necessary.

Sample Spreadsheet

	A	*B*	*C*	*D*
01	value1	value2	added	multiplied
02	100	200	300	20000
03	15	60	75	900

Because spreadsheets can be linked to outside data and are easy to format, some people use them to organize information (like a database) and to create calendars,

---

[3]In most programs, the equal sign (=) begins the formula; the cell in which the calculation appears is assumed to be to the left of the equal sign. So the assumption is C2=A2+B2; notice that formulas usually do not have blank spaces.

[4]This formula adds a range of cells; in this example, the range is only two cells long, but you could add an entire row with this formula: =sum(A2:Z2).

timetables, lists, and other documents, even when they do not need any mathematical calculation.

For More Information

A future assignment calls for use of a spreadsheet to track and summarize time at various tasks. There are many Internet sites describing the use of spreadsheets and databases; see, for example, http://www.k12.hi.us/~tethree/01-02/tutorials/ss/home3.html. For tutorials on use of the Microsoft products Access and Excel, visit http://office.microsoft.com/en-us/products/FX100487411033.aspx?pid=CL100571081033.

---

3. Presentation Software

Presentation software, such as Microsoft PowerPoint, is used to display information on a screen (although the presentation may be printed as a handout), normally in the form of a "slide show." The software typically includes three major functions: an editor that allows text to be inserted and formatted, a method for inserting and manipulating graphic images, and a slide-show system to display the content. Increasingly law firms are using presentation programs in court, during client meetings, or for related reasons in place of older visual aids such as handouts, chalkboards, flip charts, posters, photographic slides, and overhead transparencies.

Many presentation programs come with predesigned images (clipart) or have the ability to import graphic images, such as digital pictures and videos. A program may have the ability to link to another document, for example, to a page in a deposition transcript on which a witness makes an important statement. Custom graphics can also be created in other programs and imported.

C. Hardware

The applications described in the previous section are tools that enable you to use hardware to create a "product," such as a document. Many firms spend a significant amount of money acquiring, maintaining, and updating the hardware described in the following sections. To get the most out of that investment, hardware and applications must be regularly evaluated, as described in Exhibit 2-4 at the end of this chapter.

1. Printers, Fax Machines, Copiers, and Scanners

Printers, fax machines,[5] copiers, and scanners are the **peripheral** equipment connected to a computer to enable it to produce or input documents. Smaller law

peripheral
Equipment (hardware) connected to computer to increase functionality

---

[5]Fax machines, which have the ability to copy and transmit documents using telephone lines, can create unique challenges with respect to confidentiality and are discussed in depth in Chapter 3 and 4.

offices may use a single combination printer/fax/copier/scanner unit. Large offices may have multiple machines to serve different purposes. Some of the characteristics relevant to all of these devices include the following:

- Speed — usually expressed in pages per minute. High speed may come at the cost of the ability to make color prints or high-resolution documents.
- Color — a law office may need to produce color documents or exhibits for trial.
- Resolution — often expressed in terms of number of dots per inch. High resolution can be expensive, but it may be necessary for tasks such as enlarging photographs for trial exhibits.
- Document size — can include traditional document sizes such as 8½ × 11 to large pictures or charts for trial exhibits.
- Duplexing — ability to input or produce two-sided documents.

Some copiers have additional features:

- Ability to enlarge or reduce the size of print documents.
- Ability to sort (collate) and staple documents.

Because copiers capable of handling high volume are expensive, many firms lease rather than purchase copy machines. Whether leasing or buying, the firm has to consider the cost of "consumables," such as toner (ink), the availability and cost of support and repair, and ability to upgrade if the firm needs additional features in the future.

Because a firm might sometimes need high-volume printing of medium quality and other times need high-quality printing of less volume, some firms invest in different machines for different purposes. The devices may be networked, so that users can access the right equipment for a particular use.

One of the biggest trends in the legal field is the paperless office. A scanner is a device that converts a paper document to an electronic document. Creating and using electronic documents is about far more than saving trees and reducing the space devoted to filing cabinets. Having documents in electronic form makes them much easier to retrieve, search, **redact**, and manage for purposes of **discovery** (see Exhibit 2-3). With courts moving toward e-filing and even e-service, and with communication moving to e-mail (with attached graphic files for correspondence, court papers, attachments, and exhibits), scanners are becoming essential to the well-equipped law office.

redact
To remove

discovery
Pretrial process of sharing evidence

Example

It is December 23, and you have to review boxes full of documents that have just been found in a warehouse in Alaska. They are important to an antitrust case, and there is no time to waste. Even if it were possible to fly to Alaska, spend the next two weeks in a hotel, and go through the documents, imagine the expense and wasted time. Wouldn't it be better to review the documents in the comfort of your own home or office? For this type of situation, many firms now set up "virtual war rooms" (for litigation) or "virtual deal rooms" for business transactions. Scanned images of the documents are placed on a site in an extranet or intranet and those who need to review the documents are granted access. The site provides additional benefits — once a document is on the site, there is no chance of its being "lost" or hidden.

Some of the basic terminology and options associated with these scanners include the following:

- Flatbed scanners — these scanners function much like copiers, with a glass plate over a scanning element or lens. Some are equipped with an automatic document feeder; a flatbed is necessary for scanning books or other bound volumes, photographs, film, or slides. Sheet-fed scanners have no plate and work like a fax machine. Some can scan both sides at once (duplex). They can be significantly more expensive than flatbed scanners but are useful for high-volume scanning (for example, document productions). There are units that combine the characteristics of both.
- Compatibility — not all scanners work with every operating system. Some are compatible only with Windows-based computers or with recent versions of Windows; others work with a wide selection of operating systems.
- Connection — many scanners use USB connections, but there are other options.
- Color depth — refers to the number of possible colors. There is a difference between the number of colors a machine will scan in and what it will print, so ask to see a printed page if color quality is a feature important to your firm.
- Maximum scan area — consider whether you will ever scan any original larger than 8½ × 11 inches. For specialty uses, you can get larger or smaller units. For example, you can buy a paperback-sized unit to scan cards or receipts. Some of these will automatically enter the information on business cards into the correct fields to generate a database of contacts that you can export to your computer.
- Duty cycle — refers to the number of scans per month the scanner is designed to handle. Be sure your choice of scanner matches your anticipated volume. Also consider warranty, service, and support.
- Software application — do you want your scanned text to be searchable or able to be marked and edited (as opposed to an image of the document)? If so, you need **OCR** software. Adobe Acrobat is generally considered the standard for document exchange and provides for OCR. Many state courts have systems for electronic filing using Adobe PDF, and the federal courts are also moving to a PDF system. (Don't confuse Adobe Acrobat with Acrobat Reader, a free program available on the Internet that makes PDF files readable.) When you scan a paper document, Adobe Acrobat converts it to PDF for storage; for outgoing documents created on your own computer, Word and WordPerfect contain drivers to convert (publish) word processing files to PDF files for storage. It's important to set up a good system of folders and subfolders for storing the documents on your system, but it is very easy to search for scanned documents.
- Output — do you want scanned material saved and available to all office workstations throughout the network (as opposed to available only at a dedicated computer)? Do you want scanned materials transferred directly to storage media, such as a CD or a DVD? Do you want the scanner to directly fax or e-mail scanned materials?

OCR
Optical character recognition, electronic conversion of printed text into editable format

Exhibit 2-3
Scanners and E-Discovery

Some lawsuits are notorious for the number of documents involved. First, read Cat Lazaroff, DOE Ordered to Release Energy Documents, Feb. 28, 2002, http://www.ens-newswire.com/ens/feb2002/2002-02-28-07.asp. Then, suppose that you are the paralegal responsible for discovery in the case described in Lazaroff's article. You have just "won" access to 7,584 pages of documents relating to energy policy. A scanner is essential to either producing or receiving that many documents.

PROBLEMS WITH HARD COPY

The documents must be marked with an identification number so that a record can be kept of the document's origin, handling, location, and authentication. This is often called **Bates stamping** and may be done by hand with a device that automatically moves to the next number each time a document is stamped. While hand stamping is still done, it presents difficulties. You may not have the flexibility to use descriptive numbering. For example, you might want to identify all documents arriving from Tanker Transport as TT-xxxx while identifying all documents received from SuperKlean as SK-xxxx, which would necessitate having special stamps. In addition, you may not want to stamp an original document. You would have to either make a copy (be sure you never remove staples for copying unless an attorney directs you to do so — it could create an impression of tampering), mark the back of the document, or attach and mark a sticker.

There is also the problem of redacting **privileged** material so that it is not accidentally disclosed. Working with hard copy, this is often done by simply using a marker to cover privileged material. Finally there is the problem of filing paper copies so that they are retrievable. Do you file the document by its subject (ownership of the contaminated property versus source of contamination), its author, its date, or its type (letter, internal memo)? Or do you make multiple copies and file it in each category, with the resulting waste of resources (bad for the environment)? Almost any system of filing hard copies will be inefficient if thousands of documents are involved. All of these problems, along with the tedious work of copying and stamping, can be minimized by scanning the documents so that they can be stamped, redacted, and filed electronically. Many of the litigation support software packages discussed in later chapters include document **coding** functions. With electronic coding, a document can be identified by several **fields** that can be searched: date, originator, recipient, subject. Identification of these common fields and the beginning and end of multipage documents or multidocument sets (**document unitization**) is called **objective coding**.[6] A paralegal or other individual

Bates stamping
Method of marking documents for identification

privileged
Protected from discovery in litigation

coding
Marking document for identification based on characteristics

fields
Discrete pieces of information

document unitization
Identification of beginning and end of document

objective coding
Marking document for identification based on document characteristics

---

[6]Documents can be stored and organized according to pages, but the concept of a "page" is often not useful in dealing with documents in image format.

EXHIBIT 2-3
(continued)

with knowledge of the case at issue may be used for **subjective coding**, which can involve substantive decisions, such as identification of the issue addressed by the document, determination of relevance, and identification of privileged material.

subjective coding
Marking document for identification based on knowledge of case

---

For More Information

Scanners make it possible to work with documents located at a distance without travel, but what about working with people at a distant location? That is also increasingly being accomplished without travel. The use of teleconferencing equipment makes it possible to have a real-time conversation with people you can see and who can see you. The technology is used in some courts so that prisoners can be "present" at motions and short hearings on their cases without the expense and risk of transport in custody. In addition, video Internet depositions of witnesses are increasingly common.

---

2. Cameras and Projectors

Digital cameras are now the norm, but their use by law firms to produce exhibits involves special concerns. A digital photo is admissible as evidence under the same rules as any other photograph, videotape, or drawing — it is admissible if a witness with knowledge confirms that it fairly and accurately represents what it is being introduced to prove. Digital photos, however, can be manipulated in unique ways that can make their credibility questionable. For example, the contrast settings might be changed in an attempt to sharpen the image. To circumvent such problems, avoid changing the picture. If any touch-ups, compression, or editing are necessary for the sake of clarity, preserve the original. Clearly label the original and the edited versions.

To serve as exhibits, digital photos often must be enlarged to sizes visible from across a courtroom. The camera used must produce very sharp images. There is a camera review website (http://www.dcresource.com) from which you can print samples of pictures taken by various model cameras, using the same settings.

A firm may also have a projector and a screen for use during trials and other presentations. In addition to being reliable, a projector planned for use at offsite locations must be portable and easy to set up.

If a firm uses this type of technology only occasionally (for example, once in three years to show accident scene pictures or a "day in the life" video in a personal injury case), it may find it more economical to hire an outside professional to create and display the exhibit. Hiring an outside professional can also result in a more technically sophisticated presentation and give the presentation added credibility as objective.

3. PDAs

Personal digital assistants (PDAs) have become essential equipment for legal professionals who spend significant time out of the office. New PDAs combine cell phones, wireless e-mail, Internet access, paging, cameras, and applications such as a calendar, a contacts list, and more. Many have portable (even projection) keyboards to supplement the normally tiny keyboard on the face of the device. The PDA should be chosen to synchronize to software on the user's main computer, so that dates, contacts, and other useful information can be shared between the two devices.

Exhibit 2-4
Assessing Law Firm Technology

Assessing the technology in place or the technology needed at a law firm involves multiple considerations.

Hardware	Software	Training/ Support	Protection
Server? If so, how old? Adequate speed, capacity?	Any additional applications needed?	Do all users have needed skills? Manuals or instructions readily available?	Adequate firewalls, filters?
Desktops or client computers — adequate speed, capacity?	Duplicates of applications?	Does vendor charge for training? Where is training available?	Daily backup taken offsite?
Adequate portable devices — PDAs, cameras, cell/smart phones, projectors, notebook computers?	All licenses in place?	Is support onsite or offsite? Available outside of 9-5 weekdays? What is typical wait time on service calls?	Adequate "chain of command" responsibility for backup, website, etc.?

EXHIBIT 2-4
(continued)

Hardware	Software	Training/ Support	Protection
Multiple printers, scanners or combination printers/ scanners with different capabilities (e.g., color, speed, duplexing) tied to network for access by various users as needed or separate workstation for use of scanner or specialty printer?	Are all applications being used?	Plan in place for maintenance and upgrade?	Adequate password or other system to limit access?

Assignments 2-2 Applications and Hardware

Management Portfolio

1. The scope of this book is limited, but technology seems limitless. Help is just a few clicks away. Become familiar with some of the resources available online. Visit http://www.abanet.org and, in the search box, enter the term "printing digital photographs" or "laser printer." You will find very specific information, for example, estimating the per-page costs of various printers.

2. Partner Leona Stosh of the firm Rodan & Stosh would like to prepare courtroom exhibits for the firm's upcoming product liability trial by enlarging digital photographs of the client's injuries and the product that caused the injuries. Research digital cameras online and write a memo detailing the features necessary for taking pictures that will be enlarged to 18 × 24 inches. Based on your research, recommend a particular camera and determine the cost of that camera, purchased locally or online. Identify printers capable of producing color pictures that size. Your memo should also include the cost of having pictures printed at a local print shop or by an online service, as an alternative to buying a printer.

3. Explore freeware at http://www.openoffice.com. Determine whether there is any free download of presentation software. You may want to bookmark this site for future assignments if you do not have data management or presentation software on your computer.

Management Portfolio

PC
Short for "personal computer"; traditionally refers to an IBM-compatible computer (i.e., not a Mac)

4. Partner Ed Rodan is a bit of a techno-phobe. Newly hired paralegal Rene Miller needs a notebook computer to use while assisting at trial. Rene wants a Mac. Everyone else in the firm has a **PC**. Ed has asked you to do some online research and write a memo analyzing whether law offices ever use Macs and whether Rene will be able to share calendars, documents, and other necessary information with her PC-using colleagues.

5. Partner Ed Rodan is so impressed by your research that he decides that all of the firm's notebook computers should be replaced with Macs. Because all of the attorneys and paralegals work with notebook computers, you know there will be much resistance to the change. After reading the next section in this chapter, develop a step-by-step process for implementing the change.

D. Managing Changes in Technology

After you move into management, it's no longer "all about you." It's all about the people with whom you work, and those people may have many legitimate reasons for resisting changes in the technology for their jobs. They may resent money being spent on technology, rather than on salary and benefits; they may fear that technology will eventually eliminate jobs. Some may think that the change implies criticism of the way they have been doing their jobs. They may believe that the chosen technology is not the right fit for the office or won't work; they almost certainly will resent having to learn new technology after having mastered the old. Even tech-lovers may become exasperated when the new version of Windows appears and they had to learn new toolbars.

> Many of the barriers to effective utilization of new technology are managerial and organizational, rather than technological per se.
>
> — Mission statement of the Center for the Management of Technological Change at the Penn State Smeal College of Business

Technology does change, however, and there are ways to make transitions easier on your colleagues. In *Win Win Management* (1998), George Fuller identifies strategies for handling worker concerns about new technology:

- Communicate early and often; get input from those who will use the technology and limit the spread of "information" on the rumor mill.

- Demystify to limit technical trauma; simplify the language used to describe the new technology and its functions.
- Provide proper training.
- Overcome technical trauma by addressing worker concerns and stating the reasons and goals for change.
  - "Jim, you've always done a great job on billing with just the regular office applications. Using this new time and billing software should free you up from the end-of-the month logjam and give you more time for some of the other projects you've suggested."
  - "This new litigation support software has most of the features you asked for at the meeting last month, Liliana. We are going to send everybody to training, one at a time, so that the office will have coverage. No one will have to use the system before he or she attends training."
- Give people reasons to want to use the new technology; publicize its advantages.
- Be understanding; allow people to vent their frustrations.

Technology users should never feel that their supervisor was given a slick sales talk about equipment or a system that is not right for the job and that the burden of working with the new equipment or system is now being "dumped" on them. The best input on an office's purchasing decisions comes from those who will use the purchased item.

Out There— Paralegal Profile
The Spreadsheet that Launched a New Career?

Greg Duncan is a paralegal working in the research department of the Second District Appellate Court of Illinois. He completed two other careers before entering the paralegal field. The first was a 20-year career as an electronics technician in the U.S. Navy submarine nuclear power program. The second was a 15-year career as a technical training supervisor at several midwestern nuclear power plants. In 1991, Greg earned a M.Ed. degree in technology education from Bowling

Green State University. He completed an ABA-approved paralegal certificate program in 2004.

Being a non-traditional student, Greg was concerned about how employers would perceive him. To start networking, Greg volunteered his technology skills to a project that one of the local trial judges was supervising. The judge was gathering statistics about outcomes in child custody cases by looking at a number of factors, such as allegations of abuse. The judge did not know how to organize the information so that it could be sorted according to different factors. Greg created a spreadsheet with rows for each factor, so that the information could be sorted according to the user's needs. He subsequently created a PowerPoint presentation, with charts and graphs, to share the information with the other judges in the circuit. As a result, Greg conducted his job search armed with a letter of recommendation from a judge.

Greg's interest in technology has continued. He developed and taught a class on law office computing for the local community college and is now studying computer forensics.

Chapter Review

Discussion Questions

1. Your firm handles litigation that involves high-volume document production. How might a scanner help the firm? What kind of scanner would be a good choice for your firm's needs?
2. What is the difference between a computer's operating system and its applications programs?
3. What is the purpose of a cell in a spreadsheet program?
4. Why might a law office use presentation software, such as PowerPoint?
5. Identify important considerations in taking digital pictures for use as trial exhibits.
6. What features might be included on an extranet for clients?
7. What would be the advantage of networking two to three computers in a very small firm?
8. What is a URL, and what can it tell you about a website?
9. What is a listserv, and why might a paralegal join one?
10. What is the most common operating system?
11. What is metadata? What is the difference between native format and image format?
12. What is a server?
13. Why might employees resist new technology that might actually make their jobs easier?

ACROSS

1. programs that can be downloaded at no cost
5. a word processing short cut
7. a private version of the internet, within acompany
10. processes e-mail according to rules to eliminate spam
11. worldwide connected computers
12. data behind the data
13. to make a two-sided copy
15. a commonly used operating system
17. division into parts
19. _____-firm, really large
23. navigation element that leads to another part of document or another domain
24. allows clients and others some access to company's network
26. _____ name, identifies computers on internet
27. security to limit access to computers
29. characteristics of a printer or scanner, speed and _____
32. does mathematical calculations
33. word _____ means the software automatically moves to the next line
35. spreadsheet, word processing are examples of _____ programs
39. main computer, runs applications forclient computers
43. unsolicited, undesirable e-mail

44. structured collection of records
45. a group of connected computers and hardware
46. arrangement of computer units for particular function

DOWN

1. typeface
2. Google is a search _____
3. to make copies of data for restoration in event of loss
4. _____ system, runs applications
6. _____ copy, print version of document
8. _____ computers connect to server
9. IT= _____ Technology
12. _____ Office Suite is a package in use at many law offices
14. methods of recognizing people based on unique traits
16. _____ signature, allows assent to contract online
18. protected from discovery in litigation
20. destruction of evidence
21. permission to use copyrighted software
22. in a spreadsheet, a box for holding data
25. format in which document is created
28. electronic mailing list
30. _____ stamping, manual coding
31. e-mail= _____ mail
34. URL= Uniform _____ Locator
36. pre-made images
37. e.g., Firefox, Netscape, Outlook
38. a person with computer skills that would allow her to "break in" to files
40. to remove
41. format not subject to editing
42. iniitials, allows peripherals to be connected through a single standardized socket

Terms and Definitions

applications program: Software designed for a particular task, such as word processing
backup: Copies of data for restoration
Bates stamping: Method of marking documents for identification
biometrics: Science of identification by personal characteristics
broadband: Method of data transmission
browser: User interface on computer; allows navigation
cell: Box for holding data or formula in a spreadsheet
client computer: Connected to a server in a network
clipart: Premade images for insertion into electronic documents
coding: Marking document for identification based on characteristics
computer forensics: Specialized form of e-discovery in which an investigation is carried out on the contents of the hard drive of a specific computer

database: Organized collection of data in electronic format

digital signature: Method of authenticating electronic message using cryptography

discovery: Pretrial process of sharing evidence

document assembly software: Creates templates for legal documents

document unitization: Identification of beginning and end of document

domain name: Identifies computers on Internet

e-discovery: Electronic discovery

e-mail: Electronic mail

encryption: Process of transforming information using an algorithm to make it unreadable to anyone except those possessing a key

extranet: Private intranet extended to select outsiders

fields: Discrete pieces of information

filters: Security devices that sort e-mail according to rules

firewall: Security to limit access from outside computer or network

font: Typeface

freeware: Software available for free download

hacker: Computer user who intentionally gains access to confidential information

hard copy: Printed document

homepage: Main page of a website

hyperlinks: Navigation elements that connect user to another spot in the same document or to another document or website

image format: Preserves document as an "image" that cannot be edited

Internet: Worldwide, publicly accessible series of interconnected computer networks

intranet: Private version of Internet within organization

Internet service provider (ISP): A company or organization through which users access the Internet

IT: Information technology

license: Permission to use copyrighted software

listserv: E-mail mailing list

macro: Character or word that represents a command or a series of keystrokes

mega-firm: Extremely large firm

metadata: Data describing the properties and history of electronic documents

native format: Format in which document was originally created

network: Group of connected computers and hardware

objective coding: Marking document for identification based on document characteristics

OCR: Optical character recognition, electronic conversion of printed text into editable format

operating system: Software that allows computer to run applications

outsource: To send tasks outside the organization for completion

partition: To divide into parts

PC: Short for "personal computer"; traditionally refers to an IBM-compatible computer (i.e., not a Mac)

peripheral: Equipment (hardware) connected to computer to increase functionality

privileged: Protected from discovery in litigation

redact: To remove

scan: To convert a physical document or image to electronic form, using a scanner

search engine: Used to find information on Internet

server: A central computer that manages computer network resources; a file server stores files for users; a print server manages printers; a network server manages network traffic

spam: Unsolicited, unwanted e-mail

spoliation: Destruction, alteration, or mutilation of evidence, especially by a party for whom the evidence is damaging

spreadsheet: Software application that does mathematical calculations

subjective coding: Marking document for identification based on knowledge of case

uniform resource locator (URL):   Web address

USB-enabled: Capable of being connected to computer by universal serial bus, a standardized interface socket

web configuration: Arrangement of components to achieve particular function

wi-fi: Wireless technology used for networking

word-wrap: Word processing feature in which text automatically advances to next line

World Wide Web: Sites accessible by Internet containing images, documents, services

3

Law Office Communications: The Medium

As a Manager

You will be responsible for establishing policies to ensure effective and ethical communications with clients and others outside the firm and among members of the firm. You will train employees to follow those policies and monitor compliance. You will research and propose the purchase of equipment to best implement those policies and establish policies to secure that equipment.

Objectives

After completing this chapter, you will be able to

- Identify and discuss ethical rules pertaining to law office communications.
- Identify technology commonly used for law office communications and the unique problems associated with each.
- Describe procedures to minimize the risk of ethical problems with each type of technology.
- Use technology as it would be used in a law office.

A. **Why Law Firms Must Control Use of Communications Equipment**
B. **Phones**
   1. **Phone Equipment**
   2. **Making Calls**

It is often said that words are a lawyer's only tool. Communication is such an essential part of the practice of law that the ABA Model Rules of Professional Conduct govern several aspects of communication. For example, Rule 1.4 establishes the obligation of an attorney to communicate with the client under specific circumstances; other rules govern other aspects of the communication. This chapter and the next explore various aspects of communications and the relevant ethical rules.

A. Why Law Firms Must Control Use of Communications Equipment

New law firm employees and even their supervisors sometimes resist discussion of rules for using phones, fax machines, and electronic communications, thinking that these are a matter of "common sense" or "common courtesy." Of course, courtesy and professionalism do matter in conveying the right impression to clients, prospective clients, and others, but there is much more at stake than image. In fact, the firm's efforts to supervise and educate its employees on proper procedures can make a difference when a mistake does occur.

Example

The defendant's law firm accidentally attached a letter to a court pleading, a copy of which went to the plaintiff's law firm. The letter had been written to the defendant by an attorney in the firm. When it discovered the error, the defendant filed a motion to prevent the use of the letter at trial and require that the plaintiff's firm return the letter. The defendant claimed the letter was privileged attorney-client communication. The court declined to address the issue of privilege, finding that any privilege had been waived by the inadvertent disclosure. The court particularly noted the defendant's law firm's failure to supervise its employees or educate them about confidentiality. *Local 851 of the Intl. Bhd. of Teamsters v. Kuehne & Nagel Air Freight, Inc.*, 36 F. Supp. 2d 127 (E.D.N.Y. 1998). Not all courts take the same approach, but regardless of whether the court orders return of information disclosed by mistake, the information is no longer secret. As one court stated, in refusing to order return of confidential documents accidentally sent to the opposing party, "there is no order I can enter which erases from defendant's counsel's knowledge what has been disclosed. There is no order which can remedy what has occurred." *Intl. Digital Sys. Corp. v. Digital Equip. Corp.*, 120 F.R.D. 445 (D. Mass. 1988).

Using the website previously bookmarked, you can find your state rule concerning disclosure of confidential information. Does the rule simply say that the attorney "shall not disclose," or does it give a lawyer an affirmative obligation to protect confidential information? Regardless of the language of the rule, courts have read the confidentiality rule, in connection with the rule that makes lawyers responsible for the actions of their employees (discussed in Chapter 1), as requiring lawyers to supervise and educate employees.

Although people often use the terms "attorney-client privilege" and "confidentiality" as if the concepts were interchangeable, they are not. The attorney-client privilege is an *evidentiary rule* that applies to the question of whether a lawyer can be required to *testify* about professional communications with the client or to produce documents reflecting these communications. The privilege does not protect information received from sources other than that of the client.

Example

The attorney-client privilege may attach to confidences shared with an attorney during initial discussions between the parties even though the relationship does not continue. *Levin v. Ripple Twist Mills, Inc.,* 416 F. Supp. 876, 883 (E.D. Pa. 1976); *United States v. Nelson,* 38 M.J. 710, 715 (A.C.M.R. 1993).

The *ethical* concept of confidentiality is broader and, as defined in Model Rule 1.6, prohibits the lawyer from revealing information relating to the lawyer's representation of the client, whatever its source, without consent. While there are exceptions, generally related to preventing commission of a crime, confidentiality generally survives even the death of the client and covers *even information that may be publicly known.*[1] Law office employees, if not properly educated about the scope of confidentiality, may assume that only information that could incriminate the client, hurt the client's reputation, or result in financial harm is confidential. They might assume that facts such as the identity of a new client, that the client paid cash,[2] or that the client has good news, such as an inheritance, are not confidential. Others might assume that a client's disclosure of a terrible crime is not confidential because of the threat to society.

Keep in mind also that people outside the firm do not know what is and is not confidential. For example, imagine that you see the president of a local bank who is a longtime client of the firm during intermission at a play. The bank's relationship with your firm is well known, as is the fact that the bank is building a new facility. You walk over to shake hands and say, "Pat, it's just great the way

---

[1] *Statewide Grievance Comm. v. Heghmann,* 2004 Conn. Super. LEXIS 3794 (Dec. 20, 2004).
[2] For an overview, see Steven Good, *Identity, Fees, and the Attorney-Client Privilege,* 59 Geo. Wash. L. Rev. 307 (1991).

things are progressing on the new building. The firm has been really impressed with your construction manager." Pat may not be upset in the least, but people overhearing the exchange might think, "Wow, if I ever use that firm, my business will get discussed all over town."

Assignment 3-1
State Confidentiality and Disclosure Rules

Get the correct information for your state by visiting one of the sites bookmarked for an assignment in Chapter 1.

1. There are situations in which disclosure of a client's identity could harm a client. For example, imagine that an abused spouse visits a well-known divorce attorney and makes plans to "escape" the house while the abusive and emotionally disturbed spouse is at work. What if the abusive spouse finds out about the visit to the law firm? On the other hand, there are situations in which law enforcement officials would want that information. Imagine that a hit-and-run driver consults a lawyer to negotiate a plea before turning himself in. Has your state taken a position on whether client identity is protected by privilege?

2. What is your state's position on a client's disclosure of intent to commit a crime in the future? Does it matter whether the crime would involve death or bodily harm? Does the lawyer have options, or is disclosure mandatory in certain circumstances? Does your state recognize other exceptions?

Management Portfolio

3. Use the IRS website (http://www.irs.gov) to find Form 8300. At what dollar amount is a business required to report a cash payment? Is the form required of law offices? Does the form require disclosure of the client's name? Examine Publication 1544. What is the purpose of the disclosure requirement?

B. Phones

Many firms now have automated phone systems, so that a caller can be immediately directed to a particular extension or to the appropriate message box. Other firms have the general phone answered by a person who then transfers the call to the appropriate office. Even those that use a system generally have a receptionist to whom a caller can be transferred if the caller does not make a selection. This is a very important position. The person (or automated system) that answers the phone conveys an impression of the firm and has contact with more people in a typical day than a partner. The receptionist is the "voice of the firm" and creates an image with clients, prospective clients, and opposing counsel, some of whom will never have met the firm's lawyers. Yet the receptionist may be the lowest paid, least-trained, least-appreciated, and most junior employee of the firm.

Regardless of whether your position involves answering the phone for the entire firm (or training the person who does so), answering the phone for your supervisor and yourself, answering only your own phone, or making calls on behalf of the firm, there are guidelines you can follow (see Exhibit 3-1). Some of the guidelines for phone use are intended to protect confidentiality; others are intended to communicate respect and professionalism to outsiders.

Exhibit 3-1
Guidelines for Phone Use

Here are a few guidelines for answering the phone that might be included in an office procedures manual:

- Answer the phone before it rings for the fourth time whenever possible. Avoid having the call answered by the automated system.
- Do not just say "hello." Identify yourself and/or your organization.
- Never chew gum, eat, or drink while on "phone duty."
- Avoid unnecessary background noise. The receptionist may not use his or her personal cell phone, radio, or other device while at the desk.
- Speak slowly and clearly when answering the phone or making an outgoing call.
- Speak directly into the mouthpiece; do not attempt to balance the phone on your shoulder.
- Use the speaker phone only if absolutely necessary and never without the permission of the person on the other end.
- Take a deep breath when you answer the phone and smile. It is difficult to explain scientifically, but your voice will be more positive if you smile. A confident and friendly voice reassures the caller and predisposes them to have confidence in your law firm.
- Give the caller your full attention. Do not multitask by trying to use your keyboard or other equipment while receiving or making a call.
- Keep a positive attitude regardless of the attitude conveyed by the caller. The caller may be very stressed and may regard his or her problem as an emergency; no matter what the caller says, do not be rude. If the caller becomes abusive or vulgar, you may simply say that you have work to do and must hang up.
- Do not address the caller by his or her first name until asked to do so. While some people feel more at ease with such familiarity, in some

EXHIBIT 3-1
(continued)

cultures it is considered very rude to address a client or an older person by his or her first name. Use titles, such as Mr., Mrs. or Miss (if you know which is appropriate, otherwise Ms.), or Dr.
- Never use abrupt language or slang.

Avoid:	Try:
"Hang on" or "hold on"	"May I put you on hold?"
"Who's calling?"	"May I say who is calling?"
"I can't hear you, speak up!"	"I am having difficulty hearing you, can you please speak up?"
"Your problem"	"Your concern" or "situation"
"I can't help you."	"I am not able to take care of this for you, but I can (identify a course of action)."
"You have to," "You need to," or "Why didn't you?"	"Will you please . . ."

- Do not be untruthful to "cover" for an attorney.
- If you know that the attorney or paralegal will be unable to return the call within 24 hours, say so and ask whether the caller would like to speak to someone else.
- Do not disclose too much information. For example, it is inappropriate to say that the lawyer "hasn't made it in yet" or is "out running some errands." You may simply and politely say that the lawyer is out of the office. If pressed for information, you can say that you do not know exactly where the lawyer is or that you are not authorized to tell.
- Do not interrupt, argue, or finish thoughts for the caller. Even if you are very busy, project an impression that this call is important.
- Do not abruptly transfer a caller. Say: "I am putting you through to Ms. Janick's office." If possible, announce the call: "I am transferring a call from John Slawson."
- If you are asked to screen calls for a particular lawyer or during a particular time, be careful to avoid offending the caller. Say: "She's away from her desk; may I take your name and number?" or "May I say who's calling? Thank you. Let me check and see if he's in." Be aware of your tone of voice. Screening calls is delicate!
- If you must put a caller on hold:
  - Explain to the caller what you are doing.
  - If possible, ask the caller "May I put you on hold?" and listen to the response.
  - Push the hold button; do not simply lay the phone down.

EXHIBIT 3-1
(continued)

- - If the caller is waiting for someone else to pick up the call, return to the caller every 30-45 seconds and ask whether the caller is willing to continue to hold.
  - If the caller is waiting for you, offer to call back instead of keeping the call on hold.
  - When you return to the call, thank the caller for waiting.
- Give the client the option of leaving a written message or recording a message on the attorney's or paralegal's voice mail. "May I take a message, or would you like Ms. Smith's voice mail?" empowers the client; a client who refuses to leave detailed information with a staff person may be willing to give a detailed voice mail message, knowing only the attorney will listen to it.
- Do not, however, put calls into voice mail if the attorney is out of the office and no one is listening to messages and returning calls.
- The biggest single complaint about lawyers is failure to return phone calls. Clients may not realize that the number of calls and other obligations may force the lawyer to "triage" telephone calls, returning those with immediate needs first. This is particularly difficult if a client refuses to leave a message, saying "Just have her call me." Whenever possible, get a message; if a call is an emergency, indicate that on the message slip.
- Always get as much contact information as possible to help the lawyer or paralegal avoid playing phone tag. Get home, office, and cell phone numbers, and even an e-mail address if possible.
- If necessary, ask the caller to spell his or her name so that it is correct on the message, which should also include the date and time.
- It may be difficult to end a telephone conversation with an anxious client. Use closing phrases that indicate the action you will take, such as "I will make sure that Mr. Andrusz gets this message and knows that it is urgent." Thank the caller and say "goodbye" not "bye-bye," "okie-dokie," "alrighty," or any other slang phrase.
- Maintain confidentiality with written messages. Do not leave messages lying on the reception desk. Fold them in half so that they cannot be easily read and then put them in the appropriate box immediately.
- Set up your own voice mail message so that it sounds professional. It should be friendly and brief. State your name and position; if you will be out of the office for an extended period, state an alternate contact. If you change your outgoing message because you will be out of the office, be sure you change it again when you return.
- The outgoing message that people hear when they call outside normal office hours should give the firm's website. Many common questions may be answered on that site.

Best Practices

Many of the things that bother clients the most have to do with communications and communications technology. Fifty lawyers attending a CLE seminar were asked what they disliked most when dealing with another professional. Here are their top ten client pet peeves to avoid in the practice of law, in order of least to most important:

10. Lack of preparation.
9. Feeling rushed through appointments or conversations.
8. Missing promised deadlines.
7. Being called by first name before asking.
6. Not explaining so the client understands; use of unfamiliar professional jargon.
5. Dropping names to impress others.
4. Rude treatment by staff.
3. Failure to timely return telephone calls.
2. Interruptions during office meetings by telephone and staff.
1. Being kept waiting for office appointments.

Knowing this, a Chicago employment law firm recently sent prospective clients a small hourglass, imprinted with the firm's contact information, accompanied by a card:

> *Next Time You Have a Legal Question*
> *Call Your Current Firm,*
> *Then Call Us.*
> *Turn Over the Hourglass.*
> *Who Calls Back Before the Sand Runs Out?*

The response was incredible. It is equally important that the firm not neglect existing clients. Many firms have policies to ensure that clients hear from them at least once a month, by means of a "goodwill" letter or call. If a firm has a policy about how quickly calls must be returned or about goodwill communications, it should have a means of assessing whether the policy is working. As discussed in Chapter 12, clients should be asked for feedback on their satisfaction with communication.

---

1. Phone Equipment

There is an incredible variety of phone equipment and systems available to law firms today. Here are some of the more common optional features:

Voice mail
Technology that records incoming phone messages

- **Voice mail.** Voice mail can be part of a complete phone system or can be a feature of a firm's account with its phone service provider. Small firms may even use an answering machine connected to a phone jack in the office. Features may include separate message boxes for different people, ability to check messages from out of the office, ability to take more than one message at a time, and working even when there is a power failure.

  Encourage lawyers and paralegals in your firm to manage client expectations by recording a new outgoing message each day: "This is Collette Lemke.

Today, Wednesday the fifth, I will be out of the office all day. I will return your call as soon as possible. If this is an emergency, you may contact my assistant at . . ."

- **Caller ID**. This feature is often used for screening calls to a home number, but in a law office it is used for recording incoming numbers in case the caller fails to leave a number or states the number incorrectly.
- **Three-way calling**. Lawyers and paralegals frequently set up **conference calls**. If a firm does not have this feature, it can set up conference calls, as needed, through the operator or a teleconferencing company.
- **TDD or TTY machine**. This machine, which is portable and can be connected to any phone, allows communication with hearing-impaired callers by typing a message that is displayed on the receiving end.
- **Call waiting**. This feature signals that another call is on the line by beeping. Many attorneys do not like to have calls interrupted when someone else calls, and prefer that a call be forwarded to an assistant or voice mail when they are on the line.
- **Call forwarding**. Call forwarding directs incoming calls to another number; attorneys who are frequently out of the office sometimes forward calls to a cell phone or home number if they do not have assistants to speak to callers when they are out.

2. Making Calls

Lawyers sometimes request that staff members make or return calls, so a firm's procedures manual might include a page concerning outgoing calls (see Exhibit 3-2).

3. Keeping Contacts

Paralegals and others who work in the legal field need to be able to find contact information quickly. Some create a contact list on their computers, use a **Rolodex**, or simply turn to a phone book. Whatever your preference, it's good to have a backup.

Contacts entered into a computer have a unique advantage over those entered in a book or on file cards: they can be searched by different "fields." **Fields** include components of contact information such as last name, first name, company name, street address, city, state, ZIP code, phone, fax, and e-mail. For example, a paralegal might have this card in her Rolodex:

Seigler, Jack	Vendor
JS Land Surveyors	JSLandSurveyors.com
8255 River Road	Lebanon, IL 66042
Phone 708-555-1212	Fax 708-555-2121

caller ID
Technology that displays the phone number and/or identity of an incoming caller and stores the information for future reference

three-way calling
Technology that permits multiple parties to share a phone conversation

conference calls
A telephone call in which three or more people, at different locations, participate by means of a central switching unit

TDD or TTY machine
Device that assists hearing-impaired users of telephones by displaying messages so that they can be read

call waiting
Technology that notifies a person talking on the phone that another call is coming in, typically by making a beeping sound

call forwarding
Technology that sends a phone call directed to one phone number to another number

Rolodex
Trademark name for a rotary file of card, typically with contact information

fields
Discrete components of electronic document

Exhibit 3-2
Guidelines for Outgoing Phone Calls

- Make sure you have the correct number.
- Plan the call by jotting notes about what you want to say.
- When the other person answers the phone, immediately identify yourself and state the purpose of the call.
- Use the person's title (Mr., Mrs. or Miss, or Ms.) unless the person asks you to use his or her first name.
- If the call will take more than a few minutes of the other person's time or may require him or her to answer sensitive questions, begin the conversation by asking whether this is a good time to talk.
- Identify information you need to obtain by stating questions up front.
- Anticipate questions or objections to avoid making additional calls.
- Take notes during the call.
- Spell out any follow-up action.
- If you reach an answering machine or voice mail, leave
  - Your name, including the correct spelling, if necessary.
  - The firm name, your title, and your telephone number—say the phone number twice.
  - Date and time.
  - A brief message, including a good time to reach you.
  - A general message; do not leave confidential information on a machine.

If this paralegal instead entered the information into her computer's contact software (see Exhibit 3-3), she could then easily search for any of Jack Seigler's contact information, including his relationship to the firm ("Vendor"). Entering a field that identifies the contact's connection with the firm in a computer contacts database allows the firm to sort and create lists of clients, vendors/suppliers, co-counsel, relatives/friends. Some firms use the database application and include additional information, such as the year in which the relationship began, the primary contact person within the firm, or any other useful information. For information about keeping contacts in Microsoft Office, visit http://office.microsoft.com/training/Training.aspx?AssetID=RP011036451033.

Will a paper card in a file be useful if, while the paralegal is out of the office, the lawyer requests that the temporary replacement call "Jack, you know, the surveyor," "the surveyor we always use," or simply a surveyor? If the information is properly input on a computer, the person covering the job will be able to search by "surveyor" or even "Jack."

Exhibit 3-3
Microsoft Outlook Contacts Input

Note all of the fields on the Microsoft Outlook Contacts input template:

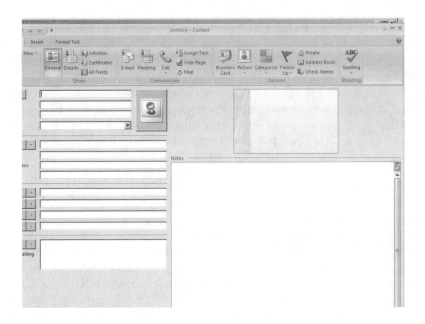

Assignment 3-2
Enter and Print Contact Information

---

1. Create a contact for your instructor on your computer. Print the contact and save it for the next assignment.
2. Discuss whether clients and others are offended by "announced calls," in which a secretary places the call, reaches the party, and says, "Please hold for Mr. More-Important-than-You."
3. In your experience in placing calls to and receiving calls from businesses, what are the most common mistakes?
4. Most firms bill clients a "per page" fee for sending and receiving faxes. Many firms bill for postage. Some bill clients for telephone usage as

soft charges
Charges for postage, phone use, etc.

well as for the lawyer's time in speaking on the phone. These expenses are sometimes called **soft charges**. Rather than calculating precise amounts, some firms add a general overhead charge that is a percentage of the bill. Determine whether your state has an ethical rule or opinion addressing whether a firm may make a profit above its cost for such services.

PDAs
"Personal digital assistant"; a small electronic device that combines various computer functions

Some law firms prohibit the use of portable storage devices, such as flash drives, in the office to avoid theft or loss of files.

text messages
Written message sent by and displayed on a phone

smart phones
Has functions, such as e-mail, not available on standard cell phones

Bluetooth technology
Short-range wireless technology that allows electronic devices to communicate

hot sync
To connect electronic devices so that they share information (e.g., PDA calendar dates are entered onto desktop computer or network calendar)

facsimile
An identical reproduction; in the law office setting, generally an electronic reproduction transmitted by phone lines

fax
Common reference to an electronic facsimile of a document

4. Cell Phones and PDAs

Many lawyers and paralegals have learned hard lessons about cell phones and **PDAs**. One of those lessons is that sometimes you have to turn them off. Many judges now impose stiff penalties when cell phones ring in court. Others may not have the ability to fine you or confiscate your phone, but they may be deeply offended if your phone rings or if you talk on the phone in their presence. Courtesy demands that you put the phone on its silent mode whenever you are with people in a business setting, never put the phone in view (for example, on a table during lunch), and, if it is necessary that you take a call, move out of the hearing of other people.

The other hard lesson is that small devices are easily lost. When a cell phone or PDA is lost, contact information and even confidential information can be lost. Confidentiality is a particular problem if the device was used for **text messages**, e-mail (a feature available on PDAs and **smart phones**), notes, or even calendars. Confidentiality agreements (see Exhibit 3-4) sometimes include specific provisions prohibiting use of portable devices for confidential communications. To limit problems associated with loss of information, it may be possible to back up your cell phone address book. Some service providers have this option for customers; other can accomplish the same thing by using **Bluetooth technology** to transfer the information to a computer.

PDAs, on the other hand, already have built-in backup features. Lawyers and paralegals who use their PDAs as personal calendars or to store other information must be sure to **hot sync** so that all important contacts, appointments, and dates are also on the firm's central system.

C. Faxes

1. Preventing Mistakes in Your Office

Rules concerning fax use concern much more than firm image. "Bad fax" stories have become legend in the legal community. Common problems with **facsimile** (**fax**) machines include locating the machine in a central area that may be open to visitors. For the sake of confidentiality, it should be moved to a private area, or the firm should have a separate machine for sending and receiving confidential faxes. A dedicated "confidential" machine can be made more secure

Exhibit 3-4
Confidentiality Agreement

I, _____ OF _____
   (name)   (address)

in the State of Florida, agree that my employment by [name of firm] ("the firm") shall be strictly on the following terms and conditions:

1. I acknowledge that I have been advised by the firm that all information and documents that I may have knowledge of or access to through my employment with the firm are strictly confidential.

2. I agree at all times to treat as confidential all information acquired through my employment with the firm, and not to disclose same except as authorized in the course of my employment or by law. I acknowledge that such information is not to be altered, copied, interfered with or destroyed, except upon authorization and in accordance with the policy of the firm. I will not discuss such information with any party, nor will I participate in or permit the release, publication or disclosure of such information, nor will I copy, photograph, scan, e-mail, distribute, or disseminate such information, except as authorized in the course of my employment or by law.

I understand that this agreement includes:

(a) never discussing the personality of a client, his or her file or any details thereof with anyone other than a member of the firm directly concerned;
(b) avoiding the use of names of clients in conversations with other clients, friends or relatives;
(c) ensuring that disclosures of information are made only to persons entitled to that information;
(d) ensuring that conversations relating to clients or other firm business are not conducted in the elevator, in the reception area, or other public areas where conversations may be heard by other than firm personnel.

3. I understand and acknowledge that, as an employee of the firm, I am required to honor and be bound by the provisions of the Rules Regulating the Florida Bar in matters of confidentiality of information in the same manner as all the lawyers in the firm, even after I have left the employment of the firm.

(a) a lawyer shall hold in strict confidence all information concerning the business and affairs of the client acquired in the course of the professional relationship, regardless of the nature or source of the information or of the fact that others may share the knowledge, and shall not divulge any such information unless disclosure is expressly or impliedly authorized by the client, or is required by law or by a court.

EXHIBIT 3-4
(continued)

(b) a lawyer shall take all reasonable steps to ensure the privacy and safekeeping of a client's confidential information.

(c) a lawyer shall not disclose the facts of having been consulted or retained by a person unless the nature of the matter requires such disclosure.

(d) a lawyer shall preserve the client's secrets even after the termination of the services.

4. I understand that compliance with the confidentiality requirements of the firm is a condition of my employment and that failure to comply with the policy may result in termination of my employment by the firm.

5. I agree to be bound by the provisions of this Agreement and will continue to be so bound following the termination of my employment.

6. I have been advised that I have the right to seek independent legal advice prior to signing this agreement. (signatures)

From the Florida State Bar Association, Law Office Management Assistance Service, reprinted with permission of J.R. Phelps.

---

encryption
Process of transforming information using an algorithm to make it unreadable to anyone except those possessing a key

key
Mechanism for scrambling and unscrambling information being encrypted

scanning
To use computer software to convert paper documents to accessible images

PDF files
"Portable document format"; a distribution format that allows electronic information to be transferred between various types of computers; secures original file and appearance and is searchable

if it is programmed to send only after the correct number is entered twice. A firm might also want to consider a machine with **encryption** capability. Encryption is a process by which a message is scrambled using complex mathematics, and only the sender and recipient of the communication can translate the scrambled message into legible text, using a **key**.[3] Other alternatives include using an Internet service that will encrypt files and send them as faxes or avoiding fax use by saving or **scanning** documents as **PDF files** that can be sent by e-mail.

Speed-dial numbers should be double checked to ensure that they have been correctly entered and labeled. The firm should use a standard **cover sheet** with a **confidentiality clause** and should train employees to use it, as appropriate.

If a fax machine is retired, the firm should retain the phone line, at least for a while, to ensure that the firm's faxes don't start showing up at a local sandwich shop. Phone companies, faced with a shortage of available numbers, may reassign numbers quickly.

---

[3]Encryption is discussed in more depth later in this chapter.

Example

Sample fax confidentiality languagee

    This fax is considered confidential and may well be legally privileged. If you have received it in error, you are on notice of its status. Please notify us immediately and then delete this message from your system. Please do not copy it or use it for any purposes, or disclose its contents to any other person. Thank you for your cooperation.

Most fax problems arise from misdirected faxes, caused by misdialing, having the wrong number, or careless use of speed-dial. Those problems can be avoided by checking the number in the display before sending and by checking and keeping the **confirmation sheet** whenever a fax is sent. But there can be other possible problems. A lawyer's failure to operate a fax machine correctly caused the European Commission to lose a multimillion-euro case. The lawyer, attempting to fax a 100-page document outlining the Commission's case, accidentally placed it face upwards in the fax machine and the court received 100 blank pages. The actual document was not received in time. With no other legal argument from the Commission, the court had to rule in favor of the opposing party.

    Could an office policy have prevented the consequences of the lawyer's mistake? Yes: when sending an especially important fax, call the recipient to ensure that the entire document arrived. Every fax should also have a cover sheet that includes the names of the sender and recipient, a number that can be called if the fax is misdirected, the date, the number of pages, and a statement that the information is confidential and should not be disclosed to unauthorized individuals.

cover sheet
Should be attached to every outgoing fax; identifies sender (with contact information), recipient, number of pages; typically includes confidentiality language

confidentiality clause
Language indicating that a communication may be privileged and should not be read by unauthorized recipients

confirmation sheet
Produced by the fax machine after a document is sent; states the time and number to which the document was sent

---

Assignment 3-3
Create a Cover Sheet and Send a Fax

1. Create a cover sheet for a two-page fax that indicates the names of the recipient and sender, the fax's confidential status, and what to do if the fax is misdirected or if the entire document is not received. Use the cover sheet to fax to your instructor the contact you created for Assignment 3-2.
2. Create an office procedures manual page for using a shared fax, located in the library/conference room of a small firm.

---

2. Responding to Mistakes by Other Offices

What should you do if a fax comes in that is not intended for your firm? May you read the document? May you use the information contained in the document? Must you return or destroy the document? Does it matter whether you read the document in good faith before realizing that it was misdirected?

In 2002, the ABA adopted Model Rule 4.4(b), which provides: "A lawyer who receives a document relating to the representation of the lawyer's client and knows or reasonably should know that the document was inadvertently sent shall promptly notify the sender." The rule does not obligate the lawyer to take any further steps, such as returning the document. The Comment to Model Rule 4.4 suggests that if any additional obligation exists, it exists solely by virtue of substantive law, not principles of legal ethics. Several state ethics opinions also require notification only, but others indicate that the receiving lawyer should also take specific steps to return or dispose of the document. Some opinions have indicated that misdirecting a communication constitutes a waiver of attorney-client privilege. At least one state has indicated that the lawyer's duty to zealously represent her own client outweighs any obligation to the opposing party and that the receiving firm need not even notify the sender.[4]

clawback agreements
Agreement between firms that confidential information, disclosed accidentally, will not be used but will be destroyed or returned to sender

To deal with the ambiguity surrounding the issue, many firms enter into **clawback agreements** at the beginning of litigation, under which they agree to notify each other of misdirected communication, to not read or use misdirected contents, and to destroy or return misdirected documents.

Assignment 3-4
Research Ethical Opinions on Misdirected Communications

1. Using the Internet, research whether any ethical opinions in your state have addressed misdirected communications.
2. Other types of communication might also be misdirected. Is there any difference when mail is misdelivered by the post office? If you are able to conduct research in federal cases, you can find cases discussing the issue.
3. Could the content of the document itself make a difference with respect to the recipient's obligation? Which ethical rules may apply?
4. Can you imagine a situation in which a firm might intentionally "misdirect" a document to gain a strategic advantage? Identify provisions of your state ethical rules that might apply to such a situation.

D. Incoming Mail

Would you consider it a problem if the mail carrier handed the daily mail to the receptionist at the desk, where it would lay until people pass the desk and pick it up? Another page for the manual! Examine Exhibit 3-5. Is there anything you would add or change?

---

[4]Philadelphia B. Assn. Prof. Guidance Comm., Op. 94-3 (June 1994).

Exhibit 3-5
Guidelines for Incoming Mail

- Mail should be sorted by recipient and not opened in a public area, to avoid the possibility of visitors seeing mail.
- Each attorney, or the attorney's secretary or paralegal (if designated by the attorney), should open and sort that attorney's mail. Every attorney must designate a backup in case the primary person is out of the office. Each attorney should state a policy concerning whether mail marked CONFIDENTIAL should be opened when she is out of the office for an extended period.
- All incoming mail should be date stamped. If an original document should not be marked, it may be date stamped on a "yellow sticky" for later removal or on the back of the document. When in doubt, consult the attorney. The attorney may want some documents copied immediately so that a copy can be inserted into the file while the original is kept elsewhere. For example, an original signed will might be kept in a safe, while a copy is kept in the client file. *When copying original signed documents, do not remove staples.* Removing staples can give the impression of tampering—that a page may have been changed.
- It is usually not necessary to save envelopes. If an attorney wants envelopes attached to correspondence, he should so instruct his paralegal or secretary.
- Mail should be sorted into correspondence from attorneys, clients, courts, periodicals, and unsolicited sources ("junk mail") so that any important dates are immediately noted and entered into the firm's **central calendar** or **docketing system**, as well as the appropriate attorney's individual calendar, before the document is filed.
- If an attorney will be out of the office for more than a day, the secretary or paralegal should make a daily mail log. When possible, mail should be filed as received, unless it requires further attention. When the attorney returns, mail logs should be reviewed and destroyed.
- Another attorney should look at the priority mail on the mail log and take care of any situations requiring immediate attention.
- "Green cards" or other receipt of mail forms should be recorded and attached to the appropriate document in the file.
- Any returned mail or change of address should be noted and entered into the system.
- Checks should be recorded as received and immediately given to bookkeeping to process as appropriate because deposits to trust accounts should be made daily.

central calendar
System by which all employees within firm can enter and check appointments, court dates, and due dates

docketing system
A system, like a calendar, for recording dates, especially related to litigation

E. E-Mail

E-mail is both a tremendous asset and a tremendous threat to law firms. Being able to communicate instantaneously in writing can solve many problems — but if people do not think before they send, that capability can also create many problems. The most obvious problem is how easily e-mail can be misdirected. The *ABA Journal*[5] recently reported that a lawyer for a major corporation had two people named "Berenson" in her e-mail address book — one was a reporter and the other was co-counsel, assisting her in confidential settlement negotiations. Many people now suspect that an e-mail accidentally sent to the wrong Berenson was a source for a front-page *New York Times* story about the negotiations.

In a presentation on the top ten causes of malpractice at the ABA Techshow 2006, e-mail problems were cited as part of the second cause of malpractice claims — lack of professionalism:

> Email is another place where being casual can be dangerous. At a minimum, you must check your spelling and your grammar, and make certain that your e-mail has a signature block at the end. Why? Again, imagine a client for whom you are acting as divorce counsel. In all likelihood, given the nature of divorce proceedings, this client will reach the end of your professional relationship feeling emotionally beaten. Now, also assume that during your representation this client received emails that were poorly written and rather cryptic. This client will tend toward what all clients do when their case doesn't end quite as expected. The client simply will try to put everything in perspective. It may be natural for this client to ask himself, "What went wrong?" Unfortunately, the client received your unprofessional e-mails, and now is thinking, "Why didn't I see this before? My own fifth grader can write better than my attorney can. She's incompetent and my loss is her fault!" Again, unprofessional behavior leads to the client questioning your competence. Mark C.S. Bassingthwaighte & Reba J. Nance, The Top Ten Causes of Malpractice — and How You Can Avoid Them, Presentation at the ABA Techshow 2006 (Apr. 20-22, 2006), http://www.abanet.org/lpm/lpt/articles/tch12062.pdf.

For untrained employees, many problems arise from how they structure their messages or from overuse. Every firm should have policies concerning use of e-mail and the Internet. Policies may cover the big picture, for example:

> The firm's equipment, including computer terminals, is for business use only. Do not use your computer for personal e-mail, shopping, etc. The firm may monitor computer use by employees to enforce this policy; employees should be aware that they have no privacy rights when using firm equipment. Violation of this policy may result in immediate termination.

Other policies may cover the details of use:

- Consider disabling the "autocomplete" feature that completes the address of the recipient after you enter a few letters, to prevent inadvertently sending to the wrong person.

---

[5]http://abajournal.com/news/lawyers_e_mail_goof_lands_on_nyts_front_page/. Posted Feb. 6, 2008. Berenson apparently later claimed that e-mail was not the source of his story.

- Be careful that you do not send messages to everyone or copy unnecessary recipients. Most people now get so many e-mail messages in a typical day that they may overlook important messages by accident. A common cause of junk e-mails is overuse of the Reply to All option. For example, a partner might send a message to "everyone," stating, "Congratulations to our paralegal manager, Terry, who presented a CLE seminar on e-mail confidentiality to the county bar association last week." You hit Reply to All and say "Terry, that's great!"
- Give careful thought to your subject line; it may prevent your message from being one of those accidentally deleted. Every business e-mail should have a subject line.
- Before forwarding an e-mail, read the entire string of messages to ensure that you are not sending confidential or other information to an inappropriate recipient.
- Do not use **emoticons** in business e-mails. Do not SHOUT by writing in all caps. Be very careful with humor—remember the reader cannot see your expression or hear your tone of voice.
- Set up your e-mail account so that your outgoing messages request a receipt when the recipient views the message.
- Write business e-mails like business letters, with a greeting, grammatically correct sentences, and a signature. Use spell-check and be sure that your punctuation is correct. Do not use text message shortcuts such as "RU ready 2 sign?" or "Thx."
- E-mail concerning business that is sent to people outside the firm should include a signature block, identifying the sender, his or her title, an e-mail address, the firm webpage URL, and the sender's telephone number. It's also a good idea to include a confidentiality statement, such as that included on fax cover sheets.
- If you can choose your own e-mail address, it should be some version of your name, such as RobertNienke@SBFKlaw.com or RNienke@SBFKlaw.com or NienkeR@SBFKlaw.com. Do not use a nickname or descriptor, such as boxingbabe@yahoo.com or beachqt@hotmail.com, for business or job search e-mails.
- If you are attaching a document to an e-mail (as opposed to including it in the body of the e-mail), consider whether it is important that the document not be altered. If so, save the document as a PDF file or use the lock feature on your word processing program before sending the document.
- Check your e-mail at least twice a day; if you cannot do so because you will be out of the office, use the help feature to learn how to set up a "rule" that will send an automatic reply containing alternate contact information. For example: "Pat Paralegal will be out of the office until October 12. If you need assistance before that time, contact Chris Coworker at ccoworker@SBFKlaw.com or 888-555-1212."
- Keep in mind that e-mails are never completely gone. They remain on some **server** long after you delete—it may be your firm's server, the server of the recipient or sender, or the **Internet service provider (ISP)** server—but they are out there and can be found and even **subpoenaed**. Do not send an e-mail unless you would be willing to have people other than the

emoticons
Symbols, such as smiley faces, used to express emotions in e-mail

Note: Follow the instructions below (for inserting confidentiality language) or use the Help feature of your e-mail account to find instructions for inserting a business card or a signature block in your outgoing e-mails.

server
A central computer that manages computer network resources; a file server stores files for users; a print server manages printers; a network server manages network traffic

Internet service provider (ISP)
A company or organization through which users access the Internet

subpoenaed
Court order requiring party to give testimony or produce evidence

recipient read it. As stated on the blog Death By Email (http://www.deathbyemail.com), if your email contains a phrase such as "delete this immediately" or "I could get in trouble for telling you this," don't send it!

- Be kind to your server. Delete (or save to other folders) long messages and messages with attachments (especially pictures, slide shows, and videos) as soon as possible to save valuable storage space. Don't forget to delete from your Sent items and Deleted items files every two to three months.
- If you will refer back to e-mail messages you have saved, either amend the subject line or "categorize" them to avoid wasting time searching.
- Keep your messages as short as possible and, if possible, limit the message to a single subject.
- Consider whether a message should be printed and added to the client's file so that others working on the file have equal access to the message. Some people do not print e-mails in an effort to protect confidentiality, but e-mails are subject to discovery under the same rules that apply to hard copy and, unlike messages originating on paper, cannot be totally destroyed.
- Be cautious about opening e-mails and using preview panes that automatically open your e-mails so that you can "preview" part of the message. When in doubt, ask your **IT department**. Opening an e-mail from an unknown source can subject your computer and the entire **network** to a **virus**.
- Use a confidentiality clause, as with a fax, at the beginning of the message so that it will be seen before the message is read. An easy way to ensure that the clause appears in every message is to use a form or a macro.

Best Practices

To create an e-mail template with a confidentiality clause, your signature, and even a firm logo, if you are using Microsoft Outlook:

- Start at http://office.microsoft.com
- Click the tab for "products" and navigate to the "help and how-to" pages for your version of Outlook
- Click "E-mail," then "Customizing E-Mail Messages"

IT department
Information technology staff

network
Group of connected computers and hardware

virus
Program designed to copy itself into the other programs on a computer; may cause a program to operate incorrectly or corrupt computer's memory

firewalls
Security system to prevent unauthorized users from gaining access to network or computer

hackers
Computer user who intentionally gains access to confidential information

e-mail retention policy
Policy concerning deletion of e-mail

e-mail clients
Computer application that allows user to send and receive e-mail

Every firm should use **firewalls** to protect itself from **hackers** and have an **e-mail retention policy**. Your firm should regularly back up its electronic information so that it will be safe in case of a disaster such as a fire, flood, or tornado, and should encrypt sensitive e-mails.

There are several mechanisms for encrypting e-mail. Once encrypted, the only part of the message that remains readable are the sender and recipient fields, necessary for routing the mail from source to destination. Encryption is valuable not only for protecting confidentiality when sending, but also for verifying authenticity of information received. Most major **e-mail clients** include options for encrypting messages.

With symmetric, or "secret key" encryption, the sender of the encrypted information must have a secure means of sending the key to the recipient separately from the confidential information itself. Public key, or asymmetric, encryption has, therefore, become more widely used.

Public key encryption works like this: Firm A wants to send Firm B a secure message. Firm A uses Firm B's public key to encrypt the message; Firm B will be able to open the message using the private key corresponding to that public key. Only Firm B has the private key that corresponds to its public key. It is like Firm A putting a letter into an open mail slot that drops into a locked box at Firm B. Anybody can put something in the slot, but only Firm B can take it out, using its private key. Does Firm A have any concerns? Yes, it must make sure that the public key definitely originated with Firm B; this may be done by means of a digital signature or a **digital certificate**. The parties might use a public key ring server — a trusted place where users keep their public keys.

digital certificate
Electronic "credit card" that establishes credentials when doing business or other transactions on the Internet

While hackers do pose a threat to confidentiality, sometimes it is the simplest mistakes that result in the most damage — for example, a client asks to use the computer of a paralegal who is out of the office to check e-mail. To avoid such mistakes, computer terminals should be password protected if practicable.

F. Loss of Communications Technology

Portable communications devices such as notebook computers, PDAs, and cell phones are particularly vulnerable to loss because they are generally used outside the office. Safeware Insurance (http://www.safeware.com), which provides coverage for technology, states that the number one cause of loss is accidental damage; the number two cause of loss is theft. Both are on the rise, and 97 percent of stolen computers are never recovered.

Users can prevent the loss of their portable devices by using various locks or engraved identification tags, and increasing their vigilance. Losing the data stored on portable devices is more serious. To prevent the loss of data, users should perform regular backups, avoid keeping confidential information on portable devices if possible, and use encryption and passwords. Tracking software is also available for notebook computers. When activated by notification, the software sends a signal so that the computer's location can be traced, and, upon request by the owner, data on the hard drive can be erased remotely.

Assignment 3-5
Office Policy for Lost Devices

Management Portfolio

Ed Rodan is very concerned about the firm's notebook computers being stolen. He has asked for a memo addressing the following:

1. What are the firm's obligations if a stolen computer contained confidential client information that might make identity theft possible? Research state and federal law at http://www.consumersunion.org/

campaigns//financialprivacynow/002215indiv.html or http://www.ftc.gov/bcp/edu/microsites/idtheft/business/data-breach.html.

2. What tracking software options are available, and might there be special concerns about using that software on a law firm computer? Research using the following websites:
   - http://www.ztrace.com
   - http://www.lojackforlaptops.com/products
   - http://www.absolute.com
   - http://www.forbes.com/2005/08/19/digilife-lojack-laotops-cx_daa_0819digilife.html

3. Should the firm have policies about how electronic devices are carried, stored, etc.? Research using the following websites:
   - http://www.microsoft.com/atwork/stayconnected/laptopsecurity.mspx
   - http://www.microsoft.com/smallbusiness/resources/technology/security/how-to-protect-your-laptop-from-thieves.aspx#Howtoprotectyourlaptopfromthieves
   - http://www.abanet.org/lpm/lpt/articles/tch10081.shtml

Out There — Paralegal Profile
But That's Not My Job!

When you finish your paralegal education, you will have every reason to be proud of your accomplishment. You may feel competent to immediately take on the most challenging substantive assignments. You might feel that answering the phone, opening the mail, or sending faxes would be a misuse of your time. The reality, however, is that you will have to do these things at some point in your career. It's not only the economics of practice, it's how firms determine those things that are not necessarily reflected in your grades: ability to work well with others, "team spirit," and reliability. Completing the less challenging tasks with competence, a positive attitude, and attention to detail will move you toward your "dream job."

Nola Sayne is a Labor and Employment/Employee Benefits and Executive Compensation paralegal with the prestigious Seyfarth Shaw firm in Atlanta. She is student growth coordinator for the Georgia Association of Paralegals and has been part of an ABA site team, evaluating a college for ABA approval of its paralegal program. Nola is quick to point out that she did not start at the top. She worked as a corporate secretary and a legal secretary before completing her paralegal education and being promoted to her current position.

Nola likes to tell paralegal students: "There are four ways to get your foot in the door with little or no previous experience: (1) *Network and*

become involved! Join your local paralegal association and tell others that you are available. Local paralegal organizations also have pro bono opportunities. You can volunteer to work on pro bono cases and gain valuable experience handling client intake, navigating the court system, and the processes involved in different areas of law (especially family and criminal). Also, it's an opportunity to give back to the community and help those in need. In most cases you are required to have attorney supervision and it's possible that you just might be volunteering with your future employer! (2) *Scout out small firms that may be willing to train.* I started at a two-attorney firm and handled most everything. I was the point of contact for all clients, I handled all initial drafts of all documents, maintained the files, and even scrubbed the toilet. (3) *Many firms and government offices offer internships.* The paralegal program you attended may have internship information. (4) *Look at entry-level positions.* Don't be too proud to take a job as a file clerk, a case assistant, or a legal secretary. These positions give you a chance to show team spirit, a willingness to learn and can give the opportunity to work with many people in different departments."

Chapter Review

Discussion Questions

1. Explain how e-mail encryption works.
2. Explain how a firm can protect the confidentiality of its outgoing faxes.
3. What should a firm do when it receives a misdirected confidential fax? Is the answer different if the firm receives misdelivered mail?
4. What steps should be taken in handling incoming mail?
5. Describe how you would handle a phone call from an obviously distraught client who insists on talking to an attorney who is out of the office until tomorrow.
6. What is the benefit of keeping contact information on a computer rather than in a Rolodex?

7. A client has retained your supervising attorney to get a divorce, but has not yet notified her husband. She is afraid he will become violent. The attorney has asked you to call the client and ask her to come in to sign the petition. What will you say when she picks up the phone? What will you say if an answering machine picks up?

8. What are the benefits of saving a document as a PDF file or in a similar format?

9. Do you think the firm is within its rights to monitor and limit employee use of the Internet?

10. Do you think the firm would benefit from having all employees sign a confidentiality agreement, in which they acknowledge that they have been informed about the ethical rules of confidentiality and agree to abide by those rules?

ACROSS

3. every fax should have a _____ sheet
5. _____certificate, establishes credentials for doing business online
8. a call involving multiple parties
9. _____ mail, replaced the old-fashioned answering machine
12. may "infect" a computer
13. _____phone, has features such as e-mail
16. security system to keep unauthorized users out of computer network
17. computers linked together
19. to transform information so that it can be read only with a key
21. shortened reference to an electronic facsimile

DOWN

1. manages computer network resources
2. desktop rotary file with contact information
4. wireless technology that allows electronic devices to communicate
6. "hot _____" PDA to office computer
7. after sending a fax, you should get this from your machine

10. a smiley face, for example
11. system, like a calendar, particularly for court dates
14. to use software to convert documents to computer images
15 one who gains unauthorized access to computer network
18. initials, device to enable hearing-impaired to use phones
20. a format that preserves original file for transfer on Internet (initials)

Terms and Definitions

Bluetooth technology: Short-range wireless technology that allows electronic devices to communicate

call forwarding: Technology that sends a phone call directed to one phone number to another number

call waiting: Technology that notifies a person talking on the phone that another call is coming in, typically by making a beeping sound

caller ID: Technology that displays the phone number and/or identity of an incoming caller and stores the information for future reference

central calendar: System by which all employees within firm can enter and check appointments, court dates, and due dates

clawback agreement: Agreement between firms that confidential information, disclosed accidentally, will not be used but will be destroyed or returned to sender

conference call: A telephone call in which three or more people, at different locations, participate by means of a central switching unit

confidentiality clause: Language indicating that a communication may be privileged and should not be read by unauthorized recipients

confirmation sheet: Produced by the fax machine after a document is sent; states the time and number to which the document was sent

cover sheet: Should be attached to every outgoing fax; identifies sender (with contact information), recipient, number of pages; typically includes confidentiality language

digital certificate: Electronic "credit card" that establishes credentials when doing business or other transactions on the Internet

docketing system: A system, like a calendar, for recording dates, especially related to litigation

e-mail client: Computer application that allows user to send and receive e-mail

e-mail retention policy: Policy concerning deletion of e-mail

emoticons: Symbols, such as smiley faces, used to express emotions in e-mail

encryption: Process of transforming information using an algorithm to make it unreadable to anyone except those possessing a key

facsimile: An identical reproduction; in the law office setting, generally an electronic reproduction transmitted by phone lines

fax: Common reference to an electronic facsimile of a document

fields: Discrete components of electronic document

firewall: Security system to prevent unauthorized users from gaining access to network or computer

hacker: Computer user who intentionally gains access to confidential information

hot sync: To connect electronic devices so that they share information (e.g., PDA calendar dates are entered onto desktop computer or network calendar)

Internet service provider (ISP): A company or organization through which users access the Internet

IT department: Information technology staff

key: Mechanism for scrambling and unscrambling information being encrypted

network: Group of connected computers and hardware

PC: Short for "personal computer"; traditionally refers to an IBM-compatible computer (i.e., not a Mac)

PDA: "Personal digital assistant"; a small electronic device that combines various computer functions

PDF file: "Portable document format"; a distribution format that allows electronic information to be transferred between various types of computers; secures original file and appearance and is searchable

Rolodex: Trademark name for a rotary file of card, typically with contact information

scanning: To use computer software to convert paper documents to accessible images

server: A central computer that manages computer network resources; a file server stores files for users; a print server manages printers; a network server manages network traffic

smart phone: Has functions, such as e-mail, not available on standard cell phones

soft charges: Charges for postage, phone use, etc.

subpoena: Court order requiring party to give testimony or produce evidence

TDD or TTY machine: Device that assists hearing-impaired users of telephones by displaying messages so that they can be read

text message: Written message sent by and displayed on a phone

three-way calling: Technology that permits multiple parties to share a phone conversation

virus: Program designed to copy itself into the other programs on a computer; may cause a program to operate incorrectly or corrupt computer's memory

voice mail: Technology that records incoming phone messages

4

Law Office Communications: The Message

As a Manager

You will be responsible for establishing guidelines for oral and written communications to support your firm's professional image and comply with ethical rules, and for ensuring that employees understand and follow those guidelines.

Objectives

After completing this chapter, you will be able to

- Identify what steps to take to avoid ethical and legal mistakes in oral and written communications.
- Identify the characteristics of various documents commonly prepared by paralegals.
- Prepare for an interview.
- Write a letter to a client, in proper format and consistent with the ethical obligations of a law office.

A. Oral Communications
   1. Can We Talk?
   2. Location, Location, Location
   3. Identifying Yourself and Your Position
   4. Do Not Assume the Attorney's Role
   5. Control the Conversation, But . . .

A.   Oral Communications

Now wait a minute, you know how to hold a conversation, right? That may be true, and you may be terrific at making people feel at ease, finding common ground, and being charming. As you might have guessed, however, speaking to a client, opposing counsel, a witness, or even your coworkers in the context of working in a law office involves ethical concerns unique to the legal field. These concerns should be dealt with from the beginning of the conversation.

1.   Can We Talk?

Your first concern is whether you can have a conversation with a particular individual. Imagine that it's 4:30 in the afternoon. You are getting ready to leave for the day when the phone rings. The caller is Barrie, the buyer in a residential real estate deal you've been working on. The purchase is scheduled to close tomorrow at 9:00 in the morning. Unfortunately, Barrie is not your firm's client. Your firm represents Sal, the seller, but it has been a cordial relationship, and there appear to be no problematic issues. Barrie has a simple question: "I know I shouldn't be calling you, but my own lawyer has been in court all day and his assistant is out sick. I know he e-mailed me the closing figures, but my computer crashed and I cannot retrieve them. I have to go get a check right now so that I won't delay the closing. Can you tell me the amount I have to bring?"

In all likelihood, you would know the number that Barrie needs, but it is equally likely that you should not be having this conversation. Most states have a rule similar to ABA Model Rule of Professional Conduct 4.2 that prohibits communication with a person represented by another lawyer without the consent of that lawyer. The ABA Model Rule refers to a "person," not a "party," and, in some places, is interpreted as applying to a witness as well as to an opponent. Let's change the situation a bit. Barrie does not have a lawyer, so there is nothing to prevent your firm from taking the call. While talking to Barrie, your supervising attorney becomes aware that Barrie believes that buying the house will create a huge tax break. Barrie thinks that a personal residence can be depreciated, which is not true. Is the attorney under an obligation to correct Barrie's mistake? Probably not, if a rule patterned after ABA Model Rule 4.1 applies. The rule prohibits an attorney from making a false statement and, relevant in this case, requires disclosure only if necessary to prevent fraud or a crime. Your state's rule may be different.

Assignment 4-1
Ethical Rules Concerning Communications

---

1. Using the website you bookmarked or added to your Favorites for an earlier assignment, find your state's equivalent of ABA Model Rule 4.2. Under what circumstances does it permit communication with a person represented by other counsel? Now find the equivalent of ABA Model Rule 4.1, concerning truthfulness. Is the state rule more stringent than ABA Model Rule 4.1?
2. Find the rule that applies if Barrie does not have a lawyer. What special concerns apply to such a situation? How might you deal with Barrie's call regarding the amount of his closing check if you believe that supplying him the answer would violate the rule? Remember, if Barrie does not come to the closing with the correct amount of money, your firm's client, Sal, may not be able to close the sale of the house.
3. Standing on the sidewalk outside your office, you see an accident. A distracted driver, talking on her cell phone, made a right turn on red and hit a pregnant woman, legally in the crosswalk. The driver jumps out of the car and begins berating the pedestrian, who is sitting on the pavement looking confused. The driver seems to be attempting to get the woman to say that she, the pedestrian, must have seen the car and should have gotten out of the way. Your impulse is to say: "Don't say a word! You need a lawyer! I can get a great lawyer here in two minutes." Find the state rule that applies to this situation.

---

2. Location, Location, Location

Some conversations can be held by phone or even by e-mail, but preliminary interviews with clients and witnesses and interviews with job applicants should be held in person whenever possible. In choosing a location, convenience and "ambience" are not the primary considerations. The legal professional must confine all conversations concerning client matters to locations where confidentiality will be protected. This means that those conversations should not take place in elevators, in restaurants, on a train or a bus, or even in the firm's reception area. An office or conference room is usually the best location for a conversation with a client, a witness, a colleague, or anyone with information about a client matter, even if the conversation is being held by phone. If the other party is with you, make sure that there are not open files, documents lying on your desk, or even a document on your computer screen that might compromise the confidentiality of another matter. Make sure that the door is closed.

While you are thinking about confidentiality, consider educating the client about confidentiality. Many clients are unaware that lawyers and paralegals may not reveal information given in confidence, except under very limited circumstances. Telling the client about the protection will make the client more comfortable about telling the whole truth about his situation. In addition, you must educate the client that the value of confidentiality and even the existence of attorney-client privilege can be lost if the client fails to keep the matter confidential. Because many people come to a law office accompanied by a friend or relative, educating the client about confidentiality may need to start at the door. While some other relationships, such as doctor-patient, penitent-clergy, and husband-wife involve **privilege**, many other supportive relationships, such as friends and siblings, do not enjoy privilege.

privilege
Rule that keeps information confidential and presents its use as evidence

---

Example

As a general rule, disclosures in the presence of third parties destroy the confidentiality of the communication, thus rendering the communication unprotected by the privilege. *United States v. Landof*, 591 F.2d 36 (9th Cir. 1978); *United States v. McCluskey*, 6 U.S.C.M.A. 545 (1955); *United States v. Nelson*, 38 M.J. 710, 715 (A.C.M.R. 1993); 1 *McCormick on Evidence* §91 (4th ed. 1992); *Wigmore on Evidence* §§2311, 2326 (3rd ed. 1983).

---

3. Identifying Yourself and Your Position

Whenever you have a conversation with someone outside the firm who does not know your role, you should introduce yourself with a firm handshake, sustained eye contact, and a statement similar to this one: "I am _____, Attorney Brown's paralegal. I am going to be assisting Attorney Brown in handling this matter." Identifying yourself as a paralegal is essential to avoid unauthorized practice of law and to avoid giving others a false impression.

Don't be surprised if the person to whom you are speaking does not know what a paralegal is or even becomes a little angry that she is not speaking to only lawyers. People dealing with the legal system are often under a lot of stress; you must stay calm and respond within the bounds of your position.

4. Do Not Assume the Attorney's Role

To avoid usurping the attorney's role, the paralegal must not establish or control the essential attorney-client relationship. This means that the paralegal may not decide whether to accept the case, set the fee, or give legal advice. The paralegal may communicate information concerning these matters, but not originate or explain the decision.

What is legal advice? That is a difficult question, but in general it involves two component parts: knowledge of the law plus individualized guidance. If a client asks, "What is attorney-client privilege?," he is requesting only generalized legal information. If, however, a client asks, "Will attorney-client privilege apply when I have already retained another lawyer?," she is requesting legal advice. When in doubt, err on the side of caution. In some cases, a question may be worded as a general inquiry but amount to a request for advice.

Assignment 4-2
Privilege

1. Find your state's rule on confidentiality and identify the circumstances under which a lawyer may disregard confidentiality.
2. Find the case *In re Jury Proceedings,* 103 F.3d 1140 (3rd Cir. 1997), *cert.den.* 520 U.S. 1253 (1997). Is there a parent-child privilege in your state?
3. Recall the situation from the previous assignment. Suppose that the pedestrian had seen you walk out of a law office and, after being hit by the car, had said to you: "I need a lawyer. Can you help me?" What would be the appropriate response?
4. Read the excerpts from the disciplinary case in Exhibit 4-1. How might a lawyer and a paralegal "innocently" fall into a similar situation? Is there any kind of firm that presents a particular risk?

EXHIBIT 4-1
Disciplinary Board v. Nassif, 547 N.W.2d 541 (N.D. 1996)

...The record in the current disciplinary proceedings demonstrates a continuing pattern of gross incompetence, neglect of client matters, negligent supervision of office staff, failure to maintain adequate records, and mishandling and conversion of client funds. . . .

The record demonstrates an unacceptable lack of supervision by Nassif of his office staff. Nassif allowed untrained "paralegals," whom he deemed to be independent contractors and not his employees, to, in effect, practice law under his license. These paralegals were allowed to recruit and advise clients, negotiate fee agreements with clients, and perform legal work for clients, with little or no supervision by Nassif. One of these paralegals was held out to a client as a licensed attorney practicing with Nassif. Nassif routinely split fees with the non-lawyer paralegals, and candidly admitted cashing a retainer check from a client and giving half of the cash to his paralegal. . . .

Nassif also mishandled and converted client funds. Nassif's financial recordkeeping was virtually nonexistent. He had no trust account for client funds, kept inadequate or no records of receipt of client funds, and commingled client funds in his general office account. He kept inadequate records of client billings, and allowed his office staff to handle financial transactions, including receipt and expenditure of client funds, with no

EXHIBIT 4-1
(continued)

supervision. He converted client funds, kept unearned fees, and failed to refund those fees to clients. Nassif also entered into oral contingent fee agreements with clients.

The hearing panel concluded, and we concur, that Nassif's conduct violated the following provisions of the North Dakota Rules of Professional Conduct: . . . Rule 5.3, NDRPC, which requires a lawyer to properly supervise non-lawyer assistants to ensure compliance with ethical obligations; Rule 5.4, NDRPC, which prohibits a lawyer from sharing fees with a non-lawyer; and Rule 5.5, NDRPC, which prohibits a lawyer from assisting a non-lawyer in the unauthorized practice of law. . . .

. . . Nassif's assistance in the unauthorized practice of law by his office staff, and sharing in fees generated therefrom, violated a duty owed to the profession with intent to obtain personal benefit.

. . . We order that Delayne G. Nassif be disbarred. Nassif is ordered to pay the costs of these proceedings in the amount of $6,854.35. Nassif is also ordered to pay restitution. . . .

5.   Control the Conversation, But . . .

Any conversation that warrants a face-to-face meeting or a phone call requires preparation. Most people (including you, probably) react poorly when they feel their time is being wasted. Clients, for instance, may become upset if they believe that their highly paid legal professionals are disorganized or distracted. Witnesses kept waiting in person or at the end of a phone line may become less cooperative. And legal professionals — among whom busy schedules and time constraints are universal — may have the least amount of patience of all when their colleagues are ill prepared.

Whether you will be talking to a client, a witness, opposing counsel, or another work colleague, you should plan for a conversation that includes some introductory talk, an organized and thorough list of questions, and satisfactory closure. Planning a list of questions that will get the information you need requires, first of all, substantive knowledge of the legal matter. Second, it requires general knowledge about human nature and differences in communication styles, as well as specific knowledge about the background of your client or visitor. And, most important, it requires good listening skills. Many studies have shown that the average person is able to recall only a small percentage of what was said in a presentation, even immediately after the presentation[1]. The reasons range from

---

[1]For example, people watching the evening news could recall only 17.2% of content when not cued and no more than 25% if cued. Stauffer, Frost & Rybolt 1983 as quoted by International Listening Association, www.listen.org

anxiety to the fact that people think much faster than they talk, giving listeners time to let their minds wander. Your supervising attorney or client won't care that you are only an average person or why you don't recall half of what was said, so you must train yourself to be an effective listener.

Here are several things you can do to prepare for a successful face-to-face interview with a client or witness:

1. Think about your goal in conducting the interview. Once you have identified the information you need, you can determine whether any of that information can be obtained by other means. Next, identify general topics for categorizing the information you need to develop an organized list of questions. Consider whether there are any relevant documents or other materials that should be available during the interview.

2. Prepare the location. If the interview will take place at your office, in addition to considering confidentiality, consider whether the room you will use has a neat and professional appearance. Is there a comfortable seating arrangement? If your interviewee arrives early and waits in the reception area for a few minutes, will someone offer her a beverage? Do employees know that they should never discuss office or personal business in the reception area?

3. Start the meeting on a positive note. Greet people by their titles (Mr., Mrs., or Ms.) and last names, using their first names only if asked to do so. If you are at your own office, offer a beverage if someone has not done so. If you are even a few minutes late, have someone apologize and assure your interviewee that you have not forgotten the appointment. If the visitor is a client and will likely have a long-term relationship with others in the office, perform relevant introductions. If the interviewee is a witness, be sure to ask whether he is represented by an attorney and whether this is the first interview he has given. If it is not the first interview, ask for a copy of what was said in the previous interview.

4. Be prepared to record what is said. Are you able to take thorough and accurate notes without being distracted from paying attention to the speaker? If not, you may want to record the interview, but be sure to tell the interviewee that you are doing so.

If you are concerned about recording or reducing to writing statements that might be harmful to your client's position, ask your supervising attorney whether the recording or document would be protected under the **work product doctrine**. The doctrine originates in attorney-client privilege and allows the attorney to refuse to produce physical items prepared in anticipation of litigation. However, the doctrine is subject to an exception when the party seeking the documents or items shows "substantial need." Of course, communication from the client is directly covered by attorney-client privilege, and courts most particularly guard against the disclosure of an attorney's "mental impressions, conclusions, opinions or legal theories." But documents or recordings directly from, or containing information from, outside sources can be subject to the exception.

work product doctrine
Part of attorney-client privilege; protects certain documents from discovery

5. Get all of the information. Limit interruptions that may disturb the flow of the conversation. Structure the meeting so that easier topics are covered first. This will sometimes mean beginning with some "small talk" about the weather or traffic, or it may mean getting basic information such as contact information. Your firm may have a standard intake form for obtaining such information. Depending on the topic of the interview, you may want to ask the client or witness for a "bare bones" chronology of events before asking detailed questions.

Ask open-ended questions, such as "What happened next?" rather than questions that can be answered "yes" or "no." Speak in a conversational tone and avoid legal terms. For example, if you tell a client that you want to discuss her "appearance" at a deposition, you may simply mean her being present at the deposition. She may think you are referring to her clothing and hair. If you tell a divorcing spouse that he is likely to be required to pay "maintenance," he may think you are talking about repairs to the house, rather than support of his ex-wife. Do not use shorthand expressions, such as S-O-L for "statute of limitations."

Be friendly and empathetic, but do not react with emotion. Try to avoid communicating any judgment of what is said, even a reaction of extreme sympathy or outrage at something that happened to the speaker. Remember, your facial expressions, posture, and even your actions, such as suddenly taking notes, can convey emotion. Do not reveal personal information about yourself or your opinions.

Listen to the response and watch for non-verbal clues. Remember to consider whether cultural differences, stress, physical discomfort, or other factors may contribute to a person's reactions. For example, people in some cultures nod and even say "uh-huh, okay," simply to indicate that they are listening. They do not intend to communicate that they agree with you. When in doubt, "mirror" what you believe was said: "You agree that Ms. Nash was not present at that meeting?"

Don't ignore "hidden clues." For example, a speaker may say, "I was so lucky to have that job." You may think this is an insignificant expression of emotion. But if you were to follow up by saying "Why do you think so?" the answer might surprise you — perhaps she was the only woman ever promoted to a management position in the company. Don't allow yourself to get impatient; many people find it difficult to just recite the most important facts. They prefer to describe a situation by way of narrative, complete with emotions, descriptions, and occasional irrelevant observations. One of the most effective interview techniques is silence: give the other person an opportunity to reflect and expand on what has been said.

You may have to revisit some issues. The speaker's body language, your own intuition, or the nature of the question may lead you to question whether the answer was accurate. For example, people tend to guess about questions involving judgment, such as "How far were you from the truck?" or "How long did it take?" If you are concerned about the accuracy of the first answer, follow up with, "How did you judge the distance?" or "What made you think that ten minutes had passed?" If you think the speaker is being evasive, she may need to be reminded about confidentiality, if it applies.

Move from topic to topic without wasting time by guiding the speaker. "We've been talking about your history with the company. Now let's talk about your efforts to find a new job since you left."

6. End the meeting on a positive note. An interview can be comfortably tied up with a summary of what has been accomplished and, even more important, with what will happen next. For example, "Thank you, Mr. Lopez, I think we have enough information to allow us to prepare your corporate documents. I'll be in touch in about two weeks and then we will . . ." If appropriate, remind the interviewee of his next step: "I'd appreciate it if you would locate those tax records and get them to me this week." Subtle body language, such as slowly rising from your seat and extending your hand, will move the meeting to a close if necessary. Always escort the interviewee out.

7. **Follow up.** After talking to a client or a witness, immediately prepare a summary for the file. A letter may be appropriate after a meeting with a client, to confirm any decisions that were made or any expected follow-up.

Some Thoughts on the First Meeting or First Letter

- Do the words communicate the difference between hiring a lawyer to do specific work and hiring a lawyer to obtain a specific result? A lawyer cannot promise results.
- Make sure the client has copies of all documents she has signed. If the client is an individual (rather than a business), give her a labeled file folder containing those documents and explain that documents you send in the future should be kept in the same folder.
- Have you discussed how future communications will be handled? Does the client check e-mail frequently? Can the client accept calls at work? Do others have access to the client's phone messages, e-mail, or mail? Does your firm have a policy concerning attachments sent to the firm by e-mail (to protect against viruses)?

B. Written Communication

Written communication is a huge part of almost every paralegal job. Those written communications may include documents such as wills, contracts, deeds, and trusts, intended to implement goals. They may be **adversarial** and argue a particular position, or they may be **objective**. Adversarial documents are generally directed to an opponent (**demand letter**) or a court (**appellate brief** or **trial memo**). Objective documents, including **interoffice memoranda** and **opinion letters**, are generally directed at clients or others within the law firm. For some documents, such as appellate briefs, following particular rules of format is critical; for others, such as a memo to a coworker, format is less important.

Some firms maintain style manuals that include the preferred formats for memoranda, contracts, and even templates for creation of regularly used documents. The style manual may include the requirements of local courts.

Regardless of the format of the written communication (letter, court pleading, memo, will, trust, contract), documents generated by a law office have some traits in common. Law office documents tend to use defined terms and other unique features and must be absolutely accurate. Law office documents are often produced from forms or templates to increase efficiency and must be saved so that they can be quickly located and retrieved.

adversarial
Argues a position

objective
Does not argue a position; typically analyzes a situation and predicts result

demand letter
Typically sent before suit on debt; requests payment

appellate brief
Formal document presenting arguments to reviewing court

trial memo
Directed to trial court; typically argues a position

interoffice memoranda
Intended for use within firm; typically objective and often covered by privilege

opinion letters
Letter giving legal advice or predicting outcome

1. Unique Features

To ensure that the parties are on the "same page," legal documents often include **recitals**, **defined terms**, and **incorporation by reference**. Recitals are most often used in contracts, and they recite the events or goals that led to the agreement. Recitals are sometimes prefaced by the word "Whereas."

recitals
State the background; typically in a contract

defined terms
Shorthand references to important subjects in document

incorporation by reference
Makes an outside document part of the document at hand

Example

Whereas the undersigned parties, Jane M. Lehmann of 555 Chestnut Street, Lebanon, Mo. (hereinafter "Jane"), and Paul H. Lehmann of 12W774 Pinery, Bevent, Wis. (hereinafter "Paul") are sister and brother, each unmarried, and have entered a contract to purchase, as tenants in common, a condominium at 666 N. Lake Shore Drive, Chicago, Ill. (hereinafter "the Condominium");

Whereas Paul and Jane wish to resolve, in advance, matters relating to the sale or inheritance of the Condominium;

Now, therefore, Paul and Jane agree as follows:

1. Paul and Jane each contributed Ten Thousand Dollars ($10,000) to the total earnest money paid pursuant to the contract to purchase the Condominium, dated January 21, 2009, attached to and made a part of this agreement.

Notice the use of parenthesis and "hereinafter" to create defined terms so that the document need not contain repeated references to "the 666 N. Lake Shore Drive Condominium." There are different styles for creating defined terms; for example, some people omit the word "hereinafter." If a document, such as a complicated contract, has many terms that require definition, the document should contain a separate section for definitions.

Notice also that paragraph 1 makes reference to the contract to buy the condominium and makes that contract a part of this agreement. Attachments are sometimes called exhibits.

2. Need for Accuracy

Lawyers know that many contracts, wills, trusts, and other legal documents end up in litigation because of mistakes in drafting those documents. Here are a few guidelines to help avoid mistakes in drafting:

- Think about your audience. Who will ultimately read this document, and how will they use it? This will help you achieve the correct tone. While your supervising lawyer may review your work, it would be inappropriate to write a contract at a level appropriate for a lawyer if it will ultimately be used by a first-time legal client who is starting an auto detailing business.
- Think about the appropriate level of specificity. In a will you might want to refer to "any vehicle I own at the time of my death," but in a divorce settlement you want to say that wife gets the "2002 Subaru Outback."

- Any document is less likely to result in trouble if all interested parties actually read it. Nobody wants to read a long legal document. Keep it short.
- If the document is unavoidably long, make it easier on the eyes. Break up large blocks of print; use headings or bullet points to organize your thoughts and guide your reader to important points.
- Keep related concepts together.
- If a document is long, test for consequences and inconsistency. Read it point by point and ask yourself, "What if . . . ?" What if this does not happen? What if I were someone who wanted to get out of this contract?
- Use short sentences. Eliminate unnecessary words and phrases such as "it should be noted that . . . " or "clearly."
- Explain your position point by point to encourage a detailed response.
- Use straightforward, concise language, but avoid a "chatty," casual tone.
- Avoid legalese, such as "party of the first part," especially in writing to non-lawyers. Legal terms of art, such as "deposition," that have very specific meanings can help keep your document concise.
- Be especially careful of **boilerplate**; those "standard clauses" aren't necessarily standard and can be disastrous in some situations.

  boilerplate
  Provisions standard or common to type of document

- Use active verbs and identify actors. Write "The builder shall purchase and maintain casualty and liability insurance . . . " instead of "The property shall be insured . . . " Who is obliged to obtain insurance under the second example?
- Never use a word or phrase unless you know its meaning.
- Avoid redundancies such as "have, own, possess, and keep." If it can be said with one word, say it with one word.
- Avoid quotation; quotation may be necessary, for example, when analyzing the exact language of a statute, but most of your writing should be in your own words.
- If you are working on a long, complicated document, give yourself enough time to walk away from it after completing a first draft. Begin your final draft with a fresh mind.
- A paralegal is not a copy machine; your employer does not want you to simply retype forms and samples you find. You must analyze and evaluate what you find to apply it to specific situations.

The Tricky Concept of Tone

Tone is the level of formality and is established by word choices. The right tone is important to both the reader's understanding and the reader's impression of the writer. A writer using an unsophisticated tone or a mixed tone loses credibility. Here are some examples of appropriate tone:

Tone
Level of sophistication as set by word choices

Very casual (with friends)	*Business casual*	*High formality (scholarly article, some legal documents)*
He gave in	He agreed to	He acquiesced
She can't	She cannot	She lacks the ability to
He will want help to schedule the meeting	Our client will want assistance	Our client will expect you to facilitate . . .
You need to clear this up	You need to explain	You need to elucidate
They have to pay	They must pay	They must remunerate

Even if a document is well written, it may contain errors that will be caught only during careful proofreading. Lawyers expect documents coming out of their own offices to be perfect. Even lesser mistakes cause the writer to lose credibility. It is especially common for people who use instant messaging or other forms of online or text-based communication to "slip up" and use informal (and incorrect) shortcuts, such as "thru" rather than "through" or "threw." Here are some common spelling or grammatical errors that may be missed by spell-check:

> *It's* ("it is") instead of *its* (possessive pronoun)
> *Statue* instead of *statute*
> *Trail* instead of *trial*
> *Judgement* instead of *judgment*
> *Defendent* instead of *defendant*
> Homonyms (words that sound alike), such as *to, two, too; there, they're, their; then, than; who's, whose; principal, principle;* or *weather, whether*

Other common errors relate to numbering. If a contract goes through several drafts, a previously correct reference to "notice as described in paragraph 13 of this Agreement" may have become incorrect. Numbers may be inadvertently skipped or duplicated.

If a contract is adapted from a form previously used for another client, references to the parties and terms of that contract may remain in place unnoticed. Adaptation of a contract may also result in grammatical mistakes. For example, the earlier contract may have involved two buyers, while the current contract involves a single buyer. The result could be subject/verb or noun/pronoun inconsistency, such as "Buyer have paid earnest money" or "Buyer shall be entitled to return of their earnest money if . . ."

Example

In October 2008 the *ABA Journal* reported that a federal judge in Philadelphia characterized a lawyer's submissions as "slipshod" because of typographical and other errors and slashed the amount of attorneys' fees awarded in the case. It was the second time that attorney's fees were lowered because of sloppy written work.

Read the sample case in Exhibit 4-2, taking particular note of the testimony of the attorneys. Imagine the cost of litigating this problem, which most likely arose from a typographical/proofreading error. Obviously, one attorney has potential malpractice liability. A 2005 article in the ABA publication *Law Practice Today* states that four out of five attorneys will experience at least one malpractice claim in their careers (Dan Pinnington, *Malpractice Claims Are Very Real — and Easily Preventable: The Key Is Improving Lawyer/Client Communications*, Law Prac. Today, Apr. 2005, http://www.abanet.org/lpm/lpt/articles/mgt04052.html). Lawyers frequently rely on paralegals for proofreading. If possible and permitted by your instructor, exchange papers with a classmate before submitting your next graded assignment. Proofread each other's papers to see how different it is to proof a document written by someone else. Here are some tips to help you avoid the kind of problem that led to this case:

- Avoid proofreading your own work.
- If you must proofread your own work, allow enough time so that you can set the document aside, ideally for more than 24 hours, before you proof it.
- Proofread from paper, not from your computer screen.
- Proofread at a time of day when you feel alert.
- If possible, read aloud or have someone else read aloud to you.
- To ensure that you look at each word and don't "slide" ahead, keep a piece of paper under each line as you read or touch your finger to each word.
- Proofread in a location that is quiet and free of all distractions.
- For particularly important documents, proofread twice. Read the document once, focusing on meaning and implementation; read it a second time to look for spelling and grammatical errors.
- Some people find that reading backwards, word by word, is most effective for finding spelling and grammatical errors.
- Do a final "skim" to check headings, page numbers, and other "structural components" that may have been missed.

Exhibit 4-2
In re Marriage of Johnson, 640 N.E.2d 378
(Ill. App. Ct. 1992)

Theodore and Shawna [Johnson] were granted dissolution of marriage on Theodore's petition. The settlement agreement Paragraph H stated that Respondent shall have possession of the residence; parties shall sell upon earliest of: (1) Petitioner's remarriage, (b) emancipation of younger child, or (c) agreement. Theodore remarried and demanded sale. Shawna filed a petition, alleging that paragraph H was clerical error.

Theodore had authorized [his attorney] Greaves to negotiate a settlement; his paramount concern was welfare of the children and he wished to

EXHIBIT 4-2
(continued)

minimize disruptions. He agreed to grant Shawna possession of the house so that the children had an adequate place to live. Theodore wished that Shawna having a male guest overnight would trigger sale. During negotiations, a proposed term was that Shawna's remarriage would trigger sale of the residence.

Shawna's attorney drafted a settlement which he thought contained the verbal agreement and sent a copy to Greaves. Theodore was handed the agreement at the courthouse on the day the judgment was granted, at which time he signed it. Shawna was not present, she had already signed. Theodore first testified that the terms were what he had previously agreed to. Theodore indicated "I did not wish to remain liable for . . . indebtedness on the residence when I married and sought a fresh start." Theodore guessed he adopted this rationale when he signed because "the agreement says what it says." He stated that it was not his intent to provide a place indefinitely. Shawna testified that she became aware that Theodore's remarriage would trigger sale when she received his demand; that his remarriage triggering sale was never discussed; that the agreement was that her remarriage would trigger sale; and that there was a clerical error. She did not catch the word "petitioner" instead of "respondent." She was unfamiliar with legal jargon.

Shawna's attorney, Hensley, prepared the judgment and opined that he made an error; in negotiation and after settlement. Theodore's remarriage triggering sale was never raised. Hensley would have counseled her not to sign if such suggestion had been made. Greaves believed the document represented agreement parties had reached, that Shawna's remarriage would trigger sale. Greaves testified that remarriage of Theodore was not discussed. At a post-trial hearing, Theodore testified that the document did not reflect the verbal agreement; he did not propose house be sold upon his remarriage, and that, after the settlement conference, the parties agreed that the house be sold earliest of: (1) agreement; (2) youngest child reaching age 18 years; or (3) Shawna's remarriage.

The trial court concluded the agreement contained a scrivener's error. Neither attorney noticed the error. Theodore did notice, understood, and signed, knowing it was different than agreed. The court granted Shawna's petition. Theodore appealed, claiming that the trial court erred in considering evidence of negotiations, letters between attorneys prior to final conference, and testimony as to what was agreed since the document is unambiguous and parties' intent must be gleaned solely from it. The court held that the trial court properly considered the real agreement and intentions in finding mutual mistake of fact. Even Theodore agreed that at the conference, it was Shawna's marriage which would trigger sale, indicating that he was aware there was a mistake. Affirmed.

3. Storing and Managing

In today's "going green" environment, many offices are now going "paper-less." Even if your office maintains paper files (the organization of which is discussed in Chapter 8), you will still save the electronic file on your computer and perhaps on a local area network so that it is accessible to others in the office. It is important, therefore, that you create files in virtual space. How you organize your files will depend on office policy or your personal preferences. You may have files for closed matters, administrative matters (such as tracking an attorney's CLE hours or speaking engagements), and open client matters. Within open client files, you may have a subfile for each client, identified by client name and matter, or by client number and matter number. Within each client/matter file, you may have files labeled "correspondence," "pleadings," "research," "meetings," and "expenses." Within each of these subfiles, the documents should be named in a way that makes identification easy. For example, a complaint drafted on May 15, 2009, might be named 051509 Complaint. If it is part of the Olsen personal injury file, it would then be: Openfiles\Olsen-PI\Pleadings\051509 Complaint. The subfiles will automatically be organized alphabetically within each file.

Your firm should have a standard system for organizing files and naming documents, so that any employee can find documents filed by another, if necessary. Every employee responsible for generating documents should be instructed to name and "file" all documents according to that policy as the documents are created.

For the sake of consistency and image, the firm may also wish to create forms or **templates** for documents that are generated regularly. For example, the firm may have a form **"engagement letter"** that is sent to each new client immediately after the first meeting. That form is personalized with the client's details and then saved in the client's file. A sample engagement form letter appears in Exhibit 4-3.

templates
Patterns for creating documents

engagement letter
Letter sent to client at beginning of representation

4. Letters

Associate lawyer Pat Parker has just finished an initial interview with a possible new client, Sam Shady. The client claims to have been beaten by the police while he was harmlessly walking through his neighborhood. He wants huge damages. Pat, new to delegating work, tells paralegal Lee Adams: "I don't think the guy is telling the truth. This case is an ethical violation in the making. Plus, even if it is true, the clock is running on this one. I don't know if we would have time to do the legwork and file it before the **limitations period** runs out. Just write a simple letter telling him we cannot take his case." Simple letter? *Au contraire!*

limitations period
Time within which suit must be filed

A letter is one of the lawyer's most powerful weapons. Like a cannon, it can blow up in the face of its handler; poor aim can cause devastating collateral damage. On the other hand, a well-done letter can end a dispute, achieve your ultimate objective, or establish or heal a relationship. As an office manager, or even a well-respected paralegal, you can expect others in your office to seek your help in drafting and sending letters.

Exhibit 4-3
Sample Form Letters: Engagement Letter

(Date)

(Client address)

RE: Representation by this firm

Dear (Name):

Thank you for selecting our firm to represent you. As we discussed at our meeting on (date), I have agreed to represent you in connection with (type of matter). This letter is to confirm our agreement with respect to payment of fees. You will be billed at a rate of $(fee rate) per hour for my work, $(travel rate) per hour for my travel time; and $(paralegal fee rate) per hour for work done by my paralegal, plus expenses, such as filing fees, copying costs, postage, and related expenses. As we discussed, this firm bills in ten-minute intervals. You will generally be billed monthly, depending upon the amount of work that was done on your file during the billing period. You have deposited $(retainer) for fees and costs, which will be held in a Lawyers' Trust Account. After my office mails you the monthly statement, we will apply the funds to the fees and expenses. You are responsible for paying fees and expenses in excess of funds in the account. Should we exceed the retainer, we may require deposit of additional funds into the trust account. Payment must be made within 30 days. We reserve the right to withdraw if bills are not paid.

At this point, it is difficult to estimate the amount of time and expense required to adequately represent you. As we discussed, I estimate the fee will be approximately $(estimate). I will contact you before undertaking any work that will substantially increase the cost. Please remember this is an estimate and may be subject to change.

I may send you documents and other information. Please retain these copies and bring your copy of the file to meetings so that we both have all necessary information in front of us. When I complete work on your case, I will close my file and return original documents to you. I will then store the file for approximately (years) years. I will then destroy the file unless you instruct me in writing to keep your file longer.

**EXHIBIT 4-3
(continued)**

I have included a copy of this letter for your review, signature, and return to me in the postage-paid envelope. If any of the information in this letter is not consistent with your understanding of our agreement, please contact me before signing the letter. We are happy to represent you in this matter. If you have any questions, please contact me at your convenience.

Very truly yours,

_____
(Lawyer Name)

LN/smn
Enc.: copy, firm envelope

I have read this letter, understand, and consent to it. (Lawyer Name) has proposed a course of conduct and has explained all material risks of and reasonable available alternatives to the proposed course of conduct.

_____
(Client name) (Date)

a. Getting Started

Before you write a letter, consider these issues:

- Do you really want to commit it to writing? You could be creating evidence. Consider whether you are confident of your knowledge of relevant facts (is it firsthand knowledge or hearsay?), whether a reader might be angered by the letter, and whether any of the topics might be covered by privilege. Considering privilege, make sure that you have the right address for sending confidential communications to the client. Clients may have employees, children, and spouses who are not privy to their legal situations.
- Who is the best person to sign this communication? If it includes legal advice or a legal opinion, it must be signed by or attributed to a lawyer.
- What is the best way to send this letter? Does the need for speed or the possible psychological impact justify using a messenger or a private delivery service? Is the method of sending dictated by court rules?
- Never write in a state of anger. Do not use threats, particularly threats of criminal prosecution.

ex parte communication
Contact without presence of
some interested parties

- Who should receive copies? Many lawyers send clients a copy of every letter, as part of the ethical duty to keep clients informed (see, for example, ABA Model Rule 1.4(3)). Remember, in litigation, there is generally a rule prohibiting **ex parte communication**; if the judge gets a copy, everybody gets a copy. Parties receiving copies should be listed after the "cc:" line, below the signature.

b. Format

The most common format for business letters is block style, with the text of the entire letter justified to the left. Margins are typically set at one inch on all sides (the default setting in most word processing programs). Text is single spaced, except for double spaces between paragraphs. The parts of a letter include the following:

- Identification of your firm, its address, phone number, and website URL, at the top of printed letterhead paper. If the letter requires additional pages, matching sheets without the firm name are used. If you have a direct phone line or e-mail address, you may put it at the top or under your signature.
- Date; use month, day, year format.
  - May 3, 2009 or 3 May 2009.
- Address of the person to whom the letter is directed. Many firms include the method of delivery above the recipient's name.
  - "Via First Class Mail/Copy Via Fax w/o Enclosures"
  - "Via Hand Delivery."
- Reference line.
  - Reference: Miller v. Miller, your file 09-D76
- Salutation: title and surname, followed by a colon (comma are used for personal letters only).
  - Dear Sir or Madam: (if you don't know to whom you are writing)
  - Dear Dr., Mr., Mrs., or Ms. Smith: (if you know to whom you are writing and it is a formal relationship) (*very important*: use Ms. for women unless asked to use Mrs.)
  - Dear Frank: (only if the person is a close business contact or friend)
- Body text.
  - Identify yourself if the recipient does not know you and indicate any relationship or connection. "I am the office manager and paralegal for the Jones Firm."
  - Use a professional tone.
  - Identify the reason for the letter close to the beginning.
  - Keep the letter short, simple, and well organized.
- End the letter by stating what the reader should do and what you will do to follow up.
- Do not mail documents without a cover letter listing the documents. A letter accompanied by other documents should have an enclosure line beneath the signature block.

- The signature block should include a closing and the name and title of the sender. If the person who prepared the letter is other than the person who signed the letter, it is traditional to indicate the initials of the signer followed by the initials of the person who prepared the letter.

Sincerely,

Lee Adams
Paralegal

LA/jmb

Enc.: Offer to Purchase dated May 15, 2009
cc: Cary Client

But Can He Type?

Why should he? Until the late 1980s, most lawyers had secretaries at a 1:1 ratio. Lawyers dictated documents; secretaries typed those documents. Many paralegals also had secretarial help. As computers started appearing on desks, lawyers started entering their own documents and found it faster and more efficient. The ratio at many law firms is now down to 4:1. Secretaries are more like personal assistants than typists. Although some lawyers and paralegals still like to dictate long documents, new technology will soon eliminate the need for a typist even in those situations. Voice recognition software allows the user to dictate a document into a headphone or recorder; it is processed into a document that can be edited and formatted like any other document. With these programs, the user can speak at normal speed and in a normal tone and achieve 99 percent accuracy in speech-to-text conversion. Some companies have special programs for law offices. For example, Dragon has a "legal solutions" package (http://www.1st-dragon.com/drnaleso.html). Go online and determine whether these programs can be used to "speak" the response to a lengthy e-mail.

Assignment 4-3
Letters

1. Does your state have an ethical rule concerning use of threats of criminal or administrative prosecution to gain advantage in a civil case? Identify a rule or rules that address the issue.
2. Write the letter that associate lawyer Pat Parker assigned to her paralegal Lee Adams (described above at the beginning of the section). Make up addresses and your firm's name.

Management Portfolio

3. Read the letter in Exhibit 4-3. Assume that the letter was sent to Chris Client, who retained the firm to handle his divorce and the disputed custody of his two children. Chris made a $5,000 deposit, but the deposit ran out two months ago. More than 30 days have gone by since Chris received a bill showing an unpaid amount of $600; he has not responded. Attorney Ed Rodan has continued to work on the case, and another $1,200 is now due for fees and expenses. Ed would like to have the arrearages paid immediately and have the deposit brought back to the $5,000 level, as this is a difficult case. The firm does not have a form letter for such situations. Write a letter to Chris that can be adapted for future use.

4. The firm of Rodan & Stosh is growing quickly! Two new paralegals and one new secretary will join the firm in two weeks to support the appellate practice, and you won't have time to answer all of their questions individually. Create a style manual to address the following:

- Format for letters, including how paralegals should sign letters.
- Format for an interoffice memo. Assume that your firm maintains a file containing hard copies of all legal research memoranda, organized by topic (for example, Family law — change of custody), so the heading of the memo should include a spot for the topic.
- Information for preparation of appellate briefs. Because this information is readily available online, your style manual need only include the URLs for the federal and state appellate courts with jurisdiction over your area and reminders about page limit and type-font size requirements. Start your research at http://www.uscourts.gov/courtlinks and http://www.ncsconline.org (National Center for State Courts).

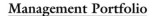

Exhibit 4-4
Fee Agreement

Sometimes a checklist is the best way to communicate complicated matters.

FEE AGREEMENT
ATTORNEY'S FEES

The attorney's fee in this matter will be set as follows:

( ) Fixed Fee of $_____
( ) Hourly Rate at $____ per hour plus ____% of amount* ( ) saved ( ) recovered

**EXHIBIT 4-4
(continued)**

( ) Estimated Fee in the range of: $_____ to $_____

( ) Contingent Fee of _____ ( ) saved ( ) recovered ( ) other *Contingent contract and statement of client's rights signed as required

( ) Fee determined on all relevant factors

( ) Minimum retainer of $_____

( ) Number of hours of attorney time covered by retainer is: _____

( ) Other: _____

This office will bill you:

( ) Monthly on _____ of each month

( ) Upon completion

( ) Other arrangement: _____

ALL BILLS ARE PAYABLE UPON RECEIPT. IF YOU DO NOT PAY WITHIN 30 DAYS OF RECEIPT, YOUR ACCOUNT WILL BEGIN TO ACCRUE INTEREST CHARGES.

RETAINERS

Retainer of $ _____ is to be applied

( ) toward fee and out-of-pocket expenses

( ) toward fee

( ) toward out-of-pocket expenses

( ) Retainer is refundable

( ) Retainer is nonrefundable

COSTS AND EXPENSES

Typical out-of-pocket expenses (NOTE: these are *not* attorney's fees) for this matter may include:

( ) Costs such as court costs, filing fees, process server fees, deposition costs, sheriff or clerk of court fees, investigator's fees, etc.

( ) Abstracting charges or title insurance premiums, clerk's recording fees

( ) Photocopying, long-distance telephone, postage, and travel costs

( ) Other: _____

( ) Estimate for costs and expenses (not including attorney's fees):( ) Expected to range between $_____ and $_____.

EXHIBIT 4-4
(continued)

( )   Not expected to exceed $_____.

( )   No expenses expected

NOTE: This is an estimate for your convenience; it is not a guarantee.

If the above properly sets forth our agreement, please sign below and keep one copy. Return the original together with your check in the amount of $ _____.

We will draw $ _____ toward attorney's fees and apply $ _____ toward out-of-pocket expenses as outlined above. If we do not receive the signed original of this agreement (you retain the copy) and your check within _____ days, we shall assume that you have obtained other counsel and shall mark our file "CLOSED" and do nothing further. Thank you.

Dated: _____   By: _____
                                                         Attorney at Law

The above is understood and agreed to by me.

Dated: _____   By: _____
                                                         Client

Reprinted with permission from J.R. Phelps, from the Florida Bar Association, Law Office Management Assistance Service.

Out There—Paralegal Profile
A "Word" with People Who Love Words

If anyone knows the importance of the written word, it is Barbara Josh, whose background includes a BS in journalism, stints as editor-in-chief of a student newspaper and copy editor for a university magazine, and a paralegal certificate from an ABA-approved program. Barb works for the Illinois Appellate Court, where she reads staff research attorneys' dispositions before they are submitted to a three-judge panel. Barb's position required a four-year college degree. While she thinks that her degree in journalism was a help, she believes her paralegal certificate has been much more valuable.

"I check for accuracy, relevance, style, and form. The errors encountered most involve caption information and/or format, citation format, inaccurate pin cites, and incorrect opinion filing dates. Since the staff research attorneys primarily use Westlaw in their research, I check all citations using the 'books' (reporters, statutes, treatises, etc.) in the court's library. If necessary, I use an outside law library. I find and report errors in case citations, spelling, and even party names. It is not unusual to find published cases containing errors in citation to precedent. In a nutshell, it is wise to thoroughly check legal sources. I also check quoted material from cited cases and transcripts. If a citation involves an ordinance, I call the city/village/county clerk to verify the 'effective' date."

"Sometimes transcripts yield odd information that sets off the 'hinky meter' and just registers a 'huh!' What would be best described as a *My Cousin Vinny* moment came when the transcript revealed that a Buick Toronado was parked at the crime scene. Most likely it was either a Buick Riviera or an Oldsmobile Toronado, but not a Buick Toronado. It's hard to believe no one caught that. Someone, somewhere, wasn't very observant. It made me wonder what else could be inaccurate. However, in such cases, all that can be done is a footnote explaining the discrepancy."

Barb's coworker, Greg Duncan (profiled in Chapter 2), adds: "In the law office, few paralegal tasks are more important than editing and proofreading legal documents. Unfortunately, using electronic spell-checkers to review documents is a mixed blessing. On the one hand, a spell-checker can quickly identify most misspelled words. On the other, without human intervention, serious errors can escape the scan of even the best spell-checker. One type of error is the merely annoying faux pas, such as using the word 'utilize' when the word 'use' would be more appropriate. An amusing situation is usually created when an intended word is misspelled in such a way that it is also a correctly spelled word. For example, a dissertation on 'pubic law' may sound intriguing; however, the reality of mind-numbing 'public law' may hold less appeal. And, last but not least, a serious punctuation error will go unnoticed by a spell-checker. For instance, consider the innocent query, 'Can we eat, Mommy?' That simple question sounds much more ominous when the comma is removed. In summary, a spell-checker is a powerful tool, but it is only one tool in the proofreader's toolbox. Please don't forget to use your primary proofreading tool—human oversight."

Chapter Review

Discussion Questions

1. Matt Peters has been a business client of the firm for many years. Last month he was in a horrible car accident. Recently released from the hospital, he is visiting the firm tomorrow to talk about a suit against the other driver. Your supervising attorney has an emergency and cannot be in the office. Describe how you would prepare to interview Matt.

2. The driver of Matt's car, his son Mark, was not injured. There is no allegation that Mark was at fault. Mark works in London and was visiting his family at the time of the accident. He stayed in town as long as he could while his father recovered, but is now unable to return for at least several months. Your boss has asked you to talk to Mark about the facts of the case. Describe how you would prepare to make the call.

3. The Chris Client divorce has finally settled! The settlement agreement is long and complicated. It was created by using a settlement from a similar case as a model. The parties are still quite hostile, so it is important that the document not contain any mistakes. You are assigning proofreading to a new paralegal. What instructions would you give?

4. Do you think the purchase of voice recognition software is a good investment for a law firm? Why?

5. Describe the differences between privilege, confidentiality, and the work product doctrine.

6. Describe the ethical concerns that govern communications with people outside your firm, in the context of working as a paralegal.

7. You may be fairly confident of your own communications skills, but as a law office manager you may supervise people whose skills are less developed (and who have not read this book). Identify topics that would be worthy of a page in a procedures manual.

ACROSS

1. pattern for creating legal documents
4. letter sent before suit is filed to collect debt
5. _____ terms, example: the building at 123 Maple Street, Elmhurst, NY (the "Office Building")
6. _____ brief, adversarial document directed to reviewing court
8. these give background, usually in a contract
10. incorporation by _____ makes an outside document part of this document
15. ex-_____, communication away from other parties
17. voice _____ software, types as you speak
18. the level at which something is written as determined by word choices
19. does not advocate a particular result
20. trial _____, goes to the judge

DOWN

2. rule that keeps certain information confidential and prevents use as evidence
3. argues a position
7. decision to send letter by special messenger has financial implications for firm and _____ implications for recipient
9. type of letter sent to new client
11. period within which lawsuit must be filed
12. standard clauses
13. an objective memo, for use within firm
14. line, identifies topic of letter
16. letter giving legal advice

Terms and Definitions

adversarial: Argues a position
appellate brief: Formal document presenting arguments to reviewing court
boilerplate: Provisions standard or common to type of document
defined terms: Shorthand references to important subjects in document
demand letter: Typically sent before suit on debt; requests payment
engagement letter: Letter sent to client at beginning of representation
ex parte communication: Contact without presence of some interested parties
incorporation by reference: Makes an outside document part of the document at hand
interoffice memo: Intended for use within firm; typically objective and often covered by privilege
limitations period: Time within which suit must be filed
objective: Does not argue a position; typically analyzes a situation and predicts result
opinion letter: Letter giving legal advice or predicting outcome
privilege: Rule that keeps information confidential and presents its use as evidence
recitals: State the background; typically in a contract
templates: Patterns for creating documents
tone: Level of sophistication as set by word choices
trial memo: Directed to trial court; typically argues a position
work product doctrine: Part of attorney-client privilege; protects certain documents from discovery

Law Offi[ce]

Conflicts a[nd]

As a Manager

You will be responsible for implementing and training others on systems to help the firm meet its ethical obligations. You may be responsible, in total or in part, for developing these systems as well.

Objectives

After completing this chapter, you will be able to

- Describe four types of conflict of interests and how they can arise.
- Describe how a firm decides whether to decline representation or employ screening in a conflict of interest situation.
- Describe how to screen an employee with a conflict.
- Describe the steps in checking for conflicts and entering new information into the firm's conflict system.
- Discuss software packages that check for conflicts and the features of those packages.
- Create a system for checking for conflicts if no dedicated software is available.
- Describe the essential features of an effective docket control system and the purpose of a master calendar.
- Describe the purpose of a tickler system.
- Set up a manual and an automated calendar system.
- Describe the advantages of docket control software.
- Describe the features available in practice management software and the considerations and comparisons relevant to purchasing it.

111

A. Why Are Tracking Systems Necessary?

Every business can benefit from systems. A system is a way of performing a set of tasks. Systems increase efficiency, provide for quality control, and make continuity possible when a worker is out. But, in the business world, law offices are unique. Unlike most other businesses, law firms are governed by regulatory agencies with specific rules (as you have already discovered), and failure to comply can be ruinous. In addition, law is a profession, so those who practice are held to a special duty of care and can be held liable for malpractice if they fail to meet that duty. The days when a lawyer could rely on her own memory and "good sense" (or the memory and good sense of an assistant) to avoid problems are long gone. To avoid ethical violations and malpractice liability, firms establish systems to comply with the ethical rules and prevent common errors. In fact, companies that provide lawyers with malpractice insurance insist that the lawyers they insure have systems (see Exhibit 5-1). The companies often dictate specifically what kind of systems and may even conduct audits to ensure that the systems are in place and up to date.

This chapter discusses two of the most common errors and systems for avoiding those errors: conflicts of interest and missed dates. (Chapters 6 and 8 discuss two other types of systems, those to avoid accounting problems and file management problems.) A well-run firm may have many systems, dealing with everything from assigning work to closing the office for the day. Systems dealing with conflicts, calendar, client files, and accounting are considered the four essential systems for any office, and, as you will learn, it is increasingly common for a single software package to integrate those four functions and more.

Exhibit 5-1
Malpractice Questions

Here are some questions typically found on an application for malpractice insurance. Notice how many relate to systems or communications.

Number of Claims/Suits/Incidents Filed Against Firm in the Past 5 Years:

* Number pending:
* Number of suits for fees in the last 2 years:
* Number of practicing attorneys:
* Number of attorneys working less than 1000 hours/year:
* Is the firm aware of any circumstance(s) or act(s) which may give rise to a claim?
* Has any attorney with the firm ever been disciplined or denied the right to practice?
* Do you maintain a Docket Control System with at least two independent data controls?
* Is a Conflict of Interest System maintained?
* Are engagement and non-engagement letters used on a regular basis?
* Have you had continuous coverage for the past 5 years?
* Does the firm share office space with another law firm?

For More Information

The ABA identifies failure to discover conflicts of interest and missed deadlines as among the top ten malpractice traps. It warns: "Calendaring errors remain a leading cause of malpractice claims" and "[e]ach firm must establish stringent procedures for identifying and resolving situations in which . . . unexpected conflicts [of interest or matter] may arise." What are the other traps? See for yourself at American Bar Association, The Top Ten Malpractice Traps and How to Avoid Them, http://www.abanet.org/legalservices/lpl/downloads/ten.pdf.

Perhaps the most important task in a first interview with a potential new client is to gather the information needed to check for conflicts of interest and to determine and enter important dates. The lawyer must evaluate both the potential for conflicts of interest and the firm's ability to do quality work within the time available before deciding whether to accept a case and before allowing the potential client to share confidential information. Most malpractice and ethical problems arise from neglect of such administrative matters rather than from lack of competence in substantive law.

B. What Is a Conflict of Interest?

A conflict of interest is any relationship that could compromise a lawyer's duty of confidentiality with respect to past or current clients or the lawyer's ability to be an advocate for a client. Ethical rules generally recognize four types of conflict of interests:

Concurrent conflict
Arises from representing opposing parties on same matter

Imputed conflict
Conflict of interest of one legal professional is contagious to others in firm

- **Concurrent conflict**—representing multiple clients in the same matter or acting against the interests of a current client, even if the matters are unrelated (see Model Rule 1.7).
- Conflict with past client—representing a party with interests materially adverse to those of a former client in the same or a substantially related matter (see Model Rule 1.9). The passage of time alone does not cure the conflict.
- **Imputed conflict**—conflicts of interest are contagious; if one member of the firm has a conflict, all have a conflict. For example, Lyn and Ben are partners in a firm; if Lyn represents the husband and Ben represents the wife in a divorce, each has an imputed conflict. If Ben accepts a case against Acme Corp. and Lyn previously worked for a firm that represented Acme, both have a conflict with a past client (see Model Rule 1.10).
- Personal conflict—this can be a direct conflict or a potential conflict. For example, a direct conflict exists if a potential client wants to sue the company that employs Ben's wife or in which Ben owns stock. A potential conflict exists if Lyn's uncle wants to employ the firm to write his will—depending on whether Lyn has any possibility of inheritance (see Model Rule 1.7).

Positional conflicts
Arises from representing parties in competition in the market or taking different positions in different matter

Although not mentioned in the ethical rules, some firms have to look for **positional conflicts** that might arise from taking different positions in different matters or representing two companies or parties that are in competition, even if the companies are not and have not been involved in litigation involving each other. For example, McDonald's might not want its firm representing Burger King.

1. Dealing with Conflicts

Potential conflicts of interest must be identified before the lawyer accepts a new client. When a conflict is not discovered and opposing parties resort to bringing a motion to disqualify, the results can be disastrous. The court must consider public perception of the legal profession, the right to have counsel of one's choosing, and the lawyer's need to make a living.

Example

Attorneys Able and Baker recently formed a new partnership. Each had previously been a solo practitioner. Able and Baker haven't taken the time yet to combine their individual conflicts systems. When each was in practice alone, Able used file cards, and Baker simply maintained a list on his computer.

On March 5, Able took on a new client, Karen Krantz, who wants to sue Sports Med, PC, for malpractice. Krantz claims that the doctors at Sports Med failed to diagnose her skin cancer during a sports physical, which allowed the disease to advance. As a result, her chances of long-term survival are reduced, and she has required treatment that has cost her a season of competition as an elite gymnast. Because she lost the season, Karen lost her scholarship to a major university and an opportunity to try out for the Olympic team.

After meeting with Krantz for the first time, Able sent Baker an e-mail about the new client's case, asking whether Baker recognized any possible conflict. He did not. What Baker did not realize, however, is that the corporation is owned by Ellen Swanson, M.D., who was formerly known as Ellen Meinke. The matter progresses, and about a year later, when Baker attends a case management conference for Able, who is on vacation, Ellen recognizes Baker. He was a young associate for the firm that represented her 15 years ago when she was sued for a similar incident. Ellen "goes ballistic," thinking that Krantz intentionally sought out a lawyer who knew her "weakness" and that her own lawyer turned on her. Smith, who is representing Ellen in the current case, moves to have the Able & Baker firm disqualified from the case. Consider:

- How will Ellen view the legal system if her former lawyer is not disqualified?
- Is it fair to Karen to have to change lawyers at this point? What about any fees she has already paid or owes to Able & Baker?
- This is a big case. If Able & Baker have to give up the fees they are owed and/or refund fees that have been paid, might it be a financial disaster for the new firm?

Many firms obtain basic information over the phone when a potential client schedules a first appointment, in order to do a preliminary check for conflicts using a system described below. Every consultation should have a file and a memo, *even if the firm is not retained*. If a possible conflict is discovered, the firm must decide what action to take. In some cases, the firm will decide that the conflict is substantial and will disqualify or **recuse** itself from the case.

recuse
To remove self or firm from case

In cases involving a concurrent conflict or a conflict with a past client, the lawyer may, under conditions described in the ethical rules, obtain **informed consent** from the clients or former client. It is, therefore, possible for a firm to represent both parties in a divorce, for example.

informed consent
Consent (to conflict of interest) based on full disclosure of potential problems

If the conflict is imputed or personal, the firm may employ **screening**, sometimes called "erecting a **Chinese Wall**." Screening involves isolating the person with the conflict from the case; it should be done in writing, and all employees should be instructed not to discuss the case with or near the screened party. Files should be flagged to ensure that the screened employee does not have access; computer access should be denied. The client should be informed of and consent to the firm's efforts. If the conflict is created by an attorney, the screened lawyer may not be allowed to share in the fee, depending on the state.

screening
Process of formally isolating a person from a case because of conflict of interest

Chinese Wall
Another term for screening

Screening is not appropriate in all cases and is not viewed favorably by all courts. Several factors are relevant to whether screening is appropriate, especially the level of the conflict. If the conflict is created by a lawyer who is opposing a client for whom she previously did significant work on a related matter, as in the

Able & Baker example, screening is likely inappropriate. On the other hand, if the conflict is created by a paralegal who had only limited involvement with the opposing party's case or if the matters are unrelated, screening may be appropriate.

Example

Can a paralegal create a conflict for his firm? Yes; in addition to any conflicts created by their personal lives, paralegals change jobs and sometimes work as independent contractors. Perhaps the most famous case is In re Complex Asbestos Litigation, 232 Cal. App. 3d 572 (1991), in which failing to deal with the conflict created by a paralegal changing jobs caused a firm to be disqualified from representing several plaintiffs in the enormously expensive asbestos litigation.

If you suspect that you may have a conflict, you must bring it to the attention of your supervisor immediately. Many firms use a form like the example in Exhibit 5-2 to add the conflict information of new employees to their systems immediately. For reasons described later, however, these systems are not perfect. Everyone who works in a law firm must be vigilant.

2. Identifying Conflicts

The starting point in avoiding or dealing with conflicts is to identify them. Every law firm must have a database or list of potential conflicts. The information on that list concerns people and organizations that work at the firm or interact with the firm.

3. Employee Conflicts

Every firm should include in its conflicts system information about its partners' and employees' past employers and past representations, personal relationships with other legal professionals, and involvement with businesses and organizations. Would even more information be potentially helpful? Yes; imagine, for example, that Pat Paralegal is married to Lou, assistant superintendent of School District 301. Pat's firm recently accepted a new matter: several families want to sue District 301 for failure to provide adequate services to their disabled children. It would likely be a conflict for Pat to work on the case, but would the firm's list disclose the problem?

Exhibit 5-2
Form for Identifying Employee Conflicts

Only to be given to an attorney once the decision has been made to hire!

Preemployment Conflict of Interest Form

To avoid potential conflicts of interest within our practice, we ask that you carefully complete this form to the best of your ability. Attach additional pages if necessary.

An internal conflict check will be generated from your information to determine if your affiliation conflicts with clients in our practice. If you have any questions about this form or any of the information requested, please let us know.

DO NOT Disclose Any Confidential Client Information in Completing This Form.

1. Full name (including maiden name or other legal names you may have used):

_____

2. Position sought with the firm: _____

3. Identify all employers (including law firms, private or governmental legal departments, and courts), positions (including attorney, judicial extern or intern, summer law clerk, legal assistant, paralegal or legal secretary), and dates employed for every position you have held in a capacity of providing legal services. (Attach a copy of your resume or additional sheets of paper.)

4. If in the interest of the client, identify the clients you have served in the last five years, describing generally the nature of the work, but without disclosing any confidential information: _____

_____

5. If a partner or Of Counsel, list the major clients of your former firm(s):

_____

_____

6. Are you aware of any clients of your former firm(s) who have had dealing with or litigation involving this firm? If so, identify them:_____

_____

**EXHIBIT 5-2
(continued)**

7. If you were a judicial clerk in the last five years, identify the matters in which you were personally and substantially involved in which this firm acted as counsel for one of the parties: _____

_____

8. Identify each directorship, general partnership, and office you hold with any commercial or nonprofit entity, including the name of the entity, its business, whether it is publicly held, the directors and officers, errors and omissions insurance it carries, and whether you have an investment interest in the entity:

_____

_____

9. Identity any close relatives (i.e., spouse, parent, child, or sibling) or close associates who either practice law or are employed by a law firm or legal department and indicate whether you live with any of these relatives or close associates:

_____

_____

10. Are you or any of your relatives (or their employers) involved in litigation where this firm is representing another party? If so, describe

_____

_____

Reprinted with permission from Florida Bar Association.

4. Information from Clients and Potential Clients

Even if the firm prescreens potential new clients, additional information should be gathered at the first meeting for a check against information already in the conflicts system and for addition to that system. Examine Exhibit 5-3, which shows information that should be obtained based on the type of matter involved. In addition, many lawyers consider the following:

- *Who is the client?* This question has two parts. It can refer to the possibility that the person appearing at the firm is an imposter. Some lawyers require that new clients produce identification. It can also refer to the possibility that one person is paying the bill and another needs representation. Suppose that Dad, a longtime client, brings his daughter to the firm for representation in a divorce with contested custody. Dad plans to pay the bill and makes several comments indicating that his goal is to have his daughter get full custody of her children. Daughter later confides that she believes that her husband would take better care of the boys and that she would rather not fight for custody.

- *Fear of commitment.* Does the potential client claim to be "just exploring her options"? Is she lawyer-shopping? Some people will visit several law offices to create conflicts so that their opponents cannot retain those firms. Some "phantom clients" attempt to obtain legal assistance without even visiting the law office, by asking questions at social events or in other settings. Has the potential client been represented by other lawyers in the past? Any of these situations can raise a red flag.

- *Two for the price of one.* Sometimes potential clients with potentially adverse interests will insist that there is no conflict. A divorcing couple may insist that they are going to remain friends and agree on everything; a buyer and seller may claim that they "just want someone to write the agreement." In an attempt to avoid dual representation problems, some attorneys will agree to represent one of the parties and document that the other has been advised to seek independent counsel. The non-client elects to proceed without representation. Unfortunately, the conversation with the unrepresented party can establish an unintended attorney-client relationship and undo the precautions taken.

- *Wanting more than legal assistance.* Lawyers should be wary of getting involved with clients' businesses and finances beyond offering legal services, for example, by accepting stock in the client's company as payment for legal services.

After the necessary information has been obtained, names must be checked against data already in the system. The new information must be added to the system, even if the attorney decides to decline representation. In addition, the information should be circulated within the firm, by memo or e-mail, to identify potential conflicts that may not show up in the system. Many firms employ a conflicts memo, such as shown in Exhibit 5-4, to document that the check was actually run. The individual responsible for assigning file numbers will not assign a number until the conflicts check has been run. The information may have to be updated as the matter progresses. For example, a cross-claim might name an additional opposing party, an opposing party may retain a new lawyer, or a new expert witness may be obtained.

5. Types of Systems

Before the introduction of computers, many law firms had conflicts systems that consisted of cards, each containing the name of a person or organization

Exhibit 5-3
Collecting Names for the Conflicts List

Matter Type	Names: birth names, former names, "aka's," related entities
BANKRUPTCY	
Client & Spouse	
Creditors	
BUSINESS & PROPERTY	
Client & Spouse	
Owner & Spouse	
Partners/Shareholders/ Members	
Directors/Officers	
Affiliated Businesses	
Key Employees	
If Sale: Buyer/Seller	
Opposing Parties	
Opposing Counsel	
CIVIL LITIGATION & WORKERS' COMPENSATION	
Plaintiffs & Spouses	
Defendants & Spouses	
Insurer/Insured	
Guardians	
Witnesses	
Opposing Counsel	
CRIMINAL	
Client	

EXHIBIT 5-3
(continued)

Victim	
Witnesses	
DIVORCE	
Husband	
Wife	
Children	
Opposing Counsel	
ESTATES	
Client & Spouse	
Decedent & Spouse	
Executor/Administrator	
Heirs/Beneficiaries	
Guardians	
Opposing Counsel	
DECLINED REPRESENTATION	
Party	
Opponent	

---

with a relationship to the firm, organized in alphabetical order. Despite the drudgery of adding new information and the potential for mistakes, some firms continue to use paper-based systems. Many firms use the database program that came with the firm's computers to check conflicts. Still other firms use dedicated software to check conflicts. Although there are programs used exclusively for conflicts checks, the function is usually integrated into case management software that serves a variety of functions. Whatever system is set up, it should be easy to use and readily accessible.

Exhibit 5-4
Request for Conflicts Check

In some firms, particular employees handle conflicts checks and entry of new information into the system at the request of the attorney dealing with the potential new client.

REQUEST FOR CONFLICT SEARCH AND SYSTEM ENTRY

FILE NUMBER: _____ DATE: _____

CLIENT NAME: _____

ATTORNEY: _____

Names to be checked/added

NAME   RELATIONSHIP

_____

_____

_____

_____

_____

_____

                                               [ ]   NEW MATTER (to open new file)

                                               [ ]   ADDITIONAL INFORMATION (to update file)

                                               [ ]   SEARCH ONLY (do not add any information)

[ ] NO CONFLICT FOUND

[ ] NAMES FOUND AS FOLLOWS:

Searched by: _____ Search Date: _____

Assignment 5-1
Avoiding Conflicts of Interest

---

1. A simple conflicts system: Create the table below in your word processing program, with a row for every student in the class. Each student should provide information for one row, using his or her own name as "attorney" and using the first names only of his or her mother and father as "client & spouse." Each student should enter the first names of his or her siblings, children, or two close friends as opposing parties. For the opposing firm column, enter the first names of all of the paralegal instructors you have had since starting the paralegal program. In the "witnesses/guardians" column, enter your two favorite first names. The "matter #" and "updated" columns can be left blank. Now, assume that potential new clients have appointments. Their names are Jason, Jennifer, Michael, Alex, and Rachel. Use the Search or Find and Replace function to find potential conflicts with each name.

Att'y	Matter #	Client & Spouse Name(s)	Opposing Parties	Opposing Firm & Attorney Names	Witnesses Guardians	Updated
Laurel		Edward, Gail	Peter, Elise	Maureen, James	Lora	

Management Portfolio

2. Your firm, Rodan & Stosh, has decided to purchase case management software that will handle conflicts of interest and time and billing. The package must be compatible with the Blackberry PDAs issued by the firm. Because the firm handles corporate clients, it would be ideal if the program could trace the relationships between companies (for example, parent/subsidiary), perhaps using DUNS numbers.[1] Conduct research online to determine which packages might meet your firm's needs and write a memo to Leona Stosh.
3. Discuss why it is necessary to circulate a memo or an e-mail to notify everyone at the firm of new clients, even after a conflicts check has been run. What are the inherent imperfections of even a well-maintained system?
4. Examine your state's ethical rules and identify all of the rules that pertain to conflicts of interest.

---

[1]A DUNS (Data Universal Numbering System) number is assigned by Dunn & Bradstreet to each business in the D & B database and is widely used by governments and private industry. With a DUNS number, separate corporate entities, which have no official relationship, can be identified as one unit by having one DUNS number for affiliated companies.

5. After several years as a successful paralegal with a major law firm, you decide to open a freelance business. You will advertise your services as a contract paralegal in the county bar association newsletter. What system can you use to avoid conflicts of interest?

C. Docketing

Have you ever had the nightmare that it's finals week and you have just realized that there's a class you've never attended or prepared for? Lawyers have a similar nightmare — missing a statute of limitations deadline. Yet, despite being the cause of a great number of problems for lawyers, missed deadlines are the easiest to prevent. The law firm must have a system with the following characteristics:

- All dates of importance to the firm should be kept on a *single master calendar*. The master calendar should contain information on matters that would have to be covered if an individual attorney became unable to attend to her files: statute of limitations dates, court hearings, and filing dates. Individual lawyers and paralegals should keep *personal calendars* that include relevant dates from the master calendar plus less urgent matters, such as appointments and meetings. Each calendar should contain *all* relevant dates. A firm that lets individual lawyers keep separate calendars without coordinating them to the master calendar or a lawyer who keeps a home calendar, an office calendar, and sticky notes all over are invitations to disaster.
- Each personal calendar and the master calendar should have a *backup*. Computers can crash or be stolen, datebooks fall out of briefcases. Many malpractice insurance carriers insist that lawyers they insure have duplicate systems. The backup can be as simple as regularly printing hard copy of an electronic calendar or synchronizing a mobile device such as a PDA to the firm's office system. The backup should not be stored at the same location as the main system. If you back up to disks or to hard copy, store it offsite in case of a fire or other disaster at your office location.
- Every attorney's personal calendar should be duplicated in the personal calendar of the attorney's secretary or paralegal; the secretary or paralegal should have a system for updating the duplicate calendar regularly. Many attorneys hold regular brief "calendar meetings" with their teams.
- Each calendar of court dates, filing dates, meetings, and appointments should be supplemented by or should incorporate **ticklers**, which are advance reminders of future deadlines. Tickler dates must take into account the time required to complete a task, time for mailing or service, and other obligations of the person assigned to the task. For example, if an appellate brief is due on May 15, an attorney might want a reminder every week, depending on her work habits. Ticklers should include follow-up dates to determine whether opposing parties (and others outside the firm) have responded to requests and filings.

ticklers
Reminders

- The master calendar should be *accessible* to everyone in the firm, and each personal calendar should be accessible to at least one other person. Lawyers do, in fact, sometimes have accidents or sudden illnesses, and their employees must be able to arrange coverage for urgent matters.
- One person (and a backup) should have responsibility for making sure that important dates are coordinated with the reminders on the tickler system (if the firm does not have software that automatically handles this function) and *checking the calendar daily* to ensure that all important matters are covered. Larger firms historically often had a docket coordinator or a docket department and forms for requesting entry of a date on the master calendar. If the firm has a computer network, a separate department and request forms are not necessary. Important dates can be entered at the desktop of the attorney handling the matter or that attorney's assistant.
- As noted in Chapter 3, dates from incoming mail should *be entered as soon as they are known*. So, for example, if the mail includes a notice of motion, the date of the motion hearing should be immediately entered on the calendar, and the person making the entry should mark the document to indicate that it has been docketed.

1. Advantages of Automated Docketing

Historically, firms used paper-based systems. A typical firm might have a book or other paper master calendar, with a column for each attorney. That book or calendar sheet would be copied regularly, depending on how often information changed, so that each person in the firm would have a copy. The system would be supplemented and backed up by a tickler system that often consisted of a small box, with a divider for each month, and cards for each day within the month, containing important dates and reminders. While entering information on the date cards, the user would have to consult a calendar to ensure that important tasks were not "tickled" on dates that fall on weekends or holidays. Because one of the purposes of the master calendar is to enable lawyers to cover each others' court dates and other important matters in emergency situations, each entry had to contain essential information including the time and location, the case name, the type of matter, and identification of the attorney scheduled to handle the matter. In addition, the cards had to be pulled every day and the information communicated to lawyers and paralegals so that appropriate action could be taken. As you can imagine, such a system is time-consuming to maintain and has a high potential for mistakes. As a result, many firms now use computers to manage their calendars. In fact, some malpractice insurance carriers offer discounts for the use of such programs.

A computerized calendar system may be a simple manual-entry system that works much like a paper calendar (see Exhibit 5-5). The user enters each hearing, task, meeting, appointment, reminder, and follow-up separately. The resulting schedule can be printed easily in an easy-to-read format, but the system has many of the weaknesses of a paper system.

Many firms, therefore, used automated computer programs. Even if the program is not specifically designed for the functions of a law office, it can make life easier by enabling you to schedule recurring events automatically (for example, a board meeting that occurs on the first Monday of every month). You can ask the system to "remind" you in advance of scheduled events with a pop-up on your computer screen. Some systems will alert the user to scheduling conflicts and to holidays. You can create your own tickler system.

With some systems, you can categorize entries as fixed or flexible. You can sort your entries into appointments (time when you are busy), meetings (tied into the calendar of another person in your firm), events (reminders, such as "Ann's birthday" that appear in a particular time period, such as a single day, but do not block off your time), or tasks (for your to-do list, described in Chapter 10). You may even be able to color code your schedule.

If you are using the Calendar function of a networked e-mail client, such as Outlook (as shown on Exhibit 5-5), you can check the schedules of others within your firm, put appointments on their calendars, or invite them to meetings. Of course, you can also block off your own schedule to reflect when you are busy and when you are free, to allow others to schedule meetings with you.

For instructions on how to set up reminders using Microsoft Outlook, visit http://office.microsoft.com/en-us/help/HA011164291033.aspx.

2.   Attorney-Specific Programs

Programs designed for the legal profession, especially programs with calendaring functions as part of a case management system, can offer many advantages because they "anticipate" the unique needs of legal professionals. These programs can help move cases along and prevent things from "falling through the cracks."

Law firm calendaring software can often make one or more additional entries or ticklers into the calendar based on a key date. With many programs, if the key date changes, all corresponding deadlines are automatically adjusted by the software, with adjustments for weekends and holidays. For example, if you have a trial set for March 3, you can program reminders to file trial briefs 30 days ahead of the trial date, 60 days ahead for supplemental discovery, and so on. If the trial is postponed, you simply change the key date and all the dependent dates change as well. These calendars also are called **rules-based calendars**.

rules-based calendars
Programmed to automatically respond when change is made to date or other matter on which other dates or matters are dependent

---

For More Information

It is possible to obtain rules-based software tied to a particular jurisdiction or area of practice. Your state bar association may have resources, or it may be possible to create your own template of rules. LawToolBox (http://www.lawtoolbox.com) offers a service that will mine courts' databases for deadlines and then e-mail them to you so that you can export them into Outlook, or into software specific to law offices, such as Time Matters, or Amicus Attorney (discussed further, later in this chapter). Similarly, CompuLaw (http://www.compulaw.com/rules/rules.htm) has rules in place for most states and for many legal specialties, such as intellectual property.

If your firm has software with special case management features, take the time to learn those features. The program may have an "inactivity watch" that can alert

Exhibit 5-5
Calendar Systems: Paper versus Automated

It's 8:00 a.m. and you get a call that your boss, Attorney Vietzen, has been in a car accident. Attorney Vietzen is a sole practitioner, and you must arrange coverage for any court calls or closings, reschedule appointments and meetings, and check to make sure that no deadlines will be missed. If Attorney Vietzen keeps a paper calendar, it might look like this:

8:00 am	
8:30 am	
9:00 am	tents closing Land Title → (rescheduled 9/15)
9:30 am	
10:00am	
10:30am	Roy Rosalind, here, re: 6661 Brown St.
11:00am	
11:30am	
NOON	Lunch Al's - Kalland
1:00 pm	
1:30 pm	conference J. Hallock - RM101 JC
2:00 pm	recorder's office - pickup releases
2:30 pm	work
3:00 pm	due next wk.
3:30 pm	
4:00 pm	LARA
4:30 pm	
5:00 pm	BAR ASSOC CLE
5:30 pm	
6:00 pm	
6:30 pm	
7:00 pm	
7:30 pm	
8:00 pm	

Notes: closing docs for Kappler — review
respond - Lynch Foreclosure complaint

If Attorney Vietzen uses Outlook's calendar, you can read the entries easily and note that:

- The appointments are tied to contacts. You need only click a link to get the phone number to reschedule Mr. Rosalind's appointment. Note that the Rosalind appointment is color coded; Attorney Vietzen uses the Categorize feature to code her day so that she knows whether she has to wear a suit!
- The symbol on the Bar Association meeting indicates this is a recurring event, scheduled for every month; the symbol on "Peterson file" indicates

EXHIBIT 5-5
(continued)

that Attorney Vietzen saved an e-mail from Attorney Kalland, requesting that they meet at Al's to review the file. After opening the e-mail, Attorney Vietzen simply chose "Move to Calendar."

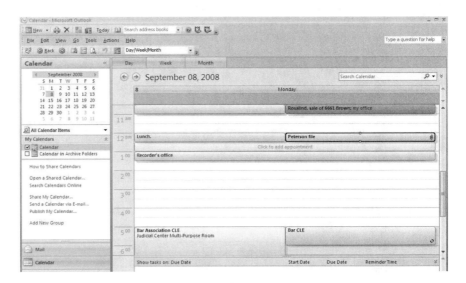

By clicking on an appointment you can get contact information.

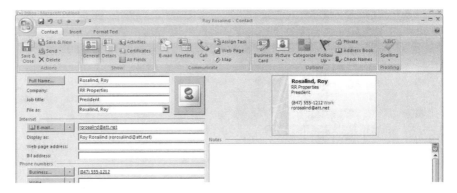

EXHIBIT 5-5
(continued)

- Clicking on the task pad gets you into Attorney Vietzen's to-do list.

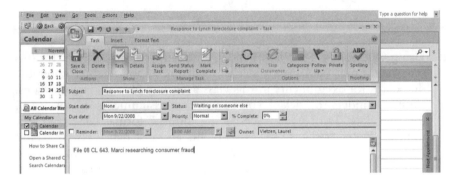

- By clicking on a task, you can get details, such as the file number and due date.

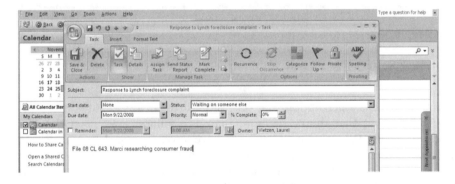

you when a case has not had any activity within a certain period of time. What better way to ensure that you don't let a case languish. This feature can then be used to generate a goodwill letter to let the client know that nothing is happening, but her case has not been forgotten.

Another example: you send a letter to a doctor requesting medical records. When you use case management software to generate the letter, an entry is automatically made into the calendar system to "tickle" for a response. If you do not receive a response by that date, the case management system will "remind" you and may even generate another follow-up request. Of course, any system is only as good as the person who uses it. What if you forget to make the entry indicating that the response has been received?

To avoid such problems, legal professionals must set aside a regular time to conduct docket review. Look at the week ahead and anticipate any problems and what needs to be done. Use the time to create a task list, as described in Chapter 10 on time management.

Assignment 5-2
Using Systems

1. Using Outlook or a similar calendar function, create a calendar for this semester. Enter your class times as recurring appointments. Enter the due dates for assignments in this class as events for the relevant dates. Enter reminders to "tickle" you to work on assignments in advance of the due date. Print your calendar in "month" format (one page per month). Enter "ticklers" for assignments and test dates. Use the Find feature to find the date of a particular assignment and print the results. (Microsoft Outlook Training can be found at http://office.microsoft.com/training.)
2. Determine whether CompuLaw has rules-based software available for your state.

D. Software Packages

Although there is a perception that only large firms invest in software packages, the ABA reports that there are more than 1.1 million lawyers in the United States, and more than half of all law firms have fewer than six lawyers.[2] With that size of a market, software providers are anxious to serve small firms.

These packages can help with far more than the essential law firm functions of checking conflicts, calendaring, and billing. Imagine, for example, that a lawyer considering whether to take additional work from a client can readily access that client's payment history and discover that the client is a "slow pay." A firm that is considering expanding its family law practice can do a quick analysis of whether that practice area is as profitable as its other areas of practice. A firm can quickly generate labels of all its conflicts to send out a newsletter, greeting cards, or other marketing material.

Software packages may include case management software or **practice management software**. Case management software provides attorneys and paralegals with a shared database containing all case- and client-specific information, conflict of interest searching, office-wide calendars, and task management systems. Practice

practice management software
"Law office in a box"

---

[2]American Bar Association, Market Research Department, Statistical Resources, http://www.abanet.org/marketresearch/resource.html#Demographics.

management software is a "law office in a box" that organizes both front- and back-office functions. Practice management software typically has more features than case management software and often includes office accounting tools, time and billing software, and customer relationship management (CRM) features. Despite these differences, the terms "practice management" and "case management" are often used interchangeably, so don't get "hung up" on the terminology. Research the features a particular package offers rather than its name.

How do you research software? There are a number of factors to consider. The first step is to consider the nature of the firm's practice. If your firm is purely a litigation firm, trust management applications would have no purpose for you. If you are a transactional practice, there is no point in paying for discovery support features. Next, start gathering information from the people who will work with the package. Any package is only as good as the information entered into it. If the people working at the firm resist using the package or find it difficult to use, it will have little value. Ask the following questions:

- What processes would users like to automate? For some firms, auto-mating every possible function might not make sense. For example, a firm that deals with a very limited client base would have different needs (for example, conflicts checking) than a firm with a regular turnover of clients.
- What features (design, compatibility with other software systems, etc.) have users liked or disliked about other software systems?
- How many users will there be? Packages are often priced on a "per user" basis.

With that information, start evaluating packages on the market. Rather than accepting the generic answers you may get from vendors, you may want to actually visit firms using the package to evaluate how it really works. With respect to basic features, consider these questions:

- How hard will it be to learn to navigate the system? Is its design intuitive? Many programs use the same Windows-based design found on the Microsoft Office and Corel WordPerfect programs. The design feels familiar to most users, so that they can easily navigate and locate key features.
- What training is available? Are there any options for face-to-face training, or is it done by phone or on the Internet? Is there any additional charge for training?
- What technical support is available, and what is the cost?
- How difficult is remote access?
- What happens when the package goes to a new edition? Will your firm be able to upgrade easily and at a reasonable cost, or will you be left with an "orphan" package?
- What are the security features? Will each user have an individual password and be required to use it each time she accesses the software? Can system administrators restrict user access to sensitive, confidential or case-specific information?

- Will the system integrate with your office's existing software and work with your hardware? For example, if you create a pleading in Word or WordPerfect, does the system index it so that it will be included in future searches for case-related documents? Can you have a trial run before you commit to a purchase?
- Does the system include "everyday" features such as spell-check and grammar-check in all applications? Does the spell-check feature include legal terms? Does the software sync with PDA devices? Does the system perform validation, for example, by preventing incorrect spelling of a party's name or transposition of the numbers in a case's docket number?
- Does the time and billing application support various billing and payment options (described in the next chapter), allow for customizing bills (for example, with the firm logo), allow for e-billing, and track payment history?
- Do the accounting applications allow you to generate the particular financial reports your firm needs, as described in the next chapter?
- Does the calendar/task application recognize holidays? Does it allow group use, so that users can send and receive alerts, check schedules of others for meeting availability, or perform similar functions? How difficult is it to add a rule so that certain tasks automatically trigger other tasks or reminders? For example, if a deposition date is added to the calendar, can the system trigger reminders for sending notice, scheduling a court reporter, or reserving a conference room?
- Will you be able to enter information only once and have it available for multiple applications? For example, if you are using an expert witness you have used on a previous case, will the system link all of the information previously entered concerning the witness to the new case? Will the system automatically change dependent dates when a date is changed?
- Is the data entry form on the client and contact database customizable or comprehensive, including fields for all the information you normally collect? Consider fields for Social Security number, e-mail address, properties owned, bank accounts, and so on. Is the entry form for billing adequately detailed?
- Which special features do you want? Some of the options are
  - Integrated financial package (i.e., one that includes not only time and billing but general ledger, check writing, and/or payroll as well).
  - Pop-up timers.
  - Multiple language capability.
  - Forms to summarize, archive, and access notes from meetings, phone calls, depositions, and other important events; can such information be called up on a single page for managing client relationships? Imagine, for example, that a client with a problem calls the office when his usual contact is on vacation; wouldn't it be nice if the person taking the call could quickly skim a summary of recent calls and meetings, rather than making the client repeat the entire story?
  - Full text searches—advanced and Boolean searches (AND, OR, NOT) that allows searching by partial words or names.
  - Coordination of court rules—allows you to enter a court date or discovery deadline on the system's calendar and all other court dates,

statutes of limitations, and other court deadlines and events are calculated for you. Users can receive e-mail alerts for all upcoming court and case deadlines.

- Real-time access to bank balances.
- Tax forms.
- Features for unique practice areas such as trust management, bankruptcy, or contract compliance.
- File review — will the system note any file that has had no activity for a prescribed time period?

By the time this book is in print, software developers will likely have developed new features and packages. Existing packages will have been made more user-friendly. Because technology changes so quickly, learning the features of any one package before using it is not as important as knowing what is possible and where to go for information.

Assignment 5-3
Researching Systems

Management Portfolio

Ed Rodan has heard that all the "best firms" use practice management software, but he is not sure what to look for. Use a search engine to search for law office practice management software. Choose three products, identify what each identifies as its major selling points, and write a memo outlining your findings and recommendations.

Out There — Paralegal Profile
The System for Success

Cary Hansing is attending an ABA-approved paralegal program to gain additional skills and knowledge for his current position. The importance of systems and how to choose systems are among Cary's favorite topics. Here's what he has to say about them.

"I currently serve as the director of operations and senior analyst for Bankruptcy Advisory Services, Inc. (BAS). BAS specializes in tasks vital to a successful bankruptcy reorganization under Chapter 11 or a liquidation under Chapter 7. One of my responsibilities at BAS is to advise our executive director on the best system choice for managing tasks in a client engagement. This can be an adoption of a simple report form that is currently used by the client, use of prepackaged software, or the creation of a customized, reporting system."

"When I talk about a system, I define it as a process of inventorying information requested from the client, along with information about legal proceedings. The goal is to be able to match or code the system with the client's objectives and to be able to report on status. The right system will give you a 'snap shot' of progress at any time, whether it is the progress of an entire proceeding or a specific task. When it comes to advising our executive director, I consider three questions. First, what task or tasks does the client want us to perform? Second, which system provides the greatest benefit to the client at the most reasonable cost? Third, how can I link it to the other systems being used on different engagements to maximize the productivity of our office? Balancing these questions with the objectives of the client and the relevant available inventory of information allows us produce the desired result for the client in a cost effective and efficient manner. It is partly an art form to make the correct choice."

"After a system is chosen, it must be implemented. The first step I take is to compare the objectives of this engagement with other engagements we have had in the past. If I can find a match, I will pull my notes and solicit feedback from the attorneys and other professionals in our office about the system used previously. The second step is to modify or incorporate any unique features that are required for this client, including status reports for the court, weekly summary reports to the client, and internal progress reports used for billing and scheduling purposes. The third step is to rate the success of the system once the engagement ends, noting features that worked well, specific requirements of the court with respect to reports, and things that did not work that need to be modified before we'd use that process or system again in the future. It's a dynamic cycle that will produce results equal to the time committed to making system determinations."

"We have created a customized reporting system that gathers data from all of our engagements and centralizes that information. This is a significant benefit for our company. This system provides an easy search process, from which we can determine conflicts of interest, allows contact information on opponents from previous matters to be used currently, improves time management by generating a list of dates for all matters, and produces reference lists when we search for items or information from previous engagements. By planning and using an efficient system to manage the tasks of an engagement, we are able to efficiently manage a client engagement and maximize time and resources, which are always necessary considerations to running a successful and profitable business."

Chapter Review

Discussion Questions

1. Describe the five ways in which a conflict of interest can arise.
2. Describe the requirements for effective screening.
3. Describe the information that must be collected from a new client to effectively check for conflicts. When and why must that information be updated?
4. Why might a conflict of interest go undiscovered despite a careful search in the firm's database?
5. Why might an attorney want to be careful to *not* learn confidential information during an initial consultation with a client?
6. Explain how rules-based docketing software would benefit a firm.
7. Identify at least five factors that should be considered in choosing a software package.
8. Identify at least three major practice management packages on the market.
9. What are the important characteristics of a firm's master calendar?
10. Your supervising attorney loves her PDA and is constantly entering new dates and contacts on the device. What must you make sure she does regularly?

ACROSS

1. _____ management software is especially useful for discovery
5. conflict of interest arising from representing parties in competion
6. _____ management software is "law office in a box"
8. to remove self or firm from case
9. conflict of interest arising from representing opposing parties at the same time
11. data-behind-data, shows, for example, when a document was altered (yes, from an earlier chapter!)
15. formal process of isolating person from case
16. in addition to keeping records of clients, firm should keep records of people for whom it has _____ representation
17. _____ client can cause a conflict in a current matter

DOWN

2. every firm should have a single _____ calendar
3. _____-based calendars can automatically update dependent dates when one changes

4. software function, e.g., spell check
5. conflict that would arise from writing your father's will
7. reminders
10. conflict spreads to entire firm if one member has a conflict
12. acronym, number that identifies business and affiliates
13. _____ managment software, stores all information relating to each client matter
14. _____ wall, isolating person from case

Terms and Definitions

Chinese wall: Another term for screening
concurrent conflict: Arises from representing opposing parties on same matter
imputed conflict: Conflict of interest of one legal professional is contagious to others in firm
informed consent: Consent (to conflict of interest) based on full disclosure of potential problems
positional conflict: Arises from representing parties in competition in the market or taking different positions in different matter
practice management software: "Law office in a box"
recuse: To remove self or firm from case
rules-based calendar: Programmed to automatically respond when change is made to date or other matter on which other dates or matters are dependent
screening: Process of formally isolating a person from a case because of conflict of interest
ticklers: Reminders

6

◆ ◆ ◆

Law Office Accounting

◆ ◆ ◆

As a Manager

You will be responsible for overseeing accounting systems and possibly for selecting and implementing those systems. You will train employees on keeping time, handling funds, and paying bills, and implement policies to increase firm profits.

Objectives

After completing this chapter, you will be able to

- Describe the methods of billing in use in most law offices.
- Explain the advantages of and basis for billing for paralegal time.
- Discuss ethical rules applicable to billing and to handling client funds.
- Describe various methods of tracking time for billing.
- Evaluate software available for law office accounting functions.
- Correctly use terminology applicable to generally accepted accounting practices.
- Use common accounting terminology correctly.
- Accurately track and record your own time on task.
- Describe procedures for paying bills.

A. Accounting Functions

If you are like many people, you may have chosen a career in the legal field because you are a "word" and "language" person. Maybe you even have an aversion to math! Like any business, however, a law office involves some accounting. Even though some firms are now outsourcing some of these functions, you must have a basic understanding of what those functions are and the ethical obligations that accompany them. Some accounting functions include the following:

- Payroll
- Paying bills for office expenses (general ledger/accounts payable)
- Payment of taxes
- Financial reports to determine the firm's profitability
- Tracking time on task
- Billing clients (accounts receivable)
- Trust/escrow accounting

Beyond the operation of the law office, many client matters require that legal professionals understand how financial calculations are made and how financial records are kept. Any type of civil litigation requires calculation of damages or settlement; business and real estate transactions require calculations; estates often involve calculation of taxes and valuations. It's usually more than just calculation; clients often do not keep good records, and legal professionals must find the underlying information, organize it, summarize it, and then do the calculations.

There are many ways of organizing and recording financial information, ranging from a checkbook register to sophisticated software. This chapter discusses some of those methods, but primarily focuses on the terminology and ethical obligations associated with these functions.

1. Basic Accounting Terminology

Like any other profession, accounting has its own language, and knowledge of common terms is essential to law office management. Many law office managers perform some accounting functions, but even if your firm has an accountant or a bookkeeper to handle these functions, the law office manager must be able to communicate with those individuals. Keep in mind that the purpose of accounting is not only to keep track of money, but also to analyze patterns as a basis for making business decisions.

accounting cycle: The period over which financial records are kept — may be a **calendar year** (January 1 to December 31), a **fiscal year** (12 consecutive months not starting in January), or some other period.

accounts payable: Money owed to others and not yet paid; the bill for malpractice insurance, due next week, is an account payable.

accounts receivable: Money owed for work performed by the firm for which a bill has been sent, but for which payment has not been received. Most firms have a system in place, which may be as simple as a calendar note, to check whether bills have been paid within a certain period after being sent.

accounts receivable schedule: A monthly report showing how much money is owed by each client.

accrual accounting: This method of accounting is the "opposite" of cash basis accounting (see below). With accrual accounting, income and expenses are recorded when billed or incurred rather than when payment is made. While small to mid-size law firms generally use cash-basis accounting, large firms may use the accrual method. Firms with very high levels of income may be required, by IRS regulations, to use the accrual method.

aging: Analysis of how long billings stay in accounts receivable before payment is received. Accounts receivable aging analysis is essential to the profitable practice of law. (Accounts *payable* aging analysis, how long each account payable has remained unpaid, may be used to determine the schedule for paying outstanding bills.)

assets: Things of value

balance sheet: A "snapshot" showing the assets and liabilities of a firm on a given date (see Exhibit 6-1).

cash basis accounting: This method reflects only payments actually received and is the basis of most small firm accounting.

cash flow projection: Many firms consider this the most important financial report. A cash flow projection is often done as a spreadsheet with several months listed across the top; revenue and expense items are listed in two sections, top to bottom. Amounts anticipated to be spent and taken in are entered in the cell where the column for the relevant month and the row for the relevant type of expense or revenue (e.g., rent) intersect. Expenses are entered as negative numbers, so that rows and columns can be totaled at the end of the year (or as often as desirable) to get the "big picture." A **variance report** is typically created every month to show the difference between income and expenses projected and what actually happened. The variance report can be a separate report or it can be done in the form of changes to the original projection.

daily cash report: Shows money taken in and money paid out on a daily basis.

depreciation: An expense recorded to reflect the use of an asset and thereby spread its cost over its useful life. Depreciation is an example of a **paper loss;** no actual money is lost as result of the entry of the expense.

double entry accounting: A system under which every transaction affects, and is therefore recorded in, two accounts. Every transaction that causes a **debit** in one account must be balanced against a **credit** in another account. For example, the purchase of a scanner might reduce (debit) the cash account by $300, but would increase (credit) the office equipment account.

Exhibit 6-1
Balance Sheet

A balance sheet is essential to determine the value of ownership when a partner enters or leaves the firm. A series of balance sheets might be compared to identify patterns and plan accordingly. For example, the firm might identify a pattern that cash is high at the end of most years and low during summer months, perhaps because of year-end settlement of contingency cases.

Torok Law Offices
Balance Sheet   Date:

Assets	
Long-Term:	
Building	760,000
Land	140,000
Current:	
Cash	57,000
Personal Property	87,000
Investments	126,000
Total	1,170,000
Liabilities	
Long-Term:	
Mortgage	490,000
Current:	
Accounts Payable	46,000
Total	536,000
EQUITY:	634,000

personal property
Moveable items, with a tangible physical existence

equity: The value of assets minus liabilities.

expenses: Costs of operations, including rent, salaries, supplies, utilities, insurance, and similar items.

GAAP: Generally accepted accounting principles.

hours worked: Many firms prepare this regular report to compare actual hours billed to the goals set for billing.

income: Profits remaining after expenses are subtracted from **revenue**. Revenue is all money coming into the firm. If a firm is using a cash basis method of accounting, these concepts "built in" to the system. A firm using the accrual method may do a **profit and loss (P&L) statement** (also called an **income statement**) to show the actual financial health of the firm.

ledger: Record for an individual account (see Exhibit 6-2).

liabilities: Claims that outsiders have against assets.

Exhibit 6-2
Sample Ledger Sheet

Ledger page for a client whose fees and costs are paid from a retainer kept in a client funds account. The client replenishes the account. On 3/15, the client gave the firm a retainer; on 5/1 the firm billed the client for $900 in fees and $325 in costs and withdrew that amount from the client's fund. The client replenished the fund on 5/12. The client's checks to that account and checks coming out of that account would also be reflected on the journal for the client funds account.

Client: Rezner, Rae   File   09-D-157
Matter: Rezner v. Rezner
Contact at: 325 N. Bluff St.
           Dundee, IN 49071
           224-401-1111

| | | | Fees | | | | Costs | | | Trust | |
Date	Description	Ck #	Charge	Rec'd	Bal	Adv	Rec'd	Bal	Rec'd	Pd	Bal.
3/15/	Retainer	3123							5,000.00		5,000.00
5/1/	Bill, April		900.00		900.00	325.00		325.00			
5/1/	Pmt	636		900.00			325.00	0		1,225.00	3,775.00
5/12/	From client	3138							1,225.00		5,000.00

one-write system (pegboard system): Using stacking check, journal, and ledger sheets, with carbon paper, writing a transaction one time causes it to be recorded on all relevant records.

posting: The transfer of information from a chronological listing of transactions, called a **journal**, to a ledger.

prorate: To allocate an amount between two accounts. For example, if a $1,200 tax bill is to be prorated between a buyer who will own the house for three months and a seller who has owned it for nine months, the seller's account will be responsible for payment of $900 and the buyer will be responsible for $300.

reconciliation: Also called balancing; the comparison of a bank statement with the firm's account records.

write-offs: A report of time that did not get billed or that was billed but will not be paid, perhaps because the client complained and a compromise was negotiated.

2. The Mechanics

Although learning the definitions is a good starting point, actually doing the job requires more. You will learn the "mechanics" of real estate prorations, estate valuation and tax forms, and litigation settlements in other substantive paralegal classes. The specifics of handling payroll accounting are discussed in Chapter 9. With respect to accounting for the firm's finances and for money it holds on behalf of clients, you will first have to know what kinds of accounts your firm maintains. A law firm typically has a business account, into which income is deposited and from which expenses such as rent, utilities, and supplies are paid; one or more trust accounts (discussed in depth later in this chapter); and a payroll account (unless the firm hires an outside payroll services company to handle its payroll). You will also have to learn whether your firm uses a paper system or an automated system (these are also discussed later). You will then have to learn the steps in the process with respect to both income and outflow. In general, each financial transaction is first recorded chronologically, as it occurs (for example, **petty cash** is taken to the post office to send a registered letter, a client pays her bill). Each transaction is then posted to the particular account it affects: the petty cash account and the client's account. Later, these accounts may be summarized, reconciled, and analyzed. With these concepts in mind, let's first examine how law firms obtain revenue.

petty cash
Money kept on hand for small purchases

B. Law Firm Finances

Billing is one of the hottest topics in the legal field. Both clients and lawyers are increasingly dissatisfied with the status quo. Flat fees and contingency arrangements present too much risk for many lawyers; hourly billing is a disincentive to efficiency. ABA Model Rule 1.5 prohibits unreasonable fees, and there is a huge body of authority on what constitutes reasonable fees. Because paralegals do not set fees, however, the topic of what is reasonable is beyond the scope of this book.

1. How Lawyers Are Paid for Their Work

Traditionally, lawyers have been paid in one of three ways: a flat fee, an hourly rate, or a contingency fee.

flat fee
Agreed in advance

A **flat fee** is often available for routine transactional work, such as closing a real estate sale, forming a corporation, or drafting a will or trust. Although the flat fee is most easily understood by clients, the distinction between the lawyer's fee and costs or expenses must be made clear. Imagine, for example, a legally unsophisticated client who requests that a law firm form a corporation for her dog grooming business. The client is told that the lawyer's fee is $700 and agrees to the fee. The client subsequently receives a bill for $950 — $700 for the lawyer and $250 for the fees charged by the secretary of state's office for registering the corporation. The client may feel she has been deceived, but the lawyer may think that this is just "common knowledge." The agreement should also address what will happen if an unanticipated problem changes the nature of the work. (Consider: if a flat fee were charged for certain litigation or negotiation matters, would the client be less motivated to accept a reasonable settlement?)

Hard costs (also called "direct costs") include the filing fee, paying the court reporter, and other payments attributable to a specific client matter. **Soft costs** include postage, photocopies, and supplies, sometimes considered part of the firm's **overhead**. Some firms allocate soft costs to individual clients, for example, by charging a "per page" fee for copies and faxes; other firms add a percentage to every client's bill to cover these costs. Some firms just figure these costs into determining the hourly rates for attorney and paralegal work. To avoid unhappy clients—and possibly unpaid bills—these policies should be fully explained to the client during the first meeting.

An hourly fee is typically charged for litigation and complex transactional matters. In most firms, each person working on a case has a different billing rate, depending on that person's status (partner, associate, paralegal) and experience; less commonly a firm may "blend" the billing rates of all lawyers and paralegals assigned to the firm and charge a single rate for all hours. A firm may charge different hourly rates for different types of tasks. The client should be informed about the amount of the hourly fee as well as what it includes. Costs not included in the fee and whether paralegal fees are billed separately should be stated. The client may also want an estimate of time or an agreement that he will be notified before a certain limit is passed. The firm can agree to place a cap (upper limit) on the fees. The client should be told how often he will be billed and when payment is expected. A client who does not receive a bill for more than a month may conclude that his case is not being worked on.

Hourly clients should be advised of how the hour is broken down and whether calls are billed. For example, if a lawyer bills at $300 per hour and bills in 1/4 hour **increments**, a 5-minute phone call will cost $75; if the lawyer bills in 1/10 hour increments, it will cost $30. Some lawyers permit a few short phone calls without billing.

A **contingency fee** arrangement means that the lawyer will not be paid for her time unless she wins the case. This arrangement is often used in personal injury and civil rights cases, where the plaintiff may not have money to pay a lawyer before the case is resolved but has the potential for a large award. A successful lawyer gets a percentage of the award; the percentage is negotiable and may depend on whether the case is settled or goes to trial. Some states set the rate for certain cases, such as workers' compensation cases, by statute. The client must be informed about how costs will be handled and how the percentage is calculated. The client may be liable for costs even if the case is lost.

hard costs
Directly attributable to client matter, such as filing fee

soft costs
Often considered overhead, include copying, postage, etc.

overhead
Expenses attributable to doing business

increments
Portions into which whole is divided

contingency fee
Lawyer is paid with a percentage of the settlement or judgment amount

Calculation of Contingency Fee

Settlement amount: $180,000   Costs: $3,450

Using the **gross fee method**:

$$180,000$$
$$\underline{\text{minus attorney's fee } 60,000 \ (1/3)}$$
$$120,000$$

gross fee method
Contingency fee calculation — costs deducted after percentage is figured

$$\frac{\text{minus } 3,450 \text{ (costs)}}{116,550 \text{ to client}}$$

net fee method
Contingency fee
calculation — costs
deducted before percentage
is figured

Using the **net fee method**:

$$180,000$$

$$\frac{\text{minus } 3,450 \text{ (costs)}}{176,550 \text{ minus}}$$

$$\frac{\text{Minus } 58,850 \text{ attorney's fee (1/3 of 176,550)}}{117,700 \text{ to client}}$$

Although contingency fees get a lot of publicity, many lawyers never or rarely take a contingency case. Only a limited number of cases qualify for a contingency arrangement, and those that do qualify may be too expensive for a firm to handle. In taking a personal injury case on a contingency, the lawyer is agreeing to work without being paid for the years until a judgment or settlement is paid. During that time, the lawyer has to continue to pay personal and office expenses (rent, electricity, and, most important, paralegal salaries) and perhaps expenses related to the case itself. Court filing fees, deposition fees, the costs of an investigator, fees for expert opinions or witnesses, and the costs of obtaining medical records will not wait until the money comes in, and not many clients can pay those expenses while the case is pending.

Many law firms are now trying new ways of billing. Most are combinations of or variations on the three traditional methods. For example, some firms employ **value (incentive) billing**, with which the result obtained by the firm is factored into the normal hourly or flat fee. Similarly, the firm might offer a modified contingency agreement, under which the firm gets a low hourly rate plus a percentage of any winnings. Other firms are trying really innovative ideas. For example, one firm is advertising that it will not charge clients for work done by first-year associates — a response to the common complaint that clients are billed for training new lawyers[1].

value (incentive) billing
Fee is tied to result obtained

In 2002 ABA Model Rule 1.2(c) was amended to allow limitation of the scope of representation, and several states adopted similar changes. In those states, lawyers offer **unbundled legal services**. Under such an arrangement, the firm has a price list for specific services that support the client's own efforts in the matter. The firm must use a clearly worded limited services agreement so there is no doubt about what the firm is and is not doing. Unbundled services are particularly popular in divorce matters.

unbundled legal services
Lawyer performs only some
tasks to accomplish client's
goal

Firms often require a deposit called a **retainer**. In some states, lawyers are permitted to collect a "classic" nonrefundable retainer, which is not applied to future fees, costs, or expenses. Some lawyers use this arrangement to prevent "lawyer shopping." Such a retainer is the lawyer's property immediately and need not be deposited into a client funds account as described below.

retainer
Advance payment

In other cases, the retainer is an advance against future billing. Costs or legal work may be charged against this type of "security" retainer. Many lawyers

---

[1]Reported by National Law Journal, August 30, 3007, http://www.law.com/jsp/article.jsp?id=1187341325148&rss=newswire

require an **evergreen retainer**, which the client is required to keep funded at a specified level. Clients should be fully informed about whether and to what extent the retainer is refundable if not entirely used for fees, costs, and expenses.

If payment will not be drawn from a retainer, some firms accept credit cards or even PayPal or a similar service. If the firm is going to extend credit to the client (by billing after services are rendered), it may require evidence of ability to pay, such as a bank account statement, tax return, or credit card bill that shows the remaining credit line. A law firm is not simply being greedy when it asks for evidence of ability to pay. When a law firm has to sue to collect its fee, clients sometimes "strike back" with a malpractice claim.

Some states recognize a third option: an advance payment retainer, which is payment for future legal service with ownership passing to the attorney immediately. This type of arrangement might be considered if the funds to be used for payment of fees might be at risk. For example, the attorney is working for an estate and there is an outsider claiming estate funds. This arrangement does put the payment at risk to the lawyer's creditors and must be explained to the client in detail. Your state may have additional ethical requirements.

Some people assume that lawyers "pay" for cases that come into their offices by giving the person who referred the client to a firm a **referral fee**. In fact, this is rarely the case. As discussed in Chapter 1, the ethical rules in many states prohibit sharing fees with non-lawyers. Even sharing fees with lawyers outside the firm is restricted: in many states, the client must be informed of such an arrangement and/or the referring lawyer is considered responsible for the work done by the lawyer to whom the referral was made.

referral fee
Money paid to a person who sends a client to the firm

2. Handling Client Funds

If the retainer is refundable, it remains the client's property until it is earned by the attorney. A lawyer might also hold client funds for other reasons, for example, an **escrow** being held to fund a purchase or to settle the debts of an estate. Settlement checks commonly are sent to the plaintiff's lawyer; judgments may be paid from or into client funds accounts.

escrow
Money being held until a purpose is achieved

A lawyer holding property for a client is acting as a **fiduciary** and has special obligations. These obligations cannot be transferred away, so even a lawyer who is comfortable delegating work should maintain careful oversight of trust accounts. For example, a lawyer who is comfortable letting his office manager sign his business account checks or use a signature stamp typically will not do so with respect to the trust account. He may not be allowed to do so, in fact, depending on state rules. States have very specific rules about handling some funds. Many states publish lists of approved financial institutions for client funds accounts and indicate how such accounts must be titled (for example, the words "Trust Account" may be required). Other ethical rules governing client funds accounts generally require the following:

fiduciary
Relationship of trust that imposes special obligations

trust
Account being held on behalf of another

- Client money must be kept in a separate **trust** account and must never be **commingled** with the lawyer's personal or business accounts. Your state may even require that client funds accounts and business accounts not be at the same bank. Client retainer funds should be kept separately from

commingled
Funds wrongly mixed

pooled
Funds intentionally mixed in a single account

other client funds that the lawyer may administer, such as trusts for children. Although a client can have a separate escrow account, most law firms maintain **pooled** accounts into which all client funds are deposited to avoid the administrative work of opening and maintaining an account for each new client. During the financial crisis of late 2008, the American Bar Association asked the FDIC to provide unlimited insurance for client trust accounts.

- The lawyer must not profit from the client funds account. If a client's funds are substantial enough and will be held long enough to justify the expense, the client should have an individual account on which client may earn interest. To open an individual interest bearing account, the financial institution will require proof of the client's federal identification number (sometimes called **FEIN**), such as a Social Security number or employer identification number.

FEIN
federal identification number

nominal
Small in amount

- With a pooled account of **nominal** amounts or short-term funds, however, it is very difficult to determine how much interest is attributable to each account. Until the 1980s, pooled accounts generally did not earn interest. Since that time, the states have enacted **Interest on Lawyers' Trust Accounts (IOLTA)** programs so that interest generated on pooled accounts in excess of what is needed to pay bank fees can be forwarded to a fund that is used to provide low-income people with access to the legal system.

Interest on Lawyers' Trust Accounts (IOLTA)
Program in which interest generated on pooled accounts is forwarded to a legal fund

- The lawyer must regularly account to the client for money being held for the client. The lawyer may withdraw fees and expenses to which the firm has become entitled, if the client does not object after proper notice. In fact, the attorney may not wait too long to withdraw fees — this would constitute **passive commingling**.

passive commingling
Waiting too long to withdraw funds from trust account

- A trust accounting system generally consists of a checkbook register, a receipts journal, a disbursements journal, and a ledger book containing individual ledger account pages for each client having funds in a pooled account for recording each financial transaction affecting that client's funds. A ledger page should be created for the client as soon as the client retains the firm. Each transaction must be recorded in several places.

- Update trust accounts daily so that the running total for each account is up to date.

- Source documents (duplicate deposit slips, canceled checks, bank statements), written reconciliation with bank statements, client fee and retainer agreements, records justifying costs and expenses billed to clients, and copies of statements and bills sent to clients should be kept as required by your state (commonly five to seven years). Even if your state rules do not impose requirements for accounting, your firm's malpractice insurance carrier may have rules requiring hard-copy backup.

signatory
Person with access to account by signature

- Your state may have rules concerning who can act as a **signatory** for a client funds account, whether checks may be made out to cash, how often the account must be balanced, and other administrative matters.

- When checks are received for the trust account, they should be deposited on the same day. As an extra level of protection against confusing the trust account with the firm's business account, limit access to checkbooks; consider having trust account checks printed in a different color.

- Never allow a client to give you money for deposit into the trust account without a clear purpose or lawyer approval. Clients have been known to attempt to use a lawyer's trust account for **money laundering**. (For examples of prosecution of money laundering schemes involving law offices, see http://www.irs.gov/compliance/enforcement/article/0,,id=163022,00.html.)

money laundering
Actions intended to conceal the true ownership, source, location, or control of funds

- The law firm must be able to account for money actually available in the account. Suppose that on Monday a client wrote a $5,000 check as a retainer for a divorce case. On Wednesday, before the lawyer has done any work on the file, the client reconciles with his wife. The lawyer is going to refund the client's retainer. Might there be a problem with writing a check against the client funds account? Yes! If the client's retainer check has not yet cleared, the lawyer is actually "borrowing" from other clients by writing that check.

Example

If your supervisor seems particularly unwilling to delegate work concerning the trust fund, you may have an exceptionally good supervisor. Consider this news blurb from the *ABA Journal*.

Maryland lawyer Charles Jay Zuckerman thought the new paralegal he hired would clean up the mess caused by a predecessor who stole from his client trust account. But the new paralegal was also a thief, taking more money than the first, the *Daily Record* reports. In all, the two paralegals stole more than $300,000, and Zuckerman is being held accountable. The Maryland Court has suspended Zuckerman, prompting the former assistant attorney general to declare that he will never return to private practice.

Zuckerman told the newspaper he was so busy with his personal injury practice that he had to delegate responsibility. "I had hundreds and hundreds of cases," he told the *Daily Record*. "I was in court a lot. You've got to delegate things. You can't be there to sign every check. . . . You've got to have some trust in your employees," he said.

Debra Cassens Weiss, *Lawyer Suspended After Second Paralegal Steals from Client Account*, ABA J., Mar. 18, 2008.

Mishandling client funds is a major cause of attorney disciplinary actions (see Exhibit 6-3). Some states even have **audit** programs, under which attorneys, typically chosen at random, are visited by a team or an individual auditor to determine whether proper records are being maintained and whether client funds are being mishandled.

audit
Examination of accounts

Your firm may have a sophisticated computer program for tracking client funds and other accounts, but still may back it up with manual ledger sheets (see Exhibit 6-4). Remember, for a client funds account: one page for the account as a whole, and one sheet for each client, showing all deposits and withdrawals attributable to that client.

Exhibit 6-3
Coppock v. State Bar of California, 749 P.2d 1317 (Cal. 1988)

... Petitioner was admitted to practice law in 1978. He has no prior record of discipline. Petitioner met Pollock in 1979, when he agreed to defend his wife, Sandra Pollock, in a fraud action. An apparently related fraud action against Robert Pollock had been concluded in 1972, resulting in a $64 million judgment against him. Petitioner was aware of the outstanding judgment, but insists he believed Pollock was innocent of fraud. Petitioner states, "I ineptly attempted . . . Sandra Pollock's defense . . . only to cause a default to be entered in excess of 55 million dollars." Petitioner brought a motion to set aside the default. The trial court denied the motion. Petitioner attempted to appeal, but the appeal was dismissed, apparently because petitioner failed to file a timely notice.

Petitioner "had become very close to Pollock," and asserts that the Pollocks, although "dismayed to learn that I had mishandled their appeal," chose not to take action against him. Instead, Pollock sought petitioner's assistance in setting up a trust account to conceal money from creditors and enable Pollock to manage his business affairs unhampered by attempts to attach his funds. Petitioner states he agreed to set up the account because he was "beleaguered by a sense of guilt" about Sandra Pollock's default judgment.

In July 1981, petitioner opened a bank account designated "Wally Coppock, Attorney at Law, Clients Trust Account" . . . so that "Pollock could be shielded from any attempts to execute on that account." He gave total control of the account to Pollock, and supplied him with signed checks and deposit slips. Petitioner initially reviewed the monthly trust account statements, but became "lax." Pollock used the account to commit fraud against third parties. [Third-party fraud victims] applied to the State Bar Client Security Fund for reimbursement. The State Bar brought this disciplinary action against petitioner.

The hearing panel concluded that petitioner violated his duties as an attorney. . . . The review department adopted the findings, with amendments. Petitioner claims the review department's findings are not supported by sufficient evidence. He objects particularly to its findings that his trust account was opened for the purpose of defrauding Pollock's creditors, and that he allowed Pollock to use it in a "scheme to defraud" his creditors.

Petitioner never claimed to be unaware of the purpose of the account, but rather asserted that he thought the purpose (hiding funds from creditors) was not fraudulent. Although the trust account was intended to conceal Pollock's funds, petitioner insists he "naively believed that their meager income would be fully exempt from execution" by their creditors. Petitioner's assertions of naivete do not help him. . . . [E]ven accepting [a] claim that he had no "active" intent to defraud, it is clear that given Pollock's history, [petitioner] should have been more circumspect rather than accepting without corroboration Pollock's assurances. He admits intent to *conceal* funds from Pollock's creditors. This amounts to an admitted intent to deceive.

EXHIBIT 6-3
(continued)

[P]etitioner compounded his misconduct by relinquishing control of the trust account to Pollock. He failed to supervise use of the account, or even to review account statements. Because petitioner designated the account his "clients trust account," he was responsible for the funds in that account, and it was a breach of his professional duties to give complete control of the account to Pollock. In *Gassman v. State Bar* (1976) 18 Cal. 3d 125, we held actual suspension to be justified where the attorney had failed to establish an accounting procedure for his client trust account, and where this "willful failure was *a result of his knowing delegation of responsibility* to [his secretary-bookkeeper] and his *failure to supervise* adequately." (Italics added.) In this case, petitioner breached his nondelegable duty to administer his trust account properly. . . . [Petitioner] was unable to prevent the fraud precisely because he failed to supervise his account.

"[Even] if petitioner's conduct were not wilful and dishonest, gross carelessness and negligence constitute a violation of an attorney's oath faithfully to discharge his duties and involve moral turpitude." *Jackson v. State Bar* (1979) 23 Cal. 3d 509. In *Palomo v. State Bar* (1984) 36 Cal. 3d 785, the attorney gave control of his client trust account to his office manager, and then failed to examine her records or the bank statements. We stated that the attorney's failure to supervise the management of the account, or to check the records, "permitted the fact that a substantial client check endorsed by him had been misdeposited, commingled and misappropriated to escape his notice for four months. . . . Any procedure so lax as to produce that result was grossly negligent."

Petitioner argues that the discipline recommended by the review department was unwarranted in light of factors in mitigation. Petitioner attached to his brief a letter from his psychiatrist, which states that he is "confident that the public will be protected since [petitioner] has been involved in therapy and has been stabilized on Lithium since October 1981." The letter was not presented in the proceedings below, however, and we conclude it is not properly before us for this purpose. . . . Even if we were to consider it, however, it would not significantly affect our evaluation of the appropriate discipline. . . . [E]motional or "psychological disability, while it may ameliorate the moral culpability of an attorney's misconduct, does not immunize him from disciplinary measures."

Petitioner's conduct, although it did not harm his clients, nonetheless warrants discipline. . . . Petitioner also argues restitution is inappropriate because he did not profit from his conduct. Although part of the rationale for requiring restitution may be to prevent an attorney from profiting from wrongdoing, restitution is also intended to compensate the victim, and to discourage dishonest and unprofessional conduct. We adopt the recommended discipline, and order that: (1) petitioner be suspended from the

EXHIBIT 3
(continued)

practice of law for two years; (2) execution of the suspension be stayed; and (3) petitioner be placed on probation for said two years on condition that he be actually suspended for the first ninety days of said probation, and that he comply with . . . further conditions . . . payment of restitution; filing of quarterly reports with the State Bar regarding his compliance and the status of his client trust accounts; and obtaining psychiatric or psychological help. We further order that petitioner take and pass the Professional Responsibility Examination within one year of the effective date of this order.

Exhibit 6-4
Manual Ledger Sheet

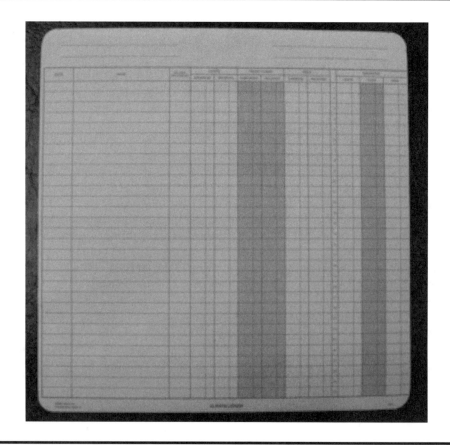

For More Information

Because trust accounts must balance to the penny, even regulatory boards encourage the use of software. The Minnesota Lawyers Professional Responsibility Board has a website that explains the use of Quicken in maintaining trust accounts. Visit it at http://www.mncourts.gov/lprb/Quicken%20Basic%202002%20color. htm.

Your firm may handle more than money for clients and has an obligation to safeguard all client property. If your firm has a safe in which it keeps client documents, evidence, or other property, it should be kept locked, and access should be limited. A log should record every time the safe is opened, who opened it, and what was removed or added. A similar log should be kept for petty cash.

If your firm does not have special software for performing accounting functions, you may have an alternative on your hard drive. Spreadsheets can be linked to accomplish multiple entries without duplication of effort. Spreadsheet templates can be developed for almost any area of practice. Some common law office applications include the following:

- **Present value** of **structured settlement**
- Value of workers' compensation claim
- Value of **retirement annuity** in estate planning or divorce
- Present value of future **lump sum** payment
- Contingent attorney's fees plus reimbursable expenses, court costs, etc.
- Value of closely held business
- Valuation of life estate, dower, and remainder interest
- **Amortization** schedules
- **RESPA** closing statement for real estate transactions
- Estate analysis
- Truth-in-Lending statement — annual percentage rate (APR) of a loan
- Value of lost earnings and wages
- Estate inventory and accounting
- Personal financial statement

present value
Value attached to money to change hands at some future date, discounted to account for the time value of money

structured settlement
Alternative to lump sum payment; financial or insurance company makes periodic payments

retirement annuity
Annual income

lump sum
A single payment that satisfies an obligation

amortization
Distribution of an amount into installments, so that it will be paid according to a schedule

RESPA
Real Estate Settlement Procedures Act

For More Information

If you are not already comfortable using spreadsheets, visit the University of Nebraska's Office of Undergraduates Studies site (http://www.unl.edu/ous/academic_ tips/instructions.shtml) and follow instructions for creating a spreadsheet to evaluate your own financial situation. This will help you too with a future assignment. There are many other excellent tutorials available. Try http://office.microsoft.com/ en-us/excel/FX100646961033.aspx or http://www.usd.edu/trio/tut/excel.

Assignment 6-1
Ethical Issues in Billing

1. Read the case summary (Exhibit 6-3) and discuss: Is it significant that the lawyer met Pollock the year after he was admitted to the bar? What might be an underlying reason for the lawyer's willingness to set up the account? If the situation had come to light before Pollock committed fraud using the account, could the lawyer have still been subject to discipline?

2. What's the big deal with commingling funds? Rules prohibiting commingling are obviously intended to prevent dishonest lawyers from borrowing or stealing client money. However, even in situations that appear harmless on the surface, commingling is prohibited and is a major cause of discipline. Discuss the following situations.

   a. Lawyer keeps a small amount of her own money in the trust account to cover bank charges. What if lawyer puts a large amount of money in the client funds account? Could there be any harm? Might lawyer be attempting to hide funds?
   b. Lawyer keeps client funds in a separate account, not labeled as a trust or escrow, but never uses the money. When clients become entitled to the money, it is promptly distributed to them. No harm done? Might the lawyer be trying to create an impression of having assets that are not hers? Why?
   c. Lawyer receives a check from an insurance company in settlement of a claim. The client has already agreed to the $60,000 settlement, in writing, and has agreed that the attorney is entitled to $23,000 in fees and costs. The attorney knows that the client is in desperate need of money and does not want the client to have to wait for the check to clear. The attorney knows that he has sufficient funds in his business account, so he deposits the check in that account and, before leaving the bank, writes a check for $37,000 to client and seals it in a stamped, addressed envelope, planning to mail it immediately. What problem could arise?

3. If you are able to do legal research, find a case from your state in which the court discusses separate billing for paralegal work in a fee reversal case.

4. In your state ethical rules, find the following:

   a. Which, if any, types of fee agreements are required to be in writing?
   b. Is there a prohibition on taking some types of cases on contingency? Is there a rule about calculation of contingency fees?
   c. Does your state have a rule prohibiting false statements about a lawyer's services? Might it apply to a "padded" bill? Does it require that legal fees be "reasonable"?
   d. Is there a list of approved institutions for client funds accounts? Are there rules concerning the title of such accounts? Are there rules

about how checks may be written from client accounts? Would it be permissible to write a check to "Cash"?

e. Are there rules about recordkeeping? Do the rules require an attorney to give the client notice when money is received for the client's account? What do the rules say about when disbursal must occur? Are there rules about how often accounts must be reconciled (balanced)? You may find these in a section concerning safekeeping of property.

f. Are there any rules concerning the refund of retainers? Are there any rules about notice the attorney must give the client before withdrawing fees and expenses?

g. What are the rules concerning handling interest on client funds? How is the IOLTA program administered?

h. Does your state have an audit program? If so, how much notice is given if an office is to be audited? Does the program have rules concerning whether the attorney must be present during an audit, which records must be made available to the auditor, or how many people visit the firm during an audit?

i. If your state has an online publication on handling client funds, download and print it for future reference.

---

3. Billing for Paralegal Time

Many lawyers have billed clients for paralegal work for years. Because the lawyer-client relationship is normally a contract with no court involvement, there were no standards for such billing; it was simply a matter of agreement between the lawyer and client. Clients were willing to agree because it resulted in a lower bill.

Example

Attorney Kappler charges $300/hour for her time; 50 percent of this is attributable to overhead (salary, benefits, etc.) and 50 percent is profit. Kappler charges $80/hour for services performed by her paralegal; 70 percent is overhead and 30 percent is profit.

If a client requests incorporation of a business, which will require 10 hours of work:

Kappler does the work alone: bill $3,000, profit to Kappler $1,500.
Kappler does 5 hours work, paralegal does 5 hours work: bill $1,900 (happier client!), profit $870.
Ah, but wait! Kappler has freed up 5 hours of her time, which she spends with another client at $300/hour, with a profit of $750, so Kappler has actually increased profit by using a paralegal.

A few years ago courts started to recognize the value of paralegals in **fee reversal** cases. In most cases in U.S. courts, each party pays her own lawyer; this is called the **American system**. There are exceptions: for example, in divorce and civil rights cases, a court often orders a party to pay the other party's fees. The court

fee reversal
Also called fee award; losing party pays winner's legal fees

American system
Each party pays own costs of litigation

Exhibit 6-5
Charges in Fee Reversal Cases

Some states have enacted statutes to make paralegal time billable in fee reversal cases:

(5 ILCS 70/1.35) (Illinois)

Sec. 1.35. Paralegal. "Paralegal" means a person who is qualified through education, training, or work experience and is employed by a lawyer, law office, governmental agency, or other entity to work under the direction of an attorney in a capacity that involves the performance of substantive legal work that usually requires a sufficient knowledge of legal concepts and would be performed by the attorney in the absence of the paralegal. A reference in an Act to attorney fees includes paralegal fees, recoverable at market rates.

In fee reversal cases, which are often subject to statutory guidelines, it is important to understand your state's restrictions on costs and expenses and keep careful records accordingly. California, for example, has the following statutory requirements:

California Code Civil Procedure §1033.5
1033.5. Items allowable as costs
(a) The following items are allowable as costs under Section 1032:
(1) Filing, motion, and jury fees.
(2) Juror food and lodging while they are kept together. . . .
(3) Taking, videotaping, and transcribing necessary depositions . . . and travel expenses to attend depositions.
(4) Service of process. . . .
(5) Expenses of attachment including keeper's fees.
(6) Premiums on necessary surety bonds.
(7) Ordinary witness fees pursuant to Section 68093 of the Government Code.
(8) Fees of expert witnesses ordered by the court.
(9) Transcripts of court proceedings ordered by the court.
(10) Attorney fees, when authorized by any of the following:
(A) Contract.
(B) Statute.
(C) Law.
(11) Court reporters fees as established by statute.

EXHIBIT 6-5
(continued)

(12) Models and blowups of exhibits and photocopies of exhibits may be allowed if they were reasonably helpful to aid the trier of fact.

(13) Any other item that is required to be awarded to the prevailing party pursuant to statute. . . .

(b) The following items are not allowable as costs, except when expressly authorized by law:

(1) Fees of experts not ordered by the court.

(2) Investigation expenses in preparing the case for trial.

(3) Postage, telephone, and photocopying charges, except for exhibits.

(4) Costs in investigation of jurors or in preparation for voir dire.

(5) Transcripts of court proceedings not ordered by the court.

(c) Any award of costs shall be subject to the following: . . .

(3) Allowable costs shall be reasonable in amount.

If a party paid an expert witness who was not ordered by the court, would the payment be recoverable under this statute? The answer is likely "no." *See United States Fiduciary & Guaranty Co. v. Scott Cos.*, 2007 U.S. Dist. LEXIS 71100 (D. Cal. Sept. 18, 2007)

must approve the bill and examines the lawyer's hourly rate as well as how many hours were billed before granting approval. Courts are not willing to approve high hourly rates or an unreasonable number of hours, so lawyers must try to control costs. One way is to use paralegals (see Exhibit 6-5). If the lawyer uses a paralegal but must absorb the cost of the paralegal as part of the overhead built in to her hourly rate, the bill will be lower and more likely to approved, but the lawyer's profit may not be great. If the lawyer uses a paralegal and can bill for the paralegal's time, the bill will be reasonable and the lawyer will make a fair profit.

Since the Supreme Court's 1989 decision in *Missouri v. Jenkins*, 491 U.S. 274, courts routinely approve awards in which paralegal time is billed on an hourly basis, rather than included as part of the lawyer's overhead expenses. Those awards have generally been at **market rate**, the hourly rate at which attorneys bill their own clients for paralegal services, including a profit for the attorney, rather than at **cost**, which covers only the attorney's overhead in employing the paralegal. The practice is so well accepted that in 1995 the Illinois legislature enacted a statute that states that an award of attorney's fees is to include paralegal fees.

market rate
Rate paid by private clients; includes profit

cost
Price actually paid

In 2008 the Supreme Court affirmed its position in *Jenkins*, addressing the limited issue of whether paralegal fees may be awarded at market rate, rather than at cost, in cases under the Equal Access to Justice Act (*Richlin Security Service Co. v. Chertoff*, http://www.supremecourtus.gov/opinions/07pdf/06-1717. pdf). The Court stated that "[i]t seems more plausible that Congress intended all 'fees and other expenses' to be recoverable at the litigant's 'reasonable cost,' subject to the proviso that 'reasonable cost' would be deemed to be 'prevailing market rates' when such rates could be determined."

Example

Fee reversal case requires 100 hours of work:

Lawyer A does all of the work by himself, submits bill of $20,000 (would result in 10,000 profit)—court not happy, cuts bill to $16,000. Nobody is happy.

Lawyer B does 70 hours work, and assigns 30 hours to paralegal. Submits bill of $14,000 (lawyer time only) (would result in only $5,000 profit; this lawyer has higher overhead because she must pay paralegal). Court very happy, lawyer less happy.

Lawyer C does 70 hours work and assigns 30 to paralegal. Submits bill of $14,000 for lawyer work, $1,800 for paralegal work—total $15,800, court is happy. Lawyer's profit on this case is $7,540, plus lawyer has freed 30 hours of time to devote to other cases for an additional $3,000 in profit. Everybody is happy!

If a court permits an attorney's fee award to include paralegal billing, it will determine whether the person who did the work is a paralegal and at what rate the work may be billed. Courts have stated that clerical workers do not qualify; the person must have special skills and the work done must be skilled, not clerical, in nature (see Exhibit 6-6). A court may ask a lawyer to prove that the paralegal is qualified; proof of formal education is very helpful.

4.   Tracking Time

Lawyers and paralegals (and, at some firms, other employees) keep track of their time for several reasons. If a case is being handled on an hourly basis, time records are used to prepare the bill. Even if the case is a flat fee or contingency matter, hours worked should be analyzed periodically to determine whether the arrangement is profitable to the firm at the fee being charged. In addition, your timesheets may be part of the employee evaluation process. The firm may consult these records to determine whether a particular employee is profitable. For this reason, you may wish to keep timesheets even if your employer does not require you to do so.

The quest for billable hours has taken a real toll on many lawyers and paralegals. While 1600 billable hours per year was once considered quite acceptable, associates at large firms are now routinely expected to bill more than 2000 hours per year. Do the math: 2000 divided by 50 weeks per year (assuming only two weeks off for vacation, holiday, sick days) equals 40 billable hours per week. Billing 40 hours a week is no small feat: lunch, breaks, time spent chatting with coworkers, time spent trying to figure out your printer or organizing your desk normally cannot be billed. Experts say that perhaps 70 to 80 percent of time at work is ethically billable.

Exhibit 6-6
What Is Paralegal Work?

Many courts state that fees are recoverable for substantive legal work that would otherwise have to be performed by a lawyer. *See, e.g., First Bank & Trust v. First State Bank*, 2000 U.S. App. LEXIS 33359 (10th Cir., Dec. 20, 2000). But exactly what that means is open to interpretation.

Taylor v. Chubb Group of Insurance Cos., 874 P.2d 806, 808-809 (Okla. 1994): The court specified tasks, including interviewing clients; drafting pleadings and other documents; conducting legal research; scheduling depositions; coordinating and managing document production; locating and interviewing witnesses; organizing pleadings, trial exhibits, and other documents; preparing witness and exhibit lists; and assisting lawyers at trial.

People Who Care v. Rockford Board of Education, 90 F.3d 1307, 1315 (7th Cir. 1996): "The district court refused to award [the law firm of Futterman & Howard (F & H)] its requested $75 paralegal rate for 1991 through 1994, although it did conclude that the rate was within the range charged by other Chicago law firms. The Board's rebuttal evidence on this issue took the form of an affidavit from Cathy Heath, a former Vice President of the Illinois Paralegal Association. Ms. Heath testified that while $75 was within the range of Chicago paralegal rates for those years, the median rate for Chicago paralegals was $53 per hour. She further testified that the work done by F&H paralegals on this case was not sufficiently complex to command a higher, $75 per hour rate. In her opinion, complex paralegal work consists of duties such as 'factual investigation, conducting legal research, summarizing depositions, checking citations, and compiling statistical and financial data.' The district court agreed with Ms. Heath's conclusion, noting that the paralegal work on this case consisted mostly of 'document preparation, coding and organizing.' Thus he awarded F & H $60 for each paralegal hour. . . . The only inquiry for requested paralegal fees should be whether the work was sufficiently complex to justify the efforts of a paralegal, as opposed to an employee at the next rung lower on the pay-scale ladder. With this focus in mind, it is unclear whether 'document preparation, coding and organizing' is reasonably considered paralegal work. On remand, if the court determines these tasks to be sufficiently complex to justify the services of a paralegal, as opposed to clerical staff, then it should have no problem in awarding paralegal rates."

Firms differ on whether non-billable hours should be recorded and whether the employee gets "credit" for such time. Non-billable hours are hours spent on work for which no client is billed: pro bono work, CLE seminars, and training on new equipment are non-billable. Non-billables are part of firm overhead, so firms are generally motivated to avoid lengthy staff meetings and other activities that cut into profit. Because firms differ on how they break down the hour (increments) and billing expectations, prospective employees should always ask how many hours they will be expected to bill annually and about the firm's policy on non-billable hours and have an idea of what is reasonable.

As you might imagine, billing can present many ethical issues. Lawyers are sometimes accused of "churning" hours or padding the bill. Some people "double bill." For example, a lawyer may argue three motions on one morning in court and bill all three clients for the time spent traveling to court. Some people bill for internal mistakes or inefficiency, for example, for time spent trying to find a missing file.

Keeping track of time is one of the more burdensome aspects of working in the legal field. How you do it is not as important as *that* you do it. Profit is lost and ethical problems arise when lawyers and paralegals try to recreate a day after the fact. Profit is also lost (and careers can be jeopardized) when a new paralegal or lawyer unilaterally decides to "cut" her own hours. People new to the field sometimes think, "I was way too slow on this; it took me four hours, but I am only going to record three." If you do that, you may be cheating your firm, which sets your billing rate with the expectation that you will need a learning curve but will also cover the overhead created by your position and generate a profit. The firm may analyze the costs and income attributable to each employee (billable hours minus salary, benefits, cost of office space) — this is sometimes called a **cost-of-chair** report. Low billable hours may affect salary increases, bonuses, promotions, and even continued employment.

The firm cannot generate income and pay its own expenses unless it bills its clients. Many firms, therefore, generate regular **delinquency reports** to identify lawyers and paralegals who have not turned in time records by due dates. Firms also generate **realization reports** to show what percentage of each lawyer or paralegal's time was billed (as opposed to being a write-off).

You may track your time directly on the software application your firm uses to generate the bill (described below), or you may keep your time in a different way and later enter it into the system used for billing.

In a future assignment, you will be asked to track the time you spend on schoolwork and generate a bill, so you may want to start tracking time now, breaking it down by class (client) and activity (in class, travel time, study group, reading, in library). To download a template that can be used for tracking time, visit http://office.microsoft.com/en-us/templates/TC011445011033.aspx or http://www.timemanagementforlawyers.com/articlesdownloads.

Some people keep paper timesheets (such as shown in Exhibit 6-7 or on the sites identified above) or a blank sheet of paper on their desks, on which they jot time and task as they work. Some keep a hand-held recorder nearby so that they can pick it up and quickly record: "11 a.m, Monday March 5, began review of Konstans lease of office space." An increasing number of legal professionals are using PDAs, which have time-tracking applications. In many cases, the PDA is compatible with the firm's accounting software so that an individual's records can be entered into the system that tracks time and generates billing for the entire firm. The ABA technology help comparison chart, http://www.abanet.org/tech/ltrc/charts/time-andbilling.html, shows compatibility between accounting software and PDAs.

If you find paper too cumbersome and your firm does not have special timekeeping software, there are likely several options already available in your computer's operating system. Try the following:

- Use a spreadsheet, as described in a future assignment.

---

cost-of-chair
Analyzes costs and income attributable to employee

delinquency reports
Identifies those late in submitting time records

realization reports
Show percentage of time billed

Exhibit 6-7
Time Slip

Many small firms still use paper timesheets. Paper timesheets generally record information shown in the example and create two copies: one for billing and one for employee records.

Lawyer/paralegal ___LAV_____ Date __4/3/09_____   File # _08 PI 756_____
Client Name _Stateco Insurance_____   Time ____4_._5___ hours
Activity: ___phone   ___meeting   ___court   ___research   _X__drafting

Description: Drafted interrogatories and a request to produce to Plaintiff, specifically discovery to determine preexisting injuries as related to plaintiff's injuries from this accident. It appears that there was prior surgery and many ER visits with requests for narcotics.

Consider the description, which was drafted to communicate to the client the value of the service provided. Remember, however, that billing records may be audited and should never include confidential information.

- If you have Microsoft Office, you can use the Tasks function, which will also track expenses and mileage. If you create a to-do list at the beginning of each day, you can tie the list to tracking time. For complete instructions, visit Microsoft Office Online, http://office.microsoft.com/en-us/outlook/HA012263961033.aspx.
- Keep the Windows Notepad application open on your computer at all times, minimizing it when not in use. (You can access Notepad by going to the Start menu, selecting Programs, and then Accessories.) The F5 key is a permanent time-date stamp that will capture the times you start and end tasks. Some people prefer this because when you are using the time-date stamp function in Word, you can accidentally update the time-date too easily.

Tips for Tracking Time

Depending on your style of work and the software applications your firm has:

- Use standard codes for commonly performed tasks. However you track your time, keep the paper, recorder, PDA, or other device close at hand so that you are not tempted to skip an entry rather than look for it. Keep a clock in a spot where it is easy to see.
- Note both start and end times; do not assume that the end time for one task is the start time for another.
- Keep in mind the difference between the billable hour and the actual hour. While double billing is unethical, it is possible to ethically bill more than

an hour in an hour's time. For example, if your firm bills in 6-minute increments, and you return 12 phone calls, ranging from 3 minutes to 6 minutes in length, it might be possible to bill 1.2 hours in the span of an hour.

- If you are easily distracted, consider using a stopwatch.
- Whenever you enter your time into the system that will generate the bill, remember that your description of your work may affect how the client feels about the fairness of the bill.

Many firms now invest in software so that the time-tracking records of individuals are automatically processed into bills for clients. Some firms use accounting software, such as QuickBooks, which is not specific to law offices, but does track time, manages payment of bills and accounts receivable, generates some financial reports and tax forms. Many of these programs have optional payroll applications. Larger firms tend to use dedicated law firm software, such as Timeslips, Timematters, Tabs3, Billing Matters, Juris, Abacus, or PCLaw. If your firm does not have dedicated time-billing software, it may use the spreadsheet program that is part of its computers' operating systems.

For an idea of how one paralegal chose to track his time, see Exhibit 6-8.

Exhibit 6-8
A Week in the Life of Lou Vincennes, Paralegal

Lou was hired last year as a transactional paralegal for sole practitioner Jill Bazos. Jill told Lou to track time, but because the firm did not have dedicated software, they used paper time slips. Lou prefers to avoid paper and decided to use a spreadsheet. Lou developed a system of client codes. For example, RKW 4 is client R.K. Warner, matter number 4 (sale of residence). Lou also developed activity codes: 1=telephone; 2=meeting; 3=travel; 4=document review; 5=document drafting; 6=legal research; 7=file management; 8=factual research; 9=title search; 10=other. For the first week, Lou simply entered client, date, time, and activity, moving from task to task throughout the day. At the end of the week, Lou realized that by selecting the cell at the bottom of the Time column and pushing just one key (the "auto sum" key Σ) it was possible to track all of his billable hours:

Client	Date	Time	Activity
ABG-1	3/9/09	1.2	4 final draft of lease
RKW4	3/9/09	0.4	5 closing documents
ELW	3/9/09	0.2	1 client
ABG-1	3/9/09	0.4	3 to tenant office
ABG-1	3/9/09	2.5	2 client and tenant
ABG-1	3/9/09	0.4	3 return to office

EXHIBIT 6-8
(continued)

Firm	3/9/09	1.0	2 Ms. Jones re new hire
RKW4	3/9/09	1.4	1 title company closing figures and final docs
ELW	3/10/09	0.3	10 online reservation of LLC name
Firm	3/10/09	1.1	1 interview receptionist candidate
BAT-2	3/10/09	2.0	6 constructive eviction
RKW4	3/11/09	1.0	10 assembled and mailed client copies closing docs
BAT-2	3/11/09	0.4	2 Attorney Bazos review research
BAT-2	3/11/09	0.2	1 client re constructive eviction
Firm	3/11/09	0.3	1 offered job to J. Schulze, sent letter
JEL	3/11/09	1.0	2 new client condominium conversion, 140 Wood, Springdale
JEL	3/11/09	1.0	7 opened file on condominium conversion, conflict check
ELW	3/11/09	0.7	1 client wants to change LLC name
ELW	3/11/09	0.5	1 secretary of state re new name selection
JEL	3/12/09	0.5	1 with surveyor and title company
JEL	3/12/09	1.1	5 identified forms for condo docs, sent to Bazos
Firm	3/12/09	2.0	10 trained new receptionist
ELW	3/12/09	1.6	5 final LLC documents sent
RM	3/12/09	0.4	3 to seller's attorney's office
RM	3/12/09	1.2	2 closing purchase of 560 Manchester
RM	3/12/09	0.4	3 return to office
JEL	3/12/09	1.0	2 client & Bazos re conversion timetable and notice to tenants
JEL	3/13/09	1.2	5 draft notice to tenants
RM	3/13/09	1.0	10 assembled and mailed client copy closing docs
BAT2	3/13/09	0.5	2 transferred file to JLB for litigation
Firm	3/13/09	1.5	2 CLE presentation at bar association
MEM	3/13/09	2.0	2 new client, opening real estate sales office
		33.9	

Lou's timesheet is a journal, a chronological record. But Lou is also responsible for billing and must create a separate record for each client account. Although he is no whiz at using spreadsheets, Lou knew it would be simpler if he got the program to calculate the amount owed by each client, so he added a formula to multiply his hours by his billing rate of $90/hour. He accomplished this by adding a new column with the formula (C2*90) in the first cell and dragging the formula down. Next, he highlighted the client

EXHIBIT 6-8
(continued)

column and hit the Sort command to group all billings by client, for easy assembly of bills. Here's how it looked for two clients:

ABG-1	3/9/2009	1.2	4-final draft lease	108
ABG-1	3/9/2009	0.4	3-to tenant office	36
ABG-1	3/9/2009	2.5	2-client & tenant	225
ABG-1	3/9/2009	0.4	3-return to office	36
BAT-2	3/10/2009	2.0	6-constructive eviction	180
BAT-2	3/11/2009	0.4	2-Attorney Bazos, review research	36
BAT-2	3/11/2009	0.2	1-client, re constructive eviction	18
BAT-2	3/13/2009	0.5	2-transfer file to JLB for litigation	45

To generate bills, Lou simply developed a template that explained the activity codes and highlighted the relevant portions of the spreadsheet for pasting into the client's bill:

JILL BAZOS
Attorney at Law
51 Center Street
Bevent, IL 60201
(312) 555-1212

STATEMENT
March 31, 2009

Alpha Beta Gamma Corp.
6701 15th Street
Bevent, IL 60201

MATTER: Lease of 17th Street Warehouse
Timekeeper: Paralegal L. Vincennes:

3/9/2009	1.2	4-final draft lease	108
3/9/2009	0.4	3-to tenant office	36
3/9/2009	2.5	2-client & tenant	225
3/9/2009	0.4	3-return to office	36

Codes:

1=telephone; 2=meeting; 3=travel; 4=document review; 5=document drafting; 6=legal research; 7=file management; 8=factual research; 9=title search; 10=other.

Timekeeper: J. Bazos . . .
Total

Payment Terms . . .

About the enclosed disk:

Tabs3 is a popular integrated system that allows users to handle multiple administrative functions without making multiple entries or using different systems. When a new client is entered into an integrated system:

- Contact information is entered into an "address book" type of application.
- Information about opposing parties is entered and run through an application that checks for conflicts of interest.
- Important dates are entered into a centralized calendar application, so that alerts are triggered.
- A billing profile is set up so that as timekeepers enter their time and expenses, they are added to the client's balance at rates set for the client. The system can automatically generate bills according to the agreement with the client. The system can also report the productivity of each timekeeper.
- The client's billing account is tied to the firm's business account; the firm can generate reports concerning receivables, revenue, assets, and liabilities.
- A "ledger" is set up for the client's trust account.
- Bills can be paid from the business and trust accounts; many systems will even handle payroll accounting.
- Many systems will hold and organize client documents.

The disk is enclosed so that you can become familiar with what these systems can do, not to make you an expert user of a particular system. The likelihood that your employer will use the same software and that it will not have changed is very small, but if you know what these systems can do and are in the habit of keeping careful records of your time, expenses, dates, and other important information, you will be able to work with the system in any office.

If you will be using the disk for assignments, you must first load it to your computer. Answer NO when asked whether you want to load sample data and when asked whether you want to create icons. This will allow you to work with "blank" templates. From your Start menu, select the Tabs3 multimedia tutorials and watch the tutorials for the sections relevant to your assignments. If you have trouble with the disk or simply prefer a print version of the training, visit http://www.tabs3.com/support/docs.html.

From the Tabs3 tutorials:

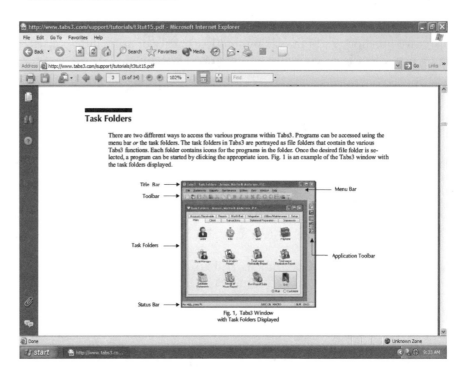

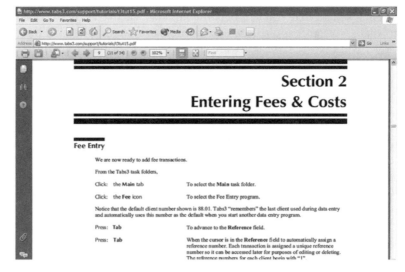

Assignment 6-2
Tracking Time and Billings

1. The purpose of this assignment is to get you in the habit of tracking and recording time and to make you aware of the features available on dedicated time-billing software. If you use time-billing software for the assignment, you need not use all of the "bells and whistles" or become an expert user. Complete one of the following assignments.

a. Explore the websites for some of the dedicated law office time-billing software discussed in this chapter. If a free trial is available, you may use any program to track the time you devote to each of your classes for the next 30 days. Make each class you are taking a client. Your tasks may include attending class, travel, library time, reading and studying, and group work. You may create codes, as done by Lou Vincennes in Exhibit 6-8. At the end of the month, print or e-mail a bill for each class.

b. If you were not able to locate a free sample of dedicated time-billing software, create a spreadsheet and, for the next two weeks, keep time for the classes you are currently taking. Each class is a "client," and your tasks may include attending class, travel, library time, reading and studying, and group work. You may create codes, as done by Lou Vincennes in Exhibit 6-8.

c. Use the TABS3 disk included with this book to track your time as follows:
   1. Watch the tutorial sections on setting up timekeepers.
   2. Starting in the Task folders, click the Setup tab, and establish your account as a timekeeper (see Screenshot A). You will be given a number with your name and initials; assign yourself level 4, paralegal.
   3. You may want to establish three billing rates: e.g., 200 for time in class, 150 for travel time, and 225 for time spent on homework or studying.
   4. Click the Tcode ("transaction code") tab and note the codes available.
   5. Create a client for each class (see Screenshot B). Start by clicking the Client tab in the Task folders. Use your instructor's name and contact information.
   6. Take note of all the features you aren't using: the ability to enter costs, to set flat fees for value billing, etc.
   7. Now start keeping time by clicking the Transactions tab, and then Fee Entry icon (see Screenshot C).
   8. At the end of the month, click the Statements tab in the Task folder, and then generate statements to print a "bill" for each client. Note that you have to select a printer, even before you preview a statement.

Screenshot A: Setting up a timekeeper (Note: You can always get back to the Task folder by clicking the icon on the toolbar.)

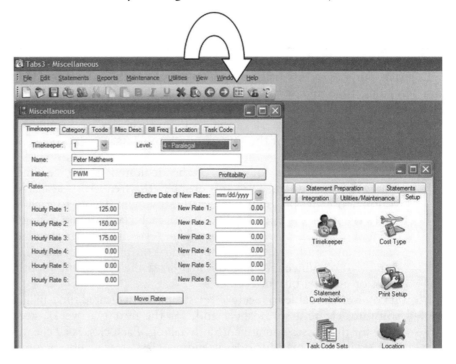

Screenshot B: Setting up a client

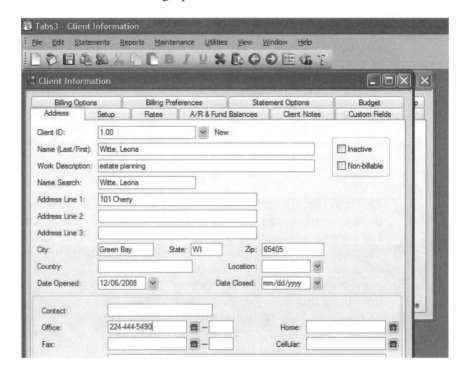

Screenshot C: Entering time

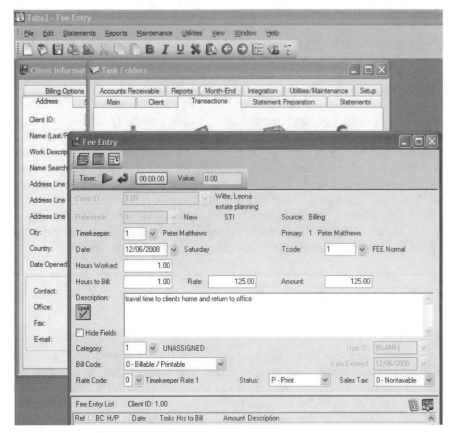

Management Portfolio

2. Now that you have explored some of the dedicated time-billing software on the market, imagine that your firm wants to purchase such software. You must research the options. The firm wants a single program that will handle time and billing, escrow accounts, and accounts payable. It should record payments to vendors, such as payment of utility bills, and should have a check-writing feature. In addition to tracking billable time for hourly, contingent, and flat-fee matters, the program should be able to create reports for individual lawyers and paralegals. The program should help prepare mandatory IRS filings. Because each lawyer has her own way of keeping time, the program must be compatible with other programs and PDAs. Prepare a chart in which you compare the features of three available software programs. A good starting point is the ABA Legal Technology Resource Center (http://www.abanet.org/tech/ltrc).

3. Determine whether your state has an arbitration system for clients who dispute lawyers' bills. If you cannot find the information on the website for the body that regulates lawyers in your state, start at http://www.abanet.org/cpr/clientpro/2006_fee_arb_survey.html.

4. Using any search engine, enter the search term *audit legal fees* and find a website for a company that audits legal fee billings.

Management Portfolio

5. Rodan & Stosh has a growing estate planning and probate practice with two paralegals. The paralegals have been complaining that they want more substantive work. Specifically, they would like to be given an opportunity to draft wills and trusts. The partner managing the team rejects their requests, saying that the firm makes more money when lawyers do that kind of work. You don't believe that is true. Most wills are billed at a flat fee of $600; complicated trusts are billed on an hourly basis. Write a short memo to attorney Amin Khan, explaining how profit could actually be increased by delegating more work. Use material in this chapter and this article: Joyce McGuiney & Lynn Grassby, *Managing for Profitability*, Prof. Legal Mgmt. Week Mag., 2008, *available at* http://www.plmw.org/ala_resources/plmwissue_08/PLMWMagazine2008-IPMA.pdf.

---

5. Billing

Clients who are not surprised or confused by their bills are more likely to pay them. To avoid surprising the client, a law firm should have and follow strict policies about how often bills are sent and expectations concerning payment. The client should be made aware of these policies, in writing, at the beginning of the relationship and in each statement. The monthly statement, which can be sent in the same mailing as the monthly accounting for the client's funds in the trust account, should clearly state how payment is to be made and the rate of interest that is charged on past-due balances. The law firm should ensure that it complies with its own policies. It should not, for example, apply a new fee structure to an ongoing client without first obtaining a new agreement.

The attorney responsible for the relationship with the client may want to review the bill before it is mailed. If the attorney believes that the bill is not fair or will be a shock to the client, he may want to make an adjustment or contact the client with an explanation.

The attorney will also want to ensure that the level of detail is sufficient to satisfy the client. Some sophisticated business clients have policies concerning the level of detail they require in billing. A law firm that wants the client's business will comply with those policies. Even a less-sophisticated legal client is unlikely to be satisfied with seeing that she is paying $700 for "review of file." As more clients also have their legal fees audited, detailed billing will become only more important.

Example

This example comes from the *ABA Journal*, March 2008:

> A Pennsylvania judge has ordered a small practitioner to pay a $5.2 million judgment, including $1 million in punitive damages, for charging unlawful

attorney fees while collecting delinquent municipal and school district property taxes. Ruling in an unjust enrichment case, Judge Mark Bernstein of the Court of Common Pleas held last week that Portnoff Law Associates had intentionally overcharged homeowners being foreclosed upon, reports the *Legal Intelligencer* in an article reprinted in *New York Lawyer*.

Because of the firm's "intentional disregard of the rule of law," Bernstein wrote, $1 million in punitive damages was merited in the class action case, in addition to a $500,000 penalty. He also is requiring the firm to pay $2,654,972.98 to reimburse unlawful attorney fees; $510,855 for unlawfully collected administrative fees; $18,493.55 in interest; and an undetermined amount of plaintiffs attorney fees.

"This cavalier attitude toward keeping the money of citizens whose homes have been sold and are entitled by law to the proceeds of the sale cannot possibly be considered mistake, misunderstanding of appellate decision or vain hope of reversal," Bernstein says in a written opinion. "This can only be considered a knowing and intentional decision to unlawfully retain improperly obtained funds."

Martha Neil, *Small Pa. Law Firm Hit With $5.2M Overbilling Judgment*, ABA J., Mar. 17, 2008, *available at* http://abajournal.com/news/small_pa_law_firm_hit_with_52m_overbilling_judgment.

6. Collecting

The agreement with the client should make clear the firm's policies about interest on unpaid balances and about whether the firm might withdraw for non-payment. In addition to having a clear agreement and carefully screening clients, the firm has to send bills in a timely fashion in keeping with the cycles by which other bills are paid. Even if the amount is small, send the bill. Sending bills late communicates the message that the firm is willing to finance the case.

When the client does not comply with the agreement, the first step is communication with the client. Unpaid balances should not be ignored in hopes that the client will pay; the longer the account is unpaid, the more likely the client will conclude that the firm does not need or perhaps does not deserve payment. Even firms that appropriately screen clients, send timely bills, and follow up on unpaid balances have write-offs of about 7 percent of their billings; once a **receivable** has been unpaid for three months, the write-off rate jumps to 30 percent.[2] So, how can you follow up? Some firms use follow-up letters. Other firms prefer telephone contact, which should include several non-confrontational inquiries:

receivable
Funds earned but not yet received

1. Have you received the invoice? This forces the client to admit that it was received. If the client says it was not received, ask to check the address and send another copy immediately. After one week, if no payment is received, contact the client again.
2. Do you understand the invoice or have any questions? If a client has questions or says he does not understand, tell the client you will have the lawyer call immediately with an explanation.

---

[2]Helen Gunnarsson, *Don't Be Afraid to Be Paid*, 96 Ill. B. J. 559 (Nov. 2008).

3. Are there any problems with the service being provided? If the answer is yes, tell the client you will have the lawyer call immediately to answer any questions.
4. If the client has received the invoice and has no questions or problems: When can we expect payment? Make note of the date and follow up if payment is not received.
5. Do not accept vague statements like "I'll see what I can do." Make certain the client gives a specific action that is going to be taken. If possible, it should include the amount to be paid and when.
6. If the promise for payment is to take more than a few days, send a short note indicating the amount to be paid and when.

If communication with the client is not sufficient, however, and a balance remains unpaid, the firm may consider withdrawing from the case. Before doing so, the firm must consider the ethical rules concerning withdrawal. In many situations, non-payment alone is not a sufficient basis for withdrawal. ABA Model Rule 1.6 requires that the lawyer consider whether:

(1) withdrawal can be accomplished without material adverse effect on the interests of the client; . . .
(5) the client fails substantially to fulfill an obligation to the lawyer regarding the lawyer's services and has been given reasonable warning that the lawyer will withdraw unless the obligation is fulfilled;
(6) the representation will result in an unreasonable financial burden on the lawyer or has been rendered unreasonably difficult by the client; or
(7) other good cause for withdrawal exists.
(c) A lawyer must comply with applicable law requiring notice to or permission of a tribunal when terminating a representation. When ordered to do so by a tribunal, a lawyer shall continue representation notwithstanding good cause for terminating the representation.
(d) Upon termination of representation, a lawyer shall take steps to the extent reasonably practicable to protect a client's interests, such as giving reasonable notice to the client, allowing time for employment of other counsel, surrendering papers and property to which the client is entitled and refunding any advance payment of fee or expense that has not been earned or incurred. The lawyer may retain papers relating to the client to the extent permitted by other law.

If the firm's own efforts to collect the balance are not successful, the firm may have to turn the account over to a collections agency or resort to litigation. Although lawyers have historically been reluctant to take such action and clients sometimes retaliate by charging the lawyer with malpractice or an ethical violation, lawyers are entitled to collect reasonable fees.

We conclude that a strict prohibition on the collection of fees, such as the one announced by the trial court, would have the unintended effect of undermining rather than strengthening public policy. The plain language of Canon 2 states that the legal profession has a duty to make counsel available, and limiting an attorney's ability to collect fees from disgruntled and recalcitrant clients would serve to discourage members of the profession from taking on cases unless payment is made in advance. Furthermore, EC 2-16 recognizes that "[t]he legal profession cannot remain a viable force in fulfilling its role in our society unless its members receive adequate compensation for services rendered, and reasonable fees should be charged in appropriate cases to clients able to pay them." Here, there was no question raised as to whether defendant was unable to pay; he simply refused to do so. Lawyers "should not be left helpless when they render valuable service and confront an alternative of a write-off or a suit."

Swanson & Lange v. Miner, 159 Vt. 327, 333 (1992).

Some lawyers wait until an unpaid bill has aged past the statute of limitations for malpractice and then send a letter telling the client that the firm has no alternative but to forgive the debt and send the client an IRS Form 1099 showing the value of services as income to the client!

7. Paying Bills

In paying bills, the top priority is to maintain a good reputation for your firm. As bills come in, they should be time-stamped and the terms of payment should be noted to ensure that the account does not go past due.

In most firms, only one person has authority to actually sign checks. Another person or even several people may prepare checks for signature, depending on how the firm divides its functions. In general it is best to have as few people as possible actually preparing and recording checks. If more people are involved with the account, it is more likely that a mistake will be made; a check may be issued but not recorded or a bill may go unpaid. On the other hand, it is a good idea to have a second person involved in balancing the account, to provide some oversight. When the account is balanced, it is important to note any checks that have not been presented for payment; those checks may have been misdirected and the payee may be wondering why the firm has not paid its bill.

Those who do not have access to the checking account may, in some cases, have to submit a **check request form** to obtain payment of an expense for which there is no bill. If a check is to be issued to a **payee** that is not a business **entity**, the firm should obtain a federal identification number, such as a Social Security or employer identification number, from the payee.

If the firm is reimbursing an employee for expenses such as cab fare, business-related meals, or attendance at conferences, the employee should be required to supply receipts to ensure that the firm is able to take tax deductions. If the firm is paying expenses that are billed out to clients, such as use of an outside courier or copy service, the person responsible for the account should make sure that the expense is added to the client's bill.

check request form
Form used to request that authorized person issue a check

payee
The person to whom payment is made

entity
A "being," such as a corporation or a limited liability company

Assignment 6-3
Maintaining Bank Records

On February 2, client Pat McNerney gave the firm a check for $5,000 for representation in her pending divorce. On February 27, the firm issued itself a check for $3,200 for fees earned during the previous month and a check to pay the costs of service of process. The transactions were reflected in: The Lawyer Trust Account Checkbook Register (along with other transactions in this pooled account)

Elgin State Bank Trust Account 14766-2

Check Number	Date	Payee or Deposit Source	Explanation	Check Amount	Deposit Amount	Balance
	1/31/09	Balance-month end				$30,600
	2/2/09	P. McNerney	09-D-97		$5,000	$35,600
	2/4/09	Pet Mart (partnership issue)	08-C-131		$2,000	$37,600
4388	2/13/09	Loni Mecum, Court reporter	08-D-65	$ 290		$37,310
4389	2/13/09	Circuit Clerk filing fee	09-D-43	$ 365		$36,945
	2/16/09	R. Kowalczyk	09-D-98		$5,000	$41,945
4390	2/27/09	Process Service Inc.	09-D-97	$ 200		$41.745
4391	2/27/09	FIRM — earned fees	09-D-97	$3,200		$38,545
	2/28/09	Balance-month end				$38,545

And in the Lawyer Individual Trust Account Ledger for this client:

Name of Client or Third Party: Pat McNerney
Legal Matter: Dissolution of Marriage
File No.   09-D-97

Date	Description	Check No.	Paid	Received	Balance
2/2/09	Retainer			$5,000	$5,000
2/27/09	Costs: service of process	4390	$ 200		$4,800
2/27/09	Fees	4391	$3,200		$1,600

At the end of the month, the firm totals all of the individual trust accounts:

Individual Trust Ledger Trial Balance
2/1/09 — 2/28/09

Client	Balance 2/28/09
Bailey, Y	$ 1,200
Fredricksen	$ 5,000
Garrity, J	$ 1,860
Kowalczyk, R	$ 5,000
McNerney, P	$ 1,600
PetMart	$ 2,000
Roberts, W	$ 1,790
Stern, L	$10,095
Tomlinsen Trust	$10,000
Trial Balance Total	$38,545

All of the individual accounts must add up to the balance in the pooled account.

The firm will receive a statement from its bank like this one:

ELGIN STATE BANK
920 SUMMIT AVENUE
ELGIN, IL 60120

Rodan & Stosh
Attorneys at Law
IOLTA Acct.
325 River Road
Elgin, IL 60120

Account: 14766-2

Opening Balance	Deposits	Interest	Withdrawals & Checks	Charges	Closing Balance
$30,600.00	$12,000.00	$20.41	$ 670.30	$0	$41,950.11

Deposits

2/2/09	$5,000.00
2/4/09	$2,000.00
2/16/09	$5,000.00

Withdrawals

2/2/09   Interest Paid to IL IOLTA for January 2009 $15.30

Checks

Item	Date	Amount
4388	2/17/09	$290.00
4389	2/19/09	$365.00

Next, the firm has to reconcile the bank statement (which does not reflect two checks that had not been presented as of the closing date for the month) against its own records:

Reconciliation

Trust Acct. 14766-2

Checkbook Balance	$38,545.00
Balance of Individual Ledgers	$38,545.00
Bank Statement Balance 2/28/09	$41,950.11
Plus outstanding deposits	0
Plus service charge	0
Plus IOLTA withdrawal	$15.30
Less outstanding checks	($ 3,400.00)
Less interest accrued	($20.41)
Adjusted Balance	$38,545.00

Management Portfolio

Prepare the checkbook ledgers for both the business and pooled trust accounts for Rodan & Stosh for March, using the samples as a starting point. You should also continue the individual ledger page for client McNerney, do a trial balance of the individual clients in the pooled account, and do a reconciliation of the pooled trust account based on the bank statement at the end of this assignment. For the firm's business account, assume an opening balance of $4,321, with no outstanding checks, withdrawals, or deposits.

What happened in March:

3/2	Roberts check for $2,000 to replenish retainer received and deposited
3/3	Stern case settles. Check 4392 to firm for $2,000 for fees earned, return balance of retainer to client (ck 4393)
3/3	Withdraw $100 for petty cash
3/6	Ck 6987 to Axelson Services for payroll, $2538.51

3/12	McNerney delivers check for $1,500 for additional retainer
3/13	Checks: 6988 Midwest Power (electric) $161.56; 6989 LAV mobile phone and landlines $154; 6990 Landlord, Inc. $1,200, rent; 4394 $300 to court reporter (McNerney case); 4395 $295 to circuit clerk, filing fees Kowalczyk
3/15	Deposit $850, ck rcvd from client Jones for real estate work billed last month
3/17	Withdraw $100, petty cash
3/20	Check 6991 to Axelson Services for payroll, $2538.51
3/23	Tomlinsen trust receives $5,000 income
3/25	Ck 4392 to Dr. Hirsch for review of Roberts medical records and examination, $1,100
3/30	Settlement check arrives for Roberts: $180,000
3/31	Deposit checks to firm for earned fees: 4397 $800 Kowalczyk; 4398 $1,700 McNerney; 4399 $600 PetMart; 4400 $1,400 Garrity; 4401 $900 Bailey. Ck 4402 to Roberts returns the balance remaining in client's trust account. Also, ck 4403 to pay to tuition on behalf of Tomlinsen beneficiary $4,300.

Let's assume that the Roberts case was taken on a contingency basis and that the trust account funds covered only costs. Why do we not see a check for $120,000 to client Roberts and for $60,000 to the firm?

From the bank, at the end of March:

ELGIN STATE BANK
920 SUMMIT AVENUE
ELGIN, IL 60120

Rodan & Stosh
Attorneys at Law
IOLTA Acct.
325 River Road
Elgin, IL 60120

Account: 14766-2

Opening Balance	Deposits	Interest	Withdrawals & Checks	Charges	Closing Balance
$41,950.11	$188,500.00	$ 17.65	$ 15,210.41	$0	$215,257.35

Deposits
3/2	$2,000.00
3/12	$1,500.00
3/23	$5,000.00
3/31	$180,000.00

Withdrawals
3/2/   Interest Paid to IL IOLTA for February 2009 $20.41

Checks

Item	Date	Amount
4390	3/2	$ 200.00
4391	3/2	$3,200.00
4392	3/3	$2,000.00
4393	3/6	$8,095.00
4394	3/16	$ 300.00
4395	3/17	$ 295.00
4396	3/27	$1,100.00

ELGIN STATE BANK
920 SUMMIT AVENUE
ELGIN, IL 60120

Rodan & Stosh
Attorneys at Law
325 River Road
Elgin, IL 60120

Account: 14766-1

Opening Balance	Deposits	Interest	Withdrawals & Checks	Charges	Closing Balance
$4,321.00	$8,250.00	$ 3.86	$ 6,792.58	$0	$5,782.28

Deposits
3/3 $2,000.00
3/17 $ 300.00
3/31 $5,400.00

Withdrawals
3/3 $ 100.00
3/17 $ 100.00

Checks

Item	Date	Amount
6987	3/16	$2,538.51
6988	3/16	$ 161.56
6989	3/17	$ 154.00
6990	3/17	$1,200.00
6991	3/23	$2,538.51

Assignment 6-4
Using Tabs3 Trust Accounting Software

- To enter the trust accounting software, click the second icon from the top on the right side of your Tabs3 screen.
- Next, click the Setup tab and establish a pooled funds bank account by clicking the Bank Account tab (Screenshot D).
- Set up a trust account within the pooled account for each of the following clients (Screenshot E) and initial deposits as of today:

Client	Initial Deposit
Bailey, Y	$ 1,200
Fredricksen	$ 5,000
Garrity, J	$ 1,860
Kowalczyk, R	$ 5,000
McNerney, P	$ 1,600
PetMart	$ 2,000
Roberts, W	$ 1,790
Stern, L	$10,095
Tomlinsen Trust	$10,000

- Now, choose which of the following transactions apply to the trust accounts and enter them by clicking Checks and Deposits from the Task folders within trust accounting (Screenshot F).
- From the TAS Tasks folder, select client trust ledger. Select your pooled account from the pull-down menu (bank acct #) and select a date range. Print the ledger for your pooled account.

Roberts check for $2,000 to replenish retainer received and deposited
Stern case settles. Check 4392 to firm $2,000 for fees earned, return balance of retainer to client (ck 4393)
Withdraw $100 for petty cash
Check 6987 to Axelson Services for payroll, $2538.51

McNerney delivers check for $1,500 for additional retainer
Checks: 6988 Midwest Power (electric) $161.56; 6989 LAV mobile phone $154; 6990 Landlord, Inc. $1,200, rent; 4394 $300 court reporter (McNerney); 4395 $295 to circuit clerk, filing fees Kowalczyk
Deposit $850, ck rcvd from client Jones for real estate work billed last month
Withdraw $100, petty cash
Check 6991 to Axelson Services for payroll, $2538.51
Tomlinsen trust receives $5,000 income
Ck 4392 to Dr. Hirsch for review of Roberts medical records and examination, $1,100
Settlement check arrives for Roberts: $180,000
Deposit checks to firm for earned fees: 4397 $800 Kowalczyk; 4398 $1,700 McNerney; 4399 $600 PetMart; 4400 $1,400 Garrity; 4401 $900 Bailey. Ck 4402 to Roberts returns the balance remaining in client's trust acct. Also, ck 4403 to pay to tuition on behalf of Tomlinsen beneficiary $4,300.

Screenshot D

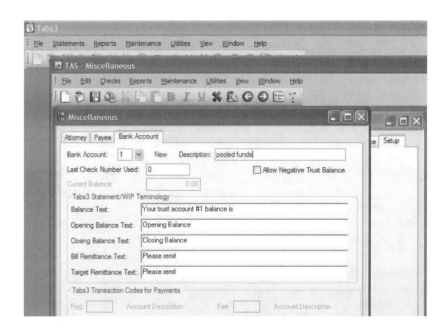

Screenshot E

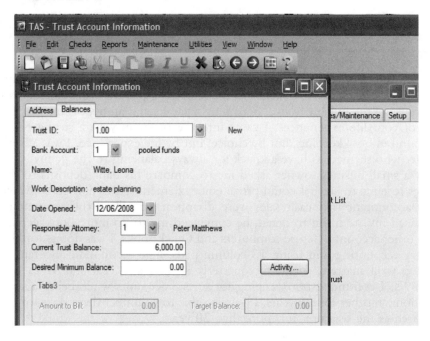

Screenshot F

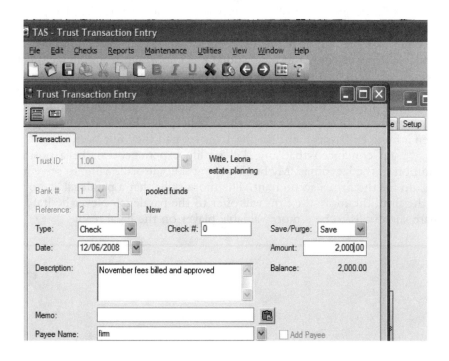

Out There—Paralegal Profile

Nancy Pickens is a paralegal with a midsized suburban firm and enjoys having special skills that make her valuable to a private firm that survives because of the billable hour. "Becoming a paralegal is an opportunity to use all of your life experiences. I came into the program with a strong background in bookkeeping, not by choice, but by life experience. I was a bank teller who seemed to have a knack for always balancing to the penny. One day a small business owner asked me to compare his bank deposits to the sales receipts to see if I could prove embezzlement. I was able to convince his accountant that cash sales were disappearing. When this accountant noticed my attention to detail, he convinced me to do more bookkeeping for other accounts. Before computers and QuickBooks, I was doing double-entry accounting and using 13-column pads. The accountant also taught me payroll matters, including quarterly reports and year-end W-2s and 1099's. I continued bookkeeping for several accounts while being a stay-at-home mother for ten years. I was also able to volunteer these skills for my church as the treasurer for more than 20 years."

"Although most bookkeeping for an attorney involves billing time and expenses, there are situations where a deeper knowledge of bookkeeping is beneficial. For example, there was a client who needed to document expenses for development of a property that would be considered as part of the sales price. This client offered receipts that included refundable deposits on equipment rental, as if they were an expense. Understanding that refundable deposits could not be included was important in stating legitimate costs. This client also submitted proof of a cash draw from a line of credit. The funds might have paid for some expenses, but just showing the draw would not prove to a valid expense, as it could also have paid for a vacation. Clients do not always understand these concepts. These errors could have been a huge embarrassment for the attorney had they not been caught."

"I am convinced that any skill or life experience can be a positive addition to the law office. My bookkeeping skills also allow me to serve as a backup for the firm's accountant. The more skills that a paralegal can offer to the firm, the more the firm will offer to the paralegal. Never hesitate to share such skills to be a more valuable player on the legal team."

Chapter Review

Discussion Questions

1. In what two places must every client funds account transaction be recorded?
2. What special rules govern contingency fee arrangements?
3. What is commingling? Passive commingling?
4. What is meant by fee reversal, and how has it made hiring paralegals more valuable to lawyers?
5. Explain how a lawyer can increase profits by having a paralegal do work that otherwise would be done by the lawyer.
6. Identify some "best practices" in tracking your time.
7. Identify some of the reports a law firm might create to assess its financial situation.
8. Identify the types of retainers.
9. What is an IOLTA account?
10. What information might you need to set up a trust account for an individual client so that the client can earn interest? In what other situation might you need similar information?
11. What must a lawyer consider before withdrawing from a client matter for non-payment? Do your state's rules differ from the ABA Model Rules in this regard? If so, how?

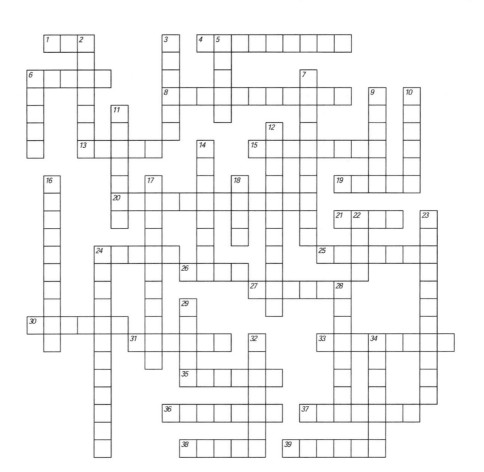

ACROSS

1. upper limit
4. special relationship
6. to whom check is written
8. lawyer is paid percentage
13. account held on behalf of another
15. fee_____, deviation from American system
19. examination of accounts
20. distribution of payment into installments
21. type of fee often for transactional work
24. an entry that reduces account
25. small amounts
26. initials, Social Security number or employer identification number
27. _____ entry accounting; every transaction recorded in 2 places
30. record of individual account
31. a legal "being," such as corporation
33. advance payment
35. money held until purpose is achieved

36. basis of accounting, not cash
37. transfer of info from journal to ledger
38. billing, also called incentive billing
39. assets minus liabilities

DOWN

2. _____ value, future payment reduced by time value
3. accounting year, not calendar
5. initials, governs interest on pooled client accounts
6. _____cash, on hand for small purchases
7. portions into which hour is divided
9. client money kept in a single account
10. entry that increases account
11. chronological listing of transactions
12. report shows percentage of time billed
14. report shows difference between cash flow projections and reality
16. settlement, not lump sum
17. practice of illegally mixing accounts
18. initials, accounting procedures in general use
22. _____ sum, single payment
23. report identifies those late in submitting time
24. a "paper loss" that spreads cost over life
28. costs of operations
29. _____-offs, accounts for time not billed
32. to allocate between accounts
34. annual income

Terms and Definitions

accounting cycle: See p. 141
accounts payable: See p. 141
accounts receivable: See p. 141
accounts receivable schedule: See p. 141
accrual accounting: See p. 141
aging: See p. 141
American system: Each party pays own costs of litigation
amortization: Distribution of an amount into installments, so that it will be paid according to a schedule
assets: See p. 141
audit: Examination of accounts
balance sheet: See p. 141
calendar year: See p. 141
cap: Upper limit
cash basis accounting: See p. 142
cash flow projection: See p. 142

check request form: Form used to request that authorized person issue a check

commingled: Funds wrongly mixed

contingency fee: Lawyer is paid with a percentage of the settlement or judgment amount

cost: Price actually paid

cost-of-chair: Analyzes costs and income attributable to employee

credit: See p. 141

daily cash report: See p. 141

debit: See p. 141

delinquency reports: Identifies those late in submitting time records

depreciation: See p. 141

double entry accounting: See p. 141

entity: A "being," such as a corporation or a limited liability company

equity: See p. 142

escrow: Money being held until a purpose is achieved

evergreen retainer: Must be replenished by client and kept at specified level

expenses: See p. 142

fee reversal: Also called fee award; losing party pays winner's legal fees

FEIN: federal identification number

fiduciary: Relationship of trust that imposes special obligations

fiscal year: See p. 141

flat fee: Agreed in advance

GAAP: See p. 142

gross fee method: Contingency fee calculation — costs deducted after percentage is figured

hard costs: Directly attributable to client matter, such as filing fee

hours worked: See p. 142

income: See p. 142

income statement: See p. 142

increments: Portions into which whole is divided

Interest on Lawyers' Trust Accounts (IOLTA): Program in which interest generated on pooled accounts is forwarded to a legal fund

journal: See p. 143

ledger: See p. 142

liabilities: See p. 142

lump sum: A single payment that satisfies an obligation

market rate: Rate paid by private clients; includes profit

money laundering: Actions intended to conceal the true ownership, source, location, or control of funds

net fee method: Contingency fee calculation — costs deducted before percentage is figured

nominal: Small in amount

one-write system: See p. 143

overhead: Expenses attributable to doing business

paper loss: See p. 141

passive commingling: Waiting too long to withdraw funds from trust account

payee: The person to whom payment is made

pegboard system: See p. 143

personal property: Moveable items, with a tangible physical existence
petty cash: Money kept on hand for small purchases
pooled: Funds intentionally mixed in a single account
posting: See p. 143
present value: Value attached to money to change hands at some future date, discounted to account for the time value of money
profit-loss statement: See p. 142
prorate: See p. 143
realization reports: Show percentage of time billed
receivable: Funds earned but not yet received
reconciliation: See p. 143
referral fee: Money paid to a person who sends a client to the firm
RESPA: Real Estate Settlement Procedures Act
retainer: Advance payment
retirement annuity: Annual income
revenue: See p. 142
signatory: Person with access to account by signature
soft costs: Often considered overhead, include copying, postage, etc.
structured settlement: Alternative to lump sum payment; financial or insurance company makes periodic payments
trust: Account being held on behalf of another
unbundled legal services: Lawyer performs only some tasks to accomplish client's goal
value (incentive) billing: Fee is tied to result obtained
variance report: See p. 141
write-offs: See p. 143

7

Office and Equipment

As a Manager

You will be responsible for acquisition of equipment and supplies; you may be responsible for locating and configuring office space. You may be responsible for ensuring that the space is ADA-compliant and has adequate space for library and other resources. You will be responsible for emergency planning.

Objectives

After completing this chapter, you will be able to

- Identify the factors that should be considered in choosing office space and in deciding to lease or purchase firm equipment.
- Define ergonomics and describe some ergonomic principles for computer work.
- Describe tax benefits available to employers for making accommodations for disabled workers.
- Describe trends in office configuration.
- Describe procedures for avoiding and dealing with workplace violence and other emergencies.
- Describe, in general terms, the print material typically found in a firm library, how that collection is updated, and procedures for keeping the collection intact.
- Identify the functions of a firm repository.

A. The Office
   1. Space Considerations
   2. Safety Considerations

A.   The Office

1.   General Considerations

While cost is often the biggest factor in choosing office space, it is not the only one (see Exhibit 7-1). Location, availability of services, and aesthetics are also very important. The location and appearance of a firm's office space reflect the practice. A litigation firm may require a location close to the courthouse; a criminal defense firm may need a location near the jail. A corporate firm may prefer a prestigious address with an impressive entry, while a legal services clinic may want to locate in a neighborhood near the clients it serves.

The inside of the office is equally important. Some design features relate to ethical concerns. For example, a firm may have conference rooms without clear windows or with special soundproofing to protect confidentiality. In addition, configuration of space is one of several factors that affect safety, efficiency, image, and worker satisfaction.

One of the biggest concerns is adequate space. A firm that rents the largest space it can afford may be reluctant to incur the expense and inconvenience of a move when its staff, records, and equipment have grown to the point of bursting the seams. Current trends for dealing with the problem on a short-term basis include storing old records offsite or going paperless (discussed in Chapter 8). If an attorney needs support, but the firm lacks space or has a limited budget for the position, consider a **virtual assistant**. A virtual assistant works from home, often using his own equipment. Virtual assistants are often willing to forgo benefits or a higher salary in order to avoid travel to an office or have the flexibility of working at home. While virtual assistants are catching on in the legal field, there are special concerns with respect to confidentiality and conflicts of interest.[1]

virtual assistant
Support staff working outside the office

---

[1] *See* Andrea Cannavina, *Working with a Virtual Assistant,* Law Prac. Today, Sept. 2008, http://www.abanet.or/lpt/articles/mgt09083.html.

2. Safety Considerations

Although offices may seem like relatively safe environments compared to workplaces like construction sites or roadways, they are not without their hazards. According to the National Institute for Occupational Safety and Health,

> Situations in offices that can lead to injury or illness range from physical hazards (such as cords across walkways, leaving low drawers open, objects falling from overhead) to task-related (speed or repetition, duration, job control, etc.), environmental (chemical or biological sources) or design-related hazards (such as nonadjustable furniture or equipment). Job stress that results when the requirements of the job do not match the capabilities or resources of the worker may also result in illness. NIOSH, Office Environment and Worker Safety and Health, http://www.cdc.gov/niosh/topics/officeenvironment/officeenvironment.html (last visited Feb. 16, 2009).

Most law office workers spend a significant amount of time each day working on computers and looking at video display terminals. The main hazards for users of computer workstations are difficult-to-diagnose **ergonomic** injuries, also called "musculoskeletal disorders." The federal **Occupational Safety and Health Administration (OSHA)** has no specific standards for computer workstations; in most cases, only a few general electrical or radiation hazards may apply. Employers should, nonetheless, be concerned because workers suffering ergonomic injuries are likely to be less productive and more prone to absence.

Cornell University hosts a website on arranging computer workstations to avoid ergonomic injuries (http://ergo.human.cornell.edu/ergoguide.html). Suggestions include

ergonomics
Study of stress on muscles and bones

Occupational Safety and Health Administration (OSHA)
Federal agency concerned with preventing work-related injuries and deaths

- Chairs with lumbar support and armrests that adjust to accommodate users' physical stature.
- Desktop (rather than laptop) computers for prolonged use, with monitors at a comfortable height and distance (straight ahead, to avoid neck turning, and about arm's length distant) and negative-tilt keyboards.
- Use of a stable work surface with a keyboard/mouse tray at a level lower than normal desk height.
- Use of a document holder.

The site includes special considerations for users with vision problems; suggestions about noise, ventilation, and lighting; and information about the newest ergonomic devices and fads. One source of office worker injuries, lifting heavy files from an incorrect posture, may become a thing of the past as offices move away from paper files.

Exhibit 7-1
Factors in Choosing Office Space

- Location
  - Practice-specific needs (e.g., near court)
  - Proximity to public transportation, restaurants, banks, post office, delivery/messenger services, health club and other services used regularly by clients and staff
  - Client-friendly location (easy to get to, safe area)
  - Nature of other businesses in the building, turnover of other tenants in building
- Cost
  - Usually based on square footage
  - Length of lease and any options to renew
  - Are utilities or services (such as cleaning) included?
- Will interior walls have to be moved or installed to meet firm needs? Will interior require painting, carpeting, or other decorating? If leasing, will the landlord handle the reconfiguration and decorating?
- Is the space immediately available, or will current tenant have to vacate? What is the time needed for reconfiguration and decorating?
- If leasing, furnished or unfurnished? Will existing furniture fit? Can it be gotten through doorways, elevators, etc.?
- Are phone jacks and data ports available in the right locations?
- Is the space large enough to provide about 150-200 square feet per person and to allow for expansion? Might it be possible to expand to additional space in the building in the future?
- Signage outside building or on interior directories
- Windows for offices
- Parking: proximity, cost, availability to visitors, security?
- Services
  - Cleaning
  - Exterior—snow removal, loading dock, trash removal
  - Security
  - Twenty-four-hour access and usability of space outside normal business hours (e.g., is building air conditioned on holidays?)
  - Shared business services (e.g., building receptionist, wi-fi, high-volume copier, insurance, mail room)
  - Quality of management company—which contractors do they use, do they respond quickly to maintenance needs?
- Need for and availability of specialty spaces
  - Client reception area
  - Conference rooms
  - Kitchen
  - Washrooms—in office suite or elsewhere in building?
  - File storage in the office or in another area of the building?

> ## Assignment 7-1
> ## Handling Workplace Challenges

Management Portfolio

1. Several legal secretaries in your firm have been complaining about aches and pains related to working at computers all day. Some have taken days off. Create a page for the office policies manual detailing procedures they can follow during the workday to reduce their physical discomfort. The page can include suggestions for short breaks and giving them the opportunity to request reasonable special equipment.

2. The landlord has raised the rent and your midsized firm is moving to a new office a few blocks away. The boss just announced that the move will occur over the weekend, in two months. A moving company has been chosen. Work with a partner and develop a list of tasks that must be completed so that the firm can be in operation on the following Monday. As directed by your instructor, exchange your plan with that of another team for comparison. Discuss what you may have overlooked. Try these resources: http://www.abanet.org/genpractice/books/busoflaw-36.pdf, http://www.buyerzone.com/office-moving/move-checklist.html, or http://www.lacba.org/showpage.cfm?pageid=2611.

3. ADA Considerations

The Americans with Disabilities Act (ADA), discussed in depth in Chapter 9, sometimes requires **reasonable accommodation** to the physical layout of the office. Reasonable accommodation refers to any change in the work environment or in the way things are customarily done that enables an individual with a disability to enjoy equal opportunities. Reasonable accommodation can benefit both disabled workers and their employers:

reasonable accommodation
Required by the ADA for persons with disabilities

> Aside from the fact that lawyers and their offices are required to be accessible, there are many other reasons why an attorney or a law firm should want to voluntarily comply with these laws. . . . Creating an accessible office will also potentially broaden a firm's client base. Individuals with disabilities are often well networked, and inform each other of businesses that address their needs. Attorneys who are accessible increase their chances of representing clients on numerous legal issues faced by individuals with a disability. Many statutes, designed to benefit individuals with disabilities, include attorney fee provisions. These provisions were designed to encourage private attorneys to act as "attorney generals" in protecting the rights of individuals with disabilities. David Michael Stokes & Daniel P. McGlinn, *Disability Law: The Accessible Law Office*, 75 Mich. Bar J. 390 (1996).

Reasonable accommodation of employees and job applicants does not mean that an employer must change an essential function of a job. A job applicant or an employee with a disability may request an accommodation with respect to the firm's equipment or facilities. In such cases, the firm may request documentation of the disability and can make a decision on a case-by-case basis, considering the employee's wishes and what will be most effective and reasonable. The firm is not required to provide the exact accommodation requested or to provide personal use items that the employee needs outside the office. What is reasonable depends on cost, the firm's size and resources, the type of facility, and the impact of the accommodation on other functions. Reasonable accommodation can often be provided at little or no cost. Typical accommodations involving the office facility might include

- Removal of barriers and/or provision of ramps for individuals in wheelchairs.
- Provision of accessible washrooms, fountains, and other physical facilities.
- Provision of software (and training), such as voice recognition software for people who have difficulty using a keyboard or screen magnification for those with vision problems.
- Adjustment of lighting and glare from windows for those with vision impairments.
- Provision of a reserved parking spot for an employee with limited mobility.

This list is far from exhaustive and is intended only to demonstrate that accommodation is often a matter of creativity, rather than of spending large amounts of money. Employers making reasonable accommodations sometimes also qualify for tax incentives (see Exhibit 7-2).

Even if the firm does not have a disabled employee or applicant, it should periodically evaluate how disability-friendly it is for non-employees. The ADA requires that new buildings meet certain accessibility standards, but older buildings may not meet those standards. Office equipment and layout considerations under the ADA include the following:

- Is the office itself accessible to visitors and employees — are ramps available to avoid steps, are doorways and aisles between workstations wide enough for a wheelchair to pass, are washrooms accessible, and do doors open easily?
- Are the firm website, intranet, and extranet accessible to individuals who use specialized software (e.g., job applicants with vision impairments who use screen reading or magnification software)?
- Does the firm have telephones and/or other voice amplification equipment for individuals with hearing impairment?
- Are emergency protocols adequate — flashing lights in addition to alarm bells and a plan for evacuation of people with limited mobility?
- Is handicapped parking available and truly usable?

For More Information

For more information about workplace safety standards, visit http://www.osha.gov. For more information about the ADA, visit http://www.eeoc.gov/types/ada.html. For interesting articles about legal professionals with disabilities, see http://www.law.com/jsp/article.jsp?id=1169200940729 and http://www.eeoc.gov/facts/accommodations-attorneys.html.

Exhibit 7-2
Tax Credits for Accessibility

There are tax incentives available to help employers cover the cost of accommodations for employees with disabilities and to make their places of business accessible.

SMALL BUSINESS TAX CREDIT: IRS CODE §44, DISABLED ACCESS CREDIT

Small businesses that in the previous year earned a maximum of $1 million or had 30 or fewer full-time employees may take a tax credit for making their businesses accessible to persons with disabilities. The credit is 50 percent of expenditures over $250, not to exceed $10,250, for a maximum benefit of $5,000. The credit is subtracted from total tax liability. The credit is available every year and can be used for a variety of costs such as:

- sign language interpreters for employees or customers who have hearing impairments;
- readers for employees or customers who have visual impairments;
- purchase of adaptive equipment or the modification of equipment;
- production of print materials in accessible formats (e.g., Braille, audio tape, large print);
- removal of barriers, in buildings or vehicles, which prevent a business from being accessible to, or usable by, individuals with disabilities; and
- fees for consulting services (under certain circumstances).

Expenses must be paid or incurred to enable a small business to comply with the requirements of the ADA. The credit does not apply to the costs of new construction, and a building being modified must have been placed in service before November 5, 1990.

ARCHITECTURAL/TRANSPORTATION TAX DEDUCTION: IRS CODE §190, BARRIER REMOVAL

All businesses are eligible to take an annual deduction for expenses incurred to remove physical, structural, and transportation (i.e., vehicle-related) barriers for persons with disabilities at the workplace. Businesses may take a tax deduction of up to $15,000 a year for expenses incurred to remove barriers for persons with disabilities. Amounts in excess of the $15,000 maximum annual deduction may be depreciated. The deduction is available every year. It can be used for a variety of costs to make a facility or public transportation vehicle, owned or leased for use in the business, more accessible to and usable by persons with disabilities. Examples include the cost of:

- providing accessible parking spaces, ramps, and curb cuts;
- providing telephones, water fountains, and restrooms that are accessible to persons in wheelchairs;
- making walkways at least 48 inches wide.

The deduction may not be used for new construction, complete renovation of a facility or public transportation vehicle, or normal replacement of depreciable property.

Small businesses may use the credit and deduction together, if the expenses qualify under both sections. Although both the tax credit and deduction may be used annually, if a business spends more than may be claimed in one year, it cannot carry over those expenses and claim a tax benefit in the next year. However, if the amount of credit the business is entitled to exceeds the amount of taxes owed, the business can carry forward the unused portion of the credit to the following year.

From U.S. Department of Labor, Office of Disability Employment Policy, Tax Incentives for Providing Business Accessibility, http://www.dol.gov/odep/pubs/fact/tifpba.htm (last visited Feb. 16, 2009).

4. Design Considerations

Law firm space is divided between offices and rooms that house support functions. Support functions for a sole practitioner may all be contained in a single outer office/reception area. A large firm may have several reception areas, several conference rooms, a dining room and kitchen, a mailroom, a library, a copy center, supply rooms, and copy rooms. Some firms even have daycare centers, gyms, and shower rooms. With changes in the economy, in client expectations, in job descriptions, and in the culture of how people work, many law firms are moving in new directions when it comes to how they use their space.

Many of the newest trends have positive effects on the bottom line, as well as how employees view their jobs.

Large firms traditionally have had "wow space," such as an ornate internal staircase, elaborately paneled conference rooms, and reception areas containing expensive art. What was once a sign of prestige is now often viewed as a sign that clients are overpaying for legal services! Some firms are eliminating such features entirely from new office space, but others are opting for one impressive public space. The availability of such a space, especially if it is configured for flexibility (for example, a conference room that can fit 30 but can also be partitioned into three rooms, each seating 10) can eliminate the need for large offices for client meetings.

That flexible space can be used for multiple purposes. Part may normally be used as the library; sections can be temporarily turned into "war rooms" or "deal rooms" for big projects. It might also be used for another trend—group or "team" space. Firms are providing places where lawyers and paralegals can work together in comfortable spaces. Some firms are even decorating team spaces with couches and comfortable chairs, coffee bars, and other amenities to encourage collegiality.

Even individual workspaces, such as cubicles for secretaries, are being designed to be more flexible and open. This reflects not only a desire to make the area seem larger, but also the fact that secretaries typically work for several lawyers or paralegals. While an open layout often provides a space with better lighting and ventilation and allows workers to feel less isolated, it also can create a noisy, stressful environment in which workers feel they have no privacy. A good design can provide the benefits of open layout without totally sacrificing the feeling of private space. Consider too whether the worker is facing a hallway and will have eye contact with people walking to the washrooms, the copier, or the break room; even the instinctive "how are you?" can be a big time-waster.

As space becomes more expensive, many firms are sending certain support functions offsite to less expensive locations and are reducing the size of individual offices. Attorney offices typically represent about one-third of a firm's space usage.

5. Workplace Violence

We have all heard the jokes: What do you call ten dead lawyers? A good start. T-shirts proclaim: "The first thing we do, let's kill all the lawyers," Shakespeare's famous quote from *Henry VI*. While these statements are meant to be funny, they are becoming less amusing as the United States sees an increase in workplace and school violence. The Bureau of Labor Statistics' 2005 Survey of Workplace Violence Prevention (http://www.bls.gov/iif/osh_wpvs.htm) indicated that 4.8 percent of private industry establishments (5.3 percent of all establishments) had experienced an incident of workplace violence within the previous 12 months. The statistics, while bad enough, do not take threats and harassment into account.

> **Examples**
>
> When people think of being injured at work, they usually think of construction accidents and other situations in which performance of the job itself involves certain physical risks. Unfortunately, usually quiet offices have recently become scenes of violence. Law offices are not immune:
>
> In October 2007 a gunman held hostages at a law firm in Alexandria, Louisiana; five people were shot and two died.
>
> In December 2006 a disgruntled client walked into a Chicago law office and opened fire, killing three people and wounding another. He apparently believed he had been cheated in applying for a patent.
>
> In spring 2005 a dissatisfied litigant entered the Chicago home of federal judge Joan Lefkow and killed the judge's mother and husband before taking his own life.
>
> In 1993 a client killed eight and wounded six after entering the San Francisco office of Pettit & Martin. The firm closed in 1995.

All offices are somewhat vulnerable to violent acts by employees with emotional problems, former employees angry at having been terminated, domestic violence partners following their victims to work, and even random strangers walking in off the street. Law offices have additional risks: clients unhappy with results and emotionally disturbed opposing parties. Law offices may be even more vulnerable to attacks by strangers than other businesses because lawyers and the legal system are common targets for emotionally disturbed individuals. In addition, law offices tend to be highly visible, with signs and even glass doors.

Reducing the threat of violence by current employees starts with careful screening before hiring, in compliance with antidiscrimination laws discussed in Chapter 9. The prehiring process should involve a detailed employment application, an interview, and reference checks. The firm may want to go further for some positions and require a criminal background check, drug screening, and even a credit check, if permitted by local law. Once employees have been hired, the firm's other policies concerning sick leave, vacation time, wellness programs, training, and recognition are important to reducing employee stress that can lead to workplace violence.

The next step is a well-written and well-implemented policy in the employee handbook. The policy should involve a zero-tolerance standard for violence and threats of violence (much like the zero-tolerance policy for sexual harassment) and should establish guidelines for reporting and investigating violations of the standard. The policy alone is not enough; the person charged with enforcement must take all reports seriously.

The person charged with enforcement must also pay special attention to events likely to trigger stress: termination, changes in job titles and descriptions, changes in benefits or office space, disciplinary action, or problems at home. The firm may be able to handle trigger events to minimize risk. For example, troubled workers often blame the person who supervises their daily work for their troubles; having someone other than that supervisor handle disciplinary actions or termination may prevent the situation from spiraling out of control. The person charged with disciplining or terminating a troubled employee should be cautious to maintain a professional tone, not argue the merits of the decision to terminate or discipline, and not threaten the employee's remaining self-esteem. Depending on the situation, the firm may want to offer the employee outplacement services, a severance package, psychological counseling, or other services. If the situation merits extra caution, the firm may want to engage special security.

Example

Workplace Violence Red Flags
The following, especially in conjunction with a trigger event such as losing a case or being fired, can be warning signs of impending workplace violence:

- Long-term dissatisfaction with job or representation
- Blaming others for problems or projecting shortcomings on others
- Verbal abuse or attempts to intimidate others
- General dissatisfaction with life and "the system"
- Lack of support from friends or family
- Low self-esteem
- Disparagement of other races, religions, ethnicities, men or women
- Feelings of persecution as an individual or as part of a class of individuals
- Concern with shortcomings of others — may keep records[2]

Employees should be trained about workplace violence and what causes it, so that they are able to recognize a coworker, a client, or anyone else who visits the firm and is under stress. Clients and opponents are most likely to be stressed by the outcome of a case or motion.

People who feel desperate and helpless are most likely to take desperate measures. Some problems with both employees and clients can be avoided by having and publicizing a policy, such as mediation, for presenting grievances.

Even a firm that has done all the right things in dealing with employees and clients can be a victim of violence. Some steps that can reduce the risk include the following:

- Configure office space to have a single point of access.
- Depending on the firm's size, location, and assessment of risk, that single point of access should be secured so that a visitor has to pass building security, be "buzzed in," or check in with a receptionist.
- Discourage "social visiting," especially by employees who may have left the firm on unhappy terms. Be sure that when an employee leaves the firm, she returns all keys, building identification badges, and similar items.
- The person who greets visitors should have a plan for dealing with suspicious individuals, such as a panic button or a code to alert others.
- Do not allow outsiders to walk around the office unattended; have a procedure for greeting visitors in reception and walking them out at the end of a meeting.
- If office space is large enough to justify, consider locking interior doors and giving employees key cards for passage.
- All employees should be trained on evacuation procedures.

---

[2]For more information, see *Violence Against Lawyers*, 23 J. Legal Prof. 197 (1998).

- If the firm is aware of a specific threat, it may want to remove its information from the building directory
- Provide building security and/or local police with information about specific threats.

6.   Preparing for Emergencies

You are working at your desk when the fire alarm rings — but your office is on the twelfth floor, and you have an injured knee. You are working at your desk and see a man walking purposefully down the hall — with a gun. You are getting ready to leave for work when you get a call from a coworker — there was a major fire in the office last night. You arrive at your office in a high-rise building and find that the building is closed; a construction crew working on a bridge over the river breached an abandoned tunnel, causing basements to flood and building systems to shut down. The partner for whom you work has had a stroke and is unable to speak or write. A husband, being represented by your firm in a divorce case, killed his entire family last night and the press is outside, waiting for information. Would you know what to do?

For More Information

There are many Internet resources that can help you and your firm plan for emergencies. Here are a few to get you started:

ABA resources: http://www.abanet.org/barserv/disaster/disasterbiblio. html
Department of Homeland Security: http://www.dhs.gov
Disaster Recovery Journal: http://www.drj.com
Federal Emergency Management Agency: http://www.fema.gov
Northeast Document Conservation Center (nonprofit providing document conservation advice and services): http://www.nedcc.org
Red Cross: http://www.redcross.org

Despite the fact that disasters do happen, as the publicity surrounding the attacks on the World Trade Center, Hurricane Katrina, and other events bear testament to, most people live their daily lives as if disasters will not happen to them. They may rationalize that they will "cross that bridge when they get to it," but law firms owe their clients a responsibility to be ready for the worst-case scenario. Clients are frequently the victims of the same forces that harm the law firm, so firms must be prepared to serve clients in times of crisis.

Every firm's procedures manual should address emergency plans in specific detail, and the plans must be available to employees who cannot get into the office. The process starts with assessing risk, taking steps to prevent emergencies to the greatest extent possible, and then planning for response and recovery.

Assessing risk involves considering disasters that would have an impact on your ability to use your office and equipment. These include natural disasters known to your geographic area (hurricanes, earthquakes, blizzards, tornadoes) and disasters possible in any area (fire, violence). Personal disasters affect an individual's ability to work.

Prevention may include the security measures discussed in the previous section. In addition the firm should have good locks, possibly an alarm system; fire-resistant cabinets for storage and fireproof safes for irreplaceable documents, evidence, and other items; a policy requiring that files be kept in these protected locations when not in use (never on the desk overnight); locks for laptops and other easily moved equipment; surge protectors for electronic equipment; virus protection and firewalls for computers; and regular safety review of the premises (for example, checking that electrical outlets are not overloaded, exits are clearly marked, bookcases are bolted to the wall, stairways are not blocked, and fire extinguishers are working).

Planning for risks will depend on the size and resources of the firm.

a. Planning for Office Emergencies

Every firm should have the following safety elements in place:

- A contact sheet with addresses, home e-mail accounts, cell phone numbers, and perhaps even emergency contact information, so that people can get in touch with each other, even if phone service is not available in areas (keep in mind that this information is of no value in case of a locked-out emergency unless people have it at home)
- An individual responsible for initiating contact in the event of a lock-out type emergency and for reviewing and updating the plan regularly
- Basic first-aid equipment, flashlights (with working batteries), canned goods, and water in a known location in the office; if the firm is large enough, it may want to invest in first-aid training for one or more employees
- A way of knowing who is in the office at any given time and a "disaster leader" to order evacuation, lock the office (if possible without risk to human safety), account for who gets out, and give the "all clear" to return
- Information about anyone who may need assistance or special medical care in the event of emergency and a plan for who will assist those people
- A protocol and contact sheet that instructs any individual on how to report a danger that may not be known to everyone in the office (fire in the kitchen, disturbed individual in the hall) and how to communicate that information throughout the firm as necessary
- An escape plan with alternatives in case primary exits are blocked and an assembly point at a safe spot outside the building (again, useless unless communicated to every person in the office)
- Emergency drills, if the size of the office justifies them
- A plan for assisting employees, if necessary, with information about counseling, medical benefits, and related services
- A way of backing up electronic data so that it is available at another location if the office becomes inaccessible and regular assessment of whether the data actually is retrievable from that location
- Adequate insurance on office and equipment, liability and business interruption insurance; consider keeping copies of policies offsite

- An updated, detailed (manufacturer, serial number, purchase cost or appraised value) inventory of property, including software licenses (again, valuable only if not destroyed in the disaster) and an individual identified as responsible for assessing damage and initiating salvage efforts as soon as possible after the disaster and communicating with insurance carriers
- A plan for removing valuables (such as pieces of art, key records) if possible to do so without risk to human safety
- A plan for offsite access to financial resources (a supply of checks kept offsite, a line of credit)
- A sign that can be placed on the door in the event of evacuation, giving emergency workers a way of contacting the disaster leader to determine whether there are people inside
- A spokesperson to speak on behalf of the firm and instructions that others should direct inquiries to the spokesperson
- A plan for operating from another site — perhaps home, if the firm is small, a "buddy" office for a larger firm, or a satellite office, if the firm is very large
- A plan for reaching and assisting clients from outside the office; this will depend on your firm's clients — if local courts close as the result of a hurricane, litigation becomes less urgent, but a local manufacturer, unable to deliver to customers in other states, may need legal advice immediately
- A plan for contacting opposing counsel on pending matters, from outside the office
- A plan for reaching other business contacts — landlord, suppliers, firm accountant, payroll company, banks
- A way of recording all steps taken and expenses incurred in dealing with the emergency
- An individual designated to handle insurance claims by contacting the insurer immediately, photographing damage, and verifying the credentials of any individuals claiming to work with insurers

b. Planning for Personal Emergencies

Sudden illness, disability, even death can affect anyone at the firm. The firm must ensure that the following systems are in place:

- Others in the firm have a way of accessing voice mail, e-mail, documents in progress, files, and calendar (a list of passwords, keys to file drawers)
- Someone has quick access to personal information about everyone in the firm — emergency contacts, medical information, numbers of any firm credit cards carried
- There is coverage available for key people — for a sole practitioner, this means having one or more "buddies" who can step in and handle client matters in the event of death or disability

B. Equipment

Imagine that the attorney for whom you have worked for many years is splitting from her partner. You will be moving to a new office and taking some of the furniture and equipment. The attorney has given you a list of furniture and equipment that will be needed for the new office and asked you to start working on acquiring the needed items. Your first question is whether to buy or lease the needed items.

1. Purchasing

Your attorney says that she wants to purchase, rather than lease, the office furnishings, so you start investigating possible sources of the various items. Some of your considerations include the following:

- If the purchase requires installation, maintenance, or repairs, check references. Ask:
  - Was the job completed on time?
  - Did the end cost meet expectations, or were there surprises?
  - Was training or training material adequate?
  - Have you been satisfied with service and repairs?
- Obtain information about the **vendor**:
  - How long has the vendor been in business?
  - Does it service the product? Onsite?
  - Does it provide loaners while repairing equipment?

  vendor
  Seller

- Tell the vendor what you want in terms of the purpose of the equipment (for example, "We need a 'workhorse' copier that produces high volume at high speed — we already have a color copier that does finishing functions"). Be open to suggestions and do not assume that you know all possibilities, but never tell the vendor that you have no idea what you need or want. The vendor should be able to provide options at various prices, with an explanation of relative advantages and disadvantages.
- Consider doing an **RFP**. If you are going to request proposals (bids), use detailed specifications so that you can do valid comparisons. Remember that delivery and setup, training, and product warranties and service contracts may be part of the package. When you get proposals, make sure that the vendors have followed your specifications and not substituted other products or manufacturers or even left out some items.

  RFP
  Request for proposals

- Do not let the vendor sell you a product or service if you do not understand the reason for it.
- A firm can save a lot of money by buying last year's model, an "off" brand, or a reconditioned piece of equipment, but must consider several factors. The likelihood that replacement parts and support will be available in the future can justify paying for "name" brands and for buying latest model equipment. Another reason for considering name brands is the likelihood of being able to obtain service if your particular vendor goes out of business.

The cost of supplies, such as pens, paper, staples, tabs, and binders can quickly add up and hurt the firm's bottom line, especially if people are being careless or using supplies for personal tasks. Even in a small firm, loss can be reduced by implementing simple practices such as keeping supplies in a central, locked

The majority of office workers (58%) have taken office supplies for their personal use (http://research.lawyers.com/ Majority-of-Office-Workers-Have-Stolen-Supplies.html).

location and requiring that people request what they need from the person charged with keeping and ordering the supplies. Such a system also ensures that the person charged with ordering supplies is aware of inventory and the need to reorder.

2. Leasing

Now let's imagine that your attorney tells you that she does not have sufficient funds to buy furnishings and is nervous about committing to big purchases at this time. It is estimated that about eight out of ten U.S. companies lease some or all of their business equipment. For some firms, leasing equipment is a way of ensuring that they will upgrade office technology on a regular schedule. Buying new equipment every couple of years can be too expensive for the solo practices and small firms where almost half of U.S. lawyers work. Most equipment leases allow the lessee to purchase the equipment for a set price at the end of the lease (buyout option). Equipment leases, therefore, are generally considered a form of financing an acquisition. Unlike a rental that has no characteristics of a purchase (for example, renting a carpet steamer for a day), an equipment lease can place many risks and obligations on the lessee.

capital assets
Assets expected to be in use for a year or more, used to generate income

Leasing also has tax implications. While **capital assets** such as computers can be depreciated at tax time, the business can generally deduct lease payments for the years in which those payments are made, which can be a greater tax advantage. The owner must also consider whether the equipment will be used for personal purposes; if so, lease payments may have to be prorated. In some circumstances, the IRS will treat a lease as a sale. The tax ramifications can be complicated, and the owner may wish to consult an accountant or tax professional.

Factors for evaluating an equipment lease include these:

lessor
Owns property and leases to others

- What is the reputation of the **lessor**?
- Who is responsible for routine maintenance and repair?
- What are the rights of the firm if the equipment becomes unusable?
- Does the firm have the right to move equipment to new location?
- May the firm modify the equipment? If it does, can any modifications be removed, or do they become property of the lessor?
- Does the lease contain an early termination option or an early buyout option?
- Does the lease contain an option to renew or an automatic renewal?
- Does the firm have the right to sublease or assign the lease?
- Who pays cost of return (removal, shipping, insurance), and when must the equipment be ready for removal?
- If the lease refers to fair market value, how is that determined?
- If the lease covers several pieces of equipment, can the lessee purchase less than all equipment at the end of the term?

3. Going Green

One of the biggest trends in managing all types of offices is "going green": implementing sustainable, environmentally friendly practices. Going green tends to improve staff morale, presents a good public image, and often saves the business money. The concept of "sustainability" refers to maintaining economic growth while minimizing impact on the environment.

There are several easy office policies that can make a difference:

- Keep heating and cooling at reasonable levels. Workers should not have to wear sweaters in August.
- Office computers waste about $1 billion in electricity each year.
  - Unless your tech staff tells you otherwise, turn off computers and printers at the end of the workday.
  - Set computers to automatically "go to sleep" after a period of inactivity — screen savers are not energy savers.
  - When you replace electronic equipment, look for energy efficient replacements; donate old equipment to charitable organizations or find a reputable recycler that follows safety guidelines (the Environmental Protection Agency has e-cycling resources at http://www.epa.gov/epawaste/conserve/materials/ecycling/index.htm).
  - Go paperless, when possible. When printing, avoid color copies, print two-sided copies, and print in "draft" mode whenever possible. Recycle ink and toner cartridges and purchase refilled cartridges. Use paper with a high percentage of post-consumer recycled content.
- Artificial lighting accounts for 44 percent of the electricity use in office buildings.
  - Turn off the lights when leaving a room for 15 minutes or more and use natural light when you can.
  - Buy Energy Star-rated light bulbs and fixtures, which use at least two-thirds less energy than regular lighting, and install timers or motion sensors that automatically shut off lights when not needed.
- Travel Policies:
  - Some companies give employees "perks" such as reserved parking for carpooling and subsidies for riding public transportation.
  - Allow staff members to work from home when possible.
  - Encourage teleconferencing or videoconferencing over face-to-face meetings.
- In the kitchen:
  - Discourage staff from using individual drink containers such as water bottles by having cold filtered water and fresh coffee available.
  - Do not provide disposable cups and utensils, but encourage staff to bring their own cups, glasses, and eating utensils.
  - Place recycling bins in convenient spots so that people will use them.
  - Purchase non-toxic cleaning products; avoid use of paper towels.

Assignment 7-2
Making Wise Equipment Decisions

1. One of the vendors law offices deal with regularly is the U.S. Postal Service. Using its website, find the list of authorized providers of postage meters; find out how it is possible to track the delivery of certified mail using the Internet. What is "registered mail," and what other methods are available for verifying delivery?

2. Leona Stosh wants to go green. Visit http://www.plmw.org (the International Professional Legal Management Week website) and listen to a webinar on going green. Or try this resource: http://www.p2pays.org/ref/05/04040.pdf. What tools are recommended for developing and implementing a law office sustainability policy? Write a short memo to Leona, recommending a course of action.

C. Library

While large firms still have libraries and law librarians, the advent of Internet legal research has caused many law firms to downsize their law libraries. Few firms have completely eliminated print libraries, however, because some materials still cannot be accessed online, and others, while available online, are difficult to search online. Some firms have decentralized their collections, for example, housing the books on real estate law near the offices of lawyers and paralegals in the real estate practice group. Other firms have kept traditional central libraries, believing that they provide a peaceful haven for lawyers and paralegals to focus on research projects and serve as an important "image" booster.

1. Library Resources

primary authority
Sources of law

secondary authority
Helps find or explain sources of law

Law libraries contain both **primary authority** and **secondary authority** resources (see Exhibit 7-3). And of course, they need librarians to help run them.

Librarians serve many functions, but if your firm does not have a librarian, you may be required to perform the following tasks:

- Assess the firm's needs and plan for acquisitions (and elimination of unneeded materials)
- Budget for acquisitions, subscriptions, equipment, and furnishings
- Maintain or create a catalog of the library's resources; it is also a good idea to maintain a list of libraries that have resources not in your library and information about using those libraries

- Keep materials updated (for example, by ordering necessary **pocket parts** or looseleaf pages)
- Discard material that is out-of-date and donate or discard material no longer in use; space is expensive
- Establish policies for checkout of materials and for reshelving of books
- Keep the library organized
- Circulate information about copyright compliance
- Support the use of library materials by providing orientation and training for new employees
- Manage the firm's accounts for **CALR**, which may include researching subscription costs, managing password distribution, and arranging for training on Lexis, Loislaw, Westlaw, or another subscription service

pocket part
Common method of updating law books

CALR
Computer-assisted legal research

Before making decisions about acquisitions and elimination of material, obtain input from the people who use the library. The fact that something is available online does not necessarily mean you can eliminate the print version. For example, state and federal legislation is available online, but researchers often prefer to work with print materials so that they can examine the layout of a particular chapter or section without moving from screen to screen. Many researchers also prefer the print versions of looseleaf service materials, encyclopedias, digests, and formbooks. Consider whether there might be a more efficient way to acquire, store, and access materials such as periodicals, perhaps by purchasing a **CD-ROM** subscription or saving the material on **microfilm**, **microfiche**, or **ultrafiche**.

CD-ROM
Compact disk, read-only-memory

microfilm
Media for photographic reduction

microfiche
Media for photographic reduction

ultrafiche
Media for photographic reduction

Exhibit 7-3
Resources Necessary for Legal Research

Primary Authority

The law originates from five sources of primary authority: constitutions, legislation, judicial decisions, administrative agencies, or the executive branch. Even small law firms typically have print versions of their state's statutes and court rules. These sets are typically organized by topic and updated by pocket part. Many firms also have **reporters** containing judicial decisions from their state courts. Firms that do federal work may also have the U.S. Code (federal statutes) and reporters of federal court cases.

reporters
Contain published judicial decisions

Although there are some case reporters for specialty areas of practice, state and regional case reporters are not organized by topic and are of little use without secondary authority to lead the researcher to the correct cases.

Secondary Authority

Secondary authority is material that helps a researcher find, understand, or use primary authority. Often, when presented with a legal issue, the researcher does not have the name of a case or any reference to a statute, regulation, order, or constitutional provision that addresses the issue and must use secondary authority to get started.

Textbooks, legal periodicals (law reviews published by law schools, bar association magazines), practice manuals, formbooks, digests, and encyclopedias are all forms of secondary authority. Many are not available online or are available only with expensive subscription services. Almost all secondary authority in print form comes with an index and is updated by pocket part or looseleaf pages. Which type of secondary authority a researcher uses depends on the goal.

For an overview or a basic understanding of an area of law, a text or an article in a legal publication is usually a good starting point.

If the goal is to perform a specific legal task such as drafting a store lease or petitioning for an international adoption, a practice manual or formbook is a good starting point. Formbooks are samples of various documents, including pleadings, contracts, and government documents.

If the researcher has some understanding of the issue but is not sure of the answer to a specific question, a finding tool can lead to primary authority. Finding tools include encyclopedias and digests, which include alphabetically arranged topics, with references to primary law and, in some cases, explanation and discussion of each topic.

Keeping individual books from disappearing into offices and briefcases can be one of the most difficult aspects of managing a library. Some firms use sign-out sheets. Others attach pockets to the inside cover of each book and insert checkout cards with the book's title and other relevant information; the person checking the book out either signs the card or inserts the card into a file or box with the borrower's name. Some firms place bar codes on books.

2. Firm Repository

repository
Facility for storage

Many firm libraries also house the firm **repository** of forms and work product so that there is no duplication of effort the next time the firm encounters the same issue or need.

Traditionally, the form bank contained court forms and business forms (for example, a deed) in use in the area in which the firm practiced. Many court forms are now available online, but a firm may retain copies (either in print or stored on the computer network) for use in case the Internet is not working or for use in areas in which the forms are not available online.

The other purpose of the repository is to preserve and organize work done by members of the firm for future use.

Examples

Last year one of the partners did a CLE presentation on the new bankruptcy law, complete with a Microsoft PowerPoint presentation. It is stored on her laptop computer, and only one other member of the firm was present and is aware of the presentation. An associate drafted condominium conversion documents that are stored in the firm's filing cabinets and on the firm intranet, in the developer's client file. Only the partner, secretary, and paralegal who worked with the associate are aware of the existence of those documents. A paralegal and an associate worked together on pro bono project — a podcast for the local legal aid website, describing the rights of a homeowner in foreclosure. No other member of the firm is aware of the podcast. All of these may have value in the future, but will the people who need them be aware of the resources and able to find them?

The firm's work product resources can be stored as hard copy in files or binders or in digital form on the computer network. The resources should be stored so that they are in a location within the firm's control. The legal aid society may take the podcast off the website, and the partner's laptop computer may crash. The documents that exist in client files or on the firm's intranet need not be duplicated or physically moved. The most important consideration is having a good database so that material can be located easily. Maintaining an index by creating a database or simply creating a searchable table in a word processing program is much easier than maintaining a print index. Consider the table you created and searched for Chapter 5's assignment on conflicts of interest. The same technique will work. The author of the brief, memo, form, or presentation can suggest terms under which the material can be categorized. For example, the pro bono podcast might be referenced under "foreclosure," "mortgage," "pro bono," "legal aid," "podcast," and "homeowners."

Assignment 7-3
Running an Effective Library

Contact the librarian for your local county law library and ask which resources he or she believes must be available in print form. Which print resources can be eliminated first? What is the annual budget for updates (pocket parts)?

Out There—Paralegal Profile
Tale of Two Libraries

Julie Melvin is the reference librarian for the Chicago office of one of the largest firms in the country. She has both an MLIS and a JD degree, is the author of several articles, and is very active in professional associations. She has used her education in a number of diverse settings. Julie and her colleagues cover all aspects of business, legal, and general research and even handle some more complex docket issues. "We are trained and experienced in many tools that lawyers and paralegals probably have never heard of. This is as it should be—none of us can be experts in everything, but librarians' best strength is how and where to find something in the most efficient, cost-conscious and factually reliable fashion. Our role is to HELP you NOT report you to the partners, so no lawyer will hear from a librarian that a paralegal 'asked a stupid question.'" Because new lawyers and paralegals often don't know what the librarians can do or are afraid of looking stupid, they sometimes seek help as a last resort, rather than as a first stop, according to Julie, who likes to be brought in on a project as early as possible.

Asked about the continued need for a print collection, Julie said that many people believe that all useful information is available for free on the Internet, and this misperception is a major problem for librarians. Many firms are reducing print holdings as a cost savings measure and relying on academic institutions to fill the void. However, law schools are feeling pressure for teaching space and are also reducing print collections, leaving researchers at the mercy of proprietary database holders. In the legal field, our most reliable, and therefore necessary, information comes from subscription databases that cost a substantial amount of money. In some cases, buying alternate years or editions of print resources is more reliable and cost-effective than subscribing to particular electronic sources. Finally, sometimes the fastest way to find a useful answer is just to look at the index of a print resource/book, according to Julie; electronic search mechanisms have a long way to go before they become as sophisticated as the human mind. As part of her ongoing "battle for budget," Julie appreciates lawyers and paralegals who share credit and acknowledge the important role of the library and its staff.

Meanwhile, about 30 miles away, Halle Cox is the librarian for a suburban county law library. She earned her undergraduate degree in English and an MLS before obtaining her position more than 14 years ago. Halle says that even in an affluent area outside a major city, few law firms have substantial libraries, and none have librarians. While many have a CALR subscription (Fastcase is free as part of membership in the state bar association), the lawyers regularly need to use the statutes and practice materials in the county library. Halle says that most researchers find the statutes difficult to search online and that most practice materials (such as forms) are not available online at all. Lawyers often send their non-lawyer assistants to the library, and Halle is happy to help. Because law school is focused on identifying issues and legal theories, rather than on the hands-on use of research materials, she often helps young lawyers too. Many lawyers don't realize how far Halle is willing to go in assisting them: she is willing to respond to requests by phone or e-mail and fax resources or e-mail links to those who cannot get to the library. Halle is especially proud of the self-help center in the library, dedicated to assisting those who cannot afford lawyers

Chapter Review

Discussion Questions

1. Identify factors to be considered in leasing office equipment.
2. What can a firm do to reduce the risk of office violence?
3. What is the difference between secondary and primary authority? How are most law books updated?
4. What types of things would be collected in a firm repository?
5. What would be the "top ten" things you would put into a firm's emergency plan?
6. What would be the "top three" things you would check for in considering a firm's ADA compliance?
7. Identify two trends in law office design.
8. What is meant by "ergonomics"?
9. Identify factors to be considered in purchasing office equipment.
10. Identify three companies that provide CALR subscriptions.

ACROSS

2. _____ authority, helps find or explain the law
4. injuries to muscle/skeletal system
5. _____ part, updates law books
7. _____ tolerance policy for violence
8. for security, an office should have a single point of _____
12. reasonable _____, required for people with disabilities
13. initials, federal law dealing with disabilities
14. landlord
15. initials, legal research done online
17. work done to accommodate disabilities may have _____ advantages
18. _____ authority; the law

DOWN

1. contain cases
3. collection of work product, forms, etc.
6. initials, federal agency dealing with workplace safety

9. _____ sheet, essential in emergency
10. a way of storing material, such as publications, to save space
11. seller
16. space increasingly favored over large private offices

Terms and Definitions

CALR: Computer-assisted legal research
CD-ROM: Compact disk, read-only-memory
capital assets: Assets expected to be in use for a year or more, used to generate income
ergonomics: Study of stress on muscles and bones
lessor: Owns property and leases to others
microfiche: Media for photographic reduction
microfilm: Media for photographic reduction
Occupational Safety and Health Administration (OSHA): Federal agency concerned with preventing work-related injuries and deaths
pocket part: Common method of updating law books
primary authority: Sources of law
reasonable accommodation: Required by the ADA for persons with disabilities
reporters: Contain published judicial decisions
repository: Facility for storage
RFP: Request for proposals
secondary authority: Helps find or explain sources of law
ultrafiche: Media for photographic reduction
vendor: Seller
virtual assistant: Support staff working outside the office

8

Records Management

As a Manager

You will be responsible for implementing, and possibly creating or updating, your firm's system for organizing and storing files. You will also be responsible for training others to use the system.

Objectives

After completing this chapter, you will be able to

- List the advantages and disadvantages of keeping only paper files or only electronic files.
- Identify the characteristics of alphabetical, numerical, and alphanumeric filing and the advantages of each system.
- Use the commonly accepted rule of alphabetical filing.
- Organize electronic documents.
- Identify the steps that are essential to opening a new client file.
- Identify the steps essential to closing a file and disposal of documents within the file.
- Describe technology available for organizing, tracking, and locating files and evidence.

A. Filing System

Lawyers tend to document everything, but storing all of that documentation is expensive in terms of office space, supplies, and personnel hours. Although many firms are moving toward a paperless environment, others still maintain a paper file for every client and every administrative matter. This chapter focuses on filing client records. Most law firms keep administrative files (personnel records, equipment warranties, and the like) separate from client files, but they usually use a similar filing system.

Regardless of whether a firm is in an all-paper or no-paper mode, or somewhere in between, the system of managing client files must have certain characteristics. The system must be used consistently, filing must not be allowed to build up, and the system must include rules for preventing and discovering mistakes. These characteristics are achieved in different ways for paper files and electronic files. Every firm, regardless of how small, should have a written explanation of filing procedures.

1. Paper Files

centralized
In a central location, rather than dispersed

There are several variables in how firms maintain paper files. Some firms keep all files in a **centralized** location; others store files at various locations, near or in the offices of those who work on the files. A firm may control access to files; no one can remove a file without making a request through the file clerk. Other firms have a checkout system, similar to the system employed for library books. A firm may organize files alphabetically, so that direct access is possible for anyone knowing the client's name, or it may code files so that access is indirect and requires reference to a chart or index. In either case, protecting confidentiality is a top priority, and files must never be left where they can be seen by outsiders.

a. Storage Equipment

When selecting file storage equipment, consider the following:

- Number of files (take into account future growth)
- Space available
- Building code regulations

Many small to midsized firms use vertical filing cabinets with four or five drawers. A typical four-drawer cabinet can store 100 linear inches of files using 25 inches of aisle space, be moved easily, and be locked for security. Lateral filing cabinets, also called horizontal or open-sided files, also are popular in small offices. Files are accessed horizontally instead of vertically. A typical four-drawer lateral cabinet stores about 130 linear inches of files. They can be locked for file security and moved easily.

Open shelving is usually found in large offices with secure central file rooms; it resembles open bookshelves and allows for rapid retrieval and refiling. An open system saves space as compared to closed cabinets. When space is at a premium, firms sometimes use high-density mobile aisle systems on tracks that move back and forth to conserve floor space.

Within each client-matter file, there will be folders. For example, a litigation file might have folders for attorney-client relationship (fee agreement, intake interview), correspondence, pleadings, research, notes, memoranda, and discovery. The folders usually have prongs on inside surfaces to attach documents so that the most recent documents are on top. These folders should be kept in the same order in each client file for the same type of matter, so, for example, you will know that correspondence is always at the front. Also, folders are available in a variety of colors to easily identify the type of matter, the attorney assigned to the case, or the type of documents within.

b. Organizing Alphabetically

Paper files must be organized according to a consistent system and labeled for easy filing and retrieval. Files can be organized alphabetically, numerically, or by some combination. Many small firms use the simplest system — organizing client files alphabetically, typically by the client's **surname**. But for a business client, such as Marilyn Kramer Baskets, Inc., the name is filed as stated (Marilyn before Kramer), with the exception that "the" is moved to the end. The system is intuitive and easy to remember, but must include rules for common problems. Certain rules are considered standard for all businesses and make it possible for new people to come into a firm and continue the same system and find files organized by a predecessor. **ARMA International**, a not-for-profit professional association, has established "best practices" for managing paper and electronic records and information (http://www.arma.org).

surname
Also called "family name" or "last name," as distinguished from "given name" or "first name"

ARMA International
Professional organization; sets standards for records retention

---

Example

Examples of common rules for consistent alphabetical filing:

- Even if your client is defendant (Harper v. Andrews), file by your client's name (Andrews).
- File "nothing" before "something" (Andrews, S. before Andrews, Steven)

- Think in terms of units:

Unit 1	Unit 2	Unit 3	Unit 4
Andrusz	Steven	Casimir	
Andrusz	Joan	V	
Marilyn	Kramer	Baskets	Inc.
House	of	Style	The
A[1]	Dog's	Life	Inc.
Andrusz II	Steven	Casimir	

Alphabetizes to

A	Dog's	Life	Inc.
Andrusz	Joan	V	
Andrusz	Steven	Casimir	
Andrusz II	Steven	Casimir	
House	of	Style	The
Marilyn	Kramer	Baskets	Inc.

- Ignore hyphens and other punctuation (Pike-Biegel= Pikebiegel; J & B Decks=JB Decks; A.A.A. Automotive = AAA Automotive; Dog's World = Dogs World)
- File Arabic and Roman numbers before alphabetic characters; "65 or Better Club" before "Sixty-Five or Better Club."
- File **acronyms**, abbreviations, and radio or TV call letters as one unit (WFLD).

acronym
Abbreviation of several words

Other common problems can occur because of clients who have the same or similar names (Nicholson/Nicholsen), use unusual spellings (e.g., Steven Andrusz, pronounced "Andrews"), have business and personal matters (Marilyn Kramer, owner of the basket company, may be going through a divorce), and who change names. Some clients are commonly known by acronyms: the Elgin Country Club is called ECC. Sometimes the client is one of several parties in a case; for example, Merle Wilmoth may be one of the plaintiffs in the case *Stagner v. Quackenbush*. The firm may represent all or several of those plaintiffs. A cross-reference chart is needed to deal with these situations. Misfilings can be difficult to detect.

Now let's assume that Mr. Andrusz has a file for an auto accident case, a file for his estate planning matters, and a file for his purchase of land. In some firms, the Andrusz file would have three subfiles, organized alphabetically by subject or by the attorney handling the matter. Other firms might have all of the personal

---

[1]While most systems move "the" to the end unit, other prepositions, conjunctions, and articles usually stay in order

injury files in one place, all of the estate planning files in another place, and all of the real estate files in their own spot. Some firms may use color coding of either the files[2] or the labels in conjunction with the alphabetical system, so that, for example, all litigation files might be red, all real estate files green, and all estate planning files brown. Suppose Mr. Andrusz decides to transfer the land he purchased into the trust he created as part of his estate plan. Another reason to cross-reference!

c. Organizing Numerically

Firms that maintain paper files often prefer a numerical filing system that avoids rearranging file drawers when new clients are added to the system. Using numbers can also add a layer of confidentiality protection. Numeric filing also has drawbacks: it can require that those working on the files either consult an index or memorize the file number for each client; it may require an extra step in coding, as described below; in recording file information, it is very easy to transpose or omit numbers.

The system may be as simple as straight numbering (the firm's first client matter is number 1); straight numbering can be combined with color coding to show the type of matter or the supervising attorney. The disadvantage is that a single client may have files scattered throughout the system; an index is obviously necessary.

The numbers in a coded system represent characteristics of the file. For example, numbers could be coded to tie into the alphabet, so that the name "Abate" would be 1-2-1-20-5. The number assigned may be coded by fields and any combination is possible. The number may incorporate some combination of the year, the month, the date, a code describing the type of case, a unique code assigned to and retained by each client, a number representing the attorney supervising the file, and a sequential number:

File 09-11-16-31-121 may tell you this:

Year	Month	Date	Attorney	Sequential number
09	11	16	31	121

Or

Year	Matter type	Attorney	Client	Sequential Number
09	11	16	31	121

---

[2]Sometimes color coding is achieved by affixing colored "dots" to the file.

d. Organizing Alphanumerically

alphanumeric
System that identifies files by combination of letters and numbers

Alphanumeric arrangements use both alphabetic and numeric characters; the label may be random or may provide some information about the file contents.

> 09 PI 312 RKW 122 may refer to a file opened in 2009, for a personal injury matter being handled for client number 312 by attorney RKW, sequential number 122.
>
> 09 PI 354 may just mean that this is the 354th personal injury file opened in 2009.

The firm can make it as simple or complicated as fits its needs. The system should reflect the priorities of the firm. For example, in a small firm, a general practitioner will typically ask for a file by the client's name. The client's name or number should be the most significant factor in where and how the file is kept. In a large firm, however, any number of attorneys may be working on a personal injury file, and all of those attorneys work only on personal injury files. The matter type is the priority for filing. Any of the systems can be combined with color coding, which can be done on the file's tabs or labels.

Midsized to large firms designate a person to assign file numbers to avoid any chance of duplication. In some firms, that file number may be different from the client/matter number. Imagine that client number 7654, Fuller Builders, Inc., has had five real estate purchase matters (code 11) in 2009. The firm might designate the files 09-11-7654-1 through 09-11-7654-5, if it codes by year, matter type, and client number. On the other hand, the firm may assign all files sequential numbers that do not identify client and matter at all. Perhaps the firm has a large central file room where files are assigned space according to where it is available; those files might be in five separate spaces and might be given file numbers that describe the space rather than the client and matter.

Common filing problems include:

- Jammed drawers
- Overflowing subfiles
- Papers piling up in the "miscellaneous" subfile
- Labels difficult to read or worn out folders/tabs
- Lost files

If a file cannot be found, it is often because it is on someone's desk or in someone's briefcase. A checkout system that makes it easy to track files is an essential part of an effective filing system. Many firms use large "OUT" cards. A card (or file, which can hold documents pending return of the file), roughly the size of a file folder, is inserted into the file's spot in the file drawer when a file is taken out. The person taking the file signs the last line on the card. In addition to indicating that the file is out and where it is, the card makes it easy to replace the file in the proper spot. Some out cards are designed so that the person taking the file can simply insert a business card into the slot.

Large firms are moving to bar coding systems. You are probably familiar with bar coding, which is used in grocery stores for tracking inventory and scanning prices, in libraries for tracking books and other materials, and by delivery services such as the U.S. Postal Service and UPS for tracking packages. A bar code, printed on an adhesive label, can be affixed to a file and scanned when a file is taken so that the file's new location can be entered into the computerized system.

Lost files are such a major cause of wasted time[3] that some firms now invest in electronic tracking devices that can "sense" when a file is in a particular zone or on a particular desk. But finding a lost file does not always require advanced technology. Here are some tips for searching for lost files:

1. Look completely through the correct folder, and then in front of and behind the correct file or folder.
2. Look between the files and under files; the document may have slipped to the bottom of the drawer or shelf, especially when using suspended filing systems.
3. Check the transposition of names and numbers and commonly misread letters (is that a small l or a capital I?).
4. Look for other units of a filing segment; "Taylor, Cassidy A" may have been filed as "Cassidy, Taylor A."
5. Check alternate spellings: Peterson/Petersen, Sharon/Sharron, and even nicknames or Anglicized versions (Kasimir is called Casey by everyone in the office).
6. Look in the year preceding or following the one in question, if files are organized by year; look in a related subject if working with subject files.
7. Be aware that the file may be in the sorter, waiting to be filed, in storage, being transferred, or pulled for disposition or conversion to electronic format.

For More Information

To learn more about electronic tracking device technology, visit http://www.rfid-legal-file-tracking.com or http://www.filetrail.com/WS_Home/index.asp. Also, the National Archives and Records Administration has an excellent selection of records management publications, including information about how federal agencies prepare records for transfer to electronic format and recover documents after a disaster. Visit http://www.archives.gov/publications/records-mgmt.html.

---

[3]File Trail Inc., a provider of tracking devices, indicates that its clients believe that 6 to 10 percent of staff time is wasted on looking for files. http://www.alanet.org/publications/issue/sepoct07/OffTheShelf.pdf

Assignment 8-1
Organizing Paper Files

Management Portfolio

1. You work for a sole practitioner who keeps a file card box with a card for each file as a master file index. Design a card that would contain all necessary information about each file. (Have you been using the Microsoft Template site? http://office.microsoft.com/en-us/templates/FX100595491033. aspx. Search "client information" for some helpful hints.)
2. Use the Internet to determine whether bar code adhesive labels can be printed on an office printer using special software and the cost of a hand-held scanner.

2. Electronic Files

There are countless articles about "the paperless law office," but few firms do away with paper files entirely. Many firms are unwilling to invest the time to go back and transfer old files to electronic format, and there is the problem of dealing with original documents. A more appropriate title might be "the electronically organized law office."

a. Advantages of Electronic Files

The transition to an electronically organized office has more benefits and fewer problems than many firms initially expect. There is less need for original documents than some firms anticipate, even for use in litigation (Exhibit 8-1), and many firms scan documents and send the originals to the client. The task of filing becomes largely obsolete, and because electronic documents are easily searched, misfiling becomes a thing of the past. In fact, the same document can be stored in several different files with little extra effort and no need for extra space. There is never any need to move bulky files because there is no more room in the drawer.

Let's imagine several different scenarios, first in a paper environment:

- A letter arrives from opposing counsel. You locate the file, pull out the correspondence folder, make copies of the letter, two-hole punch the letter, pull back the metal prongs, find the correct chronological place in the folder, push back the prongs, and return the folder to the file and the file to its cabinet.
- Attorney is leaving for a hearing, locates the heavy, bulky file, and places it in a rolling document case. This is a particular nuisance if the attorney has to travel by plane. If an important document arrives after attorney

leaves or if attorney has accidentally left part of the file in the office, the firm may have to pay for a messenger service.

- Client calls—he has misplaced several important letters from the firm. You find the file, dig through the folders, locate and remove the letters, use the firm's expensive copier to make copies, put the letters in the correct order on the prongs, replace the folder, and file. Now, address an envelope and mail the copies.
- The correspondence folder in the Smith file has gotten too big to manage. You decide that it would be easier to manage if organized according to who originated the correspondence and spend an hour creating and organizing new folders.
- The Marden file is ready to be closed. You spend several hours closing the file (as described later in this chapter) and then send the file to storage.

Now let's imagine the same scenarios in an electronic environment:

- You scan the letter to Adobe Portable Document Format (PDF) and save to the appropriate folder. The filing is done.
- Attorney is leaving for a hearing, saves the file to a CD or other memory device, and opens documents as needed from her laptop computer. If attorney needs something more, she can access it from the firm extranet or have a paralegal send it as an e-mail attachment.
- You e-mail client the letters, as attachments.
- You create a new correspondence folder in the electronic Smith file and simply "drop and drag" the documents into the appropriate folder.
- You do a "drop and drag" to move the Marden file to the virtual storage site for closed files.

Is there a downside to using electronic files? Yes, electronic devices and storage media can become obsolete quickly. Remember the 5-inch floppy disk? If a firm does not take care to either preserve old equipment or convert and/or transfer files as new devices and software upgrades become available, the files might become inaccessible during the time the firm is required to keep them.

For More Information

Got a 5-inch floppy? If you need to retrieve old data, there are private collectors and museums that have everything from the Commodore 64 and the original Mac to today's PDAs. Many companies that provide electronic discovery services also provide data retrieval services. See, for example Data Recovery Systems, http://www.datarecoverysystems.com/. For an overview of working with obsolete data, see Law and Technology Resources, http://www.llrx.com/columns/fios3.htm.

To make the transition from a print to an electronic filing environment, the firm must first make several decisions, including: Will active files be converted or will the change apply to new files as they arrive? Who will have responsibility for converting active files? Will the firm continue to organize files in the way it has organized paper files, either by assigning a unique numeric or alpha-numeric identifier for each client/matter or by client name/matter? Will everyone at the firm be trained to scan every incoming document and every executed document originating at the firm (court filings and some transactional documents have to be signed and even notarized—a copy of the document as signed and witnessed should be scanned to the file) and to save every document coming into or originating at the firm using the same system?

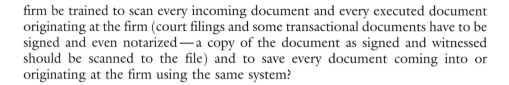

Exhibit 8-1
Federal Rules of Evidence

Can a scanned image be printed and used as evidence? The Federal Rules of Evidence provide for electronically produced copies:

ARTICLE X. CONTENTS OF WRITINGS, RECORDINGS, AND PHOTOGRAPHS

Rule 1001. Definitions

For purposes of this article the following definitions are applicable:

(1) **Writings and recordings**. "Writings" and "recordings" consist of letters, words, or numbers, or their equivalent, set down by handwriting, typewriting, printing, photostating, photographing, magnetic impulse, mechanical or electronic recording, or other form of data compilation.

(2) **Photographs**. "Photographs" include still photographs, X-ray films, video tapes, and motion pictures.

(3) **Original**. An "original" of a writing or recording is the writing or recording itself or any counterpart intended to have the same effect by a person executing or issuing it. An "original" of a photograph includes the negative or any print therefrom. If data are stored in a computer or similar device, any printout or other output readable by sight, shown to reflect the data accurately, is an "original."

(4) **Duplicate**. A "duplicate" is a counterpart produced by the same impression as the original, or from the same matrix, or by means of photography, including enlargements and miniatures, or by mechanical or electronic re-recording, or by chemical reproduction, or by other equivalent techniques which accurately reproduces the original.

Rule 1003. Admissibility of Duplicates

A duplicate is admissible to the same extent as an original unless (1) a genuine question is raised as to the authenticity of the original or (2) in the circumstances it would be unfair to admit the duplicate in lieu of the original.

b. Organizing Electronic Files

Consistency in saving documents is key to making the system work. Even if you do not have case management software, you can create virtual filing cabinets (both described below). Even if you do not create digital filing cabinets but store everything in a single, unsubdivided folder, you can find what you need quickly by using a consistent naming system. For example, all discovery might use "discovery" as a first word. A motion to compel might have its component documents named "discovery - compel - motion," "discovery - compel - memo," "discovery - compel - affidavit in support," and so on. You could also keep all the related documents together by scanning or combining them into a single PDF file, such as "discovery - compel - motion - all."

You can also create a virtual "cabinet" for active files (Exhibit 8-2); you may want to create additional cabinets for closed files and non-client files. If your firm is networked, the network is configured so that each computer can access this virtual cabinet and the files it contains. Within each cabinet, you can create a file for each client matter. In a paper-based office, each file would contain folders with labels identifying contents, such as "correspondence," "pleadings," "notes," and "research"; within the folders, documents are organized chronologically. Similarly, you can create folders within each file in your electronic cabinet for each type of document and organize documents chronologically.

Example

Here is one example of a file path: G:\Active\Lehmann\Estate\Correspondence. This indicates that on the network's G-drive there is a category for active files, a file for client Lehmann's estate planning matter, with a folder for correspondence. Within that folder, the documents will automatically organize alphabetically, so you may wish to impose order within the folder by naming the documents by date. You may wish to add more descriptive information, such as a description of the document or the initials of the originator. A letter sent by attorney Robert K. Warren to Ms. Lehmann on March 3, 2009, concerning her estate plan, might be G:\Active\Lehmann\Estate\Correspondence\090303rkw

---

Some of the documents in each folder may have been created in a native format such as Microsoft Word or Corel WordPerfect and converted to PDF. Although this is called "printing to PDF," it does not involve an actual printer, paper, or toner. The advantage of making the conversion before saving and filing is that the file copy looks just like what would come out of a physical printer. This can be particularly important for documents with complex formatting, such as pleadings, if the document might be sent to others by different means (e-filing, hard copy to the client, an attachment sent to co-counsel) so that the formatting might not remain intact in native format.

Using the same set of folders for each file involving the same type of matter simplifies the process of opening a "new matter" and creates consistency in the system. For example, you can create a master litigation folder set that contains the file structure for new litigation matters. The subfolders are empty. When opening a new litigation file, simply highlight the NewFileLit folder and then copy and then paste the file structure onto the folder created for the client. Now every

Exhibit 8-2
Electronic File Folders

Here is one example of how to create an electronic file folder: Open your computer's My Documents folder, go to the File menu, select New, and create a folder named "Active files." Open the folder, select New from the File menu, and create your client files (Screenshot A).

Screenshot A

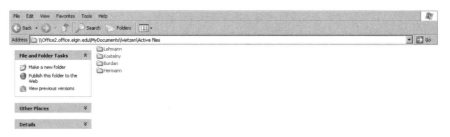

Open one of the client files ("Lehmann" in Screenshot B) and create folders for correspondence, client intake documents, pleadings, research, and notes.

Screenshot B

Notice that the intake folder contains a spreadsheet, a Word document, a document scanned and saved as a PDF file, and a saved e-mail message (Screenshot C).

Screenshot C

litigation file has the same filing structure. Similar predefined folder sets are maintained for transactional and other matters.

c. Document Management Software

Even with a careful system for creating files and folders and for naming documents, it can be difficult to locate a particular document in a large folder. **Document management software** such as iManage and Worldox works with your word processing software to prevent this problem. After a document is saved, a document profile window appears. This profile contains fields such as document name, author, client/matter number, document type, description, and document history. When the profile is completed, the document is automatically added to the firm's document library (also called a firm repository, discussed in Chapter 7).

Case management and practice management systems (discussed in depth in Chapter 5) often combine document organization, management, and assembly (template creation) functions with features for calendaring, accounting, time and billing, task management, and notes. Sophisticated programs can search through all documents in the system for conflicts of interest.

document management software
Creates a "profile" of document characteristics to make retrieval easier

---

Assignment 8-2
Organizing Electronic Files

Organize the documents you have created for school on your computer. Create a file called "school," with a folder for each class. Place the assignments you have done, along with other relevant material (e-mails from instructor or fellow students, a copy of the syllabus) in appropriate folders. You may print your directory to show that you have completed the assignment or, with the directory open, hit the "print screen" key at the top/right of your keyboard. This will put the directory in the clipboard so that you can paste it into an e-mail.

B. Client Files

1. Opening New Client Files

New clients and new matters for current clients call for new files. Files should be opened, even if they are immediately closed, for those who come in for consultation but do not retain the firm. Opening a file is a way to make sure the names and pertinent information are entered into your firm's database for conflicts checks. The firm should have a check list of documents that should appear in every file, which will usually include the following:

- A client intake form (as shown in Exhibit 8-3)

- Documentation of conflict of interest check
- A letter of engagement documenting fee agreements, assigned attorney, and a statement of the firm's file retention policy
- Documentation that statute of limitations and other dates have been entered into the calendar or tickler system

Add information about each new file to a spreadsheet or master index of files, with creation and destruction dates, and storage location. Many firms create or purchase new matter forms that produce multiple copies that can be distributed as needed. Case management software may generate a new matter form automatically. Typically one copy would go into or on the file itself (as a case cover sheet), another to the master index of files, another to the accounting/billing department, and perhaps another to the keeper of the calendar. A new matter form would typically include

- Intake date,
- Client name and billing address,
- Client number,
- Identification of attorney with primary responsibility and others assigned to the matter,
- Matter type,
- Matter number,
- Billing information (hourly, contingency, rates quoted, and client's own file reference number if it must be included on billing),
- Opposing party, if relevant, and how the matter will be identified (e.g., *Meinke v. Dolenga*),
- Opposing attorney and contact information,
- Who referred the client,
- Initials of person who completed conflicts check,
- Initials of person who calendared important dates,
- Closure date (to be added when the file is closed) and information about disposition of closed file.

Best Practices

Consider keeping your own file of cases you are working on or have worked on. This not only will provide you with a quick reference should you need information while not actively working on the file, but can also serve as your own "database" for checking for conflicts of interest if you should change jobs.

---

2. Maintaining Files

Some lawyers keep every note, every draft of every document, letter, phone message, voice mail record, and bill, at least until the representation is concluded. Others are minimalists, keeping only bare essentials. Scan or copy original documents so that they can be returned to the client or filed with the appropriate court or agency as soon as possible.

Exhibit 8-3
Client Intake Form

The purpose of an initial consultation is for the attorney to advise you, the prospective client, what, if anything, may be done for you and what the minimum fee therefore will be. The purpose is not to render a definitive legal opinion as it may be impossible to fully assess a matter within the time frame allotted for a consultation or with the information or documents that you may be able to provide at the initial consultation.

One of three outcomes is possible following your consultation.

A) You and the Attorney mutually agree to the terms of representation, or *(After a separate document called an Agreement for Representation is signed a copy will be provided to you.)*

B) The Attorney declines representation, or

C) You decide not to use the services of the Attorney.

Note: The following questions will help us to understand the reason for your visit today. Your responses are protected by attorney/client privilege and will be held in strict confidence.

Name _____

        Last   First   Middle or Maiden

Address _____

        Number   Street   City   State   Zip

Home
Phone (———) ——————————

Briefly explain what you may need advice about or assistance with today:

_____

Are there any parties involved? (Examples: a friend, an employer, a neighbor, signor of a contract, etc. This should include parties on either side of your issue.)

Party_____ Relationship_____

Party_____ Relationship_____

Party_____ Relationship_____

On the lines below, list documents (papers) that you think may help us to understand the issues.

1) _____

2) _____

3) _____

EXHIBIT 8-3
(continued)

(Note: Any documents you supply that are important to your matter will be photocopied, with your permission, and your originals returned to you at the conclusion of the initial interview.)

Ideally, if things turn out precisely the way you want, what would the outcome be?

_____

Knowing that there are no guarantees, what can you accept?_____

Please classify your urgency in concluding this matter? (check one)

[ ] Critical — Personal safety or continuation of business depends on it.
[ ] Very important — severe hardship, personal or financial inconvenience if matter is not resolved quickly.
[ ] Important — Matter interferes with business or personal financial stability.
[ ] Needs to be done, but no immediate hardship in the interim.
[ ] Just thought I'd see if it was worth pursuing, but I'm not counting on anything.
[ ] Just wanted to know what my rights are. I'll then let you know after I think about it.

If the matter involves payment of money you feel you are owed, how long can you wait before not getting paid? _____ (Days, Weeks, Months, Years)

Are we the first attorneys you have consulted regarding this matter? [ ] Yes [ ] No
If No — Why didn't you hire their services? _____
Have you ever been represented by an attorney before? [ ] Yes [ ] No
If Yes — Please state the circumstances _____

How will you pay for your attorney's fees in this matter?
[ ] Check today [ ] Cash today [ ] Contingency Fee [ ] On Account
[ ] Credit Card Credit Card No. _____ Expr. Date _____

Marital Status: [ ] Married [ ] Single [ ] Divorced [ ] Widowed [ ] Separated
Drivers License # _____ Social Security #_____
Are you known by any other names? [ ] Yes [ ] No
If yes, name(s) _____
(A fictitious name, a nickname, a former name, your maiden name etc.)

EXHIBIT 8-3
(continued)

Where are you employed?_____

May we contact you there? [ ] Yes [ ] No Phone No. (_____) _____

If your mail is returned as undeliverable or telephone service terminated, please provide the name of someone (friend or relative) you believe will always know how to contact you.

Name_____ Relationship_____

Address _____ Phone No. (_____) _____

_____ State & Zip _____

How did you learn of our office? [ ] A friend [ ] Yellow Pages [ ] Bar Referral

[ ] Our Web Page (http:/www.yourfirm'spage.com) [ ] Former Client [ ] Other

PLEASE READ CAREFULLY & Sign Below

Following your initial interview, if you agree to hire the Attorney, and the Attorney agrees to represent you, you will both sign an Agreement for Representation. The Agreement for Representation will set forth the terms and conditions of representation.

If the Attorney is willing to represent you and you decide not to sign an Agreement of Representation today, you are strongly urged to schedule a second appointment with the Attorney at the earliest possible time or to immediately consult with other legal counsel to protect your rights.

NOTICE: This office does not represent you with regard to the matters set forth by you herein in this information sheet or discussed during your consultation unless and until, both you and the Attorney execute a written Agreement for Representation.

If the Attorney does not agree to represent you, this includes not representing you with regard to the matter set forth by you on this information sheet, or any other matters you may discuss with the Attorney during your consultation. If your legal problem(s) involve a potential lawsuit, it is important that you realize a lawsuit must be filed within a certain period of time called a Statute of Limitations. Therefore, the Attorney strongly urges you to immediately consult with another attorney to protect your rights. The Attorney's decision not to represent you should not be taken by you as an expression regarding the merits of your case. Your signature acknowledges

**EXHIBIT 8-3
(continued)**

only that you received a copy of this completed information sheet and does not mean you have hired the Attorney.

SIGNATURE _____ DATE ___/___/___

This portion to be completed by the Attorney
[ ] Will represent (see New Case Memo and Agreement for Representation attached)
[ ] Will investigate and report (Schedule a follow-up conference for _____ days)
[ ] Representation declined — Letter of declination will be sent.
[ ] Party "will think about it" and get back with us — No action to be taken and party was so informed.
[ ] Client declined Representation at this time.

Interviewed by _____ this ___ day of _____

NOTES:_____

Reprinted with permission from J.R. Phelps, from the Florida Bar Association, Law Office Management Assistance Service.

---

lien
Legal claim against property to secure payment of an obligation

The firm is the custodian of the file, but not the owner. The ethical rules in most states indicate that the file and associated work product are the client's property, subject to the attorney's **lien** for fees. The lawyer has an obligation to safeguard client property and to avoid prejudicing clients' interests by withholding information.

The firm should have a policy about asking clients who request their files why they are changing firms. The reason may be simple; for example, the client could be moving to another state. If the client is dissatisfied with the firm, it is best to discover the problem as early as possible. The attorney may want to attempt to resolve the client's issues or, if the problem is more serious than dissatisfaction, notify the malpractice insurance carrier to "trigger" coverage. Always ask clients to sign and date a receipt for documents or files they take.

3. Closing Files

When may a firm close a file and when may it finally dispose of the documents in a file? The answers depend on many factors, including state ethics rules. The rule in Illinois, for example, is this:

A lawyer shall hold property of clients or third persons that is in a lawyer's possession in connection with a representation separate from the lawyer's own property. Funds shall be kept in a separate account or accounts maintained in the state where the lawyer's office is situated, or elsewhere with the consent of the client or third person. Other property shall be identified as such and appropriately safeguarded. Complete records of such account funds and other property shall be kept by the lawyer and shall be preserved for a period of seven years after termination of the representation. Ill. Rules of Prof. Conduct R. 115(a), *available at* http://www.iardc.org.

Other factors include

- Preferences of the attorney and client.
- Ages of the parties. Matters involving minor children, for example, will require longer retention.
- State statutes of limitation on attorney malpractice and grievances. Some states have a "discovery rule," under which the time begins to run when the client discovers the problem, regardless of when the representation occurred.
- Likelihood that the file will have to be revisited; some matters have a clear-cut end, while others never reach final resolution.

In some situations, the file can be closed even though the matter is not complete. For example, suppose a firm prepares a ten-year lease for a client that contains an **option** to renew. After the lease is executed, the file can be closed, but it should be kept so that it can be accessed in case of problems between landlord and tenant. In addition, the date for exercise of the option should put on the calendar (with a tickler) and should include information about where the file can be found.

option
Right to do an action (purchase property, renew lease) at an agreed price

The firm should have a procedure for closing a file, which will typically start with a review to ensure that all tasks relating to the representation have been completed, decisions and results have been documented, and any future actions docketed. A preliminary **purge** should remove unneeded duplicate copies of documents, supplies (legal pads containing one page of notes), and any other items that should not have been placed in the file, and any original documents, which should be returned to the client. Documents that are available elsewhere (such as pleadings that have been filed) may be removed to reduce bulk. Drafts of a document that is now in final form can generally be discarded. Copies of case law, briefs, and memos may be sent to the firm's form file or repository. Remaining documents should be secured with prongs so that none are lost. Electronic files also take up space—on the server—and may be stored to a disk, CD ROM, or other storage media.

purge
To systematically permanently remove items

A final "disengagement" letter to the client should identify any future actions the client needs to take and restate the firm's file retention policy. After the file is clearly labeled for storage, the master file index should be marked with the file's new location and dates for final review and destruction. Finally, submit time records for final billing.

While it is true that a client may be more likely to return to the firm knowing that the firm has a complete history and file, the firm takes on a responsibility in keeping the file. Recently closed files often are stored onsite, sometimes using storage systems that compress the files to save drawer space. Long-term storage offsite is more economical but also more subject to loss or damage. The firm must be careful to store paper files where they are protected from water, wind, fire, sunlight, insects, rodents, mold, and curious third parties. Rather than store paper files, some firms either convert the remaining documents to electronic format or microfilm.

When the attorney in charge of a file does make the decision to destroy a file, another review should be conducted to ensure that no original or irreplaceable documents remain in the file. To protect confidentiality, documents containing client information must not be "dumped" but should be shredded. Documents not containing client information can be recycled.

Law firms can go out of business and, in such situations, must provide for any files in storage. Sole practitioners, in particular, need to provide for the future care, custody, and control of client files. Many "solos" enter into agreements with other sole practitioners or firms to take charge of the files if the attorney becomes unable to practice.

Assignment 8-3
Retaining Client Files

Find your state's rule on retention of files. It may be the equivalent of ABA Model Rule 1.15.

C. Handling Evidence and Discovery

Any firm that handles important client documents and case evidence should have a way to protect the documents and evidence from theft, fire, and other physical damage. Most attorneys do not have space or resources to store everything in fireproof cabinets, but there are some things that are worth the additional investment. A "one-of-a-kind" piece of evidence or an original executed will should be kept in a fireproof safe. Evidentiary photos should be stored separately from the negatives.

Assignment 8-4
Handling Evidence

Management Portfolio

The firm of Rodan & Stosh often handles evidence for civil trials. Write a page for the procedures manual, indicating how evidence should be logged in, tracked, and kept.

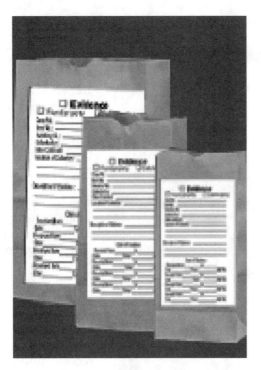

Many firms and police departments purchase evidence bags (paper or plastic?) with preprinted labels for indicating the source of the evidence, who has handled it, its original condition, and other relevant information.

Out There—Paralegal Profile
A Perspective on Records Management

Lynette Nichols Newman has worked almost 30 years in federal government positions. After starting as a file clerk with the Department of the Army, she attended an ABA-approved paralegal program and worked her way up to a paralegal position with the Securities and Exchange Commission, where she has been for the past 20 years. In addition to not having to track time, Lynette says that the top advantages to working for a government agency are the excellent pay and benefits and job security. The quality of life benefits are also great—flexible work hours and the ability to work various compressed work schedules (such as nine-hour days with one day off every two weeks or ten-hour days four days a week). Lynette takes advantage of the agency's very liberal telework program and likes the satisfaction of knowing that she is helping to protect the public from those who commit fraud in the securities markets.

The main disadvantage to working in the government is dealing with the bureaucracy, according to Lynette. It's sometimes hard to cut through

the red tape to get support or supplies for a project. Government agencies are limited on how much they can pay; raises are regulated and controlled, so managers cannot just give you a raise for a job well done. There are no "perks" like in law firms—no free lunches, and employees pay for their own coffee and holiday parties. There are no end-of-year bonuses. While Lynette does draw from many resources—online databases, research sources, computer and office supplies, it depends on the budget approved every year by Congress.

Concerning records management, Lynette says, "We've gone from all paper filing and records into computerized record keeping. Our office uses an electronic discovery and document management program for document productions, depositions, transcripts, and other electronic media. As far as paralegal duties go, document management is one area where strong organizational skills are a real asset. We use Concordance, but I've learned that whatever program is used, it's important think through how the documents will be searched and how we want to use them. There are a few quirks of electronic document management. Handwritten notes cannot be OCR'd [scanned for optical character recognition] with any accuracy, so handwritten documents need to be identified and coded so those documents can be reviewed for relevance. Documents also need to be unitized [identification of beginning and end of document in electronic environment without limitations of page size] correctly so each document can be separately searched and tagged as needed. Unitizing is also important in order to keep the integrity of the original production (if produced in hard copy). We work with a vendor who scans and downloads the documents, so we need to know how we want the documents separated, what fields we want for each document, and decide whether to use existing bates numbers or assign new numbers."

Chapter Review

Discussion Questions

1. Describe how you would organize, for alphabetical filing, files belonging to clients Robin Ann Smith, Robert E. Smith, The James T.
   Cook Foundation, Sheri Ramsay-Croy and her son Samuel T. Croy,
   Matthew Thomas Childs and Child's World Books, Inc.
2. Your firm, which has traditionally kept paper files organized by case
   numbers consisting of year-client number-matter type number-and
   case number, has decided to move toward a paper-free environment.
   Describe the decisions that will have to be made and the steps that will
   follow.
3. Describe the steps for closing a file and eventually destroying the file.
4. What is the downside of electronic files?
5. Describe the folders that would be typically found in a litigation file
   and how those folders would be organized.
6. How can a firm prevent files from being carelessly misplaced by lawyers
   and paralegals working on those files?

ACROSS

1. document _____ software creates a document profile for easy search
4. form prepared in first interview
6. legal claim against property to secure payment of obligation
7. hold papers within folders
10. filing system that protects confidentiality well
13. type of coding that can be scanned
14. downside to electronic storage, equipment can become _____
15. states have different rules concerning _____ of files
20. system of identifying files by combination of letters and numbers
21. PDF stands for a(n) _____ file

DOWN

2. AAA is an example
3. system, all files in one place
5. common cause of misfiling, _____ of numbers, letters
8. simplest filing system

9. should be disregarded in alphabetical filing
11. type of coding making file identification easier
12 when filing records of an individual alphabetically, this is the first unit considered
14. right to purchase property for an agreed price
16. initials, sets best practices for filing
17. a person's middle name would typically be the _____ for filing alphabetically
18. to remove material
19. word commonly moved to the end unit of a corporate name

Terms and Definitions

acronym: Abbreviation of several words

alphanumeric: System that identifies files by combination of letters and numbers

ARMA International: Professional organization; sets standards for records retention

centralized: In a central location, rather than disbursed

document management software: Creates a "profile" of document characteristics to make retrieval easier

lien: Legal claim against property to secure payment of an obligation

option: Right to do an action (purchase property, renew lease) at an agreed price

purge: To systematically permanently remove items

surname: Also called "family name" or "last name," as distinguished from "given name" or "first name"

9

Employees

As a Manager

You may be responsible for overseeing and, possibly, implementing the processes for hiring and evaluating employees. Depending on the firm, you may be responsible for obtaining documents from new employees.

Objectives

After completing this chapter, you will be able to

- Prepare a job description that provides objective criteria for hiring and interview questions that do not touch on discriminatory topics.
- Identify resources and strategies for finding a job as a paralegal or finding the right person for a paralegal position.
- Plan an orientation for a new employee.
- Describe policies a firm should have in place with respect to employees and describe the characteristics of a well-written sexual harassment policy.
- Describe the taxes an employer must withhold or pay and procedures for compliance.
- Identify the agencies responsible for workers' compensation and unemployment in your state.
- Identify the requirements of FMLA, ERISA, and COBRA.
- Describe procedures for employee evaluation and termination.
- Turn the differences inherent in a diverse workplace into assets for you and your firm.
- Understand how to effectively work with all attorneys, experienced and new, at your firm.

A. Hiring

If you are not already working in a legal setting, you will likely have to get your "foot in the door" before you find a job with substantial management responsibilities. Although you cannot do anything about the state of the economy or the number of legal employers in your area, you can overcome some of the challenges in finding that first job by understanding the process from an employer's point of view. Many of the resources most useful to employers are also very helpful to job seekers.

Hiring should be a process, not a reaction. Even if the firm badly needs someone as soon as possible, the process should be followed; the consequences of hiring the wrong person can be disastrous.

1. Describe the Job

The first step in the hiring process is defining what the job requires. The first step in looking for a job is deciding what you want in a job and being realistic about what you can do. A good job description provides objective criteria for hiring and reduces the likelihood that hiring decisions will be based on inappropriate, discriminatory characteristics or that a candidate will be unable to perform or unhappy with the job after accepting it (see Exhibits 9-1 and 9-2).

Exhibit 9-1
Job Descriptions

A job description should include a:

- Job Title
- Job Objective or Overall Purpose Statement — This statement is generally a summary designed to orient the reader to the general nature, level, purpose, and objective of the job. The summary should describe the broad function and scope of the position and be no longer than three to four sentences.
- List of Duties or Tasks Performed — The list contains an item by item list of principal duties, continuing responsibilities, and accountability of the occupant of the position. The list should contain each and every essential job duty or responsibility that is critical to the successful performance of the job. The list should begin with the most important functional and relational responsibilities and continue down in order of significance. Each duty or responsibility that comprises at least five percent of the incumbent's time should be included in the list.
- Description of the Relationships and Roles the occupant of the position holds within the company, including any supervisory positions, subordinating roles, and/or other working relationships.

When using job descriptions for recruiting situations, you may also want to attach the following:

- Job Specifications, Standards and Requirements — The minimum amount of qualifications needed to perform the essential functions of the job, such as education, experience, knowledge, and skills. Any critical skills and expertise needed for the job should be included. For example, for a receptionist, critical skills may be having (1) a professional and courteous telephone manner, (2) legible handwriting if messages are to be taken, (3) the ability to handle a multiple-lined phone system for a number of staff members, and (4) the patience and endurance to sit behind a desk all day.
- Job Location — Where the work will be performed.
- Equipment to be used in the performance of the job. For example, do your company's computers run on an Apple Macintosh or PC Windows environment?
- Collective Bargaining Agreements — Agreements and terms that relate to job functions, if applicable, such as when your company's employees are members of a union.
- Non-essential Functions — Functions which are not essential to the position or any marginal tasks performed by the incumbent of the position.
- Salary Range — Range of pay for the position.

EXHIBIT 9-1
(continued)

Keep each statement in the job description crisp and clear:

- Structure your sentences in classic verb/object and explanatory phrases. Since the occupant of the job is your sentences' implied subject, it may be eliminated. For example, a sentence pertaining to the description of a receptionist position might read: "Greets office visitors and personnel in a friendly and sincere manner."
- Always use the present tense of verbs.
- If necessary, use explanatory phrases telling why, how, where, or how often to add meaning and clarity. For example: "Collects all employee time sheets on a bi-weekly basis for payroll purposes."
- Omit any unnecessary articles such as "a," "an," "the," or other words for an easy to understand point description. Using the above example, the statement could have read, "Greets all visitors and the office personnel to the building in a friendly and a sincere manner."
- Use unbiased terminology. For example: use the he/she approach or construct sentences in such a way that gender pronouns are not required.
- Avoid using words which are subject to differing interpretations. Try not to use words such as "frequently," "some," "complex," "occasional," and "several."

From U.S. Small Business Administration, Manage Employees, Writing Effective Job Descriptions, http://www.sba.gov/smallbusinessplanner/manage/manageemployees/SERV_JOBDESC.html (last visited Feb. 17, 2009).

Exhibit 9-2
Sample Job Description

Law Office Manager

Reports to:	Managing Partner	Salary Grade:	C
Hours:	M-F, 8:00 a.m. to 5:00 p.m.	Exempt/Non-exempt:	Exempt

Purpose of Position:

- Supervises and trains all non-attorney employees to ensure efficient distribution of work
- Obtains temporary help or steps in to ensure completion of work assigned to employees who are absent or temporarily unable to handle workload

**EXHIBIT 9-2
(continued)**

- Works with the firm's accountant on budget, financial reports, and employee benefits
- Handles client billing
- Works with managing partner to implement firm marketing plan
- Procures and manages office supplies and equipment

Daily Functions:

- Opens office, ensures that equipment (e.g., copier, fax) is operational
- Records absences and late arrivals by non-lawyer personnel; obtains coverage for absent employees
- Manages equipment and supplies as needed

Periodic Functions:

- Handles overflow paralegal and clerical work for litigation and transaction practice groups
- Orders supplies, replacement equipment, equipment repair and maintenance
- Pays bills as approved by managing partner
- Prepares and mails monthly client billing
- Plans and supervises firm social and training events
- Works with managing partner to recruit and interview employees
- Ensures that employees are submitting weekly timesheets
- Updates and maintains procedures manual

Minimum Qualifications:

Education: ABA-approved paralegal degree or certificate.

Experience: At least one year working in a law office; at least one year working in a supervisory capacity. Must have excellent knowledge of Microsoft Office Suite and experience using word processing, spreadsheet, database, and calendaring applications.

Physical Demands: Minimal. Must be able to speak clearly and understandably and be able to sit for prolonged periods.

Behavioral Characteristics:

- Able to work well with others
- Detail-oriented
- High tolerance for stress
- Highly organized, able to complete tasks despite interruptions
- Dependable and prompt

2. Finding People/Finding Jobs

Once you know what the job looks like, how do you find the person to fill that job? Both sides of the hiring process have two problems: finding (qualified people or job openings) and evaluating (candidates and job openings).

Top Problems Encountered by Paralegal Job Hunters

> "Every job requires experience, but how can I get experience if nobody will give me a job?"
> "There aren't many paralegal positions listed around here."
> "I don't know how to put together a resume, come up with good questions to ask during an interview, or answer questions about my salary expectations."

a. *The Experience Factor*

Consider why the employer wants to hire someone with experience. She may have no time to train or she may be worried about liability for the mistakes of a novice. How can you respond to those concerns, as a job applicant, without having been employed in a law office? How can you evaluate entry-level candidates when you are in a hiring position?

- Get or look for *something* on the resume. It may be an internship obtained through a school, a job as a law firm receptionist, or even volunteer work done for or through a local legal aid office, a public law office (defender, prosecutor), or the bar association.
- Obtain or look for references from people employers trust. Such references may be a result of volunteer work, from teachers who were particularly impressed with a student's class work, or from senior paralegals already in the field with whom the job seeker has networked (see below). Previous employers in other fields, any contacts in the legal field, and community leaders can also serve as references. The applicant should prepare and the employer should expect a professional-looking list of references, with full contact information. Listing a person as a reference without first obtaining that person's permission is a red flag that should warn the potential employer that the applicant is not a good candidate.
- Demonstrate or look for interest in advancing the profession. A candidate who has been active in a local paralegal association — by volunteering to do something (write an article, help with an event) is likely to bring that same energy and initiative to an employer. If a job seeker has made the effort to get his name "out there," those already in the field will think of him when they hear of jobs and may be willing to provide a reference.
- Provide or ask for proof of ability to do the work. An energetic candidate will put together a portfolio of pleadings, memos, letters, and other work done while in school and will refer to the portfolio in his cover letter.

b. Where Are the Jobs?

Consider that the job you want to find or to advertise may be most appropriately called something other than "legal assistant" or "paralegal" and widen your search. Law firms, corporations, and government offices often hire people with paralegal credentials to do jobs with other titles: "docket clerk," "relocation specialist," "contract compliance specialist," or "regulatory compliance analyst." Focus on candidates or employers who interest you rather than job titles.

Whether you are looking for a job or looking for job candidates, arm yourself with knowledge: salary and benefits in your geographic area, billable hour expectations, most-wanted skills, common interview questions, and on-the-job expectations. Based on that knowledge, you can create a resume and cover letters that will distinguish you from the masses or suggest a job description and compensation package that will attract the best candidates. How can you acquire that knowledge? Lucky for you, you live in the cyber era!

For More Information

The Internet has a number of resources for finding or advertising a paralegal position.

- Paralegal associations have online career centers or surveys with career information:
  - American Alliance of Paralegals: http://www.aapipara.org/Jobbank.htm
  - Association of Legal Administrators: http://www.alanet.org/jobs/current.asp
  - International Paralegal Management Association: http://www.paralegalmanagement.org/ipma/detail.asp?linkID=107&heading=Job+Bank+Details+%26+Listings
  - National Association of Legal Assistants: http://www.nala.org/Survey_Table.htm
  - National Federation of Paralegal Associations: http://paralegals.legal-staff.com/Common/HomePage.aspx?abbr=PARALEGALS
- Monster has a "virtual interview" for a paralegal job: http://career-advice.monster.com/at-the-interview/legal/Paralegal-Virtual-Interview/home.aspx.
- For an interview checklist and sample resumes, visit ParalegalGateway.com at http://www.paralegalgateway.com/interviews.html.

A portfolio can be a major factor in finding employment and in finding the right candidate. Because some employers use the portfolio as part of a pre-interview screening process and paper portfolios can be difficult to assemble and distribute, job seekers may create personal websites so that employers can view their resumes and portfolios online. Another option is to burn a CD with work samples, which was previously discussed in the first chapter of this book.

c. The Resume

When writing your resume, ask yourself the following questions:

1. Does the resume include any spelling, grammatical, or typographical errors? A person who is careless in preparing a resume is likely to be even more careless on the job.
2. Does the resume respond to the job description? For example, if the job posting requests experience with particular software, does the resume refer to that software? Large firms and corporate employers frequently feed resumes through scanners with software that searches for specific key words. If the job posting refers to graduation from an ABA-approved program, the resume must contain that phrase to advance for further consideration.
3. Does the resume reveal any substantial gaps in employment, unexpected changes in direction (for example, high school teacher, dog groomer, retail sales, paramedic, and now paralegal) or decreases in responsibility?
4. What does the resume *not* say? For example, "Purdue University, Lafayette, Ind., Journalism 1999-2003" does not actually say that the applicant graduated.

If an employer is requesting or an applicant is considering submission by e-mail, consider whether the employer can open documents saved by the applicant's word processing program and whether formatting (italics, unusual fonts, spacing) will be saved. You may want to save your resume or request that resumes be submitted in PDF or plain text format.

Here are some additional tips for writing a resume and cover letter and interviewing:

1. Tailor the resume and letter to the job and firm.
2. Proofread. Then do it again. There can be *no* typographical, spelling, or grammatical errors!
3. Edit the resume and letter to eliminate unnecessary words, and keep it short.
4. Format to emphasize your strengths. If you have a 3.9 GPA and little work experience, put education at the top. If you have worked as a legal secretary at a top firm for many years but have not yet finished your paralegal education, perhaps your work experience should be at the top.
5. Find out as much as you can about the firm before the interview.
6. Dress professionally for the interview (see Chapter 10) and carry with you copies of your resume, copies of your list of references, your portfolio, information that may be needed to complete an application (names, addresses, supervisors, dates of previous employers and schools) and a pen and pad.
7. Make sure that your cell phone is silent during the interview and that you have not smoked since dressing for the interview. Non-smokers can detect even a whiff of smoke, and many employers do not want to hire smokers.

8. Think about the questions the interviewer may ask and practice your responses in advance. Be prepared to make small talk without touching on any of the "forbidden" topics.
9. Think in advance about the salary you are willing to accept, the benefits most important to you, and the type of work you hope to do, so that you will not appear unprepared if asked about these matters.

Assignment 9-1
Finding a Job

1. Using one of the websites listed in this chapter, find a paralegal or law office management/administration position in your area or in the area in which you hope to work.
2. Using the job description for an office manager given in Exhibit 9-1, create a self-assessment form for use in the employee's evaluation. This is a "check-list" type form that the office manager will complete and submit to the evaluator before the evaluation interview and should indicate, at a glance, whether the office manager believes he has performed functions listed in the job description and the office manager's goals for improvement in the coming year.
3. Create a list of interview questions for hiring an office manager, based on the job description in this chapter.

---

3. Using the Process to Avoid Discrimination

Now you have resumes and you have screened them to determine which applicants should go to the next level (phone or in-person interview). How do you further narrow the field? Various federal and state laws prohibit discrimination in hiring (and in decisions pertaining to current employees) based on race, color, religion, sex, age, ethnic/national origin, disability, or veteran status. To avoid violation of those laws and, at the same time, to hire the best possible employees, law firms can adopt various policies.

Rather than relying solely on a resume, which is designed by the applicant to highlight his strengths and conceal any weaknesses, the firm may want to use a detailed and up-to-date employment application form. Such a form can make it easier to spot gaps in employment history. For example, a resume might simply indicate employment at a firm 2008-2009; a detailed application might disclose that the job lasted from December 15, 2008, until January 5, 2009. The application can include a verification to be signed by the applicant, including agreement to investigation of statements made in the application and release of liability for informants giving truthful information; the firm obtaining a consumer and/or investigative report; drug testing and post-offer medical examination, as permitted by law; and compliance with firm policies, if hired.

Interviews must be conducted by individuals who possess a thorough understanding of what attributes are important for the position and what information needs to be obtained in order to evaluate the candidate (see Exhibit 9-3). If possible, everyone who will work with the person ultimately hired should participate in interviews. Each interviewer should study the completed application form, resume (if available), and a current job description before the interview and develop questions and topics for discussion in advance. The primary function of the interviewers is to observe the applicant and really listen to the applicant's answers and questions to evaluate attitude and compatibility. Making the applicant comfortable and providing information about the firm and the selection process are important, but the candidate should do most of the talking.

Interviewers should be careful to ask roughly the same questions of each applicant, to get a fair comparison and must be careful not to dominate the conversation. Questions should be formulated in advance and should include questions that are specific to experience and skills, open-ended questions that will require the candidate to give longer answers, scenario questions that will probe whether the candidate can exercise independent judgment, and questions to probe the candidate's personality and ability to fit into the firm and the job.

The candidate should be asked to bring work or writing samples if a work portfolio was not used as part of the pre-interview screening process. The interview should include questions about experience and specific skills, such as these:

- Describe a time you ran into an obstacle while researching a legal issue and how you overcame it.
- What types of docket control systems have you used?
- Describe the most exciting project you've worked on in the last year and what you learned from that project.
- What is your experience in coordinating the details of a client's transaction?

Interviewers can get a sense of an applicant's personality, motivation, and work style by asking open-ended questions, such as these:

- What is important to you in a job, and how do you measure your own success?
- What do you know about this firm, and why do you want to work here?
- Describe the best supervisor you've worked for.
- Describe the traits of a difficult coworker.
- How would your coworkers describe you?
- Describe a stressful situation you've handled at work and how you dealt with it.
- What is the most useful criticism or advice you have ever received on the job?
- How long have you been looking for a job?
- How did your current supervisor or coworkers contribute to your decision to look for a new position?
- Do you prefer to communicate by phone or e-mail, and why?

Exhibit 9-3
Guidelines for Hiring a Paralegal

The ABA Standing Committee on Paralegals has a number of suggestions for recruiting and hiring paralegals:

- Determine the appropriate functions and desired qualifications of a paralegal for your practice.
- Contact paralegal education programs. An ABA-approved paralegal program has met the stringent quality Guidelines established by the Standing Committee on Paralegals.
- Contact national and local paralegal associations, such as NALA, NFPA or NALS. Most list jobs at no cost to the employer. Some also maintain resume banks, such as the AAPI Job Bank or the LAMA Job Bank.
- Advertise in newspapers and list openings on web sites.
- Interview carefully, verify credentials, and check references.
- See chapter 6 in *Paralegals, Profitability, and the Future of Your Law Practice*, by Arthur G. Greene and Therese A. Cannon.
- You want a person with excellent organizational skills, who is detail minded and able to multi-task.
- Good communication skills, both oral and written, are essential.
- A paralegal with a genuine interest in law and empathy with clients' problems will be a valuable member of the legal team.

From American Bar Association, Standing Committee on Paralegals, Information for Lawyers: How Paralegals Can Improve Your Practice, http://www.abanet.org/legalservices/paralegals/lawyers.html (last visited Feb. 17, 2009).

Sometimes "scenario" questions also work well to bring out the applicant's personality, intelligence, and ability to work independently:

- Your supervisor leaves the office at 4 p.m., with instructions that you should hand-deliver loan documents to a bank down the street before the end of the day. You discover a significant typo in one of the documents and cannot reach your supervisor. What do you do?
- Your supervising attorney is preparing for trial and is locked in her office with instructions not to disturb her. You receive a call from a client, very upset, who insists on talking to the attorney immediately. How do you deal with it?

End the interview by asking whether the candidate has questions. A good candidate is interested in much more than starting salary. Ask whether you may check references and whether the candidate would like to discuss anything that has not yet come up. Red flags during an interview include negative comments about previous jobs, indications of past "job hopping," inability to provide references, and failure to listen—a person who is constantly planning what she will say next. Interviewers must avoid questions or discussions relating to an applicant's age, race, national origin, gender, religion, political associations, arrest record,[1] children (including childcare arrangements), marriage status, and medical, physical, or injury histories. The "small talk" at the beginning of an interview can easily turn to these prohibited subjects, and interviewers must be cautious. When in doubt, ask yourself whether the comment or question relates to performance of the job—if not, or if in doubt, don't say it. Consider how you word questions. Ask, "Are you authorized to work in this country?" rather than "Where were you born?" or "Are you a citizen?". "Would you be available to travel for your job?" is acceptable, while "Are you married?" or "Do you have children?" are not. Interviewers must also avoid making statements that could be viewed as promises of employment or as misrepresentations of the job, pay, or benefits.

In addition to avoiding direct questions about physical condition, age, ethnicity, religion, family status, military service, and politics, interviewers should consider how an applicant might perceive a question, even if asked with no discriminatory intent. Examples of "small talk" topics that may be perceived as touching on prohibited topics include asking about a person's name, accent, "home," holidays, social clubs, fraternities, or sororities, all of which could be perceived as questioning national origin or religion. Questions about the names and occupations of family members and names the candidate has worked under should also be avoided.

Law firms with 15 or more employees are subject to the **Americans with Disabilities Act (ADA)** in hiring and with respect to other employment actions. The ADA prohibits discrimination against a person with a disability on the basis of that disability. A disability is an impairment that limits a major life activity, long-term. When an employer is made aware of a disability, the employer is required to make reasonable accommodation that does not involve undue hardship.

An employer should not ask an applicant whether she is disabled or about the nature or severity of a disability, or require the applicant to take a medical examination before making a job offer. The employer can determine whether the applicant is "qualified" by asking questions about ability to perform job-related functions, as long as the questions are not phrased in terms of a disability. The employer can also ask an applicant to describe or to demonstrate how, with or without reasonable accommodation, the applicant will perform job-related functions.

A job offer can be made conditional on the results of a medical examination if everyone in the same position is required to have an examination after the offer is made but before the applicant starts work. If an individual is not hired because the examination reveals a disability, the employer must be able to show that the reasons for exclusion are job related and necessary for conduct of business and

Americans with Disabilities Act (ADA) Prohibits discrimination against a person with a disability on the basis of that disability

---

[1]An arrest is not a conviction. Rejecting applicants based on arrest record may have an unfair impact on protected groups. Your state may have more protective laws. For example, California limits inquiries about misdemeanors and expunged items.

that there was no reasonable accommodation that would have made it possible for the individual to perform the essential job functions. The results of all medical examinations and information from inquiries about a disability must be kept confidential, and maintained in separate medical files.

4. Checking References and Other Screening Techniques

Checking a candidate's references is essential. Many firms also conduct background investigations on serious candidates for key positions. These duties can be outsourced to companies that will check past employer references; validate education and professional licensing claims; investigate local, state, and national criminal conviction history; validate the applicant's Social Security number; check motor vehicle and drunk driving conviction records; investigate credit/financial history; and check civil litigation records and workers' compensation history (after the employment offer is made). As with all parts of the hiring process, keep the focus on the requirements of the job. If an employee will not be handling money, is there any reason to do a credit check? It is possible that reliance on a credit check could have disparate impact on groups protected by antidiscrimination laws.

The firm should consider how it will deal with candidates who cannot provide references. Although employers in many states have a qualified privilege to communicate truthful information about employees when asked by another employer, many employers refuse to provide references, other than to confirm dates of employment and position.

If the reference is willing to answer questions, consider asking the following questions:

- What were the candidate's duties? How well were they performed? Where you satisfied with the work product?
- Were there any problems with attendance? Punctuality? Attitude?
- What are the candidate's greatest strengths and weaknesses on the job?
- Did the candidate work well with others?
- Considering this candidate's personality, which management style works best?
- If you had the opportunity, would you hire or rehire this person?

Many employers also use the Internet to gain additional insight into a candidate. Some simply "Google" the applicant's name; others look at networking sites such as Facebook and MySpace and personal blog spots.

Are we there yet? Not quite. Communication during the screening process can be very important. Communication must not be ambiguous. Does "you're our top candidate" mean that you are leading the pack or that you've been offered a job? When an offer is extended:

Verify the Social Security numbers given by new hires at http://www.ssa.gov/employer/ssnv.htm.

- Be specific about the terms of the offer—salary, start date, insurance, retirement plans, and billable hour expectations. Be realistic about opportunities for advancement and how often reviews are conducted. An employer may try to sugar-coat the situation to "snag" a good employee, and a candidate may be overly optimistic about what he needs to pay his bills, but having an employee leave after a short time can be a disaster for both parties. Follow up by e-mail or letter to confirm the conversation.

- The new hire should call other employers with whom she has interviewed and remove herself from consideration. She may be working with people at those firms in the future and should maintain goodwill.
- The candidate should acknowledge the offer and thank the employer, even if she is unsure whether she will accept. If a candidate needs more time to consider, she should communicate that to the employer and keep lines of communication open. The candidate may need to contact other employers with whom she has interviewed and ask where she stands as a candidate. The firm should set a firm date for a decision.
- If the candidate knows she will not accept the offer, she should call and thank the employer and decline the offer. An offer should never be ignored.
- The new hire should let her school know where she is working; the information is needed for accreditation and approval reports.

B. New Hires

Imagine: It's your first day on the job at the firm of Rodan & Stosh. You're proud to have earned your paralegal certificate with high honors and to have been hired by this new and growing firm, but things don't go well at the start.

You arrive a little early to make a good impression, but find the office isn't open yet. When the receptionist arrives and lets you in, he announces that your supervisor took a vacation day and won't be in. Your office isn't ready yet, so he seats you in the conference room and gives you a procedures manual to read. You sit in the conference room for several hours, trying to read, and watch as others walk by in pairs to take a break or go to lunch. Are you invisible? Finally Samone Secretary comes in and announces that her boss "dumped" you on her. She is going to show you around. Samone is apparently unhappy with her job and, as she introduces you, she whispers comments, such as "the 'late' Mr. Rodan—he hasn't been on time for anything in ten years," and "this firm is so cheap—this copier should have been replaced years ago." After the tour, Samone returns you to the conference room, where she sets up a video—the firm's orientation video—two hours of watching Leona Stosh talk about the firm's history and values. Finally, at the end of the day, Samone returns to give you your assignment for tomorrow—you are to fold, seal, and stamp the firm newsletter for mailing.

You've probably had similar experiences at jobs, but as a manager you don't want to start new employees on the wrong foot. While large firms often have formal orientation programs, even solo practitioners should provide new employees with basic information immediately. Remember, orientation is not synonymous with training; even the best-educated/trained new employee needs orientation to the following aspects of this particular firm:

- Firm employment procedures (discussed in detail, next section): paydays and use of time cards; office hours and access outside normal hours; evaluation policies; time-keeping procedures

- Office equipment and library policy: how to obtain supplies; operation of copiers, fax, phone system, computers; how to obtain maintenance or repair; charges to client accounts; ethical issues in using phone/fax — if the employee has not had formal training in law office ethics, it is essential that she be educated about confidentiality, conflicts of interest, soliciting, unauthorized practice of law, and safekeeping of client property
- Mail: how is incoming mail sorted, opened, stamped, distributed, and entered into calendars; what is the preferred format and signature policy, is there a policy on use of letterhead and on keeping hard copies or copying clients; for outgoing mail, how is postage affixed (certified mail, express mail)
- Telephone communication: how is phone answered, how are messages taken and communicated; policy regarding who returns calls and how quickly; recordkeeping on long-distance calls
- Handling money: use of petty cash; issuance of receipts; posting of transactions; reimbursement for expenses paid by employees; making deposits (if employee will deposit funds from or for clients, review ethical rules concerning commingling, etc.)
- Files: new matter form; fee agreement; organization of folders and how file number is established; firm filing rules; storage of closed files
- Specialty-specific: local rules for court filings, recorder's office, etc. as pertain to employee's position

Of course, the new employee will feel overwhelmed with information and will be relieved to receive the firm procedures manual. As an additional step to make new employees comfortable and more quickly productive, many firms assign **mentors**: senior employees in similar positions. To make a mentoring program work, it should have some formal expectations. A new employee told that she can "ask Jack whatever you need to know" is likely to feel too intimidated to ask. If, however, Jack knows that he is expected to take the new person out for a coffee break or lunch once a week, real communication may develop.

mentor
A senior person acting as an advisor or guide to a junior person

As part of orientation, the firm typically has several of its own forms that should be completed. In addition to an application for employment, the firm may require new hires to sign a confidentiality agreement; a conflicts disclosure form (discussed in Chapter 5); receipts for keys, building passes, parking passes, and similar material given at hiring; and a receipt for and an agreement to read and comply with the firm's policies procedures manual.

C. The Employer-Employee Relationship

1. Firm Policies

Every firm with employees should have written policies and procedures relating to client matters (opening and closing a file, keeping time and billing) and ethical issues (checking for conflicts, handling client funds, confidentiality, and communications), as described in previous chapters. Every firm should have security and emergency procedures (described in Chapter 7). The firm should also articulate policies relating to the employees themselves, such as these:

- Job descriptions
- Probationary period for new employees, if applicable
- Work hours, preparing time records, and tardiness
- Lunch and breaks
- Availability of alternative work schedules, telecommuting
- Paydays, salary, overtime, raises, gratuities, bonuses
- Access to and updating of personnel files
- Entitlement to and scheduling of vacation and personal days
- Jury service
- Office holidays and weather-related closings
- Entitlement to and reporting of sick days
- Entitlement to and requesting leave (FMLA leave is described later in this chapter)
- Statement of equal opportunity policy and disability accommodation policy ownership and use of firm equipment and work product
- Frequency of and policies governing employee evaluations
- Separation procedures
  - **employment at will** policy
  - notice by firm or employee
  - continuation of insurance (COBRA)
  - entitlement to accumulated vacation, sick leave
  - exit interview and return of firm property
- Billable hour expectations
- Educational benefits
- Reimbursement for job-related expenses
- Obtaining technical support and office maintenance
- Ordering supplies
- Entitlement to insurance
- Zero tolerance of sexual harassment and substance abuse (discussed below)
- Compliance with ADA
- Availability of a retirement plan

employment at will
Doctrine under which employment can be terminated at any time for no reason

Larger firms may have policies concerning service on firm committees, pro bono work, in-house education and mentoring, and CLE. Some firms may also have policies concerning use of personal property at work, keeping a neat workspace, dress codes, and other office behavior policies, as described in Chapter 10.

2. Sexual Harassment Policy

Equal Employment Opportunity Commission (EEOC)
Federal agency concerned with employment discrimination

The federal **Equal Employment Opportunity Commission (EEOC)** requires that employers take reasonable steps to prevent sexual harassment before it occurs; most states impose a similar requirement. Some states even require employers to post a sexual harassment prevention notice advising employees of their rights.

Sexual harassment includes "quid pro quo" harassment, which occurs when a condition of employment is based on an employee's submission to or rejection of sexual advances. Harassment can also result from a hostile work environment. There is no clear definition of a hostile work environment. It can occur if jokes, suggestive remarks, physical interference with movement, pictures, cartoons, or sexually derogatory comments are so pervasive or severe as to alter the circumstances of the workplace. The conduct is evaluated from the perspective of the victim, and it does not matter whether the harasser intended the conduct to be harassing or complimentary. The best policy is if conduct might be construed as harassment, it is not acceptable in the workplace.

To fulfill its obligation to take all reasonable steps to prevent harassment and to take steps to remedy harassment after it takes place, an employer should have a policy and procedures. The written policy will typically include the following:

- A broad definition of what constitutes prohibited harassment
- A statement that the firm prohibits sexual harassment and will not retaliate against those who report or support claims of harassment
- A statement of consequences of harassment (written reprimand, change of assignment, termination of employment)
- If the firm is large enough, training on prevention of harassment
- Procedures, publicized to all employees, that establish how and to whom sexual harassment should be reported (with time limits)

The firm must take all reports and observations of potential harassment seriously and investigate promptly. The investigation should proceed in a way that is impartial and that fully explores both sides of the story. The firm may need to take action even if the employee experiencing the harassment does not want to pursue the matter. The next employee to be harassed by the same individual might not be willing to ignore the situation, and the firm would almost certainly be liable if it knew about the conduct and did nothing to stop it. For the same reason, confidentiality can be promised only "to the extent possible under the circumstances." It is important to maintain reasonable confidentiality during an investigation, but sometimes a victim or witness will have no choice.

3. Governmental Requirements

Many law offices outsource payroll and related accounting functions because of the complexity of the required calculations and paperwork. Even in a firm that does not handle its own payroll, a paralegal in a managerial position should understand the terminology and functions necessary to comply with laws governing employers. The firm remains ultimately responsible for compliance with the law and must be able to oversee the functions of the company to which it delegates the work. It is also possible that you will be on the ground floor, helping a lawyer launch her own practice and hire employees. The following is an overview and does not touch on all regulatory requirements. For a more detailed exploration, dealing with matters such as required workplace posters, employee benefit plans, workplace safety, and more, visit http://www.business.gov/guides/employment/managing/first-employee.html. The site includes links for state-specific requirements.

a. Taxes

The employer is required to obtain an employer identification number (**EIN**) for itself; the number is necessary for reporting required information concerning employees. Employers are required to verify that all employees are eligible to work in the United States and to retain (not submit) **Form I-9**. In addition, under the Personal Responsibility and Work Opportunity Reconciliation Act of 1996, all employers must report certain information on newly hired employees to a designated state agency. To find the agency for your state, visit http://www.acf.hhs.gov/programs/cse/newhire/employer/contacts/nh_matrix.htm.

A new hire must fill out **Form W-4**, which provides the employer with information necessary to calculate withholding for federal income tax. Forms and requirements for state income tax and for state unemployment tax (described in the next section) differ from state to state. Other matters that differ from state to state include whether the employer is required to provide disability insurance and workplace notices required to be posted. For information about your state's requirements with respect to taxes, visit http://www.business.gov/guides/taxes/state.html.

For the federal government, each pay cycle, the employer must do the following:

- Withhold federal income tax based on employee's Form W-4
- Withhold employee's share of Social Security and Medicare taxes
- Include advance earned income credit payment in paycheck if employee requested it on Form W-5
- Deposit withheld income tax, employer social security taxes, and employer Medicare taxes

---

For More Information

How much should be withheld? When must it be deposited? Where should it be deposited? What is Form W-5? What records must be kept and for how long? (See Exhibit 9-4) Those are very good questions, but beyond the scope of this book. Luckily, there are websites with detailed instructions, such as http://www.irs.gov/pub/irs-pdf/p15.pdf. To find state-specific resources, start at http://www.business.gov/states.

Depending on the employer's total liability for federal unemployment tax, quarterly (April 30, July 31, October 31, and January 31) deposits of that tax may be required. At the end of the year, the employer must provide every employee (and the Social Security Administration) with a **Form W-2** and provide certain non-employees (such as independent contractors) with **Form 1099**.

Exhibit 9-4
Employee Tax Records

Keep all records of employment taxes for at least four years. These should be available for IRS review. Records should include the following:

- Your employer identification number
- Amounts and dates of all wage, annuity, and pension payments
- Amounts of tips reported
- The fair market value of in-kind wages paid
- Names, addresses, Social Security numbers, and occupations of employees and recipients
- Any employee copies of Form W-2 that were returned to you as undeliverable
- Dates of employment
- Periods for which employees and recipients were paid while absent due to sickness or injury and the amount and weekly rate of payments you or third party payers made to them
- Copies of employees' and recipients' income tax withholding allowance certificates (Forms W-4, W-4P, W-4S, and W-4V)
- Dates and amounts of tax deposits you made
- Copies of returns filed
- Records of allocated tips
- Records of fringe benefits provided, including substantiation

From U.S. Department of the Treasury, Internal Revenue Service, Employment Tax Recordkeeping, http://www.irs.gov/businesses/small/article/0,,id=98548,00.html (last visited Feb. 17, 2009).

---

b. Workers' Compensation

Workers' compensation laws provide fixed monetary awards for employees (or the families of deceased employees) injured or disabled on the job, eliminating the need for litigation. State laws establish this system for most employees; depending on the state and the number of employees, employers may be required to purchase insurance.

c. Unemployment Compensation

Unemployment insurance is a federal-state program that provides temporary, partial wage replacement to unemployed workers and is used to help stabilize the economy during recessions. The framework for the program is part of the Social Security Act. The program is jointly financed through federal and state employer payroll taxes. Federal aspects of the program are regulated by the Department of Labor; the Internal Revenue Service collects an annual federal employer tax. Federal revenue finances administration of the system, half of the extended benefits program, and a federal account for loans to states. The states finance their own programs, as well as their half of the extended benefits program.

Generally, employers must pay both state and federal unemployment taxes if they pay wages to employees totaling $1,500, or more, in any quarter of a calendar year or they had at least one employee during any day of a week during 20 weeks in a calendar year, regardless of whether the weeks were consecutive.

State law determines state unemployment insurance tax rates, eligibility for benefits, and amount of benefits (within the parameters set by federal law). While most states fund their programs with a tax on employers, three require employee minimal contributions.

d. Family and Medical Leave Act

Family and Medical Leave Act (FMLA)
Federal law that provides job security to employees who request time off for a family or medical reason

The **Family and Medical Leave Act (FMLA)** provides certain employees with entitlement of up to 12 weeks of job-protected, unpaid leave during any 12-month period for (1) birth and care of the eligible employee's child, or placement for adoption or foster care of a child with the employee; (2) care of an immediate family member (spouse, child, parent) who has a serious health condition; or (3) care of the employee's own serious health condition. It also requires that employee's group health benefits be maintained during the leave. The FMLA was recently amended to permit a "spouse, son, daughter, parent, or next of kin" to take up to 26 workweeks of leave to care for a "member of the Armed Forces, including a member of the National Guard or Reserves, who is undergoing medical treatment, recuperation, or therapy, is otherwise in outpatient status, or is otherwise on the temporary disability retired list, for a serious injury or illness." While the FMLA applies only to companies with 50 or more employees, some state laws have broader application. For more information about FMLA, visit http://www.dol.gov/esa/whd/fmla/index.htm. For information about state laws, visit http://www.ncsl.org/programs/employ/Familyleave.htm

e. Other Compliance Issues

Fair Labor Standards Act (FLSA)
Establishes minimum wage, overtime pay, recordkeeping, and related labor standards

Like other businesses, law firms must comply with the **Fair Labor Standards Act (FLSA)** with respect to wages, hours, overtime, and recordkeeping for covered, non-exempt workers. There is no required form for the records, but the records must include accurate information about the employee and data about the hours worked and the wages earned. To find wage and hour requirements for your state, start at http://www.dol.gov/esa/contacts/state_of.htm.

Employee Retirement Income Security Act (ERISA)
Governs insurance and retirement plans

Most private sector pension and health insurance plans are covered by the **Employee Retirement Income Security Act (ERISA)**. The Employee Benefits Security Administration of the U.S. Department of Labor is responsible for administering and enforcing these provisions of ERISA

More information on all federal compliance issues is available through the U.S. Department of Labor, http://www.dol.gov.

Assignment 9-2
Employment Laws and Benefits

Management Portfolio

a) Using one of the websites, http://www.dol.gov/esa/regs/compliance/owcp/wc.htm or
http://www.workerscompensation.com, identify the office responsible for administering your state's workers' compensation program and determine whether your state would require a law office employing two paralegals, a secretary, and a receptionist to obtain insurance.

b) Starting at http://workforcesecurity.doleta.gov/unemploy, locate the office responsible for unemployment benefits in your state. Describe how employers in your state pay the required tax.

c) Find Form I-9 online and print the list of documents acceptable for verifying eligibility.

d) Working with a group, use the Internet to locate substance abuse policies of various employers. Discuss the provisions unique to each policy and the provisions common to all or most of the policies and develop a list of provisions for a law office substance abuse policy.

e) Find your state's law on family and medical leave and describe how it differs from the FMLA. Determine which workplace posters are required in your state. See http://www.business.gov/guides/employment/managing/first-employee.html.

f) Find the most up-to-date online information concerning the use of and compensation and benefits for full-time paralegals. If possible, find the information specific to your geographic area. Some good sources of information include these: http://www.nala.org; http://www.paralegalmanagement.org; http://www.paralegals.org; and your local paralegal association's website.

- Determine what percentage of paralegals report life insurance and fully paid medical insurance as benefits. How often are paralegals typically evaluated?
- Ed Rodan wants to hire a paralegal to support two new bankruptcy lawyers the firm has hired. Determine typical billable hour expectations, rates at which paralegal time is billed to clients, whether one paralegal/two lawyers is a typical ratio, and what tasks are typically performed by a bankruptcy paralegal.
- Ed Rodan has heard that a **cafeteria benefits plan** is very attractive to talented job candidates, but he is not sure what the term means. Research the term and write a memo. A good starting point (for this and many other management and human resources issues) is http://the-source.alanet.org/portal/server.pt. Go to the Content Area and find the Human Resources page.

cafeteria benefits plan
Allows employees to choose benefits that best fit their needs

4. Evaluating Employees

The annual (or biennial) performance evaluation is often dreaded by both the evaluator and the evaluated. If both parties know what to expect, however, the process can usually be painless and benefit both the firm and the employee. Both parties can see the process as an indication of the firm's investment in and commitment to its employees, if the process is treated as "coaching" rather than criticism.

As a first priority, however, the evaluation process must be honest. In some cases it is better to have no evaluations rather than evaluations that "take the easy way out" and rate an employee's performance as acceptable when it is unacceptable. When former employees litigate their terminations, they often point to a history of good or average evaluations.

The second most important characteristic is consistency. Evaluations should occur at stated intervals for all employees and should involve the same procedures and paperwork. The person or people responsible for evaluations should prepare in advance by gathering information and input, and then write the review from an objective, balanced perspective.

The evaluation should be a two-way conversation. The evaluator should discuss the employee's strengths, weaknesses, and suggestions for improvement, with the attitude that the employee wants to do a good job and improve. The evaluator may even want to open the interview with a statement of that understanding and of the firm's interest in the employee's success. Suggestions should be specific: not "you need to work on your image," but "we would feel more comfortable giving you client contact assignments if you would dress more professionally." The employee should respond and discuss how the firm can help her improve. In a sense, the evaluation can be considered a negotiation for the coming year; what will the employee do and what will the firm do to maximize the employee's potential?

As a manager, you may encounter employees who become emotional, defensive, or argumentative during evaluations. Listen and respond in a calm, factual manner. Do not engage in argument or become defensive yourself. Being a manager sometimes means that "the buck stops here." You have to deal with problems without worrying about assigning blame or emerging as "the winner." After the evaluation meeting, the employee should be given a copy of the review. Some firms have the employee sign a copy, especially if the review is not entirely positive and the employee is being required to remediate. Signs that an employee may require remediation include these:

- Rudeness to clients, coworkers, even salespeople and messengers
- Chronic complaining
- Chronic lateness, a "Monday problem,[2]" or absence without explanation
- Inability to meet deadlines
- Overly defensive about mistakes—tries to pass blame to others
- Repeating mistakes, not attempting to improve
- Sloppy appearance

---

[2]Frequent absences or tardiness on Mondays is viewed by some experts as an indication of substance abuse or depression.

When discipline or remediation is necessary, the firm should take action as quickly as possible. A firm that permits time to pass after an employee has committed an infraction or made a major mistake may be viewed as having condoned the misconduct or waived the infraction.

Discipline should always be given privately and not in anger. The supervisor should conduct a complete and fair investigation of the facts without bias against the employee. Before any disciplinary action is taken, the employee should be told why he is being considered for discipline and be given an opportunity to present his side of the situation. In addition, the firm should ascertain how other employees who have engaged in similar conduct have been treated. Consistency of treatment for similar offenses is a basic element in fair discipline. The firm should review the employee's personnel file and be totally familiar with and consider the employee's length of service, history of successes, and history of discipline before imposing discipline. Special circumstances, such as an employee going through a divorce or serious illness in the family, should also be considered.

In no case should a firm attempt to "freeze-out" the employee rather than dealing directly with the problem, for example, by reassigning the employee's work without explanation. Discipline should be imposed with sensitivity to the employee's dignity and self-respect. Particular care should be used with respect to long-term employees. Alternatives to firing, such as training or demotion to a less stressful position, should be considered.

5. Working with a Diverse Workforce

One of the major challenges facing supervisors today is the presence of men and women of all cultures and religions and from four generations in the workplace. The differences between the motivations, experiences, and values of these people are a tremendous asset to a firm; they reflect the differences in clients, and when people accept other ways of thinking, they become more creative. At the same time, these differences sometimes can create tension.

Differences include dissimilar:

- concepts of time and timeliness,
- reactions to authority,
- comfort with and reliance on technology,
- understandings of slang,
- interpretation and use of body language and gestures,
- reactions to constructive criticism and reviews,
- needs for body space,
- grooming and dress habits,
- reactions to use of first names and to touching,
- value on individuality,
- celebration of holidays and personal events and workplace recognition,
- reactions to silence,
- concepts of privacy.

Some people "tell it like it is," while others consider directness offensive; some people vocalize their ideas as a way to promote discussion, while others find "thinking out loud" confusing. As a manager, you must be able to work with people with all of these characteristics. You cannot take a "my way or the highway" attitude, but must determine how best to communicate the firm's needs so that people are able to meet those needs.

While this book cannot possibly touch on all of the issues raised by a diverse workforce, a few examples may make you more sensitive to the issues and better able to deal with them.

Examples

Most people in the United States place responsibility for communication on the speaker. If the speaker does not communicate in a clear manner, people will ask questions. In other cultures, people consider it rude to question the speaker. People may even nod to indicate that they are listening — not that they understand, simply that they are listening. What can you do? Be very specific in checking for understanding: "Lucy, are you able to make two-sided copies based on my explanation?" "Mr. Masimoto, do you have a complete list of the documents you should bring to the meeting?"

Most people in the United States are direct; people in other cultures may place responsibility for understanding on the recipient. Office manager asks Pat Paralegal to come in on Saturday to work on a large production of documents for a pending trial. Pat says, "My father's birthday is Saturday and the family is having a big party. I would be sad to miss it." Office manager thanks Pat for being a team player and says "see you Saturday." Office manager thought Pat was seeking recognition for sacrificing a family event; Pat thought he was declining to work, without being confrontational. What can you do? Express yourself clearly, but with sensitivity. "I'm sorry, I can't come in on Saturday because of a family obligation. Would it help if I stayed late on Friday?" If you get an answer that is ambiguous, clarify: "Pat, I know you don't want to miss your father's party, but we are in a bind. Could you come in for a couple of hours in the morning?"

Age can also be a factor in creating misunderstandings. Bennie Boomer, age 60, tells Sam, age 23, "I need to have you available on Saturday because the bond deal documents might be ready to go." Sam says she will be available. Bennie is dismayed and angry to find that Sam is not in the office on Saturday. Sam is baffled — she was available by cell phone all day. Older workers tend to place more value on "face time," chain of command, and work above play. They may believe that technology is unreliable and impersonal. Younger workers have never lived in a world without instant communication; they tend to see no point to "keeping up appearances."

After Bennie and Sam resolve the misunderstanding, they begin work on the project. During the day, Sam repeatedly interrupts Bennie with questions, such as "Should this statement be redacted as privileged?" Fed up, Bennie eventually shouts, "Why do you keep interrupting me? I am the boss! Research these things! Find the answer yourself!" Sam apologizes but is mystified. She is accustomed to instant information; she believes that it is inefficient to research a question if the person in the next office may know the answer immediately. From Sam's perspective, they are working on the same project; it makes no difference that Bennie is older and is in a supervisory position. Bennie thinks Sam is disrespectful.

In an attempt to make amends, Sam posts on her blog that the firm is "da bomb," that the hours she has to work "blow," but that she "is rolling in the Gs," and that her supervisor, Bennie, "is a hottie." Sam believes that any publicity is good publicity and that she has only told the truth. Sam even thinks she has flattered Bennie and the firm. When Bennie's granddaughter shows Bennie the blog, Bennie fires Sam. Why?

Wealthy widow Rose Steiskal, age 82, is coming in to establish a trust. Legal assistant Linda, age 22, is going to do the initial interview. Ann Attorney tells Linda that the client has never before visited a law office and is very nervous. To put Rose at ease, Linda dresses casually, in khaki pants and a blouse that reveals bare skin when she raises her arms. To make the situation even less threatening, Linda takes Ms. Steiskal by the arm, guides her to a chair, saying "I hope this is comfortable for you, Rose." Linda then sits on her desk, crossing her legs, and says "Let's get rolling on this." Can you guess why the client was upset and took her business to another firm?

The next firm Ms. Steiskal visited was in the middle of an international corporate takeover. Two legal assistants from the firm's affiliate in Rome were passing through the waiting room, discussing the deal in their native language. They were loud and were using large gestures. Ms. Steiskal thought they were fighting and became frightened. In fact, they are close friends. What differences in communication styles caused the misunderstanding?

Rodan & Stosh now has many corporate clients who do business in or with China and would like to hire a bilingual paralegal. Ping Guo arrives for an interview with excellent credentials, but during the interview she sits very still, rarely responding to Ed Rodan's humorous comments and looking to the side or at the floor rather than at Mr. Rodan. Some of Ping's responses seem evasive; rather than saying yes or no, she tends to smile and say things like "that would be interesting." Ed Rodan concludes that she is hiding something and is unfriendly. To the contrary, Ping is exhibiting what would be considered excellent business etiquette in China.

6. Termination

Sometimes a single, dramatic incident justifies termination. More often, however, events that result in termination occur over a period of time and are cumulative. Unless the firm's own policies require progressive discipline, there is generally no legal requirement of written warnings, suspensions without pay, and other similar types of discipline before an employee can be terminated. A documented history of counseling and criticism with clearly expressed goals and timetables for improvement can, however, establish that the employee was treated fairly and make the termination less traumatic for both the employee and the firm. Keep in mind that the way in which an employee is terminated can affect the morale of others. The matter should be handled with dignity and discretion, but firmly. Do not become engaged in argument or discussion with the person being fired; do not create any ambiguity about what is happening.

If an employee is absent from work due to a work-related injury or an illness covered by an antidiscrimination law, the firm may be prohibited from hiring a permanent replacement. Even if those situations do not exist, the firm should avoid terminating employees who are injured or ill; if possible, these employees should be allowed to remain in a "leave status."

The firm may use a separation of employment agreement containing a general release to prevent claims of wrongful termination. The inducement to sign the agreement is generally severance pay that is otherwise not required by firm policy. The firm must avoid coercion or undue pressure. Execution of a severance agreement must be knowing and voluntary.

Upon termination, some employees (and their families, who might otherwise lose health benefits) have the right to continue group health benefits for a

Consolidated Omnibus Budget Reconciliation Act (COBRA)
Gives certain employees right to continue health insurance after termination

Health Insurance Portability and Accountability Act (HIPAA)
Federal law that protects the privacy of medical information

limited period of time. Employers may be required to provide notices of employee rights under the **Consolidated Omnibus Budget Reconciliation Act (COBRA[3])** and the **Health Insurance Portability and Accountability Act (HIPAA)**. For more information on the requirements of COBRA and HIPAA, see http://www.dol.gov/ebsa/pdf/cobraemployer.pdf and http://www.dol.gov/dol/topic/health-plans/portability.htm.

Consider creating a policy of conducting exit interviews when employees leave the firm voluntarily. These interviews can be a good source of feedback on the adequacy of the firm's training, support, supervision, compensation, and benefits.

Best Practices

When an employee leaves the firm, it is essential that you immediately terminate the individual's access to computers and other communications equipment. You must also obtain the return of any credit cards, keys, employee passes, and business cards in the possession of the former employee.

D. Teaching Attorneys to Work with Legal Assistants

It may surprise you to learn that many—perhaps most—new law school graduates have never had a job that involves delegation to and supervision of another and have no idea what paralegals can do. Be prepared to educate them. An experienced paralegal can and should educate (not dominate!) his supervisor, but a new paralegal may not be comfortable asserting himself. He should have a conversation with the new lawyer and make suggestions to help the lawyer and paralegal form an effective team.

- To avoid "hovering" and anxiety about whether assigned work is being done, the lawyer should establish a policy of how her assistant should communicate the status of projects. Does the lawyer prefer a note, an e-mail, or a meeting? Does the lawyer want daily or weekly updates?
- Until they have a comfortable working relationship, the lawyer should be very specific in describing assignments and should indicate the priority to be given each assignment. The lawyer should listen carefully to the paralegal's questions and not rush.
- To enable the paralegal to learn the lawyer's style and expectations, the lawyer should be liberal in giving feedback, especially praise for tasks done well.
- The lawyer should treat her paralegal as an important team member by introducing him to clients, court staff, and fellow professionals. Say "please" and "thank you."
- Neither the lawyer nor the paralegal should burden the other with his or her personal problems.

---

[3]COBRA generally applies to employers with at least 20 employees.

- The lawyer should tell her assistant when she is leaving, how she can be reached, and when she will return. The lawyer should not lie to the paralegal, should not ask the paralegal to "cover" for her, and should never blame the paralegal for her own mistakes.
- A good paralegal will increase the lawyer's productivity and make the lawyer look good, so the lawyer should encourage professional development and continuing education, offer to teach the paralegal new ways of doing things, and, whenever possible, explain why things are done in a particular way.
- Supervision is not micromanagement, but the lawyer must remember that she *is* the supervisor and must not allow work to leave the office without review by an attorney, put her assistant in the position of having to make decisions not appropriate to a paralegal, or ignore an employee's disregard for office policies or ethical rules. All project deadlines must include time for supervision.

Out There—Paralegal Profile
Becoming a Supervisor

Who Would You Hire?

Angela Davis completed her ABA-approved paralegal certificate program in 2004. As a paralegal she worked in the research department of a state appellate court and then for General Electric. Her responsibilities at the appellate court were cite checking, editing, and proofreading opinions prior to publication in the legal reporters. At GE, Angela was responsible for legislative tracking, due

diligence reviews, regulatory filing, legal research, and litigation support. In 2006, she decided to pursue a law degree and in September 2009, she will be an associate with a large national law firm.

Angela says: "If I was in a position to hire a paralegal today, I would look for a candidate who had very strong research and writing skills. A large part of what paralegals and attorneys do on a daily basis includes both of these skills. As a matter of fact, I chose my law school based on the exceptional reputation it has for an intense legal writing program. My undergraduate degree in English enabled me to successfully transition to legal writing. During law school, I participated in a judicial externship, which reinforced just how important it is to know how to write clearly and concisely. A paralegal who is familiar with legal research resources other than the big subscription services would be a valuable asset to a law firm as well."

Management Techniques

Franne Donovan is a paralegal with many years of experience in management. She studied business and journalism at the University of Nebraska  and was further educated in management through an exten-sive internship program sponsored by The Prudential Insurance Company of America as well as management training at Blue Cross and Blue Shield Association. She earned a paralegal certificate in 2004 and is employed in civil litigation. Franne's thoughts on "Management Techniques that Work," which follow, were originally published by the Illinois Paralegal Association and are reprinted with permission.

Paralegals managing other paralegals and/or managing large projects are becoming increasingly common and it is these paralegals who command the highest salaries in our profession. Yet many paralegals move into these posts without benefit of education in the science of management. Moreover, especially in small to mid-size firms, management of resources and employees may be more likely to follow the inklings of the controlling attorneys, whose judgment is based on their own profession and not on an understanding of organizational management. Management, very simply, is working with and through other people to achieve the objectives of an organization. Management involves having a clearly defined plan for every objective, shepherding the work it takes to complete the objective, and motivating others effectively. Understanding a few sound principles can help the new manager avoid common mistakes.

What Do You Want

Before you can manage anyone else, you need to define exactly what you and your organization want to achieve and by what time you must achieve it. Once you are clear on the objective, it must be articulated to those who work for you. From the simplest objective (move boxes to permanent storage) to the more complex (manage a mass litigation project), you, as manager, own the objective. If an employee is not functioning, it is never enough to ask why that person is not producing; the next question is, "what is the manager thinking?" To be effective, the manager who asks that boxes be moved must know when the boxes are to move and must also note whether the job is done. While this may sound simple, offices everywhere are full of managers who let loose directives without ever noting the results.

Subsequently, these same "managers" try to "solve" problems by investigating who might be at fault. A good manager avoids problems, and does not focus on assigning blame for things gone wrong.

You can often tell a manager, comfortable in his or her role, from one who is not. The former is comfortable with people, clear in spoken directives to others, and more often than not, an affirming person who fosters morale. The latter is a boss, with everything that implies. Bosses give orders, not directives. Bosses like to remind people of their rank and may use bullying and blaming tactics. Managers keep track of project development, but in a way that empowers the subordinate to do most on their own initiative. Bosses micro-manage and believe that it is their very show of bossiness that will keep control. Bosses usually engender more problems than they control.

A common concern of newly-appointed managers is whether they will have to change persona to work in a new way with those who were once their equals. The answer is no, there is no personality transformation required. Nor must you "earn credibility" by becoming impersonal — for instance, declining to talk about your children or some bit of trivia. The difference should be your own acceptance of your new rank and the willingness to exert its force when needed. This force is exerted by simply stating the facts, not by the boss behaviors described earlier. Picture yourself having a discussion about baseball with your friend and now subordinate, Sarah. It is time to change the subject. "Sarah, how's it going on that case summary memorandum Jackson needs?" Sarah replies, "I haven't started it yet." Picture yourself saying, "I'll need a good reason for that — he expects it finished tomorrow." Sarah then replies, "It's just taken me so long to get through all the pleadings Patterson needs." Your job as manager then becomes to actively engage yourself in reviewing Sarah's work on the pleadings, establishing whether or not she needs help in getting them done or whether her performance is just unacceptable. You move from that to establishing the means by which the case summary will be produced on time. A good manager coaches and helps whenever possible, but must be able to level a charge of "unacceptable" when this is called for.

Rank Has Its Privileges

Your new rank may come with very special privileges such as higher compensation, invitations to certain events or meetings, and a more interactive position. Especially if you have been promoted from within, there may be resentment for your new rank. You need to learn to ignore this: "It can be lonely at the top." This can certainly be said for head paralegals since there are often few equal-rank paralegals and because the professional divide between attorneys and paralegals often means that there is no fellowship with those above your position.

Some head paralegals are in true management roles. Others are paid more because they coordinate the efforts of other paralegals but they do not have authority to hire and fire or to lend anything more than opinions in such matters as employee reviews. Beware of positions that put you in a compromising, no-win situation. As much as you can, without alienating yourself from your own management, insist on the following: Either all work is funneled through you or none of it is. Being undermined by having others direct the work of your subordinates or rearrange the priorities of your staff means you are not really a supervisor or manager. If you find that such a situation is developing, ask for assistance or clarification. Subordinates will not respect you if they see your superiors not respecting your management role.

One Is the Magic Number

People do not do well with having many managers and trying to please them all. Attorneys trying to get their work done need to have one person who is accountable for any given task. If you are in a position to create a reporting structure, create it with these rules in mind:

1. One manager for each person.
2. The manager should be connected to the work function. In other words, you shouldn't have a paralegal supervised by a manager who does not have responsibility for the work that paralegal is doing.
3. One person responsible for a project or for a clearly defined piece of that project.

Producers Rule

This maxim is highly respected in sales organizations and ought to be in law firms. Attorneys and paralegals produce the work product and hence, the money, of law firms. "Producers rule" means that producers should have a lot to say about who works for them and how they manage their staff—in other words, they should get what they need to be effective. Human resource managers have their place and in reality, we often inherit employees and situations. But whenever possible, the producer should be involved in hiring and in other choices that could affect her productivity.

If It Moves Above You, Salute It

As much as I believe in all the principles I've described in this article, I think that this proverb—which comes from the military and speaks to respecting rank—is a needed balance. Sophisticated law firms may employ MBAs and management consultant firms. They may be as hip as any pure business organization. On the other hand, law firms may be under the control of a person or people who have styled the organization on the ancient principles of monarchy. Wherever you find yourself working, you cannot force management science on anyone unless you are in power. Therefore, respect those ranked above you for as long as you choose to remain in that organization. Do what you can to manage both people and projects well; offer suggestions when you have an opportunity; but beyond that, accept the decisions of those in more power and abide by their directives.

Chapter Review

Discussion Questions

1. Identify three paralegal associations that are good sources of career information.
2. Identify the agencies responsible for unemployment compensation and workers' compensation in your state.
3. Describe the rights created by FMLA. Does your state have a law that provides broader rights?
4. What are the "tax chores" an employer must complete each pay cycle?
5. What are Forms I-9, W-2, and W-4?
6. What is COBRA?
7. What is meant by "employment at will"?
8. What is ERISA?
9. Describe the procedures for or characteristics of a good employee evaluation.
10. Describe the characteristics of a good job description.
11. Describe some of the differences in workplace expectations between older workers and younger workers.
12. Describe communications styles that can cause misunderstandings with clients or coworkers.

ACROSS

2. large employers often feed resumes through these to look for key words
5. FLSA = Fair _____ Standards Act
6. FMLA = Family and _____ Leave Act
9. Form 1099 is for _____ contractors
12. firm should have _____ tolerance of sexual harassment
14. Form W-4 is completed when an employee is _____
15. initials, paralegal association
16. provides worker's right to continue insurance
18. initials, every employer must have
19. Form W-2 is provided this often
20. category protected against discrimination
21. Agency initials — deals

DOWN

1. employment at _____; can be terminated at any time
3. initials, law deals with handicapped people
4. a way of proving you can do the work, despite lack of employment experience

7. initials, law governs retirement plans
8. _____ system is financed through both state and federal taxes on employers
10. Form I-9 verifies _____ to work in United States
11. in addition to a resume, the firm should have the candidate complete an _____
13. _____ compensation, for injured workers
17. HIPAA = _____ Insurance Portability and Accountability Act

Terms and Definitions

Americans with Disabilities Act (ADA): Prohibits discrimination against a person with a disability on the basis of that disability

cafeteria benefits plan: Allows employees to choose benefits that best fit their needs

Consolidated Omnibus Budget Reconciliation Act (COBRA): Gives certain employees right to continue health insurance after termination

Equal Employment Opportunity Commission (EEOC): Federal agency concerned with employment discrimination

EIN: Employer identification number

employment at will: Doctrine under which employment can be terminated at any time for no reason

Employee Retirement Income Security Act (ERISA): Governs insurance and retirement plans

Fair Labor Standards Act (FLSA): Establishes minimum wage, overtime pay, recordkeeping, and related labor standards

Family and Medical Leave Act (FMLA): Federal law that provides job security to employees who request time off for a family or medical reason

Form 1099: Given to independent contractors and other payees to show payments during year

Form I-9: Used to verify eligibility to work in United States

Form W-2: Provided annually to employees; shows income and withholding

Form W-4: Used to calculate withholding; filled out when employee is hired and amended as needed

Health Insurance Portability and Accountability Act (HIPAA): Federal law that protects the privacy of medical information

mentor: A senior person acting as an advisor or guide to a junior person

10

◆ ◆ ◆

Personal and Professional Development

◆ ◆ ◆

As a Manager

In most firms your top priority will be maintaining a stable staff of motivated, satisfied workers who grow in their jobs and have excellent people skills to represent your firm. At the same time, you have to continue to grow in your profession.

Objectives

After completing this chapter, you will be able to

- Know how to dress appropriately for the legal environment.
- Understand how to avoid destructive office politics.
- Understand the etiquette for business meals.
- Recognize and avoid procrastination.
- Make and prioritize a to-do list.
- Understand how to motivate people you supervise.
- Understand how to avoid becoming stale in your own career.

A. **Your Personal Life versus Your Work Life**
   1. **Dress to Make Others Feel Confident and Comfortable**
   2. **Etiquette for Business Social Events**
   3. **Time Management**
   4. **Stress Management**

275

B. Supervising Others to Maintain a Stable Staff
   1. Causes of Turnover
   2. The Problem: Gossip and Office Politics
   3. The Solution: Happy Workers Are Productive Workers
C. Your Own Career Path
   1. Dealing with Difficult People
   2. Professionalism
   Out There—Paralegal Profile: Professional Development
   Chapter Review

---

hard skills
Skills that can be quantified, such as drafting or using computer software

soft skills
Combination of personal traits, social skills, communications skills, and attitude

Hard skills usually get a person her first job. A resume can quantify whether she speaks Spanish, is proficient at using spreadsheets, or can draft pleadings. A resume cannot quantify whether she is "presentable to clients" because she looks like a professional and has good manners or whether she is a "team player." It is those **soft skills** that will largely determine how far a person can advance after getting a foot in the door. But a firm that has hired a person with strong hard skills does not benefit from allowing that person to languish in a low-level position. Contrary to what some people believe, soft skills are not just "common sense"; they can be taught and learned.

Many people are turned off by any discussion of etiquette. They think that etiquette is a set of rigid formal rules intended to keep people on edge. In fact, etiquette is the art of appearing confident and comfortable while making others feel comfortable.

A. Your Personal Life versus Your Work Life

It's Monday morning at your firm and, as usual, the receptionist has a bit of news for you. You were unable to attend the firm's annual barbecue, held at a senior partner's family farm. "Did you hear? At the firm picnic on Saturday, that new 'floater' secretary, Lindsey, showed up wearing a halter top that left nothing to the imagination. She had two big glasses of wine, then she told a dirty joke, right in front of the partners! When she came in this morning I asked her whether she thought she still had a job and she said she didn't know what the big deal was. After all, it was a party."

Wrong. Lindsey may still have a job, but she certainly won't be invited to any events that involve client contact. And if a permanent position as an assistant to a partner becomes available, Lindsey won't be given serious consideration. She made others uncomfortable by her dress and behavior, which were inappropriate for her work life. It was a social event, but it was a *business* social event.

Let's start by looking at what Lindsey wore to the party. Employees sometimes come to work dressed inappropriately because they think that only shallow people would judge them by their clothing. But how we dress and carry ourselves can have a hugely positive impact. Think about a person walking down the street in a police officer's uniform. People are likely to approach that person to ask for directions or for help if they are in danger.

1.   Dress to Make Others Feel Confident and Comfortable

There are many resources available to those who want to "dress for success." In general they recommend that employees should reflect the style of dress of their supervisors. If the boss wears a jacket, wear a jacket. But what about the "bottom" level of employee clothing choices? An employee dressing in a very inappropriate manner could actually offend clients.

Should law firms implement dress codes? Most do not; they make decisions about a person's understanding of appropriate business attire during job interviews or simply fire people who do not meet expectations. Unfortunately, this often results in overlooking or losing a talented, hard-working employee who simply does not understand that clients may be offended by seeing a baseball cap worn indoors or a belly-button ring visible when a female employee raises her arms. According to a recent *Wall Street Journal* article[1], major firms are starting to take steps to educate their new hires: Winston & Strawn had a personal shopper and an etiquette counselor visit the firm; Cadwalader Wickersham & Taft reportedly sent employees notes asking them to change out of their boots while in the office.

The problem is not unique to law offices. In 2006 Illinois State University instituted a dress code for students in its business school. While some students did not like the requirement that they wear "business casual" attire to classes, they understood its purpose: to help them make the transition to the world of work. The Disney Corporation has long had a very detailed dress code for its employees and only recently "loosened up" to allow men to wear mustaches and women to wear open-toe shoes—with hosiery.

A dress code is not discriminatory unless it imposes an unequal burden on a group or is enforced in a discriminatory way. For example, requiring men to wear "suits with ties" while requiring women to "dress nicely" would require men to spend significantly more money on work clothing. A prohibition on facial hair, with no policy for exceptions, might discriminate against men of African descent, who may have a skin condition that is irritated by shaving. The dress codes for men and women do not have to be identical so that men have to be allowed to wear long hair and earrings if women can wear long hair and earrings. On the other hand, if a company has a dress code for both men and women but only ever disciplines women for violations, it is acting in a discriminatory manner.

Assignment 10-1
Develop a Dress Code

Management Portfolio

Work with classmates to prepare a dress code for the support staff at a midsized law firm. Instead of working with classmates you already know,

---

[1]http://online.wsj.com/article/SB120175142140831193.html?mod=home_law_more_news January 31, 2008

work with new people. Try to form a group of people who are dissimilar in age and backgrounds. This should also be an exercise in working as part of a team.

First, use the Internet to find information about the Disney dress code. Find information about a woman who sued Disney for prohibiting her from wearing a headscarf required by her religion. Next, find a medical school policy with hygiene and clothing guidelines. Finally, find at least three definitions of "business casual."

Meet with your group and discuss your findings. Do you think the definitions you found are reasonable? Do they impose a hardship? With this background information, prepare a written policy. The policy should be easily understandable to even the least-educated staff member and should not impose more hardship on any particular group. Be careful to define any terms that might be ambiguous (for example, "large" jewelry) and describe how the policy will be enforced. Consider: should the policy apply to firm social events? If so, why?

After your group finishes its policy, prepare a reflection paper in which you describe the positive contributions of each member, the problems you had reaching an agreement, any misunderstandings between members, and how you finally reached a compromise.

Next, let's look at Lindsey's mistakes in terms of the party itself. Does the firm have concerns about Lindsey's drinking and telling "dirty jokes" that go beyond "image"? Possibly.

Example

Courts differ about the liability of an employer whose employee, having become intoxicated at the employer's party, injures a third person. Compare *Halvorson v. Birchfield Boiler, Inc.*, 458 P.2d 897 (Wash. 1969) (employer absolved from liability), with *Harris v. Trojan Fireworks Co.*, 174 Cal. Rptr. 452 (Ct. App. 1981) and *Chastain v. Litton Systems, Inc.*, 694 F.2d 957, (4th Cir. 1982) (employer not absolved).

In addition, there have been a number of cases in which behavior at an office party was cited as evidence of sexual harassment.[2] Finally, although most states disagree, New York allows employees injured at employer-sponsored social events to claim entitlement to workers' compensation benefits.

2. Etiquette for Business Social Events

Do you remember ever being offended or angry about the behavior of another person in a social setting? Most behavior that is perceived as disrespectful,

---

[2]*Carver v. Waste Connections of Tenn.*, No. 3:04-CV-263 (E.D. Tenn. 2006); *Monthei v. Morton Bldgs.*, No. 4:01-CV-30510 (S.D. Iowa 2003).

discourteous, or abrasive is unintentional, and can be avoided by understanding the rules and assumptions under which others in the setting are acting. Unfortunately, for some people, that understanding comes too late to "undo" a bad first impression. Some basics for anyone attending a business social event include the following:

- Arrive on time or, if you are the host, early.
- If seated at a table, do not put your purse, briefcase, phone, or paperwork on the table. Keep them under the table or on the floor.
- Keep your right hand free for shaking hands. This means that you can hold a drink or a small plate in your left hand, but if you want to have both a drink and a plate you must find a table or surface on which you can place one or the other.
- If you see someone you've met before but cannot remember the name, approach with a smile and your hand extended. Say "I'm Chris Paralegal, I believe we've met." The person will almost always respond by saying her own name.
- In general, do not drink alcohol, but do not make a big deal of it. If you are going to have an alcoholic drink, limit yourself to one and make it last.
- Greet others as they arrive by standing and offering a firm handshake. The web between your thumb and finger should touch the web between the other person's thumb and finger (no fingertip shakes). Make good eye contact, smile, and shake only two to three times.
- When introducing people always say the name of the most important person (the client, if a client is present, or the highest ranking person in your organization) first. If possible, say something that will give the people a conversation starting point. For example, "Cal Client, I'd like to introduce Ann Associate. Ann has been reviewing your trust documents with me" or "Pat Partner, I'd like you to meet Lyn Newbie. Lyn graduated from the paralegal program at State U last month and started in our real estate department last week."
- Do not automatically hand out business cards. If asked for a card, hand it to the recipient print side up. If you want someone to remember you, make a note of where you met or what you discussed on your card. If you are handed a business card, treat it with respect. Do not just slip it into a pocket.
- If you were a guest, write a thank-you note.

Correct etiquette is important during business meals also. Follow these tips:

- Do not order or start to eat (even the bread) before others arrive and are ready.
- Follow the lead of the host or hostess in placing your napkin on your lap and starting to eat.
- Generally pass food to your right, without taking some for yourself first. Keep salt and pepper together when passing. Remember to say please and thank you! Do not butter your bread directly from the butter plate; put a small amount on your bread plate.

- If you are either a fast or a slow eater, pace yourself so that you are eating at the same speed as others.
- If you are asked a question while you have food in your mouth, just raise a finger to indicate that you need a moment.
- Don't make a big deal of your own mistakes (spilled drink, using the wrong fork) and don't ever mention mistakes made by others.
- If you need to blow your nose or take a call, leave the table. When you leave the table, place your napkin on your chair.
- Your food (salad, bread plate) and fork are on the left (note that food, fork, and left all have four letters). Your drink, knife, and spoon are on the right (all have five letters).
- When you have multiple forks or spoons, work your way inward, so use the fork furthest from your plate first (for salad).
- Any utensils at the top of the dinner plate are for dessert.
- Never put utensils back on the table after they have been used.

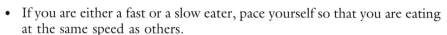

Assignment 10-2
Write Business/Social Notes

1. Your former classmate, Sasha Kurylak, has landed a job with the biggest firm in your area: Koropey, Ramsell, Garnett & Duncan at 82 Main Street. The firm has a continuing legal education lunch meeting in its conference room once a month, and you attended last month's meeting as Sasha's guest. The topic was Everyday Ethics; the lunch was an excellent seafood salad. Sasha introduced you to Ms. Linda Ramsell, the senior partner. All went well, except for a bad moment when you accidentally spilled your water on Sasha's sleeve.

- Write a thank-you note to Ms. Ramsell, keeping in mind that you might someday like to work at the KRGD firm, but don't want to appear disloyal to your current employer.
- You later hear that Ms. Ramsell was honored as "pro bono attorney of the year" by the county bar association. Write a note of congratulations.

2. The hardest type of letter to write is a condolence letter. Imagine that a coworker, Jose Martinez, has just lost his wife, Anna. Write a condolence note to Jose, remembering to include a happy memory if possible (for example, "Although I had the pleasure of meeting Anna only once, I remember that she was gracious and kind and set me at ease," or "Although I never had an opportunity to meet Anna, I know how much she meant to you because you said so often").

Management Portfolio

3. You (and others in your group) are part of a management "team" for a mega-firm that employs many young people, from high school seniors

who answer phones and run errands on weekends, all the way up to law school students working as clerks. Because the firm has a beautiful reception area, with an incredible view of the skyline, it hosts gatherings regularly, not only for its own clients, but for local charities, CLE events, press conferences, and other special events. The partners believe that the opportunity to mingle with people from all fields is very valuable for all employees, but they are concerned that the young people make a good impression. They have asked you to plan a lunch meeting at which you will introduce the young employees to some basic rules of etiquette. You know that if you stand at the front of the room and lecture about good manners, you will be greeted with eye-rolling and inattention. Identify some of the most important points from this chapter and plan some "fun" or engaging ways to convey these lessons.

4. Your firm has an annual party at the end of December. Use the Internet and prepare a list of at least ten policies or preparations that will help avoid a bad aftermath or offending certain employees.

3. Time Management

The biggest difference between a person's home life and work life is that an employer pays for time at work. When they are honest with themselves, most people know when they are procrastinating or wasting time at work and feel bad about it. Time wasting often occurs because the worker is avoiding the next task on which he plans to work: he procrastinates because he finds the task unpleasant or overwhelming.

Recognizing procrastination is the first step to avoiding it! Symptoms include the following:

- Spending the day on low-priority tasks from the to-do list
- Reading an item from a list, a request, or an e-mail repeatedly, without starting work on it
- Spending excessive amounts of time looking for things in a cluttered office or spending excessive amounts of time keeping the office obsessively neat
- Sitting down to start a task and almost immediately going off-task to make a cup of coffee or check e-mails
- Micromanaging work delegated to others or spending an unreasonable amount of time reassuring someone who has delegated work
- Leaving an important item on a priority list for a long time
- Frequently saying yes to unimportant tasks suggested by others to avoid important tasks already on the list

To deal with this behavior, the procrastinator must first determine the importance of the task being avoided. Putting off an unimportant task isn't procrastination; it may be good prioritization. Once a worker understands that the task being avoided is not immediately important, she feels free to move on to another task so that time is not being wasted. Knowing how to create a prioritized to-do list helps with this step:

- Create a routine of planning at the same time each day. Review accomplishments and what remains to be done.
- Make a written list with specific tasks. For example, "Work on Rezner file" is not as useful as "Prepare Rezner interrogatories."
- Prioritize items on your list as "A," urgent; "B," important, and "C," to be done if time permits.
- Keep a separate list of "floating tasks" that are not time-critical and may be portable. These can be used to fill in time that might otherwise be wasted, for example, waiting for an appointment.
- Learn to recognize when doing something immediately will save time in the long run. For example, if someone says, "Call me to schedule a meeting on creating those exhibits," pull out your calendar and say, "Let's set it up now to save a call." On the other hand, doing some work prematurely (for example, planning a meeting before you know the schedules of essential participants) can result in duplication of effort.
- Learn to recognize when something needs to be done very well and is, for example, worthy of a rewrite, versus something that just needs to be done quickly. A memo for a client must be done well; a memo explaining the new procedure for getting into the office on weekends just needs to be done.
- Keep only one calendar; having separate work and personal calendars creates confusion.
- Block off each day so that A priority tasks get done first, around scheduled events, and B priority tasks get done next. But do not overschedule. Allow time for emergencies, delays, unexpected events, and just thinking. Knowing what should be done during a specific block of time helps you say no to distractions.
- In planning the workday, take into account personal patterns of energy. There is no point in scheduling an urgent and challenging project for immediately after lunch if you are always sleepy at that time of day.
- Also consider that some tasks may take less time at certain times of day or in certain locations. Phone calls tend to be shorter if made right before lunch or at the end of the workday. If you need to communicate only a specific piece of non-confidential information that is not urgent, consider calling at a time when you are likely to connect with voice mail or an answering machine. If you need to meet with Lonnie-the-long-talker, go to Lonnie's office so that you can leave when you need to leave.
- Don't forget to schedule adequate time to keep stress at bay by exercising, socializing, and resting.
- As tasks are completed, cross them off to create a sense of accomplishment.
- Periodically review schedules and note deviations. Have goals proven to be realistic? Are there certain types of tasks that regularly cause trouble? If so, can the approach to those tasks be changed? What factors prevented meeting goals, how might those factors be controlled? If goals are regularly unmet, are you trying to do too much? What can be cut out or delegated?

For More Information

Time management resources are plentiful on the Internet. Many school sites, for example, give their students tips on how to better manage their time. You can conduct your own time audit by using the chart at http://www.d.umn.edu/kmc/student/loon/acad/strat/time_use_chart.html. Also, view the time management videos at http://www.dartmouth.edu/~acskills/videos/video_tm.html.

If procrastination is caused by finding a task unpleasant and the work cannot be delegated to someone else, the best strategy is motivation. A positive approach might include a reward, such as lunch at a nice restaurant rather than in the office. This works best if the procrastinator is accountable to someone else. The procrastinator can identify a coworker with whom she would enjoy sharing that lunch and ask her to check on progress on the task; tell her that the lunch is a reward. On the other hand, some people respond better to identifying the negative consequences of not completing the task.

When procrastination is the result of finding a project overwhelming, a different approach is required. Start by breaking the project into a set of smaller, more manageable tasks. Next, get some of the small or easy tasks finished, if possible, even if these aren't the logical first steps. This creates a feeling that progress is being made and that perhaps the whole project won't be so overwhelming after all.

4. Stress Management

Stress is a huge factor in the lives of legal professionals and in the lives of students, which is why states have **lawyers' assistance programs (LAPs)** and colleges have student resources such as http://www.dartmouth.edu/~acskills/videos/video_sm.html.

Unfortunately, working paralegals and other members of support staff often have to fend for themselves in controlling stress. Here are some ideas that might help you take care of yourself and advise those under your supervision:

lawyers' assistance program (LAP)
Counseling program for lawyers with substance abuse or other personal problems

- Plan every day, as described above, but do not spend time anticipating what will happen at various meetings or events. If you do visualize events, assume a realistic, positive outcome — not a glorious, unrealistic outcome, but not a negative outcome.
- Walk outside when possible; exercise, fresh air, and exposure to sun are great stress busters.
- Good sleep is essential. Go to bed and get up at the same time every day; never use bed for work, planning, reliving the day, or worrying.
- Discover what truly relaxes you and takes you outside your stress. It may be reading, it may be participating in a sport or exercise, it may be a hobby, it may be listening to audio books while walking your dog. Whatever it is, make it a required part of your schedule.
- Do not allow anger to control you; how you react to a situation is up to you, not to the other person. Forgive others when they make mistakes and learn to give constructive feedback rather than harsh criticism. Try to find humor even in situations that create trouble for you.

- Leave the junk food machine alone! You are worth the little time it takes to pack or buy a balanced meal or snack with fruits and vegetables. Limit your caffeine and drink water.

While some business gurus believe that messy offices are the cause of wasted time and lost productivity and are either a symptom or cause of stress, some people thrive in a cluttered environment. In a law office, however, your personal comfort zone is not the only consideration. Presenters at the 2006 ABA Techshow, discussing the top ten causes of malpractice, said:

> Finally, you should consider the effect created by poor housekeeping. Some of us in the legal profession view a messy and cluttered office almost as a badge of honor. These messy attorneys seem to believe that clients view the stacks of files as reflecting positively upon the attorney's workload, implying that the attorney is in demand. The reasoning extends to the desired conclusion that the client was lucky to have this particularly busy attorney agree to handle the client's matter. While this may or may not be true, what is the client's likely response when the matter takes an unexpected turn for the worse? The client is likely to conclude that the unexpected turn resulted from the attorney not devoting adequate time to representing the client. The attorney's messy office only serves to confirm the belief. Mark C.S. Bassingthwaighte & Reba J. Nance, The Top Ten Causes of Malpractice — and How You Can Avoid Them, Presentation at the ABA Techshow 2006 (Apr. 20-22, 2006), http://www.abanet.org/lpm/lpt/articles/tch12062.pdf.

If an office is seen by outsiders or if it is a source of stress to its occupant, it needs to be gotten under control. Office organization has become an industry in itself, and there are countless systems for organizing papers and files so that even the least-organized worker can have a clean desk and find anything he needs within seconds.

B. Supervising Others to Maintain a Stable Staff

The worst attitude a supervisor can have is that the workers need their jobs more than the employer needs them. High turnover at any level is costly, not only in terms of money spent on training and lost productivity, but in terms of effect on other workers and the firm's image to outsiders. Some of the causes of high turnover include the following:[3]

- Lack of orientation and/or adequate training
- Favoritism and unfair compensation systems
- No mechanism for complaints or suggestions — poor communication
- Inadequate backup for employees overwhelmed with work or in need of time off
- Unpleasant work atmosphere: negativity, office politics, and gossip; no sense of the firm as a team — individual attorneys possessive of "their" support staff and unwilling to work with others

---

[3]Ellen Freedman, *How Not to be a Staff Nightmare,* Law Prac. Today, Sept. 2008, http://www.abanet.org/lpm/lpt/articles/mgt09081.shtml.

- Attorneys with poor management skills
- Low expectations—people tend to reach toward expectations

Some of these problems can be resolved without spending money. As described in previous chapters, new lawyers should be counseled on how to work with staff; the firm should have an organizational system that is oriented to productive work flow, rather than egos; procedures manuals should be available to help employees with new tasks; and compensation and job descriptions should be based on research in the marketplace. Other problems can be resolved by creating office policies, dealing with employees who are creating problems, and modeling positive work relationships.

Keep in mind that none of these solutions or policies can be effectively implemented by a manager who is isolated from staff. Management is a hands-on pursuit: accessibility to and regular interaction with every person being supervised is essential to understanding his or her concerns, communicating, and modeling a team approach and high expectations. Remember: even the part-time receptionist can cause a disaster for the firm. Do not manage staff with a "pecking order" mentality, but with a team mentality.

1. The Problem: Gossip and Office Politics

Perhaps nothing causes stress and poisons the work atmosphere more quickly than gossip and destructive office politics. Gossip and negative "politicking" decreases productivity and hurts morale, and it can also create a hostile work environment and even result in a suit for slander. Workers often cite gossip as a pet peeve about their jobs. Employers are often desperate to control destructive gossip. Consider the case of the "Hooksett Four," four women fired in 2007 from town hall jobs in New Hampshire because a supervisor overheard them engaging in "gossip."

While the term "office politics" usually has negative connotations, the underlying reality is not always bad. People are rarely inherently "bad," but sometimes they go about attempting to achieve their goals in ways that seem bad to others. Life, office politics, and other relationships all involve goals and objectives: a high salary, professional recognition, a power position, love, trust . . . the list is long. Sometimes people are aware of their objectives, but sometimes they are not. A person might say (and might even believe) that she is not interested in recognition or promotion, but only wants to do a good job. Under the surface, however, she may crave approval and feel unappreciated. Office politics is how people attempt to achieve their objectives or "win" at the "game."

People are not always aware that their strategy for "winning" is influenced by matters such as being afraid of being seen as a "self-promoter," desire to be liked or desire to be feared, social disapproval of assertiveness by some people, or even intimidation. Winning in the workplace setting can be achieved in different ways:

- Win by natural talent, education, and skill; be the "natural" best. This works only if you were lucky enough to be born with the talent and to get the education needed to make that talent shine.

- Win by putting in the highest level of effort. Because this method can be costly in terms of other objectives (family, fun, friends) and can make coworkers perceive you as "spoiling the curve," it has its own difficulties.
- Win by creating an appearance of being the natural best or putting in the highest level of effort, even if that is not factually true.
- Win by default — make others quit or not participate.
- Win by making those around you appear to lose.
- Win by establishing a "value" that may be unrelated to talent or effort in the practice of the business (for example, marry the boss; bring in lots of clients; or be so charming that you are able to negotiate anything).

Of course, another option is to not want to win. Those who do not want to engage in any of the winning strategies might define their goal as just "not losing." So, they do their jobs and avoid being fired or reprimanded. Many people in this category are good employees and give value for their compensation. They often have objectives outside the workplace that make them "winners" in another category; but a percentage of these people nonetheless resent those who are attempting to "win" and will try to sabotage them. Some people are so convinced that they cannot win that they are most concerned with establishing a valid excuse for failure!

These strategies have different results. Some workers are actively engaged with their jobs; they feel connected and satisfied. Some workers are disengaged and essentially "sleepwalk" through the day. The worst are those who become saboteurs and actively undermine the efforts of others. Obviously, a firm is most likely to thrive when most of its employees are engaged and productive.

People who are truly "winning" in the law office environment, by means of talent, effort, or by creating a "niche" value such as "rainmaker," often say that they are not aware of office politics at their place of employment or that it has no impact on them. Those who enjoy less success will often blame their setbacks on office politics. Often they are unaware of their own motivations and strategies and oblivious to the goals and strategies of those around them.

Think back to the example at the beginning of this chapter: perhaps Lindsey, with her in-your-face, "hot chick" style of dressing is attempting to create an "excuse" for not succeeding. She is afraid her skills or her efforts won't measure up and wants to tell herself (and her friends) that "they were so tightly wound that they even got upset by things like my shoes — no way could I continue to work there."

Consider other typical law office "types," such as the long-time secretary who is resentful and hostile toward paralegals and associates because he feels that their positions reflect on his position as an inherent failure — how can he be a success when he has been at the firm for many years, but they start out in jobs "above" his? Perhaps the firm's chief gossip is subconsciously trying to make others appear inferior and to establish an alternate value for herself, as a storehouse of information. Similarly, the office control freak, vigilant organizer of the office supply closet and office spy, may be trying to make the partners value her and see her coworkers as inferior performers.

None of them are bad people, and they all do have value to the firm. How can an office manager redirect them to new strategies? One way is to recognize that every organization is political, but that the politics can work in a positive way. The first step is to analyze the existing political structure of the firm. People will engage in negative politics if they feel that that is the only way to influence decisions that will have an impact on their jobs, if they feel they need to be "protected" by affiliation with the right people, or if they feel that the firm defines achievement in terms of who likes and dislikes them. Workers who feel that they have input, that they will be treated fairly, and that their work will be evaluated objectively will not feel compelled to engage in negative politics. So, if the secretary felt that his work was appreciated and that the firm looked to him to acclimate new associates and paralegals, he might not feel resentful. If the chief gossip were valued as the person who can always find the right form, she might not need to gossip. As an office manager, you will be key to creating a culture in which employees feel that they are heard, in which fixing problems has priority over placing blame, and in which every employee is expected to grow with the firm

2. The Solution: Happy Workers Are Productive Workers

After negative factors that cause high turnover are eliminated, a good manager looks at positive factors. What makes workers productive and loyal? There are five key career motivators that give workers a greater sense of career satisfaction:

1. A job that provides an opportunity to succeed
2. An opportunity to develop and be professionally challenged
3. Integration of work life and personal life
4. A job that provides an opportunity to be creative
5. A sense of belonging to the organization

A firm can use these factors to maintain a satisfied staff without spending much money.

a. Opportunity to Succeed and Opportunity to Develop

Does the firm provide and are employees aware of opportunities for advancement? How does a file clerk become a legal secretary or a paralegal? How does a paralegal assistant become a senior paralegal?

Are employees given regular, scheduled feedback on their performance? If an employee's performance is unsatisfactory, is she given immediate feedback so that she can correct her performance before it endangers her future with the firm? Does feedback include specific suggestions? (Specific advice for conducting employee evaluations is included Chapter 9.)

Does the firm have a **mentoring** program to pair new employees with more experienced employees? Mentoring helps employees not only avoid mistakes and become productive faster, but also to feel comfortable earlier.

What opportunities are available for training, education, and CLE? Does the firm sponsor events? If it does not, would it be cost-effective to implement a program? Will the firm reimburse for attendance at classes, training, or CLE outside the firm and willingly allow employees to attend during the workday? When employees do attend educational events, are they recognized for doing so?

mentoring
Relationship between a more experienced person, the mentor, and a less experienced protégé

Are they asked to report what they learned or demonstrate new skills for the benefit of others? This can be done by way of regular group meetings or a newsletter, described later in this chapter.

If a firm handles its training in-house, the programs should be regularly assessed for effectiveness. Do the topics reflect skills that employees want and need? Do employees regard the training as too basic or too advanced?

b. Integration of Work Life and Personal Life

The most innovative employers are looking at ways of helping employees who are trying to balance work with parenthood or with care of aging parents. Other "personal life" problems that can become problems in the workplace include long expensive commutes and employee health problems.

Employers should make sure that employees know all of the benefits that are available to them. For example, some employers offer these programs:

flex time
Arrangement allowing flexibility in scheduling work time

telecommuting
Working from outside the office, via computer

concierge
Services to help with personal errands

incentives
Things that induce action

wellness programs
Assist with employees' well-being and overall good health

sick leave pool
Also called sick leave bank; enables employees to donate to and draw from a common fund of sick days

- **Flex Time**. As long as phones are covered, work is getting done, and obligations are being met, employees are allowed to arrive and leave earlier or later than normal business hours. This can be a regular thing, to help an employee who has to take a particular train, or an occasional thing, to help an employee who wants to attend her child's volleyball games. Added value: this may mean rotating employees so that they learn other jobs.
- **Telecommuting**. If an employee's job does not require face-to-face interaction with others, he may be allowed to work from home part or all of the time and avoid the expense and wasted time of a commute to the office.
- Discounts. Some employers work with tenants in the same building or nearby to obtain discounts on health club memberships, dry cleaning, and even childcare. Some even provide **concierge** service so that employees can have packages picked up and delivered at the reception desk. Some even offer **incentives** to employees who participate in **wellness programs** to lose weight or stop smoking.
- Transportation. To help the environment or make a bad commute easier, some employers offer van pools or discounted train and bus tickets.
- Employee Assistance Programs. EAPs help with counseling, consultation, and child and family services in areas such as substance abuse, marital discord, family conflicts, job stress, self-doubt/low self-esteem, adjustment to divorce, bereavement, aging parents, legal and financial problems or physical and emotional problems.
- **Sick Leave Pool**. By creating a pool to which all employees can contribute, the employer can provide additional sick leave to employees who have suffered illness or injury.

Employers should also recognize the value of longevity by having a salary structure that motivates employees to stay and grow in their jobs. The firm can also communicate that it recognizes the value of its employees by awarding bonuses in good years.

c. Opportunity to be Creative and to Feel Connected to the Organization

One of the most effective ways to make employees happy and productive is to make them feel like part of a team. Team building is a very important part of making a law office functional, but it often takes a backseat to working billable hours. But team building need not come at the expense of getting the job done. A big part of the team mentality comes from how people communicate.

A law office consists of people with different, but complementary, skills committed to a common purpose, but lawyers sometimes see only the parts played by attorneys. They may speak in ways that communicates that vision: "We are a 10-lawyer firm." But that firm may have 20 other employees who are talented, hard working, and trained to do things that many of the lawyers cannot do. "We billed 100,000 hours last year," but those hours could not have been billed without the work of the IT staff, the secretaries, the copy center, and others in the firm who do not bill hours. If a firm wants to retain and maximize the productivity of its non-lawyer staff, it has to create a culture in which those members of the staff feel like valued members of a team.

As a law office manager, you will become aware that part of the problem is that many of the lawyers only vaguely understand the skills or contributions of people with whom they do not regularly interact. Lack of knowledge not only causes lack of appreciation, but it can also lead to inefficiency. For example, if a new lawyer is not aware that Pete-the-receptionist is a gadget whiz, she may waste a lot of otherwise-billable time trying to set up her new PDA.

A good starting point is regular praise and recognition for professional accomplishments, efforts "above and beyond the call of duty," and even personal matters such as weddings, birthdays, and new babies. Recognition for professional accomplishments can include prizes or gifts, but even without any material reward, employees value acknowledgment. Acknowledgment can occur at firm or group meetings or in the firm newsletter. The firm may have an internal newsletter (which may be electronic or paper) used to describe new procedures, identify new clients, and communicate other administrative matters. By giving employees equal access to information at the same time, a newsletter makes employees feel like they are "in the loop" and can help prevent gossip and "grapevine" politics.

The firm may also have an external newsletter that it uses as a marketing tool. Would there be any value in putting information about staff achievements in a newsletter to clients? The answer is a resounding yes! Beyond the satisfaction for the employee featured in a story, there is a "human interest" value that may make clients feel more bonded to the firm. In addition, it is good for clients to see what they are paying for.

Assignment 10-3
Workplace Policies and LAP

---

1. If you have not already done so for Assignment 1-1 (see Chapter 1), find the website for your state's LAP. Write a short summary of the

program, including how it takes reports on lawyers in need of help, what types of problems it deals with, and whether it conducts interventions.

2. How can a firm define "gossip" so that if the firm has a "no gossip" policy, employees will know what is prohibited? Keep in mind that gossip is not necessarily false; what if the boss *did* get arrested for DUI over the weekend? Talk can also be positive: the boss was named pro bono lawyer of the year by the bar association. After all, the firm newsletter is a form of gossip — should there be a policy about its contents? Also keep in mind that few employees want to "drop a dime" on their coworkers; they should have a tool for avoiding gossip without having to go to a supervisor. Use the Internet to research office policies on gossip and what happened to the Hooksett Four. Work with a team of classmates to write up an office policy describing what constitutes gossip and how an employee should respond to gossip.

3. Reconvene your classmate team from the dress code assignment and discuss additional ideas and policies for improving morale and reducing the perception that success depends on a negative type of office politics. Particularly focus on respecting the cultural differences among workers; should a firm have a policy to address the fact that its employees have different religious beliefs, ethnic and economic backgrounds, political views, and family structures?

4. Reconvene your team and discuss an office policy on swearing. Prepare a position statement, but first do some research on the Internet. You may be surprised to learn that some studies have found that some swearing in the workplace has positive effects. Also consider how you will define what is prohibited.

5. Visit the websites of the **Association of Legal Administrators (ALA)** (http://www.alanet.org) and **International Paralegal Management Association (IPMA)** (http://www.paralegalmanagement.org). Determine whether there are any chapters in your local area and report to the class on the benefits of membership. Now visit http://www.plmw.org (the website of International Professional Legal Management Week) and identify the sponsoring organizations (12 at this writing). Find an article on "Improved Teamwork Yields Better Results."

6. Learn more about the theory of "total rewards" by visiting the webpage of the WorldatWork organization (http://www.worldatwork.org). How does this organization define the five elements of total compensation?

Association of Legal Administrators (ALA)
Professional organization for legal administrators and managers

International Paralegal Management Association (IPMA)
Formerly Legal Assistant Management Association (LAMA); professional organization for paralegal managers

C. Your Own Career Path

1. Dealing with Difficult People

Office managers are employees too. They have many of the same problems and needs that others in the office do, but often have one particular problem in greater doses: dealing with difficult people. As an office manager, you will deal with difficult clients, difficult suppliers, difficult lawyers, and difficult staff members. Because the legal profession is, by nature, adversarial and very competitive, you may deal with more stress, anger, and other emotions than you would in another field. Short of quitting to pursue a job in flower arranging, how do you deal with people who are regularly causing you stress?

Step One: In the Moment

Perhaps the most challenging part of dealing with difficult people is staying calm during an emotional encounter. Do not allow your instincts to take over. You must not lose control and lower yourself into the "difficult person" category. If the difficult person is a supervisor, you must not walk away; it gives the appearance of challenging authority. Keep in mind a story about the Buddha: a verbally abusive man came to see him and starting hurling insults, but the Buddha just sat there calmly. Finally the man asked the Buddha why he failed to respond. The Buddha replied, "If someone offers you a gift, and you decline to accept it, to whom does the gift belong?" Mental imagery can also help; observe the person carefully and picture any inappropriate behavior as an energy that bounces off you. Try to imagine this person as a child throwing a tantrum in a store and yourself as a calm parent, waiting for it to pass. When it does pass, suggest a time to continue the discussion later. This is especially important if the encounter is in a public place; many difficult people cannot tolerate being "challenged" in front of others.

Step Two: Analyze the Situation

If you must interact with the difficult person regularly, keep a record of problem interactions. You may see a pattern of timing, location, situation, or even your own responses that trigger difficult behavior by the other person. If the interactions involve threats, cursing, or other intolerable behavior, you may need support from above. Consider bringing in someone at the same level as or "up the chain" from the offender. Now, characterize the behavior. Which of the follow characteristics does the person display?

- Explosive — calm and rational most of the time, but occasionally loudly and aggressively angry.
- Passive-aggressive — pleasant enough in person, but never following up with agreed actions, sometimes claiming not to remember.
- Manipulative/bully — tries to identify your vulnerabilities and picks at them. Depending on the person's status relative to yours, this type may either be belligerent, belittling you openly: "Didn't you learn *anything* in your paralegal program?" or may be an envious agitator-spreading poison behind the scenes.
- Slave-driver boss — constantly piling on work so that you cannot catch up.
- Disorganized — always working under pressure, always too busy.

Based on your analysis, decide whether you should meet to discuss the person. If the person is a slave-driver boss, she may be unaware of your workload, and a meeting could benefit both of you. On the other hand, if the person is passive-aggressive, a meeting might not work. You cannot change a personality, so it may be best to focus on coping strategies.

Step Three: Strategy

An explosive employee is almost always someone over whom you have no authority, so consider how bad the problem is and how rational the person is during "good" moments. If the explosions are not terrible and the person is generally rational, a private meeting during which you lay your cards on the table may help. Focus on your own reactions rather than the other person's behavior. Take a "feel/want/will" approach: "When you yelled at me while we were assembling the exhibits, I became so upset I couldn't concentrate. I want to get things done on time, and I can do that if you will help keep the atmosphere calm."

In other situations, you may try "behavior conditioning." During an explosion, just watch the person with a befuddled look on your face; when the person handles a stressful situation without an explosion, take notice. "I admired the way you dealt with Marcy when she couldn't find the Jones file. I think she learned something from the situation without being too embarrassed." Above all, don't take this person's problems as a reflection on you. It's best to avoid such a person during times you identify as likely to be bad and, when you must deal with an explosion, be calm and stick to factual statements. At some point you may decide that you can no longer work with such a person.

If the person is manipulative and belligerent, do not bother to discuss the problem in generalities. Talk about specific incidents and the consequences. "Last week, when you asked whether I hadn't learned anything in school, you made me look bad in front of the people you expect me to supervise. If you want me to have credibility with the staff, please confine your criticism of me to private conversations." If you don't feel a meeting would be productive, respond to manipulative remarks with specific statements relating to business. In response to "Didn't you learn anything in school?" you might say, "I'm sorry, are you trying to tell me that you wanted a page-by-page summary of that deposition?" If appropriate (depending on the person's position and personality) you might even say, in a sincere tone, "Why do you say that?"

A person who appears to be passive-aggressive may be either manipulative behind the scenes or disorganized, as described below. Deal with the situation accordingly.

A person who is manipulative behind the scenes is likely someone at your own level or someone you supervise. If you have a specific incident, you may want to confront the individual. On the other hand, if you want to handle the problem without bringing others into it ("Mary said that you said that I don't know how to search title records"), you may want to try to change the person's attitude (or credibility) by killing him with kindness. Keep in mind that this type of behavior is often rooted in envy. You can often defuse the situation by making sure you never flaunt your advantages, privileges, status, or accomplishments and appropriately expressing praise or admiration for the offender.

With slave-drivers, plan a meeting so that you will not appear to be lazy or a whiner. Provide specific information about your workload and hours, perhaps examples of times you have had trouble prioritizing. Keep the tone positive: "You've always been fair, so I know you will help me work this out." Offer alternative solutions: temporary workers during crunch times, a new system for assigning work.

If the disorganized person is someone you supervise, you have the right and obligation to insist that the situation improve. Meet with the individual and make specific suggestions for organizing and prioritizing work. Set specific goals; do not discuss personality traits, but stick to behavior and specific incidents. Do not say "you are so sloppy," but "we need you to return the books to the shelves after you use them." On the other hand, if the person is a lawyer, meeting to discuss the problem would have little benefit unless you can suggest something you can do to assist the person (for example, assign help to get some filing done or reorganize files). Control your interaction with the person by planning meetings that are not in competition with her preparation for a meeting or a hearing. Confirm all important communications in writing.

Most important, focus on yourself—the only person you can really control or change. Honestly assess whether you are responsible for some part of the difficult person's behavior. Are you unhappy with your life or position, and is that reflected in your work and interactions? Do you have the ability to move on if that is the only way to deal with the situation?

How do you define you own career goals? Do you see yourself as eventually obtaining a job with a good firm and staying in that job indefinitely? Do you expect to change jobs several times, always looking for greater challenges and compensation? Only you can answer those questions, and there is no single "correct" answer. If you are a person who is always looking for the next challenge, you probably already know what you have to do to advance in your career. But if you are a person who likes stability and staying in your comfort zone, you may not realize that doing these same things can prevent you from growing bored and hitting a point of burnout. Do you view your work as a "job" or a "profession"?

2. Professionalism

The term "professionalism" can be defined as adhering to the expectations, decorum, and practices of the field. In the legal field, those expectations and practices (for both lawyers and paralegals) include the following:

- Continuing education. Even if you have achieved the highest degree or certificate that you can or want to achieve, there is always more to learn. A legal professional attends CLE, updates her technology skills regularly, and takes classes as needed for her particular job (management, a second language, medical terminology).
- Contributing to the image of the profession and mentoring new practitioners. Offer your services as a speaker at school career presentations. Join professional organizations. NALA, IPMA, ALA, or NFPA may be active in your area; there may be an independent paralegal or law office management organization. Your local bar association may have active

paralegal members. Whatever your choice of organizations, be actively involved. You will benefit the image of your profession and its newest members and you will also reap the benefits of networking, practicing leadership, and having colleagues with whom to discuss your challenges.

- Get your name in print. Getting published is easier than you think. The newsletter for your paralegal association would love an article about an interesting legal or management issue you have handled. No original ideas? Offer to write a summary of a CLE event or even a social event sponsored by the group.
- Give back. Be willing to help with pro bono work, even if it won't build your billable hours; be willing to volunteer for a local school's mock trial competition.
- Always uphold the ethics of your profession. Not only should you practice within the ethical rules, but also be alert to anything that conveys the image that the profession is not ethical.
- Always conduct yourself with dignity. Remain neutral in workplace conflicts; when you are part of a conflict, take time to seriously consider how the other person might be right. Above all, listen. Do not allow emotion or ego to control your behavior. Do not hesitate to admit that you have made a mistake or need help, but keep your personal life out of the workplace.

Out There—Paralegal Profile
Professional Development

Its a Journey, Not a Destination

Monika Bhatt is a registered attorney in India who moved to the United States and completed an ABA-approved paralegal certificate program in

 2003. She is currently working as a paralegal with Blair & Roach, LLP, a full-service law firm operating from three locations in western New York. Monika assists a team of 15 attorneys with diverse areas of practice.

Before going to work for Blair & Roach, Monika worked with a three-attorney firm in Chicago. She next worked for Legal Services, a not-for-profit organization, in Buffalo, New York. At Legal Services, she worked with another, senior, paralegal and three attorneys in the Disability Unit. Her job involved advocating for disabled clients at administrative hearings to help them receive free assistive technology, like motorized wheel chairs, from the Department of Health. The job also involved interpretation of Medicaid, Medicare, and private insurance laws; drafting; researching; and assisting healthcare professionals in writing letters of medical justification for assistive devices.

Monika says: "I have been working as a paralegal for five years now, and I thoroughly love my work. Having worked at a small law firm, a midsize law firm with 12-15 attorneys, and at legal services, it is my observation that at a small law firm there is lot of paralegal work. Paralegals often perform both secretarial and paralegal duties for a smaller salary, but it is a good starting point for the beginners to learn the nuts and bolts of working in a law firm. A large or a midsize law firm more often has defined roles and duties for a paralegal and offers more competitive salaries than a small law firm or legal services."

"A legal services job, though hard to find, offers job security, opportunity for specialization, and fulfillment of one's philanthropic goals. The disadvantage is low pay scale, compared to a private practice and lack of exposure to private practice."

Monika's paralegal certificate started her on her career path in a new country. It equipped her with the essential skills required to work in a legal environment. She has grown through her experiences in a variety of jobs. What is next? Monika plans to return to school and obtain an **LL.M** degree and a license to practice law.

LL.M
Master of law degree

Promoting the Profession

Rhonda Humphry is a litigation paralegal. She attended an ABA-approved paralegal program, and, in 1997, began her career working on the plaintiff's side of workers' compensation cases. In 2002 Rhonda began working for the defense in workers' compensation and civil litigation cases involving medical negligence and personal injury. Rhonda is interested in expanding the role of the paralegals in her area and statewide and is proud to serve as a director of the Illinois Paralegal Association. In addition, Rhonda contributes to the profession by writing articles, like the one that follows concerning billing for paralegal fees. Like many in the profession, Rhonda believes that fee awards are key to increasing use of and responsibilities given to paralegals, as well as visibility and respect for the profession. This article is reprinted with permission of Rhonda Humphry and the Illinois Paralegal

Association. The article first appeared in IPA's publication, *The Lookout*, in 2008 and has been edited for length.

Analysis of *Delgado v. Village of Rosemont*, United States District Court, N.D. Illinois, 2006 WL 3147695, concerning paralegal fees.

To determine a reasonable amount of attorneys' fees, courts use the "lodestar" method. *People Who Care v. Rockford Bd. of Educ.*, 90 F.3d 1307, 1310 (7th Cir. 1996). A court determines the "lodestar" by multiplying the hours reasonably expended on the case by a reasonable hourly rate. *Delgado v. Village of Rosemont* is a case involving Plaintiff's Motion for Attorneys' Fees and Costs. In the underlying case, plaintiffs prevailed in jury trial on a use of excessive force claim. Using the "lodestar" method, plaintiffs sought attorneys' fees in the amount of $444,830.00, including paralegal fees in the amount of $85,645.00. The paralegals' rates were $175.00 per hour and $100.00 per hour.

Awarding a total of only $272,604.84, the court criticized the practice of "block billing," or bundling tasks together. The court also noted vague language describing tasks. The court found it "impossible to evaluate whether these fees were reasonably necessary" and reduced fees by 35% due to insufficient description. The court also reduced the number of hours spent on the fee petition and litigating the merits of the case.

The court agreed with defendant's arguments relating to non-billable tasks billed by paralegals. In order to grant an award for paralegal fees, the court expects to find "the work was sufficiently complex" to justify the efforts of a paralegal. Clerical and secretarial tasks cannot be billed. The court observed that such tasks as organizing file folders, preparing documents, copying documents, assembling filings, electronically filing documents, sending materials, docketing or "logging" case events into internal case tracking system and telephoning court reporters, have all been considered clerical. The court's analysis highlights a challenge faced by paralegals daily: ensuring that their skills are used to maximum potential for the benefit of clients.

The court's itemized list of sufficiently complex tasks for which paralegals might submit a bill included: factual investigation, conducting legal research, summarizing depositions, checking citations, compiling statistical and financial data, preparing court documents, serving process, and discussing the case with attorneys.

In *Delgado*, many of the paralegals' billing entries described reviewing documents and building or updating a database. According to the court, if the paralegals had been making notes (electronic or otherwise) in order to extract pertinent information while making database entries, the work could have been correctly charged as professional time. Despite plaintiffs' protests, the work was found to be strictly clerical and the court deducted 106.80 hours (out of 490.60 hours billed). In addition, 28.70 hours of paralegal time was deducted from the fee petition for clerical tasks such as phone calls with clerks, burning CDs, filing, mailings and deliveries.

Finally, the defendant rejected the hourly billing rate of $175.00 for paralegal David Breed and suggested a rate of $90.00. Plaintiff argued the rate was based on Breed's Ph.D. and his technology expertise. Because the paralegal's degree was not in a related subject area and the computer work had been eliminated from the bill, the court reduced the rate to $125.00 per hour. The final award for paralegal services was 352.30 hours at $125.00 per hour for Mr. Breed, and 1.4 hours at $100.00 per hour for the other paralegal, minus the 35% proportionate reduction on the total.

In 2007, several cases followed *Delagado* with respect to attorney and paralegal fees:

1. *Ropak Corp. v. Plastican, Inc.*, 2007 WL 328880 (N.D. Ill.), followed *Delgado* with respect to "block-billing," holding that it had no obligation to estimate the time spent on each bundled task. Without some indication of how much time was spent on each individual task there is no way to determine whether the time spent was reasonable. The court also noted that hours billed by attorneys should be reduced to the extent that tasks could have been performed by non-attorneys.
2. In *Torres-Rivera v. Espada-Cruz*, 2007 WL 906176 (D.P.R.), the court indicated that the method most often used to compensate for block billing is a reduction of a specific percentage from the award.
3. *Lopez v. City of Chicago*, 2007 WL 4162805 (N.D. Ill.), arose from plaintiff's arrest for a murder he did not commit. Plaintiff submitted paralegal billing records and cases that satisfied his burden to support the requested rate ($105/hour) for paralegal fees. The degree of success obtained was a critical factor in determining reasonableness. In light of the nature of the case and the time span of the litigation, the court declined to reduce the lodestar amount as unreasonable, but did strike or reduce a few specific entries.

If you are a paralegal assisting with a fee petition proceeding, dealing with the "lodestar" method, or just wishing you could be more profitable for your firm, these cases provide excellent insights into court awards. Take careful note of the importance of detailed task descriptions, reflecting the professional and substantive nature of your work!

Chapter Review

Discussion Questions

1. Describe a situation in which you dealt with a difficult person.
2. What steps can a paralegal take to "grow" in the profession?
3. A newly hired paralegal is accompanying a lawyer to lunch with an important client and is very nervous. What advice would you give him?
4. Identify the factors that contribute to employee job satisfaction. What questions might you ask during a job interview, based on those factors?

5. Describes steps that should be taken to keep a firm-sponsored party from causing problems.

6. Describe steps you might take to deal with this situation: Willie, a secretary to a partner, was seriously ill for several weeks and was away from work. Willie is intensely private and has not told any coworkers about the illness. In addition, since coming back, Willie has been tired, very nervous, and short-tempered with other secretaries. Willie has been unwilling to participate in some of the "traditions" of the group, such as birthday celebrations or covering for others if they are late getting back from lunch. As a result, the other secretaries are "on the warpath." They seem to believe that Willie's time off was favoritism and that Willie is a "spy" among them. They are not violating any specific office policies, but are being very hostile to Willie. They do little things to make life difficult, such as reorganizing the supply cabinet without telling Willie.

Terms and Definitions

Association of Legal Administrators (ALA): Professional organization for legal administrators and managers

concierge: Services to help with personal errands

flex time: Arrangement allowing flexibility in scheduling work time

hard skills: Skills that can be quantified, such as drafting or using computer software

incentives: Things that induce action

International Paralegal Management Association (IPMA): Formerly Legal Assistant Management Association (LAMA); professional organization for paralegal managers

lawyers assistance program (LAP): Counseling program for lawyers with substance abuse or other personal problems

LL.M: Master of law degree

mentoring: Relationship between a more experienced person, the mentor, and a less experienced protégé

sick leave pool: Also called sick leave bank; enables employees to donate to and draw from a common fund of sick days

soft skills: Combination of personal traits, social skills, communications skills, and attitude

telecommuting: Working from outside the office, via computer

wellness programs: Assist with employees' well-being and overall good health

11

◆ ◆ ◆

Attracting and Retaining Clients

◆ ◆ ◆

As a Manager

Client satisfaction will be your job because it is the job of every person in the firm. You may also be asked to develop marketing tools to attract new clients and assess the satisfaction of existing clients.

Objectives

After completing this chapter, you will be able

- Understand the importance of and tools for assessing client satisfaction.
- Describe the ethical requirements for a lawyer wishing to terminate representation of a client.
- Know the restrictions your state imposes on advertising by lawyers.
- Describe the differences between permissible advertising and unethical solicitation.
- Assess the ethical compliance and effectiveness of a law firm website.
- Describe the First Amendment protection for lawyer advertising, as described by the Supreme Court.

A. **Existing Clients**
   1. **Assessing Client Satisfaction**
   2. **Firing Clients**
B. **New Clients**
   1. **Attracting New Clients**
   2. **Ethical Issues in Advertising**
C. **Marketing**
   1. **Assignments**

A law firm is all about clients, every day, all day. A lawyer hires paralegals to increase client satisfaction and because hiring a paralegal does not pose the risk that hiring an associate attorney presents — that the employee will leave and take clients. The relationship between the attorney and the client is the heart of the practice of law. If you always remember that the relationship is between the attorney and the client and you make clients feel like they are getting good value for their money, you will be a great asset to the firm and have a satisfying career. The best technical skills cannot overcome client issues: if you forget the nature of the relationship, you risk committing unauthorized practice of law, and if clients are not comfortable with you, you will not be valuable to the firm.

While the media often presents the image of a successful lawyer as a "shark," the key to success is not in being argumentative, tough, cunning, or tricky. Those traits may be helpful from time to time, but those traits do not necessarily win cases, and they often frighten and upset clients. Even if you assume that what clients really want is to win, both the lawyer and the client know that within our system of decision making, even the most competent and committed lawyer cannot guarantee a win. According to Stuart Forsyth, executive director of the State Bar of Arizona:

> Studies have shown that clients want their lawyers to be dedicated and communicative, and (surprisingly) they want these two things even more than they want their lawyers to be competent or fair with fees.
>
> Of course clients want quality legal services, and they do expect their lawyers to be competent. But we do not get much credit for our legal competence because that is the essence of the definition of a profession: competence. Our clients expect us to be competent precisely because we are members of the legal profession.
>
> Interestingly, what clients really want is good customer service and common business courtesy. They are willing to pay to get it. They are quite able to judge whether or not they have received it and to complain when they haven't. Many clients use customer service and courtesy — not competency — to evaluate lawyers. We know from the business world that customers want service, value and respect. Your clients want quality legal services, reasonable fees, communication from you and your commitment to them and their goals. Stuart Forsyth, *Law Practice Management: Good Client Relations = The Key to Success*, 35 Ariz. Atty. 20 (1998).

This is reflected in the fact that the first, and arguably most important, section of the ABA Model Rules is entitled "Client-Lawyer Relationship." Note that the word "client" is placed first. The section includes rules dealing with competence, the scope of representation and allocation of authority between client and lawyer, diligence, communications, fees, confidentiality, conflicts of interests, duties to former clients, clients with diminished capacity, safekeeping property, declining or terminating representation, and duties to prospective clients. You have learned about these obligations in earlier chapters, and when you accept employment in a law office, you commit yourself to upholding those rules and improving that relationship.

It's not always easy. The profession has changed, and clients themselves often fail at making the relationship work. Older lawyers may look back fondly to times when a lawyer could expect to represent a family or a business for many years. Clients valued the long-term relationship as much or more than the lawyer needed the loyalty. The paradigm changed with a sharp increase in the number of lawyers, increasingly aggressive marketing by those lawyers, and increased public awareness of the availability of specialists and of the possibility of negotiating fees. Some lawyers have struggled to adapt to a world in which law is a competitive business as much as a learned profession.

Always keep in mind that you may have knowledge and skills to improve client satisfaction that your supervising attorney does not have. While some lawyers have earned a degree in business before going to law school or had management experience in other jobs, many have not. A typical lawyer has a college degree in political science, history, or English and no management or marketing work experience. Things you've read about in this book might be unfamiliar to your supervising lawyer. Make suggestions, without being pushy or presenting yourself as a know-it-all, to help your employer.

Modernizing the Curriculum

The traditional focus of law school has been on "academic" (as opposed to practical) study of substantive law. Examine, for instance, the long list of courses offered by Harvard Law School (http://www.law.harvard.edu/academics/courses/2008-09). Harvard, arguably the most esteemed law school in the United States, does not offer a single course in law office management. This focus, however, may be changing. The U.S. law school with the largest enrollment, Thomas M. Cooley Law School, does offer such a class as an elective (http://www.cooley.edu/academics/courses.pdf). This is in keeping with a national trend to add focus on skills relevant to practicing law. Tresa Baldas, *Several Schools Adjust Their Curriculums*, Natl. L.J., Sept. 10, 2007, *available at* http://www.law.com/jsp/nlj/PubArticleNLJ.jsp?id=1189069349752.

A. Existing Clients

Why discuss existing clients before discussing how to attract clients? Satisfied clients are the best source of new clients and, of course, of repeat business. A law firm's greatest asset is its clients, yet many firms never consider how to become a client-centered firm.

Being client-centered includes many of the practices discussed in earlier chapters, such as answering the phone promptly, returning calls promptly, and sending out regular billing statements and status letters. Some practices simply amount to treating people with courtesy: smile, learn the names of the clients you work with and use them, and don't make promises you cannot or will not keep. Thank clients for their business. Remember, good results may be the client's primary objective, but many clients cannot evaluate the quality of the legal work a firm has done for them. They can evaluate the experience of working with the people. They will have an opinion about whether the firm kept them informed, discussed alternatives, took an interest in their opinions, and treated them as adult human beings, rather than as files or children. They will have a perception of the fairness of the bill, and that perception will often come from the presentation or explanation of the bill as much as from the amount billed.

Being client-centered also includes establishing business practices that make it easy for clients to do business with the firm, rather than practices that make it easy for the firm to do business. For example: if your clients are working individuals who may have trouble getting time off during regular business hours, do you have office hours in the evening or on Saturdays? Do you have the reception area covered during lunch hour, in case a client needs to drop off documents? Does someone from the firm visit your business clients at their offices to really be able to understand the businesses and their challenges?

1. Assessing Client Satisfaction

How do you determine whether your firm is client-centered? Ask the client. After a matter has been concluded, the client should be asked about satisfaction with the firm's services. There are several schools of thought on how to do this. Some firms conduct in-person or phone interviews, which conveys to the client genuine concern about satisfaction and allows for more open-ended questions. The interview can be used to strengthen the relationship between attorney and client and can help the attorney understand the client's feelings about billing and value and future needs for legal services.

Other firms believe that most people are reluctant to voice complaints in person and prefer to post surveys online so that clients can respond anonymously and without taking too much time. Online services, such as http://www.surveymonkey.com and http://www.zoomerang.com, are available to make the process easier. Still other firms prefer a mailed survey, which has more flexibility than an online survey, but still allows the client anonymity and the opportunity to respond on her own time.

If possible, at least some survey questions should be open-ended so that clients are not restricted to a choice of answers that may not include their thoughts. Questions should not focus only on the past, but should ask what the firm can do in the future.

In the following list of typical questions, note that some are open-ended while others are more suited to a checkbox type of survey. Some questions focus on satisfaction with past performance, while others ask about the future:

- How did you originally find and select this firm?
- Have you ever recommended this firm to a colleague or friend?
  - Why?
- Would you recommend this firm to others?
  - Why?
- If you have legal work in the future, are you likely to use this firm?
  - Why?
- Does your attorney have a solid knowledge of your situation and issues?

- Is your attorney accessible and efficient?
- Do you feel that your attorney listened to you, answered your questions, and kept you informed?
- Was the staffing of your case appropriate?
- Do you feel that this firm made every effort to resolve your matter promptly?
- Is our billing understandable and timely?
- Were staff members friendly and helpful?
- What can we do to improve our firm's service and make it more user-friendly?
- Is your attorney creative and flexible in assessing alternatives and solutions?
- How would you compare this firm to others with which you have dealt?
- Has this firm been proactive in helping you avoid legal problems?
- Do you find the firm newsletter informative and interesting?
- Is there anything else you would like to tell us?
- What services could we offer in the future to meet your needs?
- Rate your satisfaction with the following from very satisfied to dissatisfied
  - Overall quality of representation
  - Accessibility, promptness in response to calls and questions
  - Fees and costs
  - Attorney's substantive legal knowledge
  - Staff

Of course, a survey is of no value unless it is used for improvement. Before creating a survey, the firm should decide who will be responsible for collecting and analyzing feedback, how often it will be done, and, most important, how the results will be used to improve client service. Each question should be examined in terms of its usefulness. For example, what will the firm do if clients respond that matters are not appropriately staffed or that attorneys are not working to bring their matters to a prompt conclusion? Keep in mind that responses to open-ended questions are not easily quantified.

Attorney Satisfaction

How do people really feel about their lawyers? According to an ABA survey (http://www.abanet.org/media/perception/perceptions.pdf), 46 percent of respondents had used a lawyer within the previous five years and, of those respondents, 75 percent indicated that they were somewhat to very satisfied. Those who visited a lawyer for a transactional matter, such as preparation of a will or contract, were more likely to be satisfied. Those who visited a lawyer for reasons likely not of their own choosing or with a probability of negative results, such as a divorce, litigation, or criminal prosecution, were less likely to be satisfied.

---

2. Firing Clients

In some situations a lawyer is required to terminate representation of a client. The ABA Model Rules provide that an attorney "shall" withdraw if the representation will result in violation of an ethical rule or other law, if the lawyer is discharged, or if the lawyer's physical or mental condition materially impairs the lawyer's ability to represent the client. In situations involving a court or other tribunal, the lawyer must notify the court or tribunal of the withdrawal and, if ordered to do so, continue the representation.

In other situations, the client-attorney relationship does not work because of the client's behavior. A client may be uncooperative, missing appointments or not providing requested information. A client may be verbally abusive, constantly second-guessing the lawyer or expressing dissatisfaction. The client may insist on a course of action that the lawyer finds repugnant. Some clients are extremely needy and may call their attorneys constantly, even at home. Clients sometimes have unrealistic expectations, and the lawyer may believe that the client's plan involves criminal or fraudulent activity. The lawyer may determine that the client has used the lawyer's services to perpetrate a crime or fraud. Clients may refuse to honor their fee agreements.

A lawyer does not make the decision to terminate the relationship lightly. In addition to the obvious loss of potential income and referrals, there are ethical concerns. The ABA Model Rules require notice to any court or tribunal involved in the representation and compliance with any order to continue the representation. The lawyer must determine that withdrawal can be accomplished without material adverse effect on the interests of the client. The lawyer must take steps, as reasonably practicable, to protect the client's interests, for example, by providing notice and time to allow the client to find another lawyer and providing the client with papers, property, and unearned fees to which the client is entitled.

B. New Clients

1. Attracting New Clients

marketing
Efforts to establish and communicate firm identity to attract client

branding
Use of logos, symbols, or design to promote client awareness of firm and its services

advertising
Efforts to use media to attract public attention

solicitation
Unethical conduct to secure clients

Three important concepts apply to a firm's efforts to attract new clients: marketing, advertising, and solicitation. Also called client development, **marketing** consists of the firm's efforts to bring in new clients. Larger firms often employ individuals whose sole focus is on marketing. Marketing typically consists of efforts to create a unique identity for the firm, differentiating it from the competition, and to increase awareness of the firm in the target community. Marketing includes **branding**, image building, and public relations. It often also includes **advertising**, which must not constitute unethical **solicitation**.

2. Ethical Issues in Advertising

Many people have a negative perception of lawyers' advertising and confuse advertising with unethical solicitation by "ambulance chasers." The perception may stem from the fact that until the mid-1970s, lawyers were prohibited from advertising, based on the Sherman Act. In 1977 the Supreme Court held in *Bates v. State Bar of Arizona*[1] that the First Amendment protects the right of lawyers to advertise.

The *Bates* decision did not, however, lead to universal acceptance. Dissenting Chief Justice Warren Burger continued to speak out against advertising by lawyers[2] and even stated that the public should never engage the services of a lawyer who advertises. How advertising hurts the public perception of lawyers and the legal system remains a concern. For example, in 2007 the Pennsylvania Bar Association formed a Task Force on Lawyer Advertising, which produced a report that detailed some of the public perceptions of advertising and recommended changes to the state's rules to restore "some measure of dignity and professionalism."[3]

After the *Bates* decision, some lawyers "pushed the envelope" with ads that presented the profession in a very negative light. State regulatory authorities tried to ban the most offensive ads. Subsequent Supreme Court decisions[4] clarified that advertising is protected only if it is not misleading and does not concern an unlawful activity; states may regulate lawful advertising as reasonably required to directly advance a legitimate state interest.

Example

The classic example of misleading advertising is the statement, "If I don't win your case, you don't pay a fee," without an explanation that the client may be responsible for costs. Many states have specific disclosure requirements for advertising relating to cases taken on contingency.

Most recent decisions have focused on the mode of communication, content, timing, and even motivation in determining the boundaries of what may be prohibited. While states are generally consistent with respect to other ethical rules, they differ widely on advertising (see Exhibit 11-1).

Example

Just because it's legal . . . In 2007 Chicago lawyers advertised using a billboard that featured a male torso and female cleavage, with the words "Life is Short, Get a Divorce." The billboard was removed by the city for lack of a permit, but the state's disciplinary agency did not sanction the attorneys.

---

[1] 433 U.S. 350 (1977).
[2] Warren Burger Leaves Imprint on the Judiciary, July 1995, http://www.uscourts.gov/ttb/julttb/warren.htm.
[3] Pennsylvania Bar Assn., Report of the Pennsylvania Bar Assn., Task Force on Lawyer Advertising, May 2007, http://www.abanet.org/cpr/professionalism/050807_3082633-v3-PHILADELPHIA-PBA.pdf.
[4] *E.g., Cent. Hudson Gas & Elec. Corp. v. Pub. Serv. Commn.*, 447 U.S. 557 (1980).

Exhibit 11-1
Meeting the "Not Misleading" Standard

All communications must meet the "not misleading" standard, which states define differently. Common characters are that advertising may not create unreasonable expectations, imply improper influence with decision-making bodies, or imply promise of results. Many states specifically prohibit comparisons to other legal services and the use of ads that resemble legal documents.

In-person, phone, real-time electronic (e.g., chatroom)	*Mass media (e.g., TV, radio, phone book, newspaper, "spam")*	*Targeted communication, (e.g., mailings to recently arrested)*	*"Referral" type: (e.g., ad endorsements, referral services, prepaid legal services)*	*Letterhead, signage, business cards*
Generally prohibited, even if through a third party,[5] due to overreaching by lawyers and privacy issues. States may exempt previous clients, acquaintances, potential members of class actions, situations with no financial motive (e.g., contact by lawyer employed by insurance company).	Some states restrict dramatizations and simulations, require various disclosures and/or limit content, especially concerning fees and costs. Some states restrict paying media to appear in "news."	Generally allowed. States may impose restrictions (e.g., no contact for 30 days after accident). Many require identification as advertising, prohibit use of other than regular mail, disclosure of legal problem on envelope.	Generally allow legitimate referral services, uncompensated referrals by firm employees, and prepaid service plans. Special rules apply to lawyer-to-lawyer referrals. States generally restrict use of other endorsements and testimonials in media.	Most states restrict statements re: specialties, certification, bar admission, and that imply partnership where none exists; have rules concerning trade names and use of "of counsel."

Check individual state rules concerning other requirements concerning matters such as font size, required disclosures, prior filing, and keeping copies.

---

runner
Paid to refer individuals to an attorney

capper
Paid to refer individuals to an attorney

Read the excerpts from the two U.S. Supreme Court cases and from an FTC letter contained in Exhibit 11-2 and consider the following questions:

- What are the ways in which lawyer advertising actually benefits the public?

---

[5]A third party paid to refer potential clients is often called a **runner** or a **capper**. The practice is unethical but has often involved medical personnel, insurance adjusters, and others who see accident victims soon after the accident.

- Why do courts treat in-person solicitation differently than other types of communication?
- ABA Model Rule 7.2 states that "a lawyer may advertise services through written, recorded or electronic communication, including public media," which does not include telephone communication. In addition, Rule 7.3 states "[a] lawyer shall not by in-person, live telephone or real-time electronic contact solicit professional employment from a prospective client when a significant motive for the lawyer's doing so is the lawyer's pecuniary gain, unless the person contacted: (1) is a lawyer; or (2) has a family, close personal, or prior professional relationship with the lawyer." Why is use of the phone restricted?
- The *Zauderer* opinion refers to advertising invading the privacy of those who read it. How might that happen? Does the *Shapero* case give you a clue?
- Does it constitute "advertising" when a lawyer pays to be listed with a lawyer referral service or joins a prepaid legal services plan? Check the rules for your state.
- Many of the state rules require that lawyer advertising state that it is advertising and that it include the name and address of the lawyer responsible for the ad. Why?
- Many state bar associations originally based their restrictions on concern about the "dignity" of the profession. Why is that no longer considered an appropriate consideration?
- Consider ads you have seen on television for legal services. Do you think they were informative? In what ways might they have been misleading? Would you be more or less likely to hire a lawyer who advertised on television?
- Some states prohibit dramatizations and use of actors in ads or require disclosures indicating, for example, that the people shown are not actually lawyers or clients. What is the purpose of such a restriction?
- What do you think is the most common way for people to find a lawyer (not considering referrals)?
- Earlier chapters have presented some of the rules generally applicable to attorney letterhead. What aspects of letterhead might be considered a type of "advertising," and which rules, discussed in earlier chapters, apply?
- Why is the Federal Trade Commission interested in lawyer advertising? How is its interest different from the interests of bar associations and state regulatory bodies?

Exhibit 11-2
Limits on First Amendment Freedoms

FROM ZAUDERER V. OFFICE OF DISCIPLINARY COUNSEL, 471 U.S. 626 (1985)

An Ohio attorney ran a newspaper ad stating that his firm would represent defendants in drunk driving cases and that his clients' "full legal fee [would be] refunded if [they were] convicted of DRUNK DRIVING." He ran another ad stating willingness to represent women who had suffered injuries resulting from use of a contraceptive known as the Dalkon Shield Intrauterine Device. The ad featured a drawing of the device and stated that the Dalkon Shield had generated a large amount of lawsuits; that appellant was currently handling such lawsuits and was willing to represent other women asserting similar claims; that readers should not assume that their claims were time-barred; that cases were handled on a contingent fee basis; and that, "[i]f there is no recovery, no legal fees are owed by our clients."

The state bar association reprimanded the attorney. The Supreme Court stated that: "The reprimand is sustainable to the extent that it is based on appellant's advertisement involving his terms of representation in drunken driving cases and on the omission of information regarding his contingent fee arrangements in his Dalkon Shield advertisement. But insofar as the reprimand is based on appellant's use of an illustration in his advertisement and his offer of legal advice, the reprimand violated his First Amendment rights."

Distinguishing its decision in *Ohralik v. Ohio State Bar Assn.*, 436 U.S. 447 (1978), the Court held that appellant's ads did not implicate the same interests sufficient to justify a ban on in-person solicitation in *Ohralik*. "Although some sensitive souls may have found . . . poor taste, it can hardly be said to have invaded the privacy of those who read it. More significantly, . . . print advertising generally poses much less risk of overreaching or undue influence. State's . . . requirement that an attorney advertising . . . contingent fee . . . disclose that clients will have to pay costs even if their lawsuits are unsuccessful (assuming that to be the case) easily passes muster under this standard. Appellant's advertisement [stated] that 'if there is no recovery, no legal fees are owed by our clients.'"

FROM SHAPERO V. KENTUCKY BAR ASSOCIATION, 486 U.S. 466 (1988)

An attorney applied to the state Commission for approval to send letters "to potential clients who have had a foreclosure suit filed against them," which would advise recipients that "you may be about to lose your home," that "[f]ederal law may allow you to . . . ORDE[R] your creditor to STOP," that "you may call my office . . . for FREE information," and that "[i]t may surprise you what I may be able to do for you." Although the Commission did not find the letter misleading, it declined to approve because a Kentucky Supreme Court Rule prohibited

---

**EXHIBIT 11-2
(continued)**

---

mailing or delivery of written ads "precipitated by a specific event . . . relating to the addressee . . . as distinct from the general public."

The Court held that a state may not categorically prohibit lawyers from soliciting business for pecuniary gain by sending truthful and nondeceptive letters to potential clients known to face particular legal problems. The recipient of such advertising is not faced with the coercive presence of a trained advocate or the pressure for an immediate yes-or-no answer to the representation offer, but can simply put the letter aside to be considered later, ignored, or discarded. Although a personalized letter does present increased risks of isolated abuses or mistakes, these can be regulated and minimized by requiring the lawyer to file the letter with a state agency having authority to supervise mailings and penalize actual abuses. Scrutiny of targeted solicitation letters will not be appreciably less reliable than scrutiny of other advertisements, since the reviewing agency can require the lawyer to prove or verify any fact stated, or explain how it was discovered, or require that the letter be labeled as an advertisement, or that it tell the reader how to report inaccurate or misleading matters.

FEDERAL TRADE COMMISSION RESPONSE TO LOUISIANA STATE BAR ASSOCIATION RULES OF PROFESSIONAL CONDUCT COMMITTEE REQUEST FOR COMMENTS REGARDING PROPOSED RULES ON LAWYER ADVERTISING AND SOLICITATION, HTTP://WWW.FTC.GOV/BE/V070001.PDF

The FTC enforces laws prohibiting unfair methods of competition and unfair or deceptive acts or practices in or affecting commerce, which includes primary responsibility for stopping deceptive advertising practices. . . . [T]he Commission encourages competition in the licensed professions, including the legal profession, to the maximum extent compatible with other state and federal goals. In particular, the Commission seeks to identify and prevent, where possible, business practices and regulations that impede competition without offering countervailing benefits to consumers. . . . The FTC believes that while false and deceptive advertising by lawyers should be prohibited, imposing overly broad restrictions that prevent the communication of truthful and non-misleading information that some consumers value is likely to inhibit competition and frustrate informed consumer choice. This position is supported by research indicating that overly broad restrictions on truthful advertising may adversely affect prices paid and services received by consumers. . . .

The FTC Staff is concerned that several provisions of the Proposed Rules unnecessarily restrict truthful advertising and may adversely affect prices paid and services received by consumers. In addition, provisions regarding advertising screening and approval by a committee composed of competing attorneys may deter truthful and non-misleading advertising and present risks to competition. The FTC Staff believes that Louisiana consumers can be adequately protected

---

**EXHIBIT 11-2
(continued)**

---

from false and misleading advertising by using less restrictive means and through enforcement of narrower rules . . . particularly those involving prohibitions against certain selected forms of advertising including actor portrayals, depictions and similar dramatic techniques; comparative claims; statements about endorsements and testimonials; communications that create an expectation of results an attorney is likely to achieve; and advertisements that look like legal pleadings. . . .

---

*Assignment 11-1
Servicing New and Existing Clients*

Management Portfolio

1. Go online and search for law firm resumes and law firm client satisfaction surveys.

- Choose a firm resume that does a good job establishing the firm's identity and explain to your class why you think the resume creates a solid identity. How does the firm's website reinforce and communicate that identity?
- Identify a survey question that is creative in asking how the firm can improve in the future and share with your class.

2. Determine whether your state's rules concerning declining or terminating representation differ from the ABA rules.

Management Portfolio

3. You work for a firm that handles only divorce and child custody cases. The firm has never surveyed clients and wants to do so. Develop a one-page survey. Make enough copies for all of your classmates and distribute them. Ask your classmates to complete the surveys as "imaginary" clients. Collect the surveys and prepare a summary of the results. The purpose of this exercise is to learn to develop questions that can be answered in a way that is quantifiable.

4. Starting at http://www.abanet.org/cpr/professionalism/state-advertising.pdf, find your state's rules on lawyer advertising.

- Do the rules prohibit use of testimonials or endorsements? Dramatizations or simulations?

- Do the rules include requirements concerning statements referring to specialization or certification?
- Do the rules require filing or approval of ads?
- Are there special disclosure requirements for advertising contingent fees?
- Under what circumstances may an attorney make live telephone, in-person, or electronic contact with a prospective client?

C. Marketing

Before a firm can market its identity, it must determine that identity. Is this a general practice firm that attempts to be all things to all clients? Is this a boutique firm, focused on helping employers with problems relating to labor law? What are the credentials of the people who work here? What does this firm do that is particularly client-friendly? What types of clients has the firm represented? The answers must come from both inside and outside the firm; a firm's perception of itself is not always shared by clients and others in the legal field. A firm should never apologize for its size, but should focus on its strengths.

Determining firm identity and how to communicate it can be particularly difficult for lawyers, who tend to be cautious and like to rely on precedent — what has happened in the past. Marketing necessarily involves looking to the future. Consider what the firm wants to be rather than what it has been. Ask what your firm (and other firms) are not doing that would meet client needs, rather than what is being done.

With this information, the firm may create a firm resume, which can be distributed to potential clients, job applicants, and even vendors seeking firm business. The firm can also create a logo or a symbol for use on business cards, stationary, the office sign, and similar items to tie into its "brand." The firm can also develop a two-sentence description of the firm, so that employees know what to say when people ask about their employers.

1. Tools for Marketing

Once a firm has determined its identity, how does it spread the word? How the firm spreads the word will often depend on that identity. For example, some firms avoid media advertising and "freebies" to convey a more exclusive image. In addition to advertising, discussed above, the firm should cultivate resources already in place:

1. Employees: Attorneys and staff who work at the firm are its number-one marketing tool. Employees who are out in the community, proud to say that they work for the firm and that it's a good place to work, are priceless. Everyone who works at the firm should have well-designed business cards with the firm logo and should be encouraged to pass them out freely. Of course, business cards must clearly identify the named individual's position, and employees should be instructed not to cross the ethical line into solicitation. Encourage employees to become active in the community by supporting their participation in civic and charitable organizations (time off for meetings during business hours, even

payment of dues). Encourage employees to teach classes at local schools. Recognize and reward any extra effort that brings good publicity, such as an employee writing an article, speaking to a group, volunteering at a local school, or participating in a marathon. Send out press releases, as appropriate.

2. Clients: Make it easy for clients to "brag" about their firm. Give them lots of business cards, pens, and calendars with the firm name, and make sure that they know that you appreciate referrals. Tell them about firm services of which they may be unaware. Be sure to thank them when they do make referrals. During the first visit, provide a file or a tote, printed with the firm name, in which to keep important papers.

3. Freebies and small audience advertising: Place business cards on the bulletin board of your grocery store, your place of worship, the shop where you get a haircut, or your favorite lunch restaurant. Advertise in school, church, temple, and synagogue bulletins and in "local market" papers. Make sure that your firm is prominently identified in its building directory. Create and distribute laminated "what to do after an accident" or "what to do if you're arrested" cards with your firm's information.

4. Generosity: Donate old law books and equipment to schools and libraries, with the firm's name on the item. Help with law day or career day at local schools; volunteer to speak to local groups. Donate waiting room magazines (with the firm's name on the address label) to nursing homes. Register your firm with the bar association speakers' bureau — a speakers' bureau might, for example, provide an attorney to speak to residents of a retirement facility about identity theft.

5. Media: Write an article for a business, trade, legal or consumer publication that is distributed to a target market. For example, if your firm represents several school districts, find a publication that is distributed to school administrators; if your firm specializes in estate planning and relies on referrals from litigators, consider a bar association publication. Determine the needs, stylistic requirements, and deadlines for the publication by calling the editor.

Some firms' only interaction with the news media is electronic submission of press releases dealing with internal matters: new partners, new offices, and awards won by employees. Press releases rarely rate much space or good placement unless they involve something unique, such as an extremely well-known new partner or the opening of a "green" office. If your firm wants more, offer services to local news reporters who may need a legal expert; a local paper may even need a column explaining a current legal issue. Large firms often have media relations specialists who regularly contact local media with story ideas, particularly ideas relating to issues that interest the firm's target clients. When dealing with the news media, remember that reporters work on tight deadlines and failure to honor those deadlines can get a lawyer or law firm blacklisted from future stories.

Sometimes a reporter will contact a lawyer or law firm for background information or for a statement about a newsworthy case or matter, particularly if the matter involves one of the firm's clients. Keep in mind that the classic "no comment" will not prevent a reporter from running the story, but will only sound bad and guarantee that the story will run without your point of view. If no one is prepared to talk, promise to call the reporter back, consult with interested individuals, and come up with a statement. The information you provide might be enough to quash a negative story.

6. Mail: Constantly add to the firm's mailing list to send out holiday cards, congratulatory cards, the newsletter, birthday and anniversary cards, and clip-

pings that may interest the recipient. Every employee should be told to notify the person in charge of marketing if they become aware of any major life event involving a client (marriage, birth, death in family) or if they see an article that would be of interest to a particular client. Use the tickler system to send reminders of matters such as lease renewals and required business filings — clients will be impressed that you contact them before they contact you!

7. Newsletters: Many firms distribute newsletters, by U.S. mail or electronically. The firm may produce and distribute its own newsletter or may contract with a marketing company to do so. Newsletters are particularly useful to communicate with clients in particular industries about new developments in the law and requirements imposed by regulatory agencies. A newsletter can also be used for cross-selling services. For example, a firm that does a lot of divorce work might want to remind clients to update their wills. Some firms add a personal touch by including news about the professional accomplishments of lawyers and staff.

8. Other Legal Professionals: Encourage attorneys to network with lawyers in other practice areas through the bar association and to speak at CLE events. Many bar associations offer referral services, so that a firm can be listed on the bar association's website for a reasonable fee. Paralegals and legal secretaries should also network through their professional associations.

2. Using the Internet for Marketing

The Internet is a powerful tool for reaching potential clients with a high volume of information at low cost, but it requires special attention to ethical rules. Marketing on the Internet may include being listed on a simple attorney directory, being listed on a website through which potential clients seek and receive information or legal advice, paying for a **sponsored search**, developing a website or maintaining a **blog**. As shown in Exhibit 11-3, blogs can create special risks. Unlike a firm website, the content of which generally remains unchanged for long periods, blogs are regularly updated and often allow visitors to add comments, ask questions, and carry on a dialogue.

sponsored search
Search engine is paid to place website high on list of results when user searches particular terms

blog
Web log

For More Information

You don't need technical expertise to use the Internet for marketing. Many sites offer attorneys directory listings, websites, and assistance with design. Here are just a few that came up with a quick search:

http://www.findlaw.com
http://www.lawyers.com/
http://www.webjuris.com/hosting.htm
http://www.websitesolutionsforlawyers.com

Firm websites are subject to the same rules as other mass media communication. For example, they must not include misleading statements, such as "no recovery, no fee." They may be limited in describing specializations or certifications and may be required to list where the attorneys are licensed to practice. Remember that the site may be viewed from any location and should, therefore, comply with the strictest rules.

plagiarism
Using material of another as your own

Firm sites also present unique concerns, ranging from the name of the URL, to whether any of the material on the site has been **plagiarized**. For example, a URL entitled www.wincustody.com might imply a promise of results; www.socialsecuritylaw.com might imply some special connection with a government agency. The content must also clarify that any information contained on the site is not intended as legal advice.

If the firm website includes a "contact us" form through which potential clients may e-mail the firm, it is essential that someone check the mail every day. E-mails do not have the same level of confidentiality as an in-person meeting or even a phone call; e-mails do not allow the reader to "size up" potential new clients, accurately check for conflicts of interest, or even determine where the person is located for purposes of avoiding unauthorized practice of law in a state in which the attorney is not licensed. It is, therefore, essential that e-mails not be used to communicate anything that could possibly be construed as legal advice or as establishing the attorney-client relationship.

In *Birbrower, Montalbano, Condon & Frank v. Superior Court*,[6] a New York law firm (Birbrower) negotiated a worldwide license, on behalf of a New York client, with a California computer company. The client then created a California company to handle the work under the new licensing agreement. A dispute over the licensing rights arose, and Birbrower attorneys were brought in to resolve the matter. The case settled, but the client sued Birbrower for malpractice; Birbrower filed a cross-complaint alleging lack of payment. The client argued that no payment was due because the Birbrower attorneys were not licensed to practice law in California. Ultimately, the California Supreme Court agreed, stating:

> In our view, the practice of law "in California" entails sufficient contact with the California client to render the nature of the legal service a clear legal representation. In addition to a quantitative analysis, we must consider the nature of the unlicensed lawyer's activities in the state. Mere fortuitous or attenuated contacts will not sustain a finding that the unlicensed lawyer practiced law "in California." The primary inquiry is whether the unlicensed lawyer engaged in sufficient activities in the state, or created a continuing relationship with the California client that included legal duties and obligations. Our definition does not necessarily depend on or require the unlicensed lawyer's physical presence in the state. Physical presence here is one factor we may consider in deciding whether the unlicensed lawyer has violated section 6125, but it is by no means exclusive. For example, one may practice law in the state in violation of section 6125 although not physically present here by advising a California client on California law in connection with a California legal dispute by telephone, fax, computer, or other modern technological means. Conversely, although we decline to provide a comprehensive list of what activities constitute sufficient contact with the state, we do reject the notion that a person automatically practices law "in California" whenever that person practices California law anywhere, or virtually" enters the state by telephone, fax, e-mail, or satellite. . . . We must decide each case on its individual facts.

California subsequently amended its unauthorized practice law, but the case serves as a warning that state authority over the practice of law has not taken a backseat to global communication.

---

[6]949 P.2d 1 (Cal.), *cert. denied*, 525 U.S. 290 (1998).

Exhibit 11-3
Blog Woes

CHUBB'S POSITION ON LAW FIRM BLOGS

"The Chubb Group of Insurance Companies was recently the subject of some confusing media reports about the company's willingness to insure blogs. As a leading insurer of law firms across the country, we make it a priority to be on top of emerging trends that affect law firms," said James L. Rhyner, worldwide lawyers professional manager for Chubb Specialty Insurance. "Today, more and more law firms are establishing blogs. Chubb does insure this new form of communication—and will continue to do so within select parameters." . . .

Chubb has found that law firm blogs fall into two general classes: informational and advisory.

- An **informational blog** presents information or offers a forum for discussing issues in a neutral, unbiased way. This type of blog offers information similar to that found in an article or presented by an individual in a seminar. Informational blogs do not provide advice to a specific individual on a unique matter. Typically, these blogs pose a minimal level of risk from Chubb's underwriting perspective.

informational blog
Provides general information, not targeted to the issues of a particular individual

- In an **advisory blog**, however, a law firm offers advice. By its nature, then, it increases the risk of a malpractice lawsuit against the firm. An advisory blog can potentially establish an attorney-client relationship, possibly bypassing such safeguards as determining the suitability of a potential client and checking for possible conflicts of interest. As always, Chubb's underwriters will evaluate each submission on its own merits.

advisory blog
Provides information concerning a particular legal issue that might be construed as legal advice

Chubb provides insurance coverage for 90% of the law firms listed in *The American Lawyer*'s AM Law 200.

From Chubb's Position on Law Firm Blogs, Apr. 4, 2007, http://www.chubb.com/corporate/chubb6607.html.

LAWYER WHO CRITICIZED JUDGE IN BLOG FACES DISCIPLINE

BROWARD COUNTY - A defense attorney's law license is at risk because he posted an angry description on the Internet of embattled Broward Circuit Judge Cheryl Alemán, calling her an "evil, unfair witch." Last week, as Alemán was on trial for alleged misconduct before the Judicial Qualifications Commission, The Florida Bar signed off on its finding that Sean Conway may have violated five bar rules, including impugning the judge's qualifications or integrity.

**EXHIBIT 11-3
(continued)**

From S. Fla. Sun Sentinel, Dec. 13, 2007, *available at* http://www.tallahassee.com/legacy/special/blogs/2007/12/lawyer-who-criticized-judge-in-blog.html.

Should a firm avoid having a website if it is concerned about ethical issues or believes it won't be able to produce a "wow" site? The answer is no. A website need not be elaborate to be effective; it needs to include who the lawyers are, what they do, and how to get in touch with them. The site should provide enough information to generate cold calls from people looking for representation and to satisfy people who are checking the firm out after getting a referral from an acquaintance. Very often people who are looking for more information after finding a firm's name in a directory or getting a referral will simply move on to the next name if the firm does not have a website.

More content can add more value and utility. The site can also save valuable staff time if it includes what the firm does, directions (and even a map) to the office, profiles of lawyers, and contact information. Attorney profiles should include things like educational information, the courts in which the attorney is licensed to practice, the attorney's direct phone number and e-mail address, a photo, and a summary of the fields in which the attorney practices. Potential clients might otherwise call to ask these questions.

If the firm wants to go even further, it can include the following:

- Articles attorneys have written
- Firm newsletter
- Awards and achievements
- News stories that mention the firm or any person working there (in a positive light, of course)
- Frequently asked questions and responses
- Helpful links to other sites

Be sure to have the site professionally designed to avoid common mistakes, such as leaving it "under construction" for long periods, loading it with graphics and pictures that make it slow to load, using hard-to-read text or inconsistent format, poor planning of navigation, long pages that require readers to scroll, lack of compatibility with various **browsers**, and components that do not work correctly.

browser
Application program for looking at and interacting with websites

search optimization
Strategy for improving traffic to a website from a search engine.

The design also determines whether the site will be featured prominently when people use search engines. **Search optimization** involves several factors, including page content, keyword density (how many times a word, such as "divorce," appears on the site), titles on the pages, number of pages on the site, content-to-size ratio, inbound and outbound links, and the age of the site.

A good website can pull the firm's entire marketing plan together. It is advertising in the sense that it articulates and communicates the firm's identity to the public at large. It can include all of the writing, speaking, public service, and other public relations work done by lawyers and staff. It is an excellent source of information for current clients, other legal professionals, and even the media.

Assignment 11-2
Analyzing Marketing Materials

---

1. Obtain marketing materials from a local firm, such as the firm's brochure, and analyze how the firm complies with the ethical rules of your state, how the materials establish the firm's identity, and whether the material would be attractive, informative, and memorable to potential clients.
2. Find an attorney's blog and analyze how the attorney avoids (or fails to avoid) giving legal advice on the site and share your thoughts with the class. Find a website for a local firm and identify the features by which it complies with ethical rules for your jurisdiction.

Out There—Paralegal Profile
Marketing with the Client in Mind

Trying Something New

In 2008 Sue Robinson became marketing manager for a large Chicago firm. The interview committee was aware of her lack of legal marketing experience, but recognized and appreciated her innovative and entrepreneurial attitude, extensive marketing experience, and her enthusiasm for the legal field. Sue's history tells the story of a woman not afraid to take a chance! After receiving a bachelor's degree in English and communications, she continued to operate her own cleaning business for several years, while working part-time for a local cable television company and writing features for a local magazine. Sue sold the business after landing a job with a Chicago television show and a position as a part-time news writer for the local community college. Sue's next adventure came when she purchased a 49 percent share in an auction house, where she flourished for five years. When the business changed directions, she returned to the college as a marketing and public relations specialist. Sue took her first paralegal class and fell in love with the legal field. With her sights set on working for a law firm as a legal marketer, Sue finished master's degree and continued taking paralegal courses. Sue has considered law school, but would hate to give up the marketing field.

Keeping Clients Happy

While writing this chapter, the author corresponded with Nola Sayne, a paralegal with the prestigious Seyfarth Shaw firm in Atlanta. In res-

ponse to the question, "How do you keep clients happy?" Nola responded:

"My thoughts on keeping clients happy? I kind of think I have two clients, the external client (the client who gets a bill from Seyfarth Shaw LLP) and the internal client (the attorneys). However, keeping the external client happy keeps the internal client happy. First and foremost is communication; keeping the client informed of the progress in the matter, upcoming deadlines, upcoming projects, etc. and returning communications (phone calls, emails, etc.) in a timely manner. Also, I try to be very cost-conscious. I shop around for quality vendors that are less expensive and when I'm doing certain tasks, such as background checks, I try to use my free Internet options first. Even though it means fewer billable hours for me, I try to delegate all administrative tasks to staff so I'm not billing the client for something that a non-timekeeping staff member could do just as well. Finally, you can never be too careful. I check and recheck my work and have other people review and proof my work product, even a transmittal letter. Spelling, punctuation, grammar, and proper citations are imperative in making my attorneys and the external client look good!"

Chapter Review

Discussion Questions

1. Identify five marketing strategies that do not involve advertising in the mass media.
2. Under what circumstances do the ethical rules of your state permit personal or phone contact with a potential client?
3. What restrictions do the rules of your state impose on targeted mailings?
4. What restrictions does your state impose on media advertising (television, radio, or print media)?
5. What are the limits of First Amendment protection for advertising?
6. Why might a firm prefer to assess client satisfaction by means of a print or electronic survey, rather than a personal interview?
7. What is the FTC, and why is it concerned with lawyer advertising?
8. What are the particular risks of blogging?
9. Identify three major ethical concerns relating to law firm websites.
10. What are the advantages and disadvantages of using open-ended questions in a client satisfaction survey?
11. Describe the ethical constraints applicable to terminating representation of a client.

ACROSS

1. lawyer advertising must never have this characteristic
3. giving advice to a client in another state could constitute _____ practice of law
6. in media ads, some states restrict use of these
13. _____-time electronic communication is often treated as equivalent to in-person solicitation
14. some states place limits (e.g. 30 day wait) on _____ mailings
16. blog likely to be acceptable to malpractice insurance companies
19. blog that could constitue UPL or result in malpractice
21. _____search; search engine is paid to put site high on list of results
22. paid to refer business to lawyer

DOWN

1. plan for attracting business, including creating identity, public relations, and advertising
2. ABA rule requires termination of representation if representation would result in illegal actions or if lawyer is impaired or is _____
4. _____-ended questions in survey result in answers not easily quantified
5. FTC= Federal _____ Commission
7. unethical conduct to obtain clients
8. use of media to draw attention to business
9. search _____ can be accomplished by use of key words, etc.
10. In withdrawing lawyer may be required to notify court or _____
11. In withdrawing, lawyer must protect client _____

12. wrongful use of material created by another
15. capper is paid for _____ to lawyer
17. in-person contact may be permitted if lawyer has no _____ motive
18. computer application for looking at websites
20. a blog is a _____ log

Terms and Definitions

advertising: Efforts to use media to attract public attention

advisory blog: Provides information concerning a particular legal issue that might be construed as legal advice

blog: Web log

branding: Use of logos, symbols, or design to promote client awareness of firm and its services

browser: Application program for looking at and interacting with websites

capper: Paid to refer individuals to an attorney

informational blog: Provides general information, not targeted to the issues of a particular individual

marketing: Efforts to establish and communicate firm identity to attract client

plagiarism: Using material of another as your own

runner: Paid to refer individuals to an attorney

search optimization: Strategy for improving traffic to a website from a search engine.

solicitation: Unethical conduct to secure clients

sponsored search: Search engine is paid to place website high on list of results when user searches particular terms

INDEX

IRS, 13, 60, 149, 173, 258-259
  form 8300, 60
  publication 1544, 60
Isolation, 197
ISP, 38, 75
IT Specialists, 7, 35, 76

J.D., 5
Job
  description, 17, 242-244
  offer, 253
  titles, 247
Josh, Barbara, 106
Juris, 162

Kentucky Bar Association, 308
Keyboards, 191
Kitchen, 205

Labels, File, 219
LAP, 6, 283
Law Clerks, 12
Law Office
  atmosphere, 284
  boutique, 11
  captive, 11
  clinic type, 11
  committees, 12
  hours of operation, 302
  identity, 311
  in a box, 130
  practice groups, 11
  satellite, 11, 17
  shared space, 13-14
Law Reviews, 208
Law Tool Box, 126
Lawcrawler, 37
Lawcrossing.com, 2
Lawyer-Client Relationship, 300
Lawyers,
  assistance programs, *See LAP*
  business skills, 301
  classifications, 12
  corporate, 12
  discipline, 4
  education, 5
  generalists, 11
  image, 300
  of counsel, 13-14

reciprocity, 5
regulation, 4
solo, 11
specialists, 6, 11
supervision by, 266
Lawyers' Assistance Programs, *See LAPS*
Lawyer-Shopping, 119, 146
Leasing Equipment, 204
Leave, Family and Medical, 260
Ledger, 142, 152, 174
Legal Advice, 21, 88
Legal Advice, 88
Legal Services, New York, 294
Lending, 153
Lessor, 204
Letters, Generally, 93
  delivery of, 102
  demand, 93
  disengagement, 233
  engagement, 99, 100, 228
  format, 102
  goodwill, 129
  opinion, 93
  sample, 15
  signature, 103
Letterhead, 12, 14, 306
Levin v. Ripple Twist Mills, Inc., 59
Lexis, 207
Liabilities, 142
Liability, Vicarious, 9, 12, 17, 278
Libraries, 206
Licensing, 5, 8, 9, 32
Licensure, *See Licensing*
Lien, 232
Life Estates, 153
Lighting, 194, 205
Limitations Period, 99-100
Limited Liability Companies, 12
Limited Liability Partnerships, 12
Linux, 32
List, To-Do, 282
Listening, 90-91
Listservs, 39
LLC, 12
LLP, 12
Loans, APR, 153
Local 851 International Brotherhood of Teamsters v. Kuehne & Nagel Air Freight, Inc., 58
Location, 190